Anarchism
and Other Essays

EMMA GOLDMAN

With a new Introduction by RICHARD DRINNON

DOVER PUBLICATIONS, INC.

NEW YORK

Published in Canada by General Publishing Company, Ltd.,
30 Lesmill Road, Don Mills, Toronto, Ontario.
Published in the United Kingdom by Constable and Company, Ltd.

This Dover edition, first published in 1969, is an
unabridged and unaltered republication of the
third revised edition originally published in 1917
by Mother Earth Publishing Association, New
York. A new Introduction by Richard Drinnon
has been added.

International Standard Book Number: 0-486-22484-8
Library of Congress Catalog Card Number: 72-98540

Manufactured in the United States of America
Dover Publications, Inc.
180 Varick Street
New York, N.Y. 10014

INTRODUCTION

HARKING BACK TO THE FUTURE

IN the mid-1930's Evelyn Scott concluded a letter to Emma Goldman with the declaration: "But you to me are the future they will, paradoxically, hark back to in time." Except for some older liberals and a few young libertarians, the perceptive novelist was alone in seeing in Emma a "third attitude," one which did not represent a commitment to the unjust present nor a counter dedication "to the defeat of all personal liberty or individually achieved idealism."

Hardboiled realism was rather more to the taste of the time, a time which prided itself on its acceptance of the corporate world, on its willingness to meet those organizational problems which would be solved, it was held, by either fascist or communist managers. What right-thinking person would prefer fascist rulers? Emma's old fashioned dedication to individual freedom struck those on the left as at best irrelevant. Indeed, she had discovered this for herself during her ninety-day return from exile in 1934. On all sides, she wrote her friend Alexander Berkman, there were "young people who do not think for themselves," who "want canned or prepared stuff," who "worship at the shrine of the strong-armed man."

Two years later, seriously ill and despondent over his

v

forced inactivity, Berkman committed suicide. Somehow Emma managed to avoid utter despair over his death and over the subsequent defeat of her Spanish comrades—she had ably represented the Iberian interests in London—at the hands of Franco. Unwilling to give up ever, she crossed the Atlantic to raise money for this last lost cause. In February 1940 she suffered a stroke in Toronto and in May she died. Now merely a dead "undesirable alien," her body was allowed back in the United States by generous immigration officials. She was buried in Chicago's Waldheim Cemetery. As she had wished, she died fighting. She also died forgotten, or almost forgotten, with a crypt in the American memory almost as obscure as that of the Haymarket martyrs buried nearby.

It was once quite otherwise. In the 1890's and particularly after a concerted attempt was made to implicate her in McKinley's assassination, Emma Goldman enjoyed national notoriety: she had become a national bugaboo. S. N. Behrman has recalled that when he was a boy, "parents cited her to us constantly, using her name somewhat as English parents used Napoleon's in the first decades of the nineteenth century, to frighten and admonish." After McKinley's assassination, seven-year-old Margaret Leech wrote a poem which read:

> I am oh so sorry
>   That our President is dead,
> And everybody's sorry
>   so my father said;
> And the horrid man who killed him
>   Is a-sitting in his cell
> And I'm glad that Emma Goldman
>   Doesn't board at this hotel.

In the years that followed, Emma threw herself into a wide range of activities, most of which are represented in this collection of essays. One of the most accomplished, magnetic speakers in American history, she crisscrossed the country lecturing on anarchism, the new drama, the new school, the new woman, birth control, crime and punishment. Subject to stubborn and sometimes brutal police and vigilante attempts to silence her, she joyfully waged countless free-speech fights along lines later followed by the Wobblies (Industrial Workers of the World). Her activities moved radicals and even some liberals to action against threats to freedom of expression. In 1912 Floyd Dell recognized her function as "that of holding before our eyes the ideal of freedom. She is licensed to taunt us with our moral cowardice, to plant in our souls the nettles of remorse at having acquiesced so tamely in the brutal artifice of present day society." As for many others, especially for young women, she came to have a still more positive importance in their lives. "Emma made me what I am," once remarked Adelaide Schulkind, wife of novelist Waldo Frank and mainstay, over the decades, of the League for Mutual Aid. "Can you imagine the effect she had on an East Side girl of seventeen who knew nothing of the world of culture? She introduced me to Strindberg, Shaw, and Ibsen. I used to travel clear across town to hear her lecture Sunday nights on literature, birth control, and women."

And once again, I venture, the response toward Emma Goldman will be other than it was in the 1930's. Can you identify which of the following quotations is from her remarks on "Woman Suffrage"?

Female emancipation has not yet come. The feminists' heart-breaking struggle and incipient revolution have been aborted by male society with help from acquiescing female "Aunt Thomasinas." . . . It is the obligation of each of us to make human equality a reality, starting in our own lives. . . .

Emancipation should make it possible for woman to be human in the truest sense. Everything within her that craves assertion and activity should reach its fullest expression; all artificial barriers should be broken, and the road towards greater freedom cleared of every trace of centuries of submission and slavery.

I want full freedom and cooperation to evolve as a human being, to gain wisdom and knowledge. To be sure, I want certain rights guaranteed to me, not because I am a woman, but because I am a human being.

The second quotation is Emma's. The other two are from articles written more than a half-century later: the first by Betty Rozak, an intelligent young ballet critic, radical, mother; the third quotation expresses the thought of Gene Hoffman, a columnist for the Los Angeles *Times*.*

*See *Liberation,* Vol. XI (December, 1966), 30-31, 32.

In *Woman in the Nineteenth Century,* first published in 1845, Margaret Fuller posed the problem in almost the same words: "What woman needs is not as a woman to act or rule, but as a nature to grow, as an intellect to discern, as a soul to live freely and unimpeded to unfold such powers as were given her when we left our common home"—*Margaret Fuller: American Romantic,* Perry Miller, ed. (Garden City, N.Y., Anchor Books, 1963), p. 150. In this respect, the future we must hark back to is perhaps as remote as Aristophanes' *Lysistrata. Plus ça change.* . . .

Though Emma refers to Margaret Fuller, as you will observe in "Minorities versus Majorities," she probably had not

Emma's keen sense of the tragedy of feminine emancipation gave her essays on this topic a surprising fresh-
ness and contemporary relevance. She quite correctly
told her sisters straight out that they were settling merely
for the mechanical externalities of political equality.
Their vote fetichism, as she contended, made them less
of a real agency of social reform or revolt. Many did
become elitist, anti-labor, nativist, and racist — suffragettes in the South shyly suggested that, were they given
the vote, white supremacy would be preserved.

As you will observe, Emma practically predicted that
the first ripe fruits of enfranchisement would be Prohibition and support for the election of someone like
Harding. She would have been in immediate agreement
with the very recent comment of a spokesman of the

read her predecessor's essays. The remarkable similarities in
their lives and thoughts were rather rooted in the fact that both
were American romantics, despite their different backgrounds,
both drew on Emerson and other common sources, including
George Sand, and both confronted problems which have plagued
intelligent and sensitive women down to the present. In my
biography of Emma, *Rebel in Paradise* (University of Chicago,
1961), I should have pointed out, and did not, that these two
passionate feminists shared the conviction that true freedom
commenced with internal change, that any single doctrine or set
of institutions was imprisoning, that public disapproval could
be contemptuously dismissed, that revolutionary situations might
be joyously welcomed and courageously supported, and that the
body, in all its splendid sexuality, had to be reclaimed from the
repressive hands of the prudes and philistines. They were even
fond of some of the same imagery, as when Emma named her
magazine *Mother Earth* and when Margaret regretted that
Emerson was so abstract and "perpendicular and did not lie
along the ground long enough to hear the secret whispers of our
parent life. We could wish he might be thrown by conflicts on
the lap of mother earth, to see if he would not rise again with
added powers" (p. 198).

Women's Liberation Front: "We don't want to be equal to unfree men." Further, then as now, Emma's views could be acted upon immediately: woman simply had to assert herself as a personality and refuse the right to anyone over her body and mind. Long before Margaret Sanger, she advocated "refusing to bear children" unless women wanted them and, as a midwife and nurse, helped some woman avoid unwanted pregnancies. In 1916 she cheerfully spent some time in jail for distributing birth control information. Were she alive today, she would certainly sympathize and support her spiritual sisters in WITCH (Women's International Terrorist Conspiracy from Hell) who have proposed abortion ships, well-equipped and staffed floating hospitals to steam just beyond the twelve-mile limit and perform abortions in a decent manner and for a reasonable fee. As a modern Witch asks: "If there can be floating gambling parties for high society 'charity' balls with legal impunity, well . . . ?"

To be sure, Emma's outbursts of indignation occasionally seem excessive, sometimes even slightly ridiculous. Take, for example, her discussion of the arms race of her day, the campaign of T.R. and other militarists for a bigger and better navy and army: "It is for that purpose that America has within a short time spent four hundred million dollars. Just think of it—four hundred million dollars taken from the produce of *the people*." Just think of it: exactly this paltry sum was allotted in the defense budget of 1969-70 for "major developmental activity on no fewer than six new aircraft"; the general program in arms research and development received a total of $5.6 *billion*, which included funds for work on missiles to be snuggled down on the ocean floor —indeed, the last defense budget of the Johnson Administration came to $81.5 billion, $5.2 billion of which went simply for ammunition use in Vietnam. Yet it is, of course, our world and not Emma's indignation over the misuse of resources that is absurd. She had her eyes on a major engine of the transformation of America when she warned "that militarism is growing a greater danger here than anywhere else, because of the many bribes capitalism holds out to those whom it wishes to destroy." And she was certainly on the mark when she contrasted the puny violence of individuals with the large-scale violence of the state and put the latter in its proper, if sadly prophetic, context:

> We Americans claim to be a peace-loving people. We hate bloodshed; we are opposed to violence. Yet we go into spasms of joy over the possibility of projecting dynamite bombs from flying machines upon helpless citizens.

Along with most other radicals of the period, Emma had a blindspot when it came to the importance of race. In her attempts to come to terms with the imperialism of what was to become the American Century, she followed other radicals in grossly overestimating the importance of the capitalist drive for markets, resources, and gain. In her discussion of the Spanish-American War, for example, she did not make the obvious connection that many of the officers and men busy subjugating Filipinos had a short while before been Indian fighters, busy right up to the 1890's in killing Red rebels and in herding the rest of their tribes into those concentration camps called reservations. You will look in vain in the following pages for an illustration of Emma's magnificent outrage directed against the lynchings and oppression of Blacks. It was not because she was herself a racist. In "The Traffic in Women" she did make fleeting reference to "the brutal and barbarous persecution [of] Chinese and Japanese . . . on the Pacific Coast. . . ." When she was in the federal penitentiary in Jefferson City, Missouri, doing a two-year sentence for her activities against conscription in 1917, she related in a warm, human way to all the other inmates, Black and White, and had close friends in both groups. It was because, rather, even for someone as alert as Emma, the Blacks and their plight were essentially invisible. She and her contemporaries were more than a little blinded by the kind of pervasive economism traceable to Marxism, with all that doctrine's unfortunate inattention to racism and nationalism.

Yet, even if she remained largely unaware of the complicated interrelationships of racism and nationalism, she had a full realization that patriotic nationalism was poisonous and an intuitive sense of the still greater horrors which would be committed in its name as the twentieth century got underway. "The individual is the heart of society," she kept repeating and saw the individual's very existence threatened by increasing concentrations of economic and political power. The liberal's confidence that this threat could be met by a few managerial adjustments and his faith that the good life could be achieved through the increased application of technology struck her as dangerous nonsense. In its stead she offered the anarchism of Kropotkin, which undertook to replace authoritarian hierarchies, the coercive political state, and supernaturalistic religion by a warm humanism, a society of equals, and a polity of small organic organizations in free cooperation with each other.

She thus had a theory, one with imaginative possibilities that still remain to be explored, but she was not a theoretician. She combined her acceptance of Kropotkin's communist anarchism with a generous admixture of the individualism she found in Ibsen and then readily admitted that the result might fall short of full adequacy. Young rebels of our time must sympathize with her reply to the charge, already a cliché, that she had no "program": she made no attempt to detail the future, she explained, "because I believe that Anarchism can not consistently impose an iron-clad program or method on the future. The things every new generation has to fight, and which it can least overcome, are the burdens of the past, which holds us all as in a net." If you object to a programmed present, how can you be held responsible for programming the future? Emma's openness to new beginnings in the arts, to experimental drama, for example, and to jazz, her insistence that anarchism goes beyond economic change to *"every phase"* of life, added an esthetic dimension to Kropotkin's thought and made her thinking of immediate relevance to contemporary cultural revolutionists.

"Anarchism is the great liberator of man from the phantoms that have held him captive," argued Emma and proceeded to do her best to help out the demystification process. She and her comrades made their contributions, but they were undoubtedly sped along by the gas ovens, atomic bombs, language of overkill, napalm, colonial wars, ghetto riots, assassinations.

Events and thoughts have joined to unmask systems of totalitarian and manipulative social domination for what they are: systems of domination and repression. One result has been a world-wide renewal of interest in anarchism. A surprising number of persons, especially the young, have penetrated the escalating irrationality of nationism to see the state revealed as a death trap. They have hardly any choice but to conclude with Yakov Bok in Malamud's *The Fixer:* "If the state acts in ways that are abhorrent to human nature it's the lesser evil to destroy it." If they want-to go about it humanely, and not destroy themselves in the process, the modern prophetic minority might well hark back to Emma. Her most fundamental message was the paradoxical command to be yourself and be your own commander-in-chief. And who can dismiss her formulation of the problem?

> The problem that confronts us today, and which the nearest future is to solve, is how to be one's self and yet in oneness with others, to feel deeply with all human beings and still retain one's own characteristic qualities.

If not in her nearest future, what about ours?

RICHARD DRINNON

Milton, Pa., October, 1969

CONTENTS

EMMA GOLDMAN

> Propagandism is not, as some suppose, a "trade,"
> because nobody will follow a "trade" at which you
> may work with the industry of a slave and die with
> the reputation of a mendicant. The motives of any
> persons to pursue such a profession must be differ-
> ent from those of trade, deeper than pride, and
> stronger than interest.
>
> GEORGE JACOB HOLYOAKE.

AMONG the men and women prominent in the public
life of America there are but few whose names are
mentioned as often as that of Emma Goldman. Yet
the real Emma Goldman is almost quite unknown.
The sensational press has surrounded her name with
so much misrepresentation and slander, it would seem
almost a miracle that, in spite of this web of calumny,
the truth breaks through and a better appreciation of
this much maligned idealist begins to manifest itself.
There is but little consolation in the fact that almost
every representative of a new idea has had to struggle
and suffer under similar difficulties. Is it of any
avail that a former president of a republic pays homage
at Osawatomie to the memory of John Brown? Or
that the president of another republic participates in
the unveiling of a statue in honor of Pierre Proudhon,
and holds up his life to the French nation as a model

worthy of enthusiastic emulation? Of what avail is all this when, at the same time, the *living* John Browns and Proudhons are being crucified? The honor and glory of a Mary Wollstonecraft or of a Louise Michel are not enhanced by the City Fathers of London or Paris naming a street after them—the living generation should be concerned with doing justice to the *living* Mary Wollstonecrafts and Louise Michels. Posterity assigns to men like Wendel Phillips and Lloyd Garrison the proper niche of honor in the temple of human emancipation; but it is the duty of their contemporaries to bring them due recognition and appreciation while they live.

The path of the propagandist of social justice is strewn with thorns. The powers of darkness and injustice exert all their might lest a ray of sunshine enter his cheerless life. Nay, even his comrades in the struggle—indeed, too often his most intimate friends—show but little understanding for the personality of the pioneer. Envy, sometimes growing to hatred, vanity and jealousy, obstruct his way and fill his heart with sadness. It requires an inflexible will and tremendous enthusiasm not to lose, under such conditions, all faith in the Cause. The representative of a revolutionizing idea stands between two fires: on the one hand, the persecution of the existing powers which hold him responsible for all acts resulting from social conditions; and, on the other, the lack of understanding on the part of his own followers who often judge all his activity from a narrow standpoint. Thus it happens that the agitator stands quite alone in the midst of the multitude surrounding him. Even his most intimate friends rarely understand how solitary and deserted he feels. That is the tragedy of the person prominent in the public eye.

The mist in which the name of Emma Goldman has so long been enveloped is gradually beginning to dissipate. Her energy in the furtherance of such an unpopular idea as Anarchism, her deep earnestness, her courage and abilities, find growing understanding and admiration.

The debt American intellectual growth owes to the revolutionary exiles has never been fully appreciated. The seed disseminated by them, though so little understood at the time, has brought a rich harvest. They have at all times held aloft the banner of liberty, thus impregnating the social vitality of the Nation. But very few have succeeded in preserving their European education and culture while at the same time assimilating themselves with American life. It is difficult for the average man to form an adequate conception what strength, energy, and perseverance are necessary to absorb the unfamiliar language, habits, and customs of a new country, without the loss of one's own personality.

Emma Goldman is one of the few who, while thoroughly preserving their individuality, have become an important factor in the social and intellectual atmosphere of America. The life she leads is rich in color, full of change and variety. She has risen to the topmost heights, and she has also tasted the bitter dregs of life.

Emma Goldman was born of Jewish parentage on the 27th day of June, 1869, in the Russian province of Kovno. Surely these parents never dreamed what unique position their child would some day occupy. Like all conservative parents they, too, were quite convinced that their daughter would marry a respectable citizen, bear him children, and round out her allotted years surrounded by a flock of grandchildren, a good, religious woman. As most parents, they had no inkling what a strange, impassioned spirit would take hold of the soul of their child, and carry it to the heights which separate generations in eternal struggle. They lived in a land and at a time when antagonism between parent and offspring was fated to find its most acute expression, irreconcilable hostility. In this tremendous struggle between fathers and sons —and especially between parents and daughters—there was no compromise, no weak yielding, no truce. The spirit of liberty, of progress—an idealism which knew no considerations and recognized no obstacles— drove the young generation out of the parental house and away from the hearth of the home. Just as this same spirit once drove out the revolutionary breeder of discontent, Jesus, and alienated him from his native traditions.

What rôle the Jewish race—notwithstanding all anti-Semitic calumnies the race of transcendental idealism—played in the struggle of the Old and the New will probably never be appreciated with complete impartiality and clarity. Only now we are beginning to perceive the tremendous debt we owe to Jewish idealists in the realm of science, art, and literature.

But very little is still known of the important part
the sons and daughters of Israel have played in the
revolutionary movement and, especially, in that of
modern times.

The first years of her childhood Emma Goldman
passed in a small, idyllic place in the German-Russian
province of Kurland, where her father had charge of
the government stage. At that time Kurland was
thoroughly German; even the Russian bureaucracy of
that Baltic province was recruited mostly from German *Junker*. German fairy tales and stories, rich in
the miraculous deeds of the heroic knights of Kurland,
wove their spell over the youthful mind. But the
beautiful idyl was of short duration. Soon the soul
of the growing child was overcast by the dark shadows
of life. Already in her tenderest youth the seeds of
rebellion and unrelenting hatred of oppression were
to be planted in the heart of Emma Goldman. Early
she learned to know the beauty of the State: she saw
her father harassed by the Christian *chinovniks* and
doubly persecuted as petty official and hated Jew. The
brutality of forced conscription ever stood before her
eyes: she beheld the young men, often the sole support of a large family, brutally dragged to the barracks to lead the miserable life of a soldier. She
heard the weeping of the poor peasant women, and
witnessed the shameful scenes of official venality which
relieved the rich from military service at the expense
of the poor. She was outraged by the terrible treatment to which the female servants were subjected:
maltreated and exploited by their *barinyas*, they fell
to the tender mercies of the regimental officers, who

regarded them as their natural sexual prey. These girls, made pregnant by respectable gentlemen and driven out by their mistresses, often found refuge in the Goldman home. And the little girl, her heart palpitating with sympathy, would abstract coins from the parental drawer to clandestinely press the money into the hands of the unfortunate women. Thus Emma Goldman's most striking characteristic, her sympathy with the underdog, already became manifest in these early years.

At the age of seven little Emma was sent by her parents to her grandmother at Königsberg, the city of Immanuel Kant, in Eastern Prussia. Save for occasional interruptions, she remained there till her 13th birthday. The first years in these surroundings do not exactly belong to her happiest recollections. The grandmother, indeed, was very amiable, but the numerous aunts of the household were concerned more with the spirit of practical rather than pure reason, and the categoric imperative was applied all too frequently. The situation was changed when her parents migrated to Königsberg, and little Emma was relieved from her rôle of Cinderella. She now regularly attended public school and also enjoyed the advantages of private instruction, customary in middle-class life; French and music lessons played an important part in the curriculum. The future interpreter of Ibsen and Shaw was then a little German Gretchen, quite at home in the German atmosphere. Her special predilections in literature were the sentimental romances of Marlitt; she was a great admirer of the good Queen Louise, whom the bad Napoleon

Buonaparte treated with so marked a lack of knightly chivalry. What might have been her future development had she remained in this milieu? Fate—or was it economic necessity?—willed it otherwise. Her parents decided to settle in St. Petersburg, the capital of the Almighty Tsar, and there to embark in business. It was here that a great change took place in the life of the young dreamer.

It was an eventful period—the year of 1882— in which Emma Goldman, then in her 13th year, arrived in St. Petersburg. A struggle for life and death between the autocracy and the Russian intellectuals swept the country. Alexander II. had fallen the previous year. Sophia Perovskaia, Zheliabov, Grinevitzky, Rissakov, Kibalchitch, Michailov, the heroic executors of the death sentence upon the tyrant, had then entered the Walhalla of immortality. Jessie Helfman, the only regicide whose life the government had reluctantly spared because of pregnancy, followed the unnumbered Russian martyrs to the étapes of Siberia. It was the most heroic period in the great battle of emancipation, a battle for freedom such as the world had never witnessed before. The names of the Nihilist martyrs were on all lips, and thousands were enthusiastic to follow their example. The whole *intelligenzia* of Russia was filled with the *illegal* spirit: revolutionary sentiments penetrated into every home, from mansion to hovel, impregnating the military, the *chinovniks,* factory workers, and peasants. The atmosphere pierced the very casemates of the royal palace. New ideas germinated in the youth. The difference of sex was forgotten. Shoulder to shoulder fought the men and the women. The Russian woman! Who shall ever do justice or adequately portray her heroism and self-sacrifice, her loyalty and devotion? Holy, Turgeniev calls her in his great prose poem, *On the Threshold.*

It was inevitable that the young dreamer from Königsberg should be drawn into the maelstrom. To remain outside of the circle of free ideas meant a life of vegetation, of death. One need not wonder at the youthful age. Young enthusiasts were not then—and, fortunately, are not now—a rare phenomenon in Russia. The study of the Russian language soon brought young Emma Goldman in touch with revolutionary students and new ideas. The place of Marlitt was taken by Nekrassov and Tchernishevsky. The quondam admirer of the good Queen Louise became a glowing enthusiast of liberty, resolving, like thousands of others, to devote her life to the emancipation of the people.

The struggle of generations now took place in the Goldman family. The parents could not comprehend what interest their daughter could find in the new ideas, which they themselves considered fantastic utopias. They strove to persuade the young girl out of these chimeras, and daily repetition of soul-racking disputes was the result. Only in one member of the family did the young idealist find understanding—in her elder sister, Helene, with whom she later emigrated to America, and whose love and sympathy have never failed her. Even in the darkest hours of later persecution Emma Goldman always found a haven of refuge in the home of this loyal sister.

Emma Goldman finally resolved to achieve her independence. She saw hundreds of men and women sacrificing brilliant careers to go *v naród,* to the people. She followed their example. She became a factory worker; at first employed as a corset maker, and later in the manufacture of gloves. She was now 17 years of age and proud to earn her own living. Had she remained in Russia, she would have probably sooner or later shared the fate of thousands buried in the snows of Siberia. But a new chapter of life was to begin for her. Sister Helene decided to emigrate to America, where another sister had already made her home. Emma prevailed upon Helene to be allowed to join her, and together they departed for America, filled with the joyous hope of a great, free land, the glorious Republic.

America! What magic word. The yearning of the enslaved, the promised land of the oppressed, the goal of all longing for progress. Here man's ideals had found their fulfillment: no Tsar, no Cossack, no *chinovnik.* The Republic! Glorious synonym of equality, freedom, brotherhood.

Thus thought the two girls as they travelled, in the year 1886, from New York to Rochester. Soon, all too soon, disillusionment awaited them. The ideal conception of America was punctured already at Castle Garden, and soon burst like a soap bubble. Here Emma Goldman witnessed sights which re-

minded her of the terrible scenes of her childhood
in Kurland. The brutality and humiliation the
future citizens of the great Republic were subjected
to on board ship, were repeated at Castle Garden
by the officials of the democracy in a more savage
and aggravating manner. And what bitter disappointment followed as the young idealist began to
familiarize herself with the conditions in the new
land! Instead of one Tsar, she found scores of
them; the Cossack was replaced by the policeman
with the heavy club, and instead of the Russian
chinovnik there was the far more inhuman slave-
driver of the factory.

Emma Goldman soon obtained work in the clothing establishment of the Garson Co. The wages
amounted to two and a half dollars a week. At
that time the factories were not provided with motor
power, and the poor sewing girls had to drive the
wheels by foot, from early morning till late at
night. A terribly exhausting toil it was, without a
ray of light, the drudgery of the long day passed
in complete silence—the Russian custom of friendly
conversation at work was not permissible in the
free country. But the exploitation of the girls was
not only economic; the poor wage workers were
looked upon by their foremen and bosses as sexual
commodities. If a girl resented the advances of
her superiors," she would speedily find herself on
the street as an undesirable element in the factory.
There was never a lack of willing victims: the supply
always exceeded the demand.

The horrible conditions were made still more

unbearable by the fearful dreariness of life in the small American city. The Puritan spirit suppresses the slightest manifestation of joy; a deadly dullness beclouds the soul; no intellectual inspiration, no thought exchange between congenial spirits is possible. Emma Goldman almost suffocated in this atmosphere. She, above all others, longed for ideal surroundings, for friendship and understanding, for the companionship of kindred minds. Mentally she still lived in Russia. Unfamiliar with the language and life of the country, she dwelt more in the past than in the present. It was at this period that she met a young man who spoke Russian. With great joy the acquaintance was cultivated. At last a person with whom she could converse, one who could help her bridge the dullness of the narrow existence. The friendship gradually ripened and finally culminated in marriage.

Emma Goldman, too, had to walk the sorrowful road of married life; she, too, had to learn from bitter experience that legal statutes signify dependence and self-effacement, especially for the woman. The marriage was no liberation from the Puritan dreariness of American life; indeed, it was rather aggravated by the loss of self-ownership. The characters of the young people differed too widely. A separation soon followed, and Emma Goldman went to New Haven, Conn. There she found employment in a factory, and her husband disappeared from her horizon. Two decades later she was fated to be unexpectedly reminded of him by the Federal authorities.

The revolutionists who were active in the Russian movement of the 80's were but little familiar with the social ideas then agitating western Europe and America. Their sole activity consisted in educating the people, their final goal the destruction of the autocracy. Socialism and Anarchism were terms hardly known even by name. Emma Goldman, too, was entirely unfamiliar with the significance of those ideals.

She arrived in America, as four years previously in Russia, at a period of great social and political unrest. The working people were in revolt against the terrible labor conditions; the eight-hour movement of the Knights of Labor was at its height, and throughout the country echoed the din of sanguine strife between strikers and police. The struggle culminated in the great strike against the Harvester Company of Chicago, the massacre of the strikers, and the judicial murder of the labor leaders, which followed upon the historic Haymarket bomb explosion. The Anarchists stood the martyr test of blood baptism. The apologists of capitalism vainly seek to justify the killing of Parsons, Spies, Lingg, Fischer, and Engel. Since the publication of Governor Altgeld's reasons for his liberation of the three incarcerated Haymarket Anarchists, no doubt is left that a fivefold legal murder had been committed in Chicago, in 1887.

Very few have grasped the significance of the Chicago martyrdom; least of all the ruling classes. By the destruction of a number of labor leaders they thought to stem the tide of a world-inspiring idea.

They failed to consider that from the blood of the martyrs grows the new seed, and that the frightful injustice will win new converts to the Cause.

The two most prominent representatives of the Anarchist idea in America, Voltairine de Cleyre and Emma Goldman—the one a native American, the other a Russian—have been converted, like numerous others, to the ideas of Anarchism by the judicial murder. Two women who had not known each other before, and who had received a widely different education, were through that murder united in one idea.

Like most working men and women of America, Emma Goldman followed the Chicago trial with great anxiety and excitement. She, too, could not believe that the leaders of the proletariat would be killed. The 11th of November, 1887, taught her differently. She realized that no mercy could be expected from the ruling class, that between the Tsarism of Russia and the plutocracy of America there was no difference save in name. Her whole being rebelled against the crime, and she vowed to herself a solemn vow to join the ranks of the revolutionary proletariat and to devote all her energy and strength to their emancipation from wage slavery. With the glowing enthusiasm so characteristic of her nature, she now began to familiarize herself with the literature of Socialism and Anarchism. She attended public meetings and became acquainted with socialistically and anarchistically inclined working-men. Johanna Greie, the well-known German lecturer, was the first Socialist speaker heard by Emma

Goldman. In New Haven, Conn., where she was employed in a corset factory, she met Anarchists actively participating in the movement. Here she read the *Freiheit,* edited by John Most. The Haymarket tragedy developed her inherent Anarchist tendencies; the reading of the *Freiheit* made her a conscious Anarchist. Subsequently she was to learn that the idea of Anarchism found its highest expression through the best intellects of America: theoretically by Josiah Warren, Stephen Pearl Andrews, Lysander Spooner; philosophically by Emerson, Thoreau, and Walt Whitman.

Made ill by the excessive strain of factory work, Emma Goldman returned to Rochester where she remained till August, 1889, at which time she removed to New York, the scene of the most important phase of her life. She was now twenty years old. Features pallid with suffering, eyes large and full of compassion, greet one in her pictured likeness of those days. Her hair is, as customary with Russian student girls, worn short, giving free play to the strong forehead.

It is the heroic epoch of militant Anarchism. By leaps and bounds the movement had grown in every country. In spite of the most severe governmental persecution new converts swell the ranks. The propaganda is almost exclusively of a secret character. The repressive measures of the government drive the disciples of the new philosophy to conspirative methods. Thousands of victims fall into the hands of the authorities and languish in prisons. But nothing can stem the rising tide of enthusiasm, of self-sacrifice and devotion to the Cause. The efforts of teachers like Peter Kropotkin, Louise Michel, Elisée Reclus, and others, inspire the devotees with ever greater energy.

Disruption is imminent with the Socialists, who have sacrificed the idea of liberty and embraced the State and politics. The struggle is bitter, the factions irreconcilable. This struggle is not merely between Anarchists and Socialists.; it also finds its echo within the Anarchist groups. Theoretic differences and personal controversies lead to strife and acrimonious enmities. The anti-Socialist legislation of Germany and Austria had driven thousands of Socialists and Anarchists across the seas to seek refuge in America. John Most, having lost his seat in the Reichstag, finally had to flee his native land, and went to London. There, having advanced toward Anarchism, he entirely withdrew from the Social Democratic Party. Later, coming to America, he continued the publication of the *Freiheit* in New York, and developed great activity among the German workingmen.

When Emma Goldman arrived in New York in 1889, she experienced little difficulty in associating herself with active Anarchists. Anarchist meetings were an almost daily occurrence. The first lecturer she heard on the Anarchist platform was Dr. H. Solotaroff. Of great importance to her future development was her acquaintance with John Most, who exerted a tremendous influence over the younger elements. His impassioned eloquence, untiring energy, and the persecution he had endured for the Cause, all combined to enthuse the comrades. It was also at this period that she met Alexander Berkman, whose friendship played an important part throughout her life. Her talents as a speaker could not long remain in obscurity. The fire of enthusiasm swept her toward the public platform. Encouraged by her friends, she began to participate as a German and Yiddish speaker at Anarchist meetings. Soon followed a brief tour of agitation taking her as far as Cleveland. With the whole strength and earnestness of her soul she now threw herself into the propaganda of Anarchist ideas. The passionate period of her life had begun. Though constantly toiling in sweat-shops, the fiery young orator was at the same time very active as an agitator and participated in various labor struggles, notably in the great cloakmakers' strike, in 1889, led by Professor Garsyde and Joseph Barondess.

A year later Emma Goldman was a delegate to an Anarchist conference in New York. She was elected to the Executive Committee, but later withdrew because of differences of opinion regarding tactical matters. The ideas of the German-speaking Anarchists had at that time not yet become clarified. Some still believed in parliamentary methods, the great majority being adherents of strong centralism. These differences of opinion in regard to tactics led, in 1891, to a breach with John Most. Emma Goldman, Alexander Berkman, and other comrades joined the group *Autonomy,* in which Joseph Peukert, Otto Rinke, and Claus Timmermann played an active part.

The bitter controversies which followed this secession terminated only with the death of Most, in 1906.

A great source of inspiration to Emma Goldman proved the Russian revolutionists who were associated in the group *Znamya*. Goldenberg, Solotaroff, Zametkin, Miller, Cahan, the poet Edelstadt, Ivan von Schewitsch, husband of Helene von Racowitza and editor of the *Volkszeitung*, and numerous other Russian exiles, some of whom are still living, were members of the group. It was also at this time that Emma Goldman met Robert Reitzel, the German-American Heine, who exerted a great influence on her development. Through him she became acquainted with the best writers of modern literature, and the friendship thus begun lasted till Reitzel's death, in 1898.

The labor movement of America had not been drowned in the Chicago massacre; the murder of the Anarchists had failed to bring peace to the profit-greedy capitalist. The struggle for the eight-hour day continued. In 1892 broke out the great strike in Pittsburg. The Homestead fight, the defeat of the Pinkertons, the appearance of the militia, the suppression of the strikers, and the complete triumph of the reaction are matters of comparatively recent history. Stirred to the very depths by the terrible events at the seat of war, Alexander Berkman resolved to sacrifice his life to the Cause and thus give an object lesson to the wage slaves of America of active Anarchist solidarity with labor. His attack upon Frick, the Gessler of Pittsburg,

failed, and the twenty-two-year-old youth was doomed
to a living death of twenty-two years in the penitentiary. The bourgeoisie, which for decades had
exalted and eulogized tyrannicide, now was filled
with terrible rage. The capitalist press organized a
systematic campaign of calumny and misrepresentation against Anarchists. The police exerted every
effort to involve Emma Goldman in the act of
Alexander Berkman. The feared agitator was to
be silenced by all means. It was only due to the
circumstance of her presence in New York that she
escaped the clutches of the law. It was a similar
circumstance which, nine years later, during the
McKinley incident, was instrumental in preserving her
liberty. It is almost incredible with what amount
of stupidity, baseness, and vileness the journalists
of the period sought to overwhelm the Anarchist.
One must peruse the newspaper files to realize the
enormity of incrimination and slander. It would be
difficult to portray the agony of soul Emma Goldman experienced in those days. The persecutions of
the capitalist press were to be borne by an Anarchist
with comparative equanimity; but the attacks from
one's own ranks were far more painful and unbearable. The act of Berkman was severely criticized
by Most and some of his followers among the
German and Jewish Anarchists. Bitter accusations
and recriminations at public meetings and private
gatherings followed. Persecuted on all sides, both
because she championed Berkman and his act, and
on account of her revolutionary activity, Emma
Goldman was harassed even to the extent of in-

ability to secure shelter. Too proud to seek safety in the denial of her identity, she chose to pass the nights in the public parks rather than expose her friends to danger or vexation by her visits. The already bitter cup was filled to overflowing by the attempted suicide of a young comrade who had shared living quarters with Emma Goldman, Alexander Berkman, and a mutual artist friend.

Many changes have since taken place. Alexander Berkman has survived the Pennsylvania Inferno, and is back again in the ranks of the militant Anarchists, his spirit unbroken, his soul full of enthusiasm for the ideals of his youth. The artist comrade is now among the well-known illustrators of New York. The suicide candidate left America shortly after his unfortunate attempt to die, and was subsequently arrested and condemned to eight years of hard labor for smuggling Anarchist literature into Germany. He, too, has withstood the terrors of prison life, and has returned to the revolutionary movement, since earning the well deserved reputation of a talented writer in Germany.

To avoid indefinite camping in the parks Emma Goldman finally was forced to move into a house on Third Street, occupied exclusively by prostitutes. There, among the outcasts of our good Christian society, she could at least rent a bit of a room, and find rest and work at her sewing machine. The women of the street showed more refinement of feeling and sincere sympathy than the priests of the Church. But human endurance had been exhausted

by overmuch suffering and privation. There was
a complete physical breakdown, and the renowned
agitator was removed to the "Bohemian Republic"—
a large tenement house which derived its euphonious
appellation from the fact that its occupants were
mostly Bohemian Anarchists. Here Emma Goldman
found friends ready to aid her. Justus Schwab,
one of the finest representatives of the German
revolutionary period of that time, and Dr. Solotaroff
were indefatigable in the care of the patient. Here,
too, she met Edward Brady, the new friendship
subsequently ripening into close intimacy. Brady had
been an active participant in the revolutionary movement of Austria and had, at the time of his acquaintance with Emma Goldman, lately been released
from an Austrian prison after an incarceration of
ten years.

Physicians diagnosed the illness as consumption,
and the patient was advised to leave New York.
She went to Rochester, in the hope that the home
circle would help to restore her to health. Her
parents had several years previously emigrated to
America, settling in that city. Among the leading
traits of the Jewish race is the strong attachment
between the members of the family, and, especially,
between parents and children. Though her conservative parents could not sympathize with the
idealist aspirations of Emma Goldman and did not
approve of her mode of life, they now received
their sick daughter with open arms. The rest and
care enjoyed in the parental home, and the cheering
presence of the beloved sister Helene, proved so

beneficial that within a short time she was sufficiently restored to resume her energetic activity.

There is no rest in the life of Emma Goldman. Ceaseless effort and continuous striving toward the conceived goal are the essentials of her nature. Too much precious time had already been wasted. It was imperative to resume her labors immediately. The country was in the throes of a crisis, and thousands of unemployed crowded the streets of the large industrial centers. Cold and hungry they tramped through the land in the vain search for work and bread. The Anarchists developed a strenuous propaganda among the unemployed and the strikers. A monster demonstration of striking cloakmakers and of the unemployed took place at Union Square, New York. Emma Goldman was one of the invited speakers. She delivered an impassioned speech, picturing in fiery words the misery of the wage-slave's life, and quoted the famous maxim of Cardinal Manning: "Necessity knows no law, and the starving man has a natural right to a share of his neighbor's bread." She concluded her exhortation with the words: "Ask for work. If they do not give you work, ask for bread. If they do not give you work or bread, then take bread."

The following day she left for Philadelphia, where she was to address a public meeting. The capitalist press again raised the alarm. If Socialists and Anarchists were to be permitted to continue agitating, there was imminent danger that the workingmen would soon learn to understand the manner in which they are robbed of the joy and happiness of life.

Such a possibility was to be prevented at all cost.
The Chief of Police of New York, Byrnes, procured
a court order for the arrest of Emma Goldman.
She was detained by the Philadelphia authorities and
incarcerated for several days in the Moyamensing
prison, awaiting the extradition papers which Byrnes
intrusted to Detective Jacobs. This man Jacobs
(whom Emma Goldman again met several years later
under very unpleasant circumstances) proposed to her,
while she was returning a prisoner to New York, to
betray the cause of labor. In the name of his superior,
Chief Byrnes, he offered lucrative reward. How
stupid men sometimes are! What poverty of psychologic observation to imagine the possibility of betrayal
on the part of a young Russian idealist, who had willingly sacrificed all personal considerations to help in
labor's emancipation.

In October, 1893, Emma Goldman was tried in
the criminal courts of New York on the charge of
inciting to riot. The "intelligent" jury ignored the
testimony of the twelve witnesses for the defense
in favor of the evidence given by one single man—
Detective Jacobs. She was found guilty and sentenced
to serve one year in the penitentiary at Blackwell's
Island. Since the foundation of the Republic she was
the first woman—Mrs. Surratt excepted—to be imprisoned for a political offense. Respectable society
had long before stamped upon her the Scarlet Letter.

Emma Goldman passed her time in the penitentiary in the capacity of nurse in the prison hospital.
Here she found opportunity to shed some rays
of kindness into the dark lives of the unfortunates

whose sisters of the street did not disdain two years previously to share with her the same house. She also found in prison opportunity to study English and its literature, and to familiarize herself with the great American writers. In Bret Harte, Mark Twain, Walt Whitman, Thoreau, and Emerson she found great treasures.

She left Blackwell's Island in the month of August, 1894, a woman of twenty-five, developed and matured, and intellectually transformed. Back into the arena, richer in experience, purified by suffering. She did not feel herself deserted and alone any more. Many hands were stretched out to welcome her. There were at the time numerous intellectual oases in New York. The saloon of Justus Schwab, at Number Fifty, First Street, was the center where gathered Anarchists, littérateurs, and bohemians. Among others she also met at this time a number of American Anarchists, and formed the friendship of Voltairine de Cleyre, Wm. C. Owen, Miss Van Etton, and Dyer D. Lum, former editor of the *Alarm* and executor of the last wishes of the Chicago martyrs. In John Swinton, the noble old fighter for liberty, she found one of her staunchest friends. Other intellectual centers there were: *Solidarity,* published by John Edelman; *Liberty,* by the Individualist Anarchist Benjamin R. Tucker; the *Rebel,* by Harry Kelly; *Der Sturmvogel,* a German Anarchist publication, edited by Claus Timmermann; *Der Arme Teufel,* whose presiding genius was the inimitable Robert Reitzel. Through Arthur Brisbane, now chief lieutenant of William Randolph

Hearst, she became acquainted with the writings of Fourier. Brisbane then was not yet submerged in the swamp of political corruption. He sent Emma Goldman an amiable letter to Blackwell's Island, together with the biography of his father, the enthusiastic American disciple of Fourier.

Emma Goldman became, upon her release from the penitentiary, a factor in the public life of New York. She was appreciated in radical ranks for her devotion, her idealism, and earnestness. Various persons sought her friendship, and some tried to persuade her to aid in the furtherance of their special side issues. Thus Rev. Parkhurst, during the Lexow investigation, did his utmost to induce her to join the Vigilance Committee in order to fight Tammany Hall. Maria Louise, the moving spirit of a social center, acted as Parkhurst's go-between. It is hardly necessary to mention what reply the latter received from Emma Goldman. Incidentally, Maria Louise subsequently became a Mahatma. During the free-silver campaign, ex-Burgess McLuckie, one of the most genuine personalities in the Homestead strike, visited New York in an endeavor to enthuse the local radicals for free silver. He also attempted to interest Emma Goldman, but with no greater success than Mahatma Maria Louise of Parkhurst-Lexow fame.

In 1894 the struggle of the Anarchists in France reached its highest expression. The white terror on the part of the Republican upstarts was answered by the red terror of our French comrades.

With feverish anxiety the Anarchists throughout the
world followed this social struggle. Propaganda by
deed found its reverberating echo in almost all countries. In order to better familiarize herself with
conditions in the old world, Emma Goldman left
for Europe, in the year 1895. After a lecture tour
in England and Scotland, she went to Vienna where
she entered the *Allgemeine Krankenhaus* to prepare
herself as midwife and nurse, and where at the same
time she studied social conditions. She also found
opportunity to acquaint herself with the newest literature of Europe: Hauptmann, Nietzsche, Ibsen, Zola,
Thomas Hardy, and other artist rebels were read
with great enthusiasm.

In the autumn of 1896 she returned to New York
by way of Zurich and Paris. The project of
Alexander Berkman's liberation was on hand. The
barbaric sentence of twenty-two years had roused
tremendous indignation among the radical elements.
It was known that the Pardon Board of Pennsylvania would look to Carnegie and Frick for advice
in the case of Alexander Berkman. It was therefore
suggested that these Sultans of Pennsylvania be
approached—not with a view of obtaining their
grace, but with the request that they do not attempt
to influence the Board. Ernest Crosby offered to
see Carnegie, on condition that Alexander Berkman
repudiate his act. That, however, was absolutely
out of the question. He would never be guilty of
such forswearing of his own personality and self-
respect. These efforts led to friendly relations between Emma Goldman and the circle of Ernest

Crosby, Bolton Hall, and Leonard Abbott. In the year 1897 she undertook her first great lecture tour, which extended as far as California. This tour popularized her name as the representative of the oppressed, her eloquence ringing from coast to coast. In California Emma Goldman became friendly with the members of the Isaak family, and learned to appreciate their efforts for the Cause. Under tremendous obstacles the Isaaks first published the *Firebrand* and, upon its suppression by the Postal Department, the *Free Society*. It was also during this tour that Emma Goldman met that grand old rebel of sexual freedom, Moses Harman.

During the Spanish-American war the spirit of chauvinism was at its highest tide. To check this dangerous situation, and at the same time collect funds for the revolutionary Cubans, Emma Goldman became affiliated with the Latin comrades, among others with Gori, Esteve, Palaviccini, Merlino, Petruccini, and Ferrara. In the year 1899 followed another protracted tour of agitation, terminating on the Pacific Coast. Repeated arrests and accusations, though without ultimate bad results, marked every propaganda tour.

In November of the same year the untiring agitator went on a second lecture tour to England and Scotland, closing her journey with the first International Anarchist Congress at Paris. It was at the time of the Boer war, and again jingoism was at its height, as two years previously it had celebrated its orgies during the Spanish-American war. Various meetings, both in England and Scotland, were disturbed and broken up by patriotic mobs. Emma Goldman found on this occasion the opportunity of again meeting various English comrades and interesting personalities like Tom Mann and the sisters Rossetti, the gifted daughters of Dante Gabriel Rossetti, then publishers of the Anarchist review, the *Torch*. One of her life-long hopes found here its fulfillment: she came in close and friendly touch with Peter Kropotkin, Enrico Malatesta, Nicholas Tchaikovsky, W. Tcherkessov, and Louise Michel. Old warriors in the cause of humanity, whose deeds have enthused thousands of followers throughout the world, and whose life and work have inspired other thousands with noble idealism and self-sacrifice. Old warriors they, yet ever young with the courage of earlier days, unbroken in spirit and filled with the firm hope of the final triumph of Anarchy.

The chasm in the revolutionary labor movement, which resulted from the disruption of the *Internationale,* could not be bridged any more. Two social philosophies were engaged in bitter combat. The International Congress in 1889, at Paris; in 1892, at Zurich, and in 1896, at London, produced irreconcilable differences. The majority of Social Democrats, forswearing their libertarian past and becoming politicians, succeeded in excluding the revolutionary and Anarchist delegates. The latter decided thenceforth to hold separate congresses. Their first congress was to take place in 1900, at Paris. The Socialist renegade Millerand, who had climbed into the Ministry of the Interior, here played a Judas rôle. The congress of the revolutionists was suppressed, and the delegates dispersed two days prior to the scheduled opening. But Millerand had no objections against the Social Democratic Congress, which was afterwards opened with all the trumpets of the advertiser's art.

However, the renegade did not accomplish his object. A number of delegates succeeded in holding a secret conference in the house of a comrade outside of Paris, where various points of theory and tactics were discussed. Emma Goldman took considerable part in these proceedings, and on that occasion came in contact with numerous representatives of the Anarchist movement of Europe.

Owing to the suppression of the congress, the delegates were in danger of being expelled from France. At this time also came the bad news from America regarding another unsuccessful attempt to liberate Alexander Berkman, proving a great shock to Emma Goldman. In November, 1900, she returned to America to devote herself to her profession of nurse, at the same time taking an active part in the American propaganda. Among other activities she organized monster meetings of protest against the terrible outrages of the Spanish government, perpetrated upon the political prisoners tortured in Montjuich.

In her vocation as nurse Emma Goldman enjoyed many opportunities of meeting the most unusual and peculiar characters. Few would have identified the "notorious Anarchist" in the small blonde woman, simply attired in the uniform of a nurse. Soon after her return from Europe she became acquainted with a patient by the name of Mrs. Stander, a morphine fiend, suffering excruciating agonies. She required careful attention to enable her to supervise a very important business she conducted,—that of Mrs. Warren. In Third Street, near Third Avenue, was situated her private residence, and near it, connected by a separate entrance, was her place of business. One evening, the nurse, upon entering the room of her patient, suddenly came face to face with a male visitor, bull-necked and of brutal appearance. The man was no other than Mr. Jacobs, the detective who seven years previously had brought Emma Goldman a prisoner from Philadelphia and who had attempted to persuade her, on their way to New York, to betray the cause of the workingmen. It would be difficult to describe the expression of bewilderment on the countenance of the man as he so unexpectedly faced Emma Goldman, the nurse of his mistress. The brute was suddenly transformed into a gentleman, exerting himself to excuse his shameful behavior on the previous occasion. Jacobs was the "protector" of Mrs. Stander, and go-between for the house and the police. Several years later, as one of the detective staff of District Attorney Jerome, he committed perjury, was convicted, and sent to Sing Sing for a year. He is now probably employed by some private detective agency, a desirable pillar of respectable society.

In 1901 Peter Kropotkin was invited by the Lowell Institute of Massachusetts to deliver a series of lectures on Russian literature. It was his second American tour, and naturally the comrades were anxious to use his presence for the benefit of the movement.

Emma Goldman entered into correspondence with Kropotkin and succeeded in securing his consent to arrange for him a series of lectures. She also devoted her energies to organizing the tours of other well known Anarchists, principally those of Charles W. Mowbray and John Turner. Similarly she always took part in all the activities of the movement, ever ready to give her time, ability, and energy to the Cause.

On the sixth of September, 1901, President McKinley was shot by Leon Czolgosz at Buffalo. Immediately an unprecedented campaign of persecution was set in motion against Emma Goldman as the best known Anarchist in the country. Although there was absolutely no foundation for the accusation, she, together with other prominent Anarchists, was arrested in Chicago, kept in confinement for several weeks, and subjected to severest cross-examination. Never before in the history of the country had such a terrible man-hunt taken place against a person in public life. But the efforts of police and press to connect Emma Goldman with Czolgosz proved futile. Yet the episode left her wounded to the heart. The physical suffering, the humiliation and brutality at the hands of the police she could bear. The depression of soul was far worse. She was overwhelmed by the realization of the stupidity, lack of understanding, and vileness which characterized the events of those terrible days. The attitude of misunderstanding on the part of the majority of her own comrades toward Czolgosz almost drove her to desperation. Stirred to the very inmost of her soul,

she published an article on Czolgosz in which she
tried to explain the deed in its social and individual
aspects. As once before, after Berkman's act, she
now also was unable to find quarters; like a veritable wild animal she was driven from place to place.
This terrible persecution and, especially, the attitude of her comrades made it impossible for her to
continue propaganda. The soreness of body and
soul had first to heal. During 1901-1903 she did
not resume the platform. As "Miss Smith" she lived
a quiet life, practicing her profession and devoting
her leisure to the study of literature and, particularly,
to the modern drama, which she considers one of
the greatest disseminators of radical ideas and enlightened feeling.

Yet one thing the persecution of Emma Goldman accomplished. Her name was brought before
the public with greater frequency and emphasis
than ever before, the malicious harassing of the
much maligned agitator arousing strong sympathy
in many circles. Persons in various walks of life
began to get interested in her struggle and her ideas.
A better understanding and appreciation were now
beginning to manifest themselves.

The arrival in America of the English Anarchist,
John Turner, induced Emma Goldman to leave her
retirement. Again she threw herself into her public
activities, organizing an energetic movement for the
defense of Turner, whom the Immigration authorities condemned to deportation on account of the
Anarchist exclusion law, passed after the death of
McKinley.

When Paul Orleneff and Mme. Nazimova arrived in New York to acquaint the American public with Russian dramatic art, Emma Goldman became the manager of the undertaking. By much patience and perseverance she succeeded in raising the necessary funds to introduce the Russian artists to the theatergoers of New York and Chicago. Though financially not a success, the venture proved of great artistic value. As manager of the Russian theater Emma Goldman enjoyed some unique experiences. M. Orleneff could converse only in Russian, and "Miss Smith" was forced to act as his interpreter at various polite functions. Most of the aristocratic ladies of Fifth Avenue had not the least inkling that the amiable manager who so entertainingly discussed philosophy, drama, and literature at their five o'clock teas, was the "notorious" Emma Goldman. If the latter should some day write her autobiography, she will no doubt have many interesting anecdotes to relate in connection with these experiences.

The weekly Anarchist publication *Free Society*, issued by the Isaak family, was forced to suspend in consequence of the nation-wide fury that swept the country after the death of McKinley. To fill out the gap Emma Goldman, in co-operation with Max Baginski and other comrades, decided to publish a monthly magazine devoted to the furtherance of Anarchist ideas in life and literature. The first issue of *Mother Earth* appeared in the month of March, 1906, the initial expenses of the periodical partly covered by the proceeds of a theater benefit given by Orleneff, Mme. Nazimova, and their company, in favor of the Anarchist magazine. Under tremendous difficulties and obstacles the tireless propagandist has succeeded in continuing *Mother Earth* uninterruptedly since 1906—an achievement rarely equalled in the annals of radical publications.

In May, 1906, Alexander Berkman at last left the hell of Pennsylvania, where he had passed the best fourteen years of his life. No one had believed in the possibility of his survival. His liberation terminated a nightmare of fourteen years for Emma Goldman, and an important chapter of her career was thus concluded.

Nowhere had the birth of the Russian revolution aroused such vital and active response as among the Russians living in America. The heroes of the revolutionary movement in Russia, Tchaikovsky, Mme. Breshkovskaia, Gershuni, and others visited these shores to waken the sympathies of the American people toward the struggle for liberty, and to collect aid for its continuance and support. The success of these efforts was to a considerable extent due to the exertions, eloquence, and the talent for organization on the part of Emma Goldman. This opportunity enabled her to give valuable services to the struggle for liberty in her native land. It is not generally known that it is the Anarchists who are mainly instrumental in insuring the success, moral as well as financial, of most of the radical undertakings. The Anarchist is indifferent to acknowledged appreciation; the needs of the Cause absorb his whole interest, and to these he devotes his energy and abilities. Yet it may be mentioned that some otherwise decent folks, though at all times anxious for Anarchist support and co-operation, are ever willing to monopolize all the credit for the work done. During the last several decades it was chiefly the Anarchists who had organized all the great revolutionary efforts, and aided in every struggle for liberty. But for fear of shocking the respectable mob, who looks upon the Anarchists as the apostles of Satan, and because of their social position in bourgeois society, the would-be radicals ignore the activity of the Anarchists.

In 1907 Emma Goldman participated as delegate to the second Anarchist Congress, at Amsterdam. She was intensely active in all its proceedings and supported the organization of the Anarchist *Internationale*. Together with the other American delegate, Max Baginski, she submitted to the congress an exhaustive report of American conditions, closing with the following characteristic remarks:

"The charge that Anarchism is destructive, rather than constructive, and that, therefore, Anarchism is opposed to organization, is one of the many falsehoods spread by our opponents. They confound our present social institutions with organization; hence they fail to understand how we can oppose the former, and yet favor the latter. The fact, however, is that the two are not identical.

The State is commonly regarded as the highest form of organization. But is it in reality a true organization? Is it not rather an arbitrary institution, cunningly imposed upon the masses?

Industry, too, is called an organization; yet nothing is farther from the truth. Industry is the ceaseless piracy of the rich against the poor.

We are asked to believe that the Army is an organization, but a close investigation will show that it is nothing else than a cruel instrument of blind force.

The Public School! The colleges and other institutions of learning, are they not models of organization, offering the people fine opportunities for instruction? Far from it. The school, more than any other institution, is a veritable barrack, where the human mind is drilled and manipulated into submission to various social and moral spooks, and thus fitted to continue our system of exploitation and oppression.

Organization, as *we* understand it, however, is a different thing. It is based, primarily, on freedom. It is a natural and voluntary grouping of energies to secure results beneficial to humanity.

It is the harmony of organic growth which produces variety of color and form, the complete whole we admire in the flower. Analogously will the organized activity of free human beings, imbued with the spirit of solidarity, result in the perfection of social harmony, which we call Anarchism. In fact, Anarchism alone makes non-authoritarian organization of common interests possible, since it abolishes the existing antagonism between individuals and classes.

Under present conditions the antagonism of economic and social interests results in relentless war among the social units, and creates an insurmountable obstacle in the way of a co-operative commonwealth.

There is a mistaken notion that organization does not foster individual freedom; that, on the contrary, it means the decay of individuality. In reality, however, the true function of organization is to aid the development and growth of personality.

Just as the animal cells, by mutual co-operation, express their latent powers in formation of the complete organism, so does the individual, by co-operative effort with other individuals, attain his highest form of development.

An organization, in the true sense, cannot result from the combination of mere nonentities. It must be composed of self-conscious, intelligent individualities. Indeed, the total of the possibilities and activities of an organization is represented in the expression of individual energies.

It therefore logically follows that the greater the number of strong, self-conscious personalities in an organization, the less danger of stagnation, and the more intense its life element.

Anarchism asserts the possibility of an organization without discipline, fear, or punishment, and without the pressure of poverty: a new social organism which will make an end to the terrible struggle for the means of existence,—the savage struggle which undermines the finest qualities in man, and ever widens the social abyss. In short, Anarchism strives towards a social organization which will establish well-being for all.

The germ of such an organization can be found in that form of trades-unionism which has done away with centralization, bureaucracy, and discipline, and which favors independent and direct action on the part of its members."

The very considerable progress of Anarchist ideas in America can best be gauged by the remarkable success of the three extensive lecture tours of Emma Goldman since the Amsterdam Congress of 1907. Each tour extended over new territory, including localities where Anarchism had never before received a hearing. But the most gratifying aspect of her untiring efforts is the tremendous sale of Anarchist literature, whose propagandistic effect cannot be estimated. It was during one of these tours that a remarkable incident happened, strikingly demonstrating the inspiring potentialities of the Anarchist idea. In San Francisco, in 1908, Emma Goldman's lecture attracted a soldier of the United States Army, William Buwalda. For daring to attend an Anarchist meeting, the free Republic court-martialed Buwalda and imprisoned him for one year. Thanks to the regenerating power of the new philosophy, the government lost a soldier, but the cause of liberty gained a man.

A propagandist of Emma Goldman's importance is necessarily a sharp thorn to the reaction. She is looked upon as a danger to the continued existence of authoritarian usurpation. No wonder, then, that the enemy resorts to any and all means to make her impossible. A systematic attempt to suppress her activities was organized a year ago by the united police force of the country. But like all previous similar attempts, it failed in a most brilliant manner. Energetic protests on the part of the intellectual element of America succeeded in overthrowing the dastardly conspiracy against free speech. Another attempt to make Emma Goldman impossible was essayed by the Federal authorities at Washington. In order to deprive her of the rights of citizenship, the government revoked the citizenship papers of her husband, whom she had married at the youthful age of eighteen, and whose whereabouts, if he be alive, could not be determined for the last two decades. The great government of the glorious United States did not hesitate to stoop to the most despicable methods to accomplish that achievement. But as her citizenship had never proved of use to Emma Goldman, she can bear the loss with a light heart.

There are personalities who possess such a powerful individuality that by its very force they exert the most potent influence over the best representatives of their time. Michael Bakunin was such a personality. But for him, Richard Wagner had never written *Die Kunst und die Revolution*. Emma Goldman is a similar personality. She is a strong factor in the socio-political life of America. By virtue of her eloquence, energy, and brilliant mentality, she moulds the minds and hearts of thousands of her auditors.

Deep sympathy and compassion for suffering humanity, and an inexorable honesty toward herself, are the leading traits of Emma Goldman. No person, whether friend or foe, shall presume to control her goal or dictate her mode of life. She would perish rather than sacrifice her convictions, or the right of self-ownership of soul and body. Respectability could easily forgive the teaching of theoretic Anarchism; but Emma Goldman does not merely preach the new philosophy; she also persists in living it,—and that is the one supreme, unforgivable crime. Were she, like so many radicals, to consider her ideal as merely an intellectual ornament; were she to make concessions to existing society and compromise with old prejudices,—then even the most radical views could be pardoned in her. But that she takes her radicalism seriously; that it has permeated her blood and marrow to the extent where she not merely teaches but also practices her convictions—this shocks even the radical Mrs. Grundy. Emma Goldman lives her own life; she associates with publicans—hence the indignation of the Pharisees and Sadducees.

It is no mere coincidence that such divergent writers as Pietro Gori and William Marion Reedy find similar traits in their characterization of Emma Goldman. In a contribution to *La Questione Sociale*, Pietro Gori calls her a "moral power, a woman who, with the vision of a sibyl, prophesies the coming of a new kingdom for the oppressed; a woman who, with logic and deep earnestness, analyses the ills of society, and portrays, with artist touch, the coming dawn of humanity, founded on equality, brotherhood, and liberty."

William Reedy sees in Emma Goldman the "daughter of the dream, her gospel a vision which is the vision of every truly great-souled man and woman who has ever lived."

Cowards who fear the consequences of their deeds have coined the word of philosophic Anarchism. Emma Goldman is too sincere, too defiant, to seek safety behind such paltry pleas. She is an Anarchist, pure and simple. She represents the idea of Anarchism as framed by Josiah Warren, Proudhon, Bakunin, Kropotkin, Tolstoy. Yet she also understands the psychologic causes which induce a Caserio, a Vaillant, a Bresci, a Berkman, or a Czolgosz to commit deeds of violence. To the soldier in the social struggle it is a point of honor to come in conflict with the powers of darkness and tyranny, and Emma Goldman is proud to count among her best friends and comrades men and women who bear the wounds and scars received in battle.

In the words of Voltairine de Cleyre, characterizing Emma Goldman after the latter's imprisonment in 1893: The spirit that animates Emma Goldman is the only one which will emancipate the slave from his slavery, the tyrant from his tyranny—the spirit which is willing to dare and suffer.

HIPPOLYTE HAVEL.

New York, December, 1910.

PREFACE

SOME twenty-one years ago I heard the first great Anarchist speaker—the inimitable John Most. It seemed to me then, and for many years after, that the spoken word hurled forth among the masses with such wonderful eloquence, such enthusiasm and fire, could never be erased from the human mind and soul. How could any one of all the multitudes who flocked to Most's meetings escape his prophetic voice! Surely they had but to hear him to throw off their old beliefs, and see the truth and beauty of Anarchism!

My one great longing then was to be able to speak with the tongue of John Most,—that I, too, might thus reach the masses. Oh, for the naivety of Youth's enthusiasm! It is the time when the hardest thing seems but child's play. It is the only period in life worth while. Alas! This period is but of short duration. Like Spring, the *Sturm und Drang* period of the propagandist brings forth growth, frail and delicate, to be matured or killed according to its powers of resistance against a thousand vicissitudes.

My great faith in the wonder worker, the spoken word, is no more. I have realized its inadequacy to

awaken thought, or even emotion. Gradually, and
with no small struggle against this realization, I came
to see that oral propaganda is at best but a means of
shaking people from their lethargy: it leaves no lasting
impression. The very fact that most people attend
meetings only if aroused by newspaper sensations, or
because they expect to be amused, is proof that they
really have no inner urge to learn.

It is altogether different with the written mode of
human expression. No one, unless intensely interested
in progressive ideas, will bother with serious books.
That leads me to another discovery made after many
years of public activity. It is this: All claims of education notwithstanding, the pupil will accept only that
which his mind craves. Already this truth is recognized by most modern educators in relation to the immature mind. I think it is equally true regarding
the adult. Anarchists or revolutionists can no more
be made than musicians. All that can be done is to
plant the seeds of thought. Whether something vital
will develop depends largely on the fertility of the
human soil, though the quality of the intellectual seed
must not be overlooked.

In meetings the audience is distracted by a thousand non-essentials. The speaker, though ever so
eloquent, cannot escape the restlessness of the crowd,
with the inevitable result that he will fail to strike root.
In all probability he will not even do justice to himself.

The relation between the writer and the reader is
more intimate. True, books are only what we want
them to be; rather, what we read into them. That we

can do so demonstrates the importance of written
as against oral expression. It is this certainty which
has induced me to gather in one volume my ideas on
various topics of individual and social importance.
They represent the mental and soul struggles of
twenty-one years,—the conclusions derived after many
changes and inner revisions.

I am not sanguine enough to hope that my readers
will be as numerous as those who have heard me. But
I prefer to reach the few who really want to learn,
rather than the many who come to be amused.

As to the book, it must speak for itself. Ex-
planatory remarks do but detract from the ideas set
forth. However, I wish to forestall two objections
which will undoubtedly be raised. One is in reference
to the essay on *Anarchism;* the other, on *Minorities
versus Majorities.*

"Why do you not say how things will be operated
under Anarchism?" is a question I have had to meet
thousands of times. Because I believe that Anarchism
can not consistently impose an iron-clad program or
method on the future. The things every new generation has to fight, and which it can least overcome, are
the burdens of the past, which holds us all as in a net.
Anarchism, at least as I understand it, leaves posterity
free to develop its own particular systems, in harmony
with its needs. Our most vivid imagination can not
foresee the potentialities of a race set free from external restraints. How, then, can any one assume to
map out a line of conduct for those to come? We, who
pay dearly for every breath of pure, fresh air, must
guard against the tendency to fetter the future. If

we succeed in clearing the soil from the rubbish of the past and present, we will leave to posterity the greatest and safest heritage of all ages.

The most disheartening tendency common among readers is to tear out one sentence from a work, as a criterion of the writer's ideas or personality. Friedrich Nietzsche, for instance, is decried as a hater of the weak because he believed in the *Uebermensch*. It does not occur to the shallow interpreters of that giant mind that this vision of the *Uebermensch* also called for a state of society which will not give birth to a race of weaklings and slaves.

It is the same narrow attitude which sees in Max Stirner naught but the apostle of the theory "each for himself, the devil take the hind one." That Stirner's individualism contains the greatest social possibilities is utterly ignored. Yet, it is nevertheless true that if society is ever to become free, it will be so through liberated individuals, whose free efforts make society.

These examples bring me to the objection that will be raised to *Minorities versus Majorities*. No doubt, I shall be excommunicated as an enemy of the people, because I repudiate the mass as a creative factor. I shall prefer that rather than be guilty of the dema-gogic platitudes so commonly in vogue as a bait for the people. I realize the malady of the oppressed and disinherited masses only too well, but I refuse to pre-scribe the usual ridiculous palliatives which allow the patient neither to die nor to recover. One cannot be too extreme in dealing with social ills; besides, the extreme thing is generally the true thing. My lack of faith in the majority is dictated by my faith in the potentialities of the individual. Only when the latter becomes free to choose his associates for a common purpose, can we hope for order and harmony out of this world of chaos and inequality.

For the rest, my book must speak for itself.

Emma Goldman

ANARCHISM

WHAT IT REALLY STANDS FOR

ANARCHY.

Ever reviled, accursed, ne'er understood,
  Thou art the grisly terror of our age.
"Wreck of all order," cry the multitude,
  "Art thou, and war and murder's endless rage."
O, let them cry. To them that ne'er have striven
  The truth that lies behind a word to find,
To them the word's right meaning was not given.
  They shall continue blind among the blind.
But thou, O word, so clear, so strong, so pure,
  Thou sayest all which I for goal have taken.
I give thee to the future! Thine secure
  When each at least unto himself shall waken.
Comes it in sunshine? In the tempest's thrill?
  I cannot tell—but it the earth shall see!
I am an Anarchist! Wherefore I will
  Not rule, and also ruled I will not be!

John Henry Mackay.

THE history of human growth and development is at the same time the history of the terrible struggle of every new idea heralding the approach of a brighter dawn. In its tenacious hold on tradition, the Old has never hesitated to make use of the foulest and cruelest means to stay the advent of the New, in whatever form or period the latter may have asserted itself. Nor need we retrace our steps into the distant past to realize the enormity of opposition, difficulties, and hardships placed in the path of every progressive idea. The rack, the thumbscrew, and the knout are still with us; so are the convict's garb and the social wrath, all conspiring against the spirit that is serenely marching on.

Anarchism could not hope to escape the fate of all other ideas of innovation. Indeed, as the most revolutionary and uncompromising innovator, Anarchism must needs meet with the combined ignorance and venom of the world it aims to reconstruct.

To deal even remotely with all that is being said and done against Anarchism would necessitate the writing of a whole volume. I shall therefore meet only two of the principal objections. In so doing, I shall attempt to elucidate what Anarchism really stands for.

The strange phenomenon of the opposition to Anarchism is that it brings to light the relation between so-called intelligence and ignorance. And yet this is not so very strange when we consider the relativity of all things. The ignorant mass has in its favor that it makes no pretense of knowledge or tolerance. Acting, as it always does, by mere impulse, its reasons are like those of a child. "Why?" "Because." Yet the opposition of the uneducated to Anarchism deserves the same consideration as that of the intelligent man.

What, then, are the objections? First, Anarchism
is impractical, though a beautiful ideal. Second,
Anarchism stands for violence and destruction, hence
it must be repudiated as vile and dangerous. Both
the intelligent man and the ignorant mass judge not
from a thorough knowledge of the subject, but either
from hearsay or false interpretation.

A practical scheme, says Oscar Wilde, is either
one already in existence, or a scheme that could be
carried out under the existing conditions; but it is
exactly the existing conditions that one objects to,
and any scheme that could accept these conditions is
wrong and foolish. The true criterion of the practical, therefore, is not whether the latter can keep
intact the wrong or foolish; rather is it whether the
scheme has vitality enough to leave the stagnant
waters of the old, and build, as well as sustain, new
life. In the light of this conception, Anarchism is
indeed practical. More than any other idea, it is
helping to do away with the wrong and foolish;
more than any other idea, it is building and sustaining new life.

The emotions of the ignorant man are continuously
kept at a pitch by the most blood-curdling stories about
Anarchism. Not a thing too outrageous to be employed against this philosophy and its exponents.
Therefore Anarchism represents to the unthinking
what the proverbial bad man does to the child,—
a black monster bent on swallowing everything; in
short, destruction and violence.

Destruction and violence! How is the ordinary
man to know that the most violent element in society

is ignorance; that its power of destruction is the very thing Anarchism is combating? Nor is he aware that Anarchism, whose roots, as it were, are part of nature's forces, destroys, not healthful tissue, but parasitic growths that feed on the life's essence of society. It is merely clearing the soil from weeds and sagebrush, that it may eventually bear healthy fruit.

Someone has said that it requires less mental effort to condemn than to think. The widespread mental indolence, so prevalent in society, proves this to be only too true. Rather than to go to the bottom of any given idea, to examine into its origin and meaning, most people will either condemn it altogether, or rely on some superficial or prejudicial definition of non-essentials.

Anarchism urges man to think, to investigate, to analyze every proposition; but that the brain capacity of the average reader be not taxed too much, I also shall begin with a definition, and then elaborate on the latter.

ANARCHISM:—The philosophy of a new social order based on liberty unrestricted by man-made law; the theory that all forms of government rest on violence, and are therefore wrong and harmful, as well as unnecessary.

The new social order rests, of course, on the materialistic basis of life; but while all Anarchists agree that the main evil today is an economic one, they maintain that the solution of that evil can be brought about only through the consideration of *every phase* of life,—individual, as well as the collective; the internal, as well as the external phases.

A thorough perusal of the history of human development will disclose two elements in bitter conflict with each other; elements that are only now beginning to be understood, not as foreign to each other, but as closely related and truly harmonious, if only placed in proper environment: the individual and social instincts. The individual and society have waged a relentless and bloody battle for ages, each striving for supremacy, because each was blind to the value and importance of the other. The individual and social instincts,—the one a most potent factor for individual endeavor, for growth, aspiration, self-realization; the other an equally potent factor for mutual helpfulness and social well-being.

The explanation of the storm raging within the individual, and between him and his surroundings, is not far to seek. The primitive man, unable to understand his being, much less the unity of all life, felt himself absolutely dependent on blind, hidden forces ever ready to mock and taunt him. Out of that attitude grew the religious concepts of man as a mere speck of dust dependent on superior powers on high, who can only be appeased by complete surrender. All the early sagas rest on that idea, which continues to be the *Leitmotiv* of the biblical tales dealing with the relation of man to God, to the State, to society. Again and again the same motif, *man is nothing, the powers are everything.* Thus Jehovah would only endure man on condition of complete surrender. Man can have all the glories of the earth, but he must not become conscious of himself. The State, society, and moral laws all sing the same refrain: Man can have all the glories of the earth, but he must not become conscious of himself.

Anarchism is the only philosophy which brings to man the consciousness of himself; which maintains that God, the State, and society are non-existent, that their promises are null and void, since they can be fulfilled only through man's subordination. Anarchism is therefore the teacher of the unity of life; not merely in nature, but in man. There is no conflict between the individual and the social instincts, any more than there is between the heart and the lungs: the one the receptacle of a precious life essence, the other the repository of the element that keeps the essence pure and strong. The individual is the heart of society, conserving the essence of social life; society is the lungs which are distributing the element to keep the life essence—that is, the individual—pure and strong.

"The one thing of value in the world," says Emerson, "is the active soul; this every man contains within him. The soul active sees absolute truth and utters truth and creates." In other words, the individual instinct is the thing of value in the world. It is the true soul that sees and creates the truth alive, out of which is to come a still greater truth, the re-born social soul.

Anarchism is the great liberator of man from the phantoms that have held him captive; it is the arbiter and pacifier of the two forces for individual and social harmony. To accomplish that unity, Anarchism has declared war on the pernicious influences which have so far prevented the harmonious

blending of individual and social instincts, the individual and society.

Religion, the dominion of the human mind; Property, the dominion of human needs; and Government, the dominion of human conduct, represent the
stronghold of man's enslavement and all the horrors
it entails. Religion! How it dominates man's mind,
how it humiliates and degrades his soul. God is
everything, man is nothing, says religion. But out
of that nothing God has created a kingdom so despotic, so tyrannical, so cruel, so terribly exacting that
naught but gloom and tears and blood have ruled
the world since gods began. Anarchism rouses man
to rebellion against this black monster. Break your
mental fetters, says Anarchism to man, for not until
you think and judge for yourself will you get rid
of the dominion of darkness, the greatest obstacle to
all progress.

Property, the dominion of man's needs, the denial
of the right to satisfy his needs. Time was when
property claimed a divine right, when it came to
man with the same refrain, even as religion, "Sacrifice! Abnegate! Submit!" The spirit of Anarchism
has lifted man from his prostrate position. He now
stands erect, with his face toward the light. He has
learned to see the insatiable, devouring, devastating
nature of property, and he is preparing to strike the
monster dead.

"Property is robbery," said the great French
Anarchist Proudhon. Yes, but without risk and
danger to the robber. Monopolizing the accumulated
efforts of man, property has robbed him of his birth-

right, and has turned him loose a pauper and an outcast.   Property has not even the time-worn excuse
that man does not create enough to satisfy all needs.
The A B C student of economics knows that the
productivity of labor within the last few decades far
exceeds normal demand.   But what are normal
demands to an abnormal institution?   The only
demand that property recognizes is its own glutton-
ous appetite for greater wealth, because wealth
means power; the power to subdue, to crush, to
exploit, the power to enslave, to outrage, to degrade.
America is particularly boastful of her great power,
her enormous national wealth.   Poor America, of
what avail is all her wealth, if the individuals com-
prising the nation are wretchedly poor?   If they live
in squalor, in filth, in crime, with hope and joy gone,
a homeless, soilless army of human prey.

It is generally conceded that unless the returns
of any business venture exceed the cost, bankruptcy
is inevitable.   But those engaged in the business of
producing wealth have not yet learned even this
simple lesson.   Every year the cost of production in
human life is growing larger (50,000 killed, 100,000
wounded in America last year); the returns to the
masses, who help to create wealth, are ever getting
smaller.   Yet America continues to be blind to the
inevitable bankruptcy of our business of production.
Nor is this the only crime of the latter.   Still more
fatal is the crime of turning the producer into a mere
particle of a machine, with less will and decision
than his master of steel and iron.   Man is being
robbed not merely of the products of his labor, but

of the power of free initiative, of originality, and
the interest in, or desire for, the things he is making.

Real wealth consists in things of utility and
beauty, in things that help to create strong, beautiful
bodies and surroundings inspiring to live in. But
if man is doomed to wind cotton around a spool, or
dig coal, or build roads for thirty years of his life,
there can be no talk of wealth. What he gives to
the world is only gray and hideous things, reflecting
a dull and hideous existence,—too weak to live, too
cowardly to die. Strange to say, there are people
who extol this deadening method of centralized production as the proudest achievement of our age. They
fail utterly to realize that if we are to continue in
machine subserviency, our slavery is more complete
than was our bondage to the King. They do not
want to know that centralization is not only the death-
knell of liberty, but also of health and beauty, of
art and science, all these being impossible in a clock-
like, mechanical atmosphere.

Anarchism cannot but repudiate such a method
of production: its goal is the freest possible expression of all the latent powers of the individual.
Oscar Wilde defines a perfect personality as "one
who develops under perfect conditions, who is not
wounded, maimed, or in danger." A perfect personality, then, is only possible in a state of society where
man is free to choose the mode of work, the conditions of work, and the freedom to work. One to
whom the making of a table, the building of a house,
or the tilling of the soil, is what the painting is to
the artist and the discovery to the scientist,—the

result of inspiration, of intense longing, and deep interest in work as a creative force. That being the ideal of Anarchism, its economic arrangements must consist of voluntary productive and distributive asso ciations, gradually developing into free communism, as the best means of producing with the least waste of human energy. Anarchism, however, also recognizes the right of the individual, or numbers of individuals, to arrange at all times for other forms of work, in harmony with their tastes and desires.

Such free display of human energy being possible only under complete individual and social freedom, Anarchism directs its forces against the third and greatest foe of all social equality; namely, the State, organized authority, or statutory law,—the dominion of human conduct.

Just as religion has fettered the human mind, and as property, or the monopoly of things, has subdued and stifled man's needs, so has the State enslaved his spirit, dictating every phase of conduct. "All government in essence," says Emerson, "is tyranny." It matters not whether it is government by divine right or majority rule. In every instance its aim is the absolute subordination of the individual.

Referring to the American government, the greatest American Anarchist, David Thoreau, said: "Government, what is it but a tradition, though a recent one, endeavoring to transmit itself unimpaired to posterity, but each instance losing its integrity; it has not the vitality and force of a single living man. Law never made man a whit more just; and by

means of their respect for it, even the well disposed
are daily made agents of injustice."

Indeed, the keynote of government is injustice.
With the arrogance and self-sufficiency of the King
who could do no wrong, governments ordain, judge,
condemn, and punish the most insignificant offenses,
while maintaining themselves by the greatest of all
offenses, the annihilation of individual liberty. Thus
Ouida is right when she maintains that "the State
only aims at instilling those qualities in its public
by which its demands are obeyed, and its exchequer
is filled. Its highest attainment is the reduction of
mankind to clockwork. In its atmosphere all those
finer and more delicate liberties, which require treatment and spacious expansion, inevitably dry up and
perish. The State requires a taxpaying machine in
which there is no hitch, an exchequer in which there
is never a deficit, and a public, monotonous, obedient,
colorless, spiritless, moving humbly like a flock of
sheep along a straight high road between two walls."

Yet even a flock of sheep would resist the chicanery
of the State, if it were not for the corruptive, tyrannical, and oppressive methods it employs to serve
its purposes. Therefore Bakunin repudiates the State
as synonymous with the surrender of the liberty of
the individual or small minorities,—the destruction of
social relationship, the curtailment, or complete denial
even, of life itself, for its own aggrandizement. The
State is the altar of political freedom and, like the
religious altar, it is maintained for the purpose of
human sacrifice.

In fact, there is hardly a modern thinker who

does not agree that government, organized authority, or the State, is necessary *only* to maintain or protect property and monopoly. It has proven efficient in that function only.

Even George Bernard Shaw, who hopes for the miraculous from the State under Fabianism, nevertheless admits that "it is at present a huge machine for robbing and slave-driving of the poor by brute force." This being the case, it is hard to see why the clever prefacer wishes to uphold the State after poverty shall have ceased to exist.

Unfortunately there are still a number of people who continue in the fatal belief that government rests on natural laws, that it maintains social order and harmony, that it diminishes crime, and that it prevents the lazy man from fleecing his fellows. I shall therefore examine these contentions.

A natural law is that factor in man which asserts itself freely and spontaneously without any external force, in harmony with the requirements of nature. For instance, the demand for nutrition, for sex gratification, for light, air, and exercise, is a natural law. But its expression needs not the machinery of government, needs not the club, the gun, the handcuff, or the prison. To obey such laws, if we may call it obedience, requires only spontaneity and free opportunity. That governments do not maintain themselves through such harmonious factors is proven by the terrible array of violence, force, and coercion all governments use in order to live. Thus Blackstone is right when he says, "Human laws are invalid, because they are contrary to the laws of nature."

Unless it be the order of Warsaw after the slaughter of thousands of people, it is difficult to ascribe to governments any capacity for order or social harmony. Order derived through submission and maintained by terror is not much of a safe guaranty; yet that is the only "order" that governments have ever maintained. True social harmony grows naturally out of solidarity of interests. In a society where those who always work never have anything, while those who never work enjoy everything, solidarity of interests is non-existent; hence social harmony is but a myth. The only way organized authority meets this grave situation is by extending still greater privileges to those who have already monopolized the earth, and by still further enslaving the disinherited masses. Thus the entire arsenal of government—laws, police, soldiers, the courts, legislatures, prisons,—is strenuously engaged in "harmonizing" the most antagonistic elements in society.

The most absurd apology for authority and law is that they serve to diminish crime. Aside from the fact that the State is itself the greatest criminal, breaking every written and natural law, stealing in the form of taxes, killing in the form of war and capital punishment, it has come to an absolute standstill in coping with crime. It has failed utterly to destroy or even minimize the horrible scourge of its own creation.

Crime is naught but misdirected energy. So long as every institution of today, economic, political, social, and moral, conspires to misdirect human energy into wrong channels; so long as most people

are out of place doing the things they hate to do,
living a life they loathe to live, crime will be inevitable, and all the laws on the statutes can only increase, but never do away with, crime. What does
society, as it exists today, know of the process of
despair, the poverty, the horrors, the fearful struggle
the human soul must pass on its way to crime and
degradation. Who that knows this terrible process
can fail to see the truth in these words of Peter
Kropotkin:

"Those who will hold the balance between the
benefits thus attributed to law and punishment
and the degrading effect of the latter on humanity;
those who will estimate the torrent of depravity
poured abroad in human society by the informer,
favored by the Judge even, and paid for in clinking
cash by governments, under the pretext of aiding
to unmask crime; those who will go within prison
walls and there see what human beings become
when deprived of liberty, when subjected to the
care of brutal keepers, to coarse, cruel words, to a
thousand stinging, piercing humiliations, will agree
with us that the entire apparatus of prison and punishment is an abomination which ought to be
brought to an end."

The deterrent influence of law on the lazy man
is too absurd to merit consideration. If society
were only relieved of the waste and expense of
keeping a lazy class, and the equally great expense
of the paraphernalia of protection this lazy class
requires, the social tables would contain an abundance for all, including even the occasional lazy

individual. Besides, it is well to consider that lazi-
ness results either from special privileges, or physical and mental abnormalities. Our present insane
system of production fosters both, and the most
astounding phenomenon is that people should want
to work at all now. Anarchism aims to strip labor
of its deadening, dulling aspect, of its gloom and
compulsion. It aims to make work an instrument
of joy, of strength, of color, of real harmony, so
that the poorest sort of a man should find in work
both recreation and hope.

To achieve such an arrangement of life, government, with its unjust, arbitrary, repressive measures,
must be done away with. At best it has but imposed one single mode of life upon all, without
regard to individual and social variations and needs.
In destroying government and statutory laws, Anarchism proposes to rescue the self-respect and
independence of the individual from all restraint
and invasion by authority. Only in freedom can
man grow to his full stature. Only in freedom will
he learn to think and move, and give the very best
in him. Only in freedom will he realize the true
force of the social bonds which knit men together,
and which are the true foundation of a normal
social life.

But what about human nature? Can it be
changed? And if not, will it endure under Anarchism?

Poor human nature, what horrible crimes have
been committed in thy name! Every fool, from
king to policeman, from the flatheaded par-

son to the visionless dabbler in science, presumes
to speak authoritatively of human nature. The
greater the mental charlatan, the more definite his
insistence on the wickedness and weaknesses of
human nature. Yet, how can any one speak of it today, with every soul in a prison, with every heart fettered, wounded, and maimed?

John Burroughs has stated that experimental
study of animals in captivity is absolutely useless.
Their character, their habits, their appetites un-
dergo a complete transformation when torn from
their soil in field and forest. With human nature
caged in a narrow space, whipped daily into submission, how can we speak of its potentialities?

Freedom, expansion, opportunity, and, above all,
peace and repose, alone can teach us the real dominant factors of human nature and all its wonderful
possibilities.

Anarchism, then, really stands for the liberation
of the human mind from the dominion of religion;
the liberation of the human body from the dominion
of property; liberation from the shackles and restraint of government. Anarchism stands for a
social order based on the free grouping of individuals for the purpose of producing real social wealth;
an order that will guarantee to every human being
free access to the earth and full enjoyment of the
necessities of life, according to individual desires,
tastes, and inclinations.

This is not a wild fancy or an aberration of the
mind. It is the conclusion arrived at by hosts of
intellectual men and women the world over; a con-

clusion resulting from the close and studious observation of the tendencies of modern society: individual liberty and economic equality, the twin forces for the birth of what is fine and true in man.

As to methods. Anarchism is not, as some may suppose, a theory of the future to be realized through divine inspiration. It is a living force in the affairs of our life, constantly creating new conditions. The methods of Anarchism therefore do not comprise an iron-clad program to be carried out under all circumstances. Methods must grow out of the economic needs of each place and clime, and of the intellectual and temperamental requirements of the individual. The serene, calm character of a Tolstoy will wish different methods for social reconstruction than the intense, overflowing personality of a Michael Bakunin or a Peter Kropotkin. Equally so it must be apparent that the economic and political needs of Russia will dictate more drastic measures than would England or America. Anarchism does not stand for military drill and uniformity; it does, however, stand for the spirit of revolt, in whatever form, against everything that hinders human growth. All Anarchists agree in that, as they also agree in their opposition to the political machinery as a means of bringing about the great social change.

"All voting," says Thoreau, "is a sort of gaming, like checkers, or backgammon, a playing with right and wrong; its obligation never exceeds that of expediency. Even voting for the right thing is doing nothing for it. A wise man will not leave the right to the mercy of chance, nor wish it to prevail through the power of the majority." A close examination of the machinery of politics and its achievements will bear out the logic of Thoreau.

What does the history of parliamentarism show? Nothing but failure and defeat, not even a single reform to ameliorate the economic and social stress of the people. Laws have been passed and enactments made for the improvement and protection of labor. Thus it was proven only last year that Illinois, with the most rigid laws for mine protection, had the greatest mine disasters. In States where child labor laws prevail, child exploitation is at its highest, and though with us the workers enjoy full political opportunities, capitalism has reached the most brazen zenith.

Even were the workers able to have their own representatives, for which our good Socialist politicians are clamoring, what chances are there for their honesty and good faith? One has but to bear in mind the process of politics to realize that its path of good intentions is full of pitfalls: wire-pulling, intriguing, flattering, lying, cheating; in fact, chicanery of every description, whereby the political aspirant can achieve success. Added to that is a complete demoralization of character and conviction, until nothing is left that would make one hope for anything from such a human derelict. Time and time again the people were foolish enough to trust, believe, and support with their last farthing aspiring politicians, only to find themselves betrayed and cheated.

It may be claimed that men of integrity would not become corrupt in the political grinding mill. Perhaps not; but such men would be absolutely helpless to exert the slightest influence in behalf of labor, as indeed has been shown in numerous instances. The State is the economic master of its servants. Good men, if such there be, would either remain true to their political faith and lose their economic support, or they would cling to their economic master and be utterly unable to do the slightest good. The political arena leaves one no alternative, one must either be a dunce or a rogue.

The political superstition is still holding sway over the hearts and minds of the masses, but the true lovers of liberty will have no more to do with it. Instead, they believe with Stirner that man has as much liberty as he is willing to take. Anarchism therefore stands for direct action, the open defiance of, and resistance to, all laws and restrictions, economic, social, and moral. But defiance and resistance are illegal. Therein lies the salvation of man. Everything illegal necessitates integrity, self-reliance, and courage. In short, it calls for free, independent spirits, for "men who are men, and who have a bone in their backs which you cannot pass your hand through."

Universal suffrage itself owes its existence to direct action. If not for the spirit of rebellion, of the defiance on the part of the American revolutionary fathers, their posterity would still wear the King's coat. If not for the direct action of a John

Brown and his comrades, America would still trade in the flesh of the black man. True, the trade in white flesh is still going on; but that, too, will have to be abolished by direct action. Trade-unionism, the economic arena of the modern gladiator, owes its existence to direct action. It is but recently that law and government have attempted to crush the trade-union movement, and condemned the exponents of man's right to organize to prison as conspirators. Had they sought to assert their cause through begging, pleading, and compromise, trade-unionism would today be a negligible quantity. In France, in Spain, in Italy, in Russia, nay even in England (witness the growing rebellion of English labor unions), direct, revolutionary, economic action has become so strong a force in the battle for industrial liberty as to make the world realize the tremendous importance of labor's power. The General Strike, the supreme expression of the economic consciousness of the workers, was ridiculed in America but a short time ago. Today every great strike, in order to win, must realize the importance of the solidaric general protest.

Direct action, having proven effective along economic lines, is equally potent in the environment of the individual. There a hundred forces encroach upon his being, and only persistent resistance to them will finally set him free. Direct action against the authority in the shop, direct action against the authority of the law, direct action against the invasive, meddlesome authority of our moral code, is the logical, consistent method of Anarchism.

Will it not lead to a revolution? Indeed, it will.
No real social change has ever come about without
a revolution. People are either not familiar with their
history, or they have not yet learned that revolution
is but thought carried into action.

Anarchism, the great leaven of thought, is today
permeating every phase of human endeavor. Science,
art, literature, the drama, the effort for economic
betterment, in fact every individual and social opposition to the existing disorder of things, is illumined
by the spiritual light of Anarchism. It is the philosophy of the sovereignty of the individual. It is
the theory of social harmony. It is the great, surging,
living truth that is reconstructing the world, and that
will usher in the Dawn.

MINORITIES VERSUS MAJORITIES

IF I WERE to give a summary of the tendency of our times, I would say, Quantity. The multitude, the mass spirit, dominates everywhere, destroying quality. Our entire life—production, politics, and education—rests on quantity, on numbers. The worker who once took pride in the thoroughness and quality of his work, has been replaced by brainless, incompetent automatons, who turn out enormous quantities of things, valueless to themselves, and generally injurious to the rest of mankind. Thus quantity, instead of adding to life's comforts and peace, has merely increased man's burden.

In politics, naught but quantity counts. In proportion to its increase, however, principles, ideals, justice, and uprightness are completely swamped by the array of numbers. In the struggle for supremacy the various political parties outdo each other in trickery, deceit, cunning, and shady machinations, confident that the one who succeeds is sure to be hailed by the majority as the victor. That is the only god,—Success. As to what expense, what terrible cost to character, is of no moment. We have not far to go in search of proof to verify this sad fact.

Never before did the corruption, the complete rottenness of our government stand so thoroughly exposed; never before were the American people brought face to face with the Judas nature of that political body, which has claimed for years to be absolutely beyond reproach, as the mainstay of our institutions, the true protector of the rights and liberties of the people.

Yet when the crimes of that party became so brazen that even the blind could see them, it needed but to muster up its minions, and its supremacy was assured. Thus the very victims, duped, betrayed, outraged a hundred times, decided, not against, but in favor of the victor. Bewildered, the few asked how could the majority betray the traditions of American liberty? Where was its judgment, its reasoning capacity? That is just it, the majority cannot reason; it has no judgment. Lacking utterly in originality and moral courage, the majority has always placed its destiny in the hands of others. Incapable of standing responsibilities, it has followed its leaders even unto destruction. Dr. Stockman was right: "The most dangerous enemies of truth and justice in our midst are the compact majorities, the damned compact majority." Without ambition or initiative, the compact mass hates nothing so much as innovation. It has always opposed, condemned, and hounded the innovator, the pioneer of a new truth.

The oft repeated slogan of our time is, among all politicians, the Socialists included, that ours is an era of individualism, of the minority. Only those who do not probe beneath the surface might be led to entertain this view. Have not the few accumulated the wealth of the world? Are they not the masters, the absolute kings of the situation? Their success, however, is due not to individualism, but to the inertia, the cravenness, the utter submission of the mass. The latter wants but to be dominated, to be led, to be coerced. As to individualism, at no time in human history did it have less chance of expression, less opportunity to assert itself in a normal, healthy manner.

The individual educator imbued with honesty of purpose, the artist or writer of original ideas, the independent scientist or explorer, the non-compromising pioneers of social changes are daily pushed to the wall by men whose learning and creative ability have become decrepit with age.

Educators of Ferrer's type are nowhere tolerated, while the dietitians of predigested food, à la Professors Eliot and Butler, are the successful perpetuators of an age of nonentities, of automatons. In the literary and dramatic world, the Humphrey Wards and Clyde Fitches are the idols of the mass, while but few know or appreciate the beauty and genius of an Emerson, Thoreau, Whitman; an Ibsen, a Hauptmann, a Butler Yeats, or a Stephen Phillips. They are like solitary stars, far beyond the horizon of the multitude.

Publishers, theatrical managers, and critics ask not for the quality inherent in creative art, but will it meet with a good sale, will it suit the palate of the people? Alas, this palate is like a dumping ground; it relishes anything that needs no mental mastication. As a result, the mediocre, the ordinary, the commonplace represents the chief literary output.

Need I say that in art we are confronted with the same sad facts? One has but to inspect our parks and thoroughfares to realize the hideousness and vulgarity of the art manufacture. Certainly, none but a majority taste would tolerate such an outrage on art. False in conception and barbarous in execution, the statuary that infests American cities has as much relation to true art, as a totem to a Michael Angelo. Yet that is the only art that succeeds. The true artistic genius, who will not cater to accepted notions, who exercises originality, and strives to be true to life, leads an obscure and wretched existence. His work may some day become the fad of the mob, but not until his heart's blood had been exhausted; not until the pathfinder has ceased to be, and a throng of an idealless and visionless mob has done to death the heritage of the master.

It is said that the artist of today cannot create because Prometheuslike he is bound to the rock of economic necessity. This, however, is true of art in all ages. Michael Angelo was dependent on his patron saint, no less than the sculptor or painter of today, except that the art connoisseurs of those days were far away from the madding crowd. They felt honored to be permitted to worship at the shrine of the master.

The art protector of our time knows but one criterion, one value,—the dollar. He is not concerned about the quality of any great work, but in the quantity of dollars his purchase implies. Thus the finan-

cier in Mirbeau's *Les Affaires sont les Affaires* points
to some blurred arrangement in colors, saying: "See
l·ow great it is; it cost 50,000 francs." Just like our
own parvenus.   The fabulous figures paid for their
great art discoveries must make up for the poverty
of their taste.

The most unpardonable sin in society is independence of thought.   That this should be so terribly
apparent in a country whose symbol is democracy, is
very significant of the tremendous power of the
majority.

Wendell Phillips said fifty years ago: "In our
country of absolute democratic equality, public opinion is not only omnipotent, it is omnipresent.   There
is no refuge from its tyranny, there is no hiding from
its reach, and the result is that if you take the old
Greek lantern and go about to seek among a hundred, you will not find a single American who has
not, or who does not fancy at least he has, something to gain or lose in his ambition, his social life,
or business, from the good opinion and the votes of
those around him.   And the consequence is that instead of being a mass of individuals, each one fear-
lessly blurting out his own conviction, as a nation
compared to other nations we are a mass of cowards.
More than any other people we are afraid of each
other."   Evidently we have not advanced very far
from the condition that confronted Wendell Phillips.

Today, as then, public opinion is the omnipresent
tyrant; today, as then, the majority represents a mass
of cowards, willing to accept him who mirrors its
own soul and mind poverty.   That accounts for the

unprecedented rise of a man like Roosevelt. He em
bodies the very worst element of mob psychology.
A politician, he knows that the majority cares little
for ideals or integrity. What it craves is display.
It matters not whether that be a dog show, a prize
fight, the lynching of a "nigger," the rounding up
of some petty offender, the marriage exposition of
an heiress, or the acrobatic stunts of an ex-president.
The more hideous the mental contortions, the greater
the delight and bravos of the mass. Thus, poor in
ideals and vulgar of soul, Roosevelt continues to be
the man of the hour.

On the other hand, men towering high above such
political pygmies, men of refinement, of culture, of
ability, are jeered into silence as mollycoddles. It is
absurd to claim that ours is the era of individualism.
Ours is merely a more poignant repetition of the
phenomenon of all history: every effort for progress,
for enlightenment, for science, for religious, political,
and economic liberty, emanates from the minority,
and not from the mass. Today, as ever, the few are
misunderstood, hounded, imprisoned, tortured, and
killed.

The principle of brotherhood expounded by the
agitator of Nazareth preserved the germ of life, of
truth and justice, so long as it was the beacon light
of the few. The moment the majority seized upon
it, that great principle became a shibboleth and harbinger of blood and fire, spreading suffering and
disaster. The attack on the omnipotence of Rome,
led by the colossal figures of Huss, Calvin, and
Luther, was like a sunrise amid the darkness of the

night. But so soon as Luther and Calvin turned politicians and began catering to the small potentates, the nobility, and the mob spirit, they jeopardized the great possibilities of the Reformation. They won success and the majority, but that majority proved no less cruel and bloodthirsty in the persecution of thought and reason than was the Catholic monster. Woe to the heretics, to the minority, who would not bow to its dicta. After infinite zeal, endurance, and sacrifice, the human mind is at last free from the religious phantom; the minority has gone on in pursuit of new conquests, and the majority is lagging behind, handicapped by truth grown false with age.

Politically the human race would still be in the most absolute slavery, were it not for the John Balls, the Wat Tylers, the Tells, the innumerable individual giants who fought inch by inch against the power of kings and tyrants. But for individual pioneers the world would have never been shaken to its very roots by that tremendous wave, the French Revolution. Great events are usually preceded by apparently small things. Thus the eloquence and fire of Camille Desmoulins was like the trumpet before Jericho, razing to the ground that emblem of torture, of abuse, of horror, the Bastille.

Always, at every period, the few were the banner bearers of a great idea, of liberating effort. Not so the mass, the leaden weight of which does not let it move. The truth of this is borne out in Russia with greater force than elsewhere. Thousands of lives have already been consumed by that bloody régime, yet the monster on the throne is not appeased.

How is such a thing possible when ideas, culture, literature, when the deepest and finest emotions groan under the iron yoke? The majority, that compact, immobile, drowsy mass, the Russian peasant, after a century of struggle, of sacrifice, of untold misery, still believes that the rope which strangles "the man with the white hands"* brings luck.

In the American struggle for liberty, the majority was no less of a stumbling block. Until this very day the ideas of Jefferson, of Patrick Henry, of Thomas Paine, are denied and sold by their posterity. The mass wants none of them. The greatness and courage worshipped in Lincoln have been forgotten in the men who created the background for the panorama of that time. The true patron saints of the black men were represented in that handful of fighters in Boston, Lloyd Garrison, Wendell Phillips, Thoreau, Margaret Fuller, and Theodore Parker, whose great courage and sturdiness culminated in that somber giant John Brown. Their untiring zeal, their eloquence and perseverance undermined the stronghold of the Southern lords. Lincoln and his minions followed only when abolition had become a practical issue, recognized as such by all.

About fifty years ago, a meteorlike idea made its appearance on the social horizon of the world, an idea so far-reaching, so revolutionary, so all-embracing as to spread terror in the hearts of tyrants everywhere. On the other hand, that idea was a harbinger of joy, of cheer, of hope to the millions. The pioneers

---

* The intellectuals.

knew the difficulties in their way, they knew the
opposition, the persecution, the hardships that would
meet them, but proud and unafraid they started on
their march onward, ever onward. Now that idea
has become a popular slogan. Almost everyone is
a Socialist today: the rich man, as well as his poor
victim; the upholders of law and authority, as well
as their unfortunate culprits; the freethinker, as well
as the perpetuator of religious falsehoods; the fashionable lady, as well as the shirtwaist girl. Why
not? Now that the truth of fifty years ago has become a lie, now that it has been clipped of all its
youthful imagination, and been robbed of its vigor,
its strength, its revolutionary ideal—why not? Now
that it is no longer a beautiful vision, but a "practical,
workable scheme," resting on the will of the majority,
why not? Political cunning ever sings the praise of
the mass: the poor majority, the outraged, the abused,
the giant majority, if only it would follow us.

Who has not heard this litany before? Who does
not know this never-varying refrain of all politicians?
That the mass bleeds, that it is being robbed and
exploited, I know as well as our vote-baiters. But
I insist that not the handful of parasites, but the
mass itself is responsible for this horrible state of
affairs. It clings to its masters, loves the whip, and
is the first to cry Crucify! the moment a protesting
voice is raised against the sacredness of capitalistic
authority or any other decayed institution. Yet how
long would authority and private property exist, if
not for the willingness of the mass to become soldiers,
policemen, jailers, and hangmen. The Socialist dema-

gogues know that as well as I, but they maintain the myth of the virtues of the majority, because their very scheme of life means the perpetuation of power. And how could the latter be acquired without numbers? Yes, authority, coercion, and dependence rest on the mass, but never freedom or the free unfoldment of the individual, never the birth of a free society.

Not because I do not feel with the oppressed, the disinherited of the earth; not because I do not know the shame, the horror, the indignity of the lives the people lead, do I repudiate the majority as a creative force for good. Oh, no, no! But because I know so well that as a compact mass it has never stood for justice or equality. It has suppressed the human voice, subdued the human spirit, chained the human body. As a mass its aim has always been to make life uniform, gray, and monotonous as the desert. As a mass it will always be the annihilator of individuality, of free initiative, of originality. I therefore believe with Emerson that "the masses are crude, lame, pernicious in their demands and influence, and need not to be flattered, but to be schooled. I wish not to concede anything to them, but to drill, divide, and break them up, and draw individuals out of them. Masses! The calamity are the masses. I do not wish any mass at all, but honest men only, lovely, sweet, accomplished women only."

In other words, the living, vital truth of social and economic well-being will become a reality only through the zeal, courage, the non-compromising determination of intelligent minorities, and not through the mass.

THE PSYCHOLOGY OF POLITICAL VIOLENCE

To ANALYZE the psychology of political violence is not only extremely difficult, but also very dangerous. If such acts are treated with understanding, one is immediately accused of eulogizing them. If, on the other hand, human sympathy is expressed with the *Attentäter*,* one risks being considered a possible accomplice. Yet it is only intelligence and sympathy that can bring us closer to the source of human suffering, and teach us the ultimate way out of it.

The primitive man, ignorant of natural forces, dreaded their approach, hiding from the perils they threatened. As man learned to understand Nature's phenomena, he realized that though these may destroy life and cause great loss, they also bring relief. To the earnest student it must be apparent that the accumulated forces in our social and economic life, culminating in a political act of violence, are similar to the terrors of the atmosphere, manifested in storm and lightning.

To thoroughly appreciate the truth of this view, one must feel intensely the indignity of our social

---

* A revolutionist committing an act of political violence.

wrongs; one's very being must throb with the pain, the sorrow, the despair millions of people are daily made to endure. Indeed, unless we have become a part of humanity, we cannot even faintly understand the just indignation that accumulates in a human soul, the burning, surging passion that makes the storm inevitable.

The ignorant mass looks upon the man who makes a violent protest against our social and economic iniquities as upon a wild beast, a cruel, heartless monster, whose joy it is to destroy life and bathe in blood; or at best, as upon an irresponsible lunatic. Yet nothing is further from the truth. As a matter of fact, those who have studied the character and personality of these men, or who have come in close contact with them, are agreed that it is their super-sensitiveness to the wrong and injustice surrounding them which compels them to pay the toll of our social crimes. The most noted writers and poets, discussing the psychology of political offenders, have paid them the highest tribute. Could anyone assume that these men had advised violence, or even approved of the acts? Certainly not. Theirs was the attitude of the social student, of the man who knows that beyond every violent act there is a vital cause.

Björnstjerne Björnson, in the second part of *Beyond Human Power,* emphasizes the fact that it is among the Anarchists that we must look for the modern martyrs who pay for their faith with their blood, and who welcome death with a smile, because they believe, as truly as Christ did, that their martyr-dom will redeem humanity.

François Coppé, the French novelist, thus expresses himself regarding the psychology of the *Attentäter:*

"The reading of the details of Vaillant's execution left me in a thoughtful mood. I imagined him expanding his chest under the ropes, marching with firm step, stiffening his will, concentrating all his energy, and, with eyes fixed upon the knife, hurling finally at society his cry of malediction. And, in spite of me, another spectacle rose suddenly before my mind. I saw a group of men and women pressing against each other in the middle of the oblong arena of the circus, under the gaze of thousands of eyes, while from all the steps of the immense amphitheatre went up the terrible cry, *Ad leones!* and, below, the opening cages of the wild beasts.

"I did not believe the execution would take place. In the first place, no victim had been struck with death, and it had long been the custom not to punish an abortive crime with the last degree of severity. Then, this crime, however terrible in intention, was disinterested, born of an abstract idea. The man's past, his abandoned childhood, his life of hardship, pleaded also in his favor. In the independent press generous voices were raised in his behalf, very loud and eloquent. 'A purely literary current of opinion' some have said, with no little scorn. *It is, on the contrary, an honor to the men of art and thought to have expressed once more their disgust at the scaffold.*"

Again Zola, in *Germinal* and *Paris,* describes the tenderness and kindness, the deep sympathy with

human suffering, of these men who close the chapter
of their lives with a violent outbreak against our
system.

Last, but not least, the man who probably better
than anyone else understands the psychology of the
Attentäter is M. Hamon, the author of the brilliant
work *Une Psychologie du Militaire Professionnel,*
who has arrived at these suggestive conclusions:

"The positive method confirmed by the rational
method enables us to establish an ideal type of
Anarchist, whose mentality is the aggregate of common psychic characteristics. Every Anarchist par-
takes sufficiently of this ideal type to make it possible
to differentiate him from other men. The typical
Anarchist, then, may be defined as follows: A man
perceptible by the spirit of revolt under one or more
of its forms,—opposition, investigation, criticism,
innovation,—endowed with a strong love of liberty,
egoistic or individualistic, and possessed of great curi-
osity, a keen desire to know. These traits are sup-
plemented by an ardent love of others, a highly
developed moral sensitiveness, a profound sentiment
of justice, and imbued with missionary zeal."

To the above characteristics, says Alvin F. San-
born, must be added these sterling qualities: a rare
love of animals, surpassing sweetness in all the ordinary relations of life, exceptional sobriety of
demeanor, frugality and regularity, austerity, even, of
living, and courage beyond compare.*

"There is a truism that the man in the street seems

---

* *Paris and the Social Revolution.*

always to forget, when he is abusing the Anarchists, or whatever party happens to be his *bête noire* for the moment, as the cause of some outrage just perpetrated. This indisputable fact is that homicidal outrages have, from time immemorial, been the reply of goaded and desperate classes, and goaded and desperate individuals, to wrongs from their fellowmen, which they felt to be intolerable. Such acts are the violent recoil from violence, whether aggressive or repressive; they are the last desperate struggle of outraged and exasperated human nature for breathing space and life. And their cause lies not in any special conviction, but in the depths of that human nature itself. The whole course of history, political and social, is strewn with evidence of this fact. To go no further, take the three most notorious examples of political parties goaded into violence during the last fifty years: the Mazzinians in Italy, the Fenians in Ireland, and the Terrorists in Russia. Were these people Anarchists? No. Did they all three even hold the same political opinions? No. The Mazzinians were Republicans, the Fenians political separatists, the Russians Social Democrats or Constitutionalists. But all were driven by desperate circumstances into this terrible form of revolt. And when we turn from parties to individuals who have acted in like manner, we stand appalled by the number of human beings goaded and driven by sheer desperation into conduct obviously violently opposed to their social instincts.

"Now that Anarchism has become a living force in society, such deeds have been sometimes committed by Anarchists, as well as by others. For no new faith, even the most essentially peaceable and humane the mind of man has yet accepted, but at its first coming has brought upon earth not peace, but a sword; not because of anything violent or anti-social in the doctrine itself; simply because of the ferment any new and creative idea excites in men's minds, whether they accept or reject it. And a conception of Anarchism, which, on one hand, threatens every vested interest, and, on the other, holds out a vision of a free and noble life to be won by a struggle against existing wrongs, is certain to rouse the fiercest opposition, and bring the whole repressive force of ancient evil into violent contact with the tumultuous outburst of a new hope.

"Under miserable conditions of life, any vision of the possibility of better things makes the present misery more intolerable, and spurs those who suffer to the most energetic struggles to improve their lot, and if these struggles only immediately result in sharper misery, the outcome is sheer desperation. In our present society, for instance, an exploited wage worker, who catches a glimpse of what work and life might and ought to be, finds the toilsome routine and the squalor of his existence almost intolerable; and even when he has the resolution and courage to continue steadily working his best, and waiting until new ideas have so permeated society as to pave the way for better times, the mere fact that he has such ideas and tries to spread them, brings him into difficulties with his employers. How many thousands of Socialists, and above all Anarchists, have lost work and even the chance of work, solely on the ground of their opinions. It is only the specially gifted craftsman, who, if he be a zealous propagandist, can hope to retain permanent employment. And what happens to a man with his brain working actively with a ferment of new ideas, with a vision before his eyes of a new hope dawning for toiling and agonizing men, with the knowledge that his suffering and that of his fellows in misery is not caused by the cruelty of fate, but by the injustice of other human beings,—what happens to such a man when he sees those dear to him starving, when he himself is starved? Some natures in such a plight, and those by no means the least social or the least sensitive, will become violent, and will even feel that their violence is social and not anti-social, that in striking when and how they can, they are striking, not for themselves, but for human nature, outraged and despoiled in their persons and in those of their fellow sufferers. And are we, who ourselves are not in this horrible predicament, to stand by and coldly condemn these piteous victims of the Furies and Fates? Are we to decry as miscreants these human beings who act with heroic self-devotion, sacrificing their lives in protest, where less social and less energetic natures would lie down and grovel in abject submission to injustice and wrong? Are we to join the ignorant and brutal outcry which stigmatizes such men as monsters of wickedness, gratuitously running amuck in a harmonious and innocently peaceful society? No! We hate murder with a hatred that may seem absurdly exaggerated to apologists for Matabele massacres, to callous acquiescers in hangings and bombardments, but we decline in such cases of homicide, or attempted homicide, as those of which we are treating, to be guilty of the cruel injustice of flinging the whole responsibility of the deed upon the immediate perpetrator. The guilt of these homicides lies upon every man and woman who, intentionally or by cold indifference, helps to keep up social conditions that drive human beings to despair. The man who flings his whole life into the attempt, at the cost of his own life, to protest against the wrongs of his fellow men, is a saint compared to the active and passive upholders of cruelty and injustice, even if his protest destroy other lives besides his own. Let him who is without sin in society cast the first stone at such an one."*

That every act of political violence should nowadays be attributed to Anarchists is not at all surprising. Yet it is a fact known to almost everyone familiar with the Anarchist movement that a great number of acts, for which Anarchists had to suffer, either originated with the capitalist press or were instigated, if not directly perpetrated, by the police.

For a number of years acts of violence had been committed in Spain, for which the Anarchists were held responsible, hounded like wild beasts, and thrown into prison. Later it was disclosed that the perpetrators of these acts were not Anarchists, but members of the police department. The scandal became so widespread that the conservative Spanish papers demanded the apprehension and punishment of the

---

* From a pamphlet issued by the Freedom Group of London.

gang-leader, Juan Rull, who was subsequently condemned to death and executed. The sensational evidence, brought to light during the trial, forced Police
Inspector Momento to exonerate completely the
Anarchists from any connection with the acts committed during a long period. This resulted in the
dismissal of a number of police officials, among them
Inspector Tressols, who, in revenge, disclosed the fact
that behind the gang of police bomb throwers were
others of far higher position, who provided them with
funds and protected them.

This is one of the many striking examples of how
Anarchist conspiracies are manufactured.

That the American police can perjure themselves
with the same ease, that they are just as merciless,
just as brutal and cunning as their European colleagues, has been proven on more than one occasion.
We need only recall the tragedy of the eleventh of
November, 1887, known as the Haymarket Riot.

No one who is at all familiar with the case can
possibly doubt that the Anarchists, judicially murdered in Chicago, died as victims of a lying, bloodthirsty press and of a cruel police conspiracy. Has
not Judge Gary himself said: "Not because you have
caused the Haymarket bomb, but because you are
Anarchists, you are on trial."

The impartial and thorough analysis by Governor
Altgeld of that blotch on the American escutcheon
verified the brutal frankness of Judge Gary. It was
this that induced Altgeld to pardon the three Anarchists, thereby earning the lasting esteem of every
liberty-loving man and woman in the world.

When we approach the tragedy of September sixth, 1901, we are confronted by one of the most striking examples of how little social theories are responsible for an act of political violence. "Leon Czolgosz, an Anarchist, incited to commit the act by Emma Goldman." To be sure, has she not incited violence even before her birth, and will she not continue to do so beyond death? Everything is possible with the Anarchists.

Today, even, nine years after the tragedy, after it was proven a hundred times that Emma Goldman had nothing to do with the event, that no evidence whatsoever exists to indicate that Czolgosz ever called himself an Anarchist, we are confronted with the same lie, fabricated by the police and perpetuated by the press. No living soul ever heard Czolgosz make that statement, nor is there a single written word to prove that the boy ever breathed the accusation. Nothing but ignorance and insane hysteria, which have never yet been able to solve the simplest problem of cause and effect.

The President of a free Republic killed! What else can be the cause, except that the *Attentäter* must have been insane, or that he was incited to the act.

A free Republic! How a myth will maintain itself, how it will continue to deceive, to dupe, and blind even the comparatively intelligent to its monstrous absurdities. A free Republic! And yet within a little over thirty years a small band of parasites have successfully robbed the American people, and trampled upon the fundamental principles, laid down by the fathers of this country, guaranteeing to every man, woman, and child "life, liberty, and the pursuit of happiness." For thirty years they have been increasing their wealth and power at the expense of the vast mass of workers, thereby enlarging the army of the unemployed, the hungry, homeless, and friendless portion of humanity, who are tramping the country from east to west, from north to south, in a vain search for work. For many years the home has been left to the care of the little ones, while the parents are exhausting their life and strength for a mere pittance. For thirty years the sturdy sons of America have been sacrificed on the battlefield of industrial war, and the daughters outraged in corrupt factory surroundings. For long and weary years this process of undermining the nation's health, vigor, and pride, without much protest from the disinherited and oppressed, has been going on. Maddened by success and victory, the money powers of this "free land of ours" became more and more audacious in their heartless, cruel efforts to compete with the rotten and decayed European tyrannies for supremacy of power.

In vain did a lying press repudiate Leon Czolgosz as a foreigner. The boy was a product of our own free American soil, that lulled him to sleep with,

> My country, 'tis of thee,
> Sweet land of liberty.

Who can tell how many times this American child had gloried in the celebration of the Fourth of July, or of Decoration Day, when he faithfully honored the Nation's dead? Who knows but that he, too, was willing to "fight for his country and die for her liberty," until it dawned upon him that those he belonged to have no country, because they have been robbed of all that they have produced; until he realized that the liberty and independence of his youthful dreams were but a farce. Poor Leon Czolgosz, your crime consisted of too sensitive a social consciousness. Unlike your idealless and brainless American brothers, your ideals soared above the belly and the bank account. No wonder you impressed the one human being among all the infuriated mob at your trial— a newspaper woman—as a visionary, totally oblivious to your surroundings. Your large, dreamy eyes must have beheld a new and glorious dawn.

Now, to a recent instance of police-manufactured Anarchist plots. In that bloodstained city Chicago, the life of Chief of Police Shippy was attempted by a young man named Averbuch. Immediately the cry was sent to the four corners of the world that Averbuch was an Anarchist, and that the Anarchists were responsible for the act. Everyone who was at all known to entertain Anarchist ideas was closely watched, a number of people arrested, the library of an Anarchist group confiscated, and all meetings made impossible. It goes without saying that, as on various previous occasions, I must needs be held responsible for the act. Evidently the American police credit me with occult powers. I did not know Averbuch; in fact, had never before heard his name, and the only way I could have possibly "conspired" with him was in my astral body. But, then, the police are not concerned with logic or justice. What they seek is a target, to mask their absolute ignorance of the cause, of the psychology of a political act. Was Averbuch an Anarchist? There is no positive proof of it. He had been but three months in the country, did not know the language, and, as far as I could ascertain, was quite unknown to the Anarchists of Chicago.

What led to his act? Averbuch, like most young Russian immigrants, undoubtedly believed in the mythical liberty of America. He received his first baptism by the policeman's club during the brutal dispersement of the unemployed parade. He further experienced American equality and opportunity in the vain efforts to find an economic master. In short, a three months' sojourn in the glorious land brought him face to face with the fact that the disinherited are in the same position the world over. In his native land he probably learned that necessity knows no law —there was no difference between a Russian and an American policeman.

The question to the intelligent social student is not whether the acts of Czolgosz or Averbuch were practical, any more than whether the thunderstorm is practical. The thing that will inevitably impress itself on the thinking and feeling man and woman is that the sight of brutal clubbing of innocent victims in a so-called free Republic, and the degrading, soul-destroying economic struggle, furnish the spark that kindles the dynamic force in the overwrought, outraged souls of men like Czolgosz or Averbuch. No amount of persecution, of hounding, of repression, can stay this social phenomenon.

But, it is often asked, have not acknowledged Anarchists committed acts of violence? Certainly they have, always however ready to shoulder the responsibility. My contention is that they were impelled, not by the teachings of Anarchism, but by the tremendous pressure of conditions, making life unbearable to their sensitive natures. Obviously, Anarchism, or any other social theory, making man a conscious social unit, will act as a leaven for rebellion. This is not a mere assertion, but a fact verified by all experience. A close examination of the circumstances bearing upon this question will further clarify my position.

Let us consider some of the most important Anarchist acts within the last two decades. Strange as it may seem, one of the most significant deeds of political violence occurred here in America, in connection with the Homestead strike of 1892.

During that memorable time the Carnegie Steel Company organized a conspiracy to crush the Amalgamated Association of Iron and Steel Workers. Henry Clay Frick, then Chairman of the Company, was intrusted with that democratic task. He lost no time in carrying out the policy of breaking the Union, the policy which he had so successfully practiced during his reign of terror in the coke regions. Secretly, and while peace negotiations were being purposely prolonged, Frick supervised the military preparations, the fortification of the Homestead Steel Works, the erection of a high board fence, capped with barbed wire and provided with loopholes for sharpshooters. And then, in the dead of night, he attempted to smuggle his army of hired Pinkerton thugs into Homestead, which act precipitated the terrible carnage of the steel workers. Not content with the death of eleven victims, killed in the Pinkerton skirmish, Henry Clay Frick, good Christian and free American, straightway began the hounding down of the helpless wives and orphans, by ordering them out of the wretched Company houses.

The whole country was aroused over these inhuman outrages. Hundreds of voices were raised in protest, calling on Frick to desist, not to go too far. Yes, hundreds of people protested,—as one objects to annoying flies. Only one there was who actively responded to the outrage at Homestead,—Alexander Berkman. Yes, he was an Anarchist. He gloried in that fact, because it was the only force that made the discord between his spiritual longing and the world without at all bearable. Yet not Anarchism, as such, but the brutal slaughter of the eleven steel workers was the urge for Alexander Berkman's act, his attempt on the life of Henry Clay Frick.

The record of European acts of political violence affords numerous and striking instances of the influence of environment upon sensitive human beings.

The court speech of Vaillant, who, in 1894, exploded a bomb in the Paris Chamber of Deputies, strikes the true keynote of the psychology of such acts:

"Gentlemen, in a few minutes you are to deal your blow, but in receiving your verdict I shall have at least the satisfaction of having wounded the existing society, that cursed society in which one may see a single man spending, uselessly, enough to feed thousands of families; an infamous society which permits a few individuals to monopolize all the social wealth, while there are hundreds of thousands of unfortunates who have not even the bread that is not refused to dogs, and while entire families are committing suicide for want of the necessities of life.

"Ah, gentlemen, if the governing classes could go down among the unfortunates! But no, they prefer to remain deaf to their appeals. It seems that a fatality impels them, like the royalty of the eighteenth century, toward the precipice which will engulf them, for woe be to those who remain deaf to the cries of the starving, woe to those who, believing themselves of superior essence, assume the right to exploit those beneath them! There comes a time when the people no longer reason; they rise like a hurricane, and pass away like a torrent. Then we see bleeding heads impaled on pikes.

"Among the exploited, gentlemen, there are two classes of individuals. Those of one class, not realizing what they are and what they might be, take life as it comes, believe that they are born to be slaves, and content themselves with the little that is given them in exchange for their labor. But there are others, on the contrary, who think, who study, and who, looking about them, discover social iniquities. Is it their fault if they see clearly and suffer at seeing others suffer? Then they throw themselves into the struggle, and make themselves the bearers of the popular claims.

"Gentlemen, I am one of these last. Wherever I have gone, I have seen unfortunates bent beneath the yoke of capital. Everywhere I have seen the same wounds causing tears of blood to flow, even in the remoter parts of the inhabited districts of South America, where I had the right to believe that he who was weary of the pains of civilization might rest in the shade of the palm trees and there study nature. Well, there even, more than elsewhere, I have seen capital come, like a vampire, to suck the last drop of blood of the unfortunate pariahs.

"Then I came back to France, where it was reserved for me to see my family suffer atrociously. This was the last drop in the cup of my sorrow. Tired of leading this life of suffering and cowardice, I carried this bomb to those who are primarily responsible for social misery.

"I am reproached with the wounds of those who were hit by my projectiles. Permit me to point out in passing that, if the bourgeois had not massacred or caused massacres during the Revolution, it is probable that they would still be under the yoke of the nobility. On the other hand, figure up the dead and wounded of Tonquin, Madagascar, Dahomey, adding thereto the thousands, yes, millions of unfortunates who die in the factories, the mines, and wherever the grinding power of capital is felt. Add also those who die of hunger, and all this with the assent of our Deputies. Beside all this, of how little weight are the reproaches now brought against me!

"It is true that one does not efface the other; but, after all, are we not acting on the defensive when we respond to the blows which we receive from above? I know very well that I shall be told that I ought to have confined myself to speech for the vindication of the people's claims. But what can you expect! It takes a loud voice to make the deaf hear. Too long have they answered our voices by imprisonment, the rope, rifle volleys. Make no mistake; the explosion of my bomb is not only the cry of the rebel Vaillant, but the cry of an entire class which vindicates its rights, and which will soon add acts to words. For, be sure of it, in vain will they pass laws. The ideas of the thinkers will not halt; just as, in the last century, all the governmental forces could not prevent the Diderots and the Voltaires from spreading emancipating ideas among the people, so all the existing governmental forces will not prevent the Reclus, the Darwins, the Spencers, the Ibsens, the Mirbeaus, from spreading the ideas of justice and liberty which will annihilate the prejudices that hold the mass in ignorance. And these ideas, welcomed by the unfortunate, will flower in acts of revolt as they have done in me, until the day when the disappearance of authority shall permit all men to organize freely according to their choice, when everyone shall be able to enjoy the product of his labor, and when those moral maladies called prejudices shall vanish, permitting human beings to live in harmony, having no other desire than to study the sciences and love their fellows.

"I conclude, gentlemen, by saying that a society in which one sees such social inequalities as we see all about us, in which we see every day suicides caused by poverty, prostitution flaring at every street corner, —a society whose principal monuments are barracks and prisons,—such a society must be transformed as

soon as possible, on pain of being eliminated, and
that speedily, from the human race. Hail to him
who labors, by no matter what means, for this transformation! It is this idea that has guided me in
my duel with authority, but as in this duel I have
only wounded my adversary, it is now its turn to
strike me.

"Now, gentlemen, to me it matters little what penalty you may inflict, for, looking at this assembly
with the eyes of reason, I can not help smiling to
see you, atoms lost in matter, and reasoning only
because you possess a prolongation of the spinal
marrow, assume the right to judge one of your
fellows.

"Ah! gentlemen, how little a thing is your assembly and your verdict in the history of humanity; and
human history, in its turn, is likewise a very little
thing in the whirlwind which bears it through im-
mensity, and which is destined to disappear, or at
least to be transformed, in order to begin again the
same history and the same facts, a veritably per-
petual play of cosmic forces renewing and trans-
ferring themselves forever."

Will anyone say that Vaillant was an ignorant,
vicious man, or a lunatic? Was not his mind singu-
larly clear and analytic? No wonder that the best
intellectual forces of France spoke in his behalf, and
signed the petition to President Carnot, asking him
to commute Vaillant's death sentence.

Carnot would listen to no entreaty; he insisted
on more than a pound of flesh, he wanted Vaillant's
life, and then—the inevitable happened: President

Carnot was killed. On the handle of the stiletto used by the *Attentäter* was engraved, significantly,

VAILLANT!

Santa Caserio was an Anarchist. He could have gotten away, saved himself; but he remained, he stood the consequences.

His reasons for the act are set forth in so simple, dignified, and childlike manner that one is reminded of the touching tribute paid Caserio by his teacher of the little village school, Ada Negri, the Italian poet, who spoke of him as a sweet, tender plant, of too fine and sensitive texture to stand the cruel strain of the world.

"Gentlemen of the Jury! I do not propose to make a defense, but only an explanation of my deed.

"Since my early youth I began to learn that present society is badly organized, so badly that every day many wretched men commit suicide, leaving women and children in the most terrible distress. Workers, by thousands, seek for work and can not find it. Poor families beg for food and shiver with cold; they suffer the greatest misery; the little ones ask their miserable mothers for food, and the mothers cannot give it to them, because they have nothing. The few things which the home contained have already been sold or pawned. All they can do is beg alms; often they are arrested as vagabonds.

"I went away from my native place because I was frequently moved to tears at seeing little girls of eight or ten years obliged to work fifteen hours a day for the paltry pay of twenty centimes. Young

women of eighteen or twenty also work fifteen hours
daily, for a mockery of remuneration.   And that
happens not only to my fellow countrymen, but to
all the workers, who sweat the whole day long for a
crust of bread, while their labor produces wealth in
abundance.   The workers are obliged to live under
the most wretched conditions, and their food consists of a little bread, a few spoonfuls of rice, and
water; so by the time they are thirty or forty years
old, they are exhausted, and go to die in the hospitals.
Besides, in consequence of bad food and overwork,
these unhappy creatures are, by hundreds, devoured
by pellagra—a disease that, in my country, attacks,
as the physicians say, those who are badly fed and
lead a life of toil and privation.

"I have observed that there are a great many
people who are hungry, and many children who
suffer, whilst bread and clothes abound in the towns.
I saw many and large shops full of clothing and
woolen stuffs, and I also saw warehouses full of
wheat and Indian corn, suitable for those who are in
want.   And, on the other hand, I saw thousands of
people who do not work, who produce nothing and
live on the labor of others; who spend every day
thousands of francs for their amusement; who de-
bauch the daughters of the workers; who own dwell-
ings of forty or fifty rooms; twenty or thirty horses,
many servants; in a word, all the pleasures of life.

"I believed in God; but when I saw so great an
inequality between men, I acknowledged that it was
not God who created man, but man who created God.
And I discovered that those who want their property

to be respected, have an interest in preaching the existence of paradise and hell, and in keeping the people in ignorance.

"Not long ago, Vaillant threw a bomb in the Chamber of Deputies, to protest against the present system of society. He killed no one, only wounded some persons; yet bourgeois justice sentenced him to death. And not satisfied with the condemnation of the guilty man, they began to pursue the Anarchists, and arrest not only those who had known Vaillant, but even those who had merely been present at any Anarchist lecture.

"The government did not think of their wives and children. It did not consider that the men kept in prison were not the only ones who suffered, and that their little ones cried for bread. Bourgeois justice did not trouble itself about these innocent ones, who do not yet know what society is. It is no fault of theirs that their fathers are in prison; they only want to eat.

"The government went on searching private houses, opening private letters, forbidding lectures and meetings, and practicing the most infamous oppressions against us. Even now, hundreds of Anarchists are arrested for having written an article in a newspaper, or for having expressed an opinion in public.

"Gentlemen of the Jury, you are representatives of bourgeois society. If you want my head, take it; but do not believe that in so doing you will stop the Anarchist propaganda. Take care, for men reap what they have sown."

During a religious procession in 1896, at Barcelona, a bomb was thrown. Immediately three hundred men and women were arrested. Some were Anarchists, but the majority were trade-unionists and Socialists. They were thrown into that terrible bastille Montjuich, and subjected to most horrible tortures. After a number had been killed, or had gone insane, their cases were taken up by the liberal press of Europe, resulting in the release of a few survivors.

The man primarily responsible for this revival of the Inquisition was Canovas del Castillo, Prime Minister of Spain. It was he who ordered the torturing of the victims, their flesh burned, their bones crushed, their tongues cut out. Practiced in the art of brutality during his régime in Cuba, Canovas remained absolutely deaf to the appeals and protests of the awakened civilized conscience.

In 1897 Canovas del Castillo was shot to death by a young Italian, Angiolillo. The latter was an editor in his native land, and his bold utterances soon attracted the attention of the authorities. Persecution began, and Angiolillo fled from Italy to Spain, thence to France and Belgium, finally settling in England. While there he found employment as a compositor, and immediately became the friend of all his colleagues. One of the latter thus described Angiolillo: "His appearance suggested the journalist rather than the disciple of Guttenberg. His delicate hands, moreover, betrayed the fact that he had not grown up at the 'case.' With his handsome frank face, his soft dark hair, his alert expression, he looked the very type of the vivacious Southerner.

Angiolillo spoke Italian, Spanish, and French, but no English; the little French I knew was not sufficient to carry on a prolonged conversation. However, Angiolillo soon began to acquire the English idiom; he learned rapidly, playfully, and it was not long until he became very popular with his fellow compositors. His distinguished and yet modest manner, and his consideration towards his colleagues, won him the hearts of all the boys."

Angiolillo soon became familiar with the detailed accounts in the press. He read of the great wave of human sympathy with the helpless victims at Montjuich. On Trafalgar Square he saw with his own eyes the results of those atrocities, when the few Spaniards, who escaped Castillo's clutches, came to seek asylum in England. There, at the great meeting, these men opened their shirts and showed the horrible scars of burned flesh. Angiolillo saw, and the effect surpassed a thousand theories; the impetus was beyond words, beyond arguments, beyond himself even.

Señor Antonio Canovas del Castillo, Prime Minister of Spain, sojourned at Santa Agueda. As usual in such cases, all strangers were kept away from his exalted presence. One exception was made, however, in the case of a distinguished looking, elegantly dressed Italian—the representative, it was understood, of an important journal. The distinguished gentleman was—Angiolillo.

Señor Canovas, about to leave his house, stepped on the veranda. Suddenly Angiolillo confronted him. A shot rang out, and Canovas was a corpse.

The wife of the Prime Minister rushed upon the scene. "Murderer! Murderer!" she cried, pointing at Angiolillo. The latter bowed. "Pardon, Madame," he said, "I respect you as a lady, but I regret that you were the wife of that man."

Calmly Angiolillo faced death. Death in its most terrible form—for the man whose soul was as a child's.

He was garroted. His body lay, sun-kissed, till the day hid in twilight. And the people came, and pointing the finger of terror and fear, they said: "There—the criminal—the cruel murderer."

How stupid, how cruel is ignorance! It misunderstands always, condemns always.

A remarkable parallel to the case of Angiolillo is to be found in the act of Gaetano Bresci, whose *Attentat* upon King Umberto made an American city famous.

Bresci came to this country, this land of opportunity, where one has but to try to meet with golden success. Yes, he too would try to succeed. He would work hard and faithfully. Work had no terrors for him, if it would only help him to independence, manhood, self-respect.

Thus full of hope and enthusiasm he settled in Paterson, New Jersey, and there found a lucrative job at six dollars per week in one of the weaving mills of the town. Six whole dollars per week was, no doubt, a fortune for Italy, but not enough to breathe on in the new country. He loved his little home. He was a good husband and devoted father to his *bambina* Bianca, whom he adored. He worked and worked for a number of years. He actually managed to save one hundred dollars out of his six dollars per week.

Bresci had an ideal. Foolish, I know, for a workingman to have an ideal,—the Anarchist paper published in Paterson, *La Questione Sociale.*

Every week, though tired from work, he would help to set up the paper. Until late hours he would assist, and when the little pioneer had exhausted all resources and his comrades were in despair, Bresci brought cheer and hope, one hundred dollars, the entire savings of years. That would keep the paper afloat.

In his native land people were starving. The crops had been poor, and the peasants saw themselves face to face with famine. They appealed to their good King Umberto; he would help. And he did. The wives of the peasants who had gone to the palace of the King, held up in mute silence their emaciated infants. Surely that would move him. And then the soldiers fired and killed those poor fools.

Bresci, at work in the weaving mill at Paterson, read of the horrible massacre. His mental eye beheld the defenceless women and innocent infants of his native land, slaughtered right before the good King. His soul recoiled in horror. At night he heard the groans of the wounded. Some may have been his comrades, his own flesh. Why, why these foul murders?

The little meeting of the Italian Anarchist group in Paterson ended almost in a fight. Bresci had demanded his hundred dollars. His comrades begged, implored him to give them a respite. The paper would go down if they were to return him his loan. But Bresci insisted on its return.

How cruel and stupid is ignorance. Bresci got the money, but lost the good will, the confidence of his comrades. They would have nothing more to do with one whose greed was greater than his ideals.

On the twenty-ninth of July, 1900, King Umberto was shot at Monzo. The young Italian weaver of Paterson, Gaetano Bresci, had taken the life of the good King.

Paterson was placed under police surveillance, everyone known as an Anarchist hounded and persecuted, and the act of Bresci ascribed to the teachings of Anarchism. As if the teachings of Anarchism in its extremest form could equal the force of those slain women and infants, who had pilgrimed to the King for aid. As if any spoken word, ever so eloquent, could burn into a human soul with such white heat as the lifeblood trickling drop by drop from those dying forms. The ordinary man is rarely moved either by word or deed; and those whose social kinship is the greatest living force need no appeal to respond—even as does steel to the magnet —to the wrongs and horrors of society.

If a social theory is a strong factor inducing acts of political violence, how are we to account for the recent violent outbreaks in India, where Anarchism has hardly been born. More than any other old philosophy, Hindu teachings have exalted passive resistance, the drifting of life, the Nirvana, as the highest spiritual ideal. Yet the social unrest in India is daily growing, and has only recently resulted in an act of political violence, the killing of Sir Curzon Wyllie by the Hindu Madar Sol Dhingra.

If such a phenomenon can occur in a country socially and individually permeated for centuries with the spirit of passivity, can one question the tremendous, revolutionizing effect on human character exerted by great social iniquities? Can one doubt the logic, the justice of these words:

"Repression, tyranny, and indiscriminate punishment of innocent men have been the watchwords of the government of the alien domination in India ever since we began the commercial boycott of English goods. The tiger qualities of the British are much in evidence now in India. They think that by the strength of the sword they will keep down India! It is this arrogance that has brought about the bomb, and the more they tyrannize over a helpless and unarmed people, the more terrorism will grow. We may deprecate terrorism as outlandish and foreign to our culture, but it is inevitable as long as this tyranny continues, for it is not the terrorists that are to be blamed, but the tyrants who are responsible for it. It is the only resource for a helpless and unarmed people when brought to the verge of despair. It is never criminal on their part. The crime lies with the tyrant."*

Even conservative scientists are beginning to realize that heredity is not the sole factor moulding human character. Climate, food, occupation; nay,

---

* *The Free Hindustan.*

color, light, and sound must be considered in the study of human psychology.

If that be true, how much more correct is the contention that great social abuses will and must influence different minds and temperaments in a different way. And how utterly fallacious the stereotyped notion that the teachings of Anarchism, or certain exponents of these teachings, are responsible for the acts of political violence.

Anarchism, more than any other social theory, values human life above things. All Anarchists agree with Tolstoy in this fundamental truth: if the production of any commodity necessitates the sacrifice of human life, society should do without that commodity, but it can not do without that life. That, however, nowise indicates that Anarchism teaches submission. How can it, when it knows that all suffering, all misery, all ills, result from the evil of submission?

Has not some American ancestor said, many years ago, that resistance to tyranny is obedience to God? And he was not an Anarchist even. I would say that resistance to tyranny is man's highest ideal. So long as tyranny exists, in whatever form, man's deepest aspiration must resist it as inevitably as man must breathe.

Compared with the wholesale violence of capital and government, political acts of violence are but a drop in the ocean. That so few resist is the strongest proof how terrible must be the conflict between their souls and unbearable social iniquities.

High strung, like a violin string, they weep and moan for life, so relentless, so cruel, so terribly inhuman. In a desperate moment the string breaks. Untuned ears hear nothing but discord. But those who feel the agonized cry understand its harmony; they hear in it the fulfillment of the most compelling moment of human nature.

Such is the psychology of political violence.

PRISONS

A SOCIAL CRIME AND FAILURE

In 1849 Feodor Dostoyevsky wrote on the wall of his prison cell the following story of *The Priest and the Devil*:

" 'Hello, you little fat father!' the devil said to the priest. 'What made you lie so to those poor, misled people? What tortures of hell did you depict? Don't you know they are already suffering the tortures of hell in their earthly lives? Don't you know that you and the authorities of the State are my representatives on earth? It is you that make them suffer the pains of hell with which you threaten them. Don't you know this? Well, then, come with me!'

"The devil grabbed the priest by the collar, lifted him high in the air, and carried him to a factory, to an iron foundry. He saw the workmen there running and hurrying to and fro, and toiling in the scorching heat. Very soon the thick, heavy air and the heat are too much for the priest. With tears in his eyes, he pleads with the devil: 'Let me go! Let me leave this hell!'

" 'Oh, my dear friend, I must show you many more

places.' The devil gets hold of him again and drags him off to a farm. There he sees workmen threshing the grain. The dust and heat are insufferable. The overseer carries a knout, and unmercifully beats any-one who falls to the ground overcome by hard toil or hunger.

"Next the priest is taken to the huts where these same workers live with their families—dirty, cold, smoky, ill-smelling holes. The devil grins. He points out the poverty and hardships which are at home here.

" 'Well, isn't this enough?' he asks. And it seems as if even he, the devil, pities the people. The pious servant of God can hardly bear it. With uplifted hands he begs: 'Let me go away from here. Yes, yes! This is hell on earth!'

" 'Well, then, you see. And you still promise them another hell. You torment them, torture them to death mentally when they are already all but dead physically! Come on! I will show you one more hell—one more, the very worst.'

"He took him to a prison and showed him a dungeon, with its foul air and the many human forms, robbed of all health and energy, lying on the floor, covered with vermin that were devouring their poor, naked, emaciated bodies.

" 'Take off your silken clothes,' said the devil to the priest, 'put on your ankles heavy chains such as these unfortunates wear; lie down on the cold and filthy floor—and then talk to them about a hell that still awaits them!'

" 'No, no!' answered the priest, 'I cannot think of

anything more dreadful than this. I entreat you, let me go away from here!'

"'Yes, this is hell. There can be no worse hell than this. Did you not know it? Did you not know that these men and women whom you are frightening with the picture of a hell hereafter—did you not know that they are in hell right here, before they die?"

This was written fifty years ago in dark Russia, on the wall of one of the most horrible prisons. Yet who can deny that the same applies with equal force to the present time, even to American prisons?

With all our boasted reforms, our great social changes, and our far-reaching discoveries, human beings continue to be sent to the worst of hells, wherein they are outraged, degraded, and tortured, that society may be "protected" from the phantoms of its own making.

Prison, a social protection? What monstrous mind ever conceived such an idea? Just as well say that health can be promoted by a widespread contagion.

After eighteen months of horror in an English prison, Oscar Wilde gave to the world his great masterpiece, *The Ballad of Reading Goal:*

> The vilest deeds, like poison weeds,
>   Bloom well in prison air;
> It is only what is good in Man
>   That wastes and withers there.
> Pale Anguish keeps the heavy gate,
>   And the Warder is Despair.

Society goes on perpetuating this poisonous air, not realizing that out of it can come naught but the most poisonous results.

We are spending at the present $3,500,000 per day, $1,000,095,000 per year, to maintain prison institutions, and that in a democratic country,—a sum almost as large as the combined output of wheat, valued at $750,000,000, and the output of coal, valued at $350,000,000. Professor Bushnell of Washington, D. C., estimates the cost of prisons at $6,000,000,000 annually, and Dr. G. Frank Lydston, an eminent American writer on crime, gives $5,000,000,000 annually as a reasonable figure. Such unheard-of expenditure for the purpose of maintaining vast armies of human beings caged up like wild beasts!*

Yet crimes are on the increase. Thus we learn that in America there are four and a half times as many crimes to every million population today as there were twenty years ago.

The most horrible aspect is that our national crime is murder, not robbery, embezzlement, or rape, as in the South. London is five times as large as Chicago, yet there are one hundred and eighteen murders annually in the latter city, while only twenty in London. Nor is Chicago the leading city in crime, since it is only seventh on the list, which is headed by four Southern cities, and San Francisco and Los Angeles. In view of such a terrible condition of affairs, it seems ridiculous to prate of the protection society derives from its prisons.

---

* *Crime and Criminals.* W. C. Owen.

The average mind is slow in grasping a truth, but when the most thoroughly organized, centralized institution, maintained at an excessive national expense, has proven a complete social failure, the dullest must begin to question its right to exist. The time is past when we can be content with our social fabric merely because it is "ordained by divine right," or by the majesty of the law.

The widespread prison investigations, agitation, and education during the last few years are conclusive proof that men are learning to dig deep into the very bottom of society, down to the causes of the terrible discrepancy between social and individual life.

Why, then, are prisons a social crime and a failure? To answer this vital question it behooves us to seek the nature and cause of crimes, the methods employed in coping with them, and the effects these methods produce in ridding society of the curse and horror of crimes.

First, as to the *nature* of crime:

Havelock Ellis divides crime into four phases, the political, the passional, the insane, and the occasional. He says that the political criminal is the victim of an attempt of a more or less despotic government to preserve its own stability. He is not necessarily guilty of an unsocial offense; he simply tries to overturn a certain political order which may itself be anti-social. This truth is recognized all over the world, except in America where the foolish notion still prevails that in a Democracy there is no place for political criminals. Yet John Brown was a political criminal; so were the Chicago Anarchists; so is every

striker. Consequently, says Havelock Ellis, the
political criminal of our time or place may be the
hero, martyr, saint of another age. Lombroso calls
the political criminal the true precursor of the progressive movement of humanity.

"The criminal by passion is usually a man of
wholesome birth and honest life, who under the stress
of some great, unmerited wrong has wrought justice
for himself."*

Mr. Hugh C. Weir, in *The Menace of the Police*,
cites the case of Jim Flaherty, a criminal by passion,
who, instead of being saved by society, is turned into
a drunkard and a recidivist, with a ruined and pov-
erty-stricken family as the result.

A more pathetic type is Archie, the victim in
Brand Whitlock's novel, *The Turn of the Balance*,
the greatest American exposé of crime in the making.
Archie, even more than Flaherty, was driven to crime
and death by the cruel inhumanity of his surroundings, and by the unscrupulous hounding of the machinery of the law. Archie and Flaherty are but the
types of many thousands, demonstrating how the
legal aspects of crime, and the methods of dealing
with it, help to create the disease which is undermining our entire social life.

"The insane criminal really can no more be considered a criminal than a child, since he is mentally
in the same condition as an infant or an animal."*

The law already recognizes that, but only in rare
cases of a very flagrant nature, or when the culprit's

---

* *The Criminal*, Havelock Fllis.

wealth permits the luxury of criminal insanity. It
has become quite fashionable to be the victim of
paranoia. But on the whole the "sovereignty of
justice" still continues to punish criminally insane
with the whole severity of its power. Thus Mr. Ellis
quotes from Dr. Richter's statistics showing that in
Germany one hundred and six madmen, out of one
hundred and forty-four criminally insane, were condemned to severe punishment.

The occasional criminal "represents by far the
largest class of our prison population, hence is the
greatest menace to social well-being." What is the
cause that compels a vast army of the human family
to take to crime, to prefer the hideous life within
prison walls to the life outside? Certainly that cause
must be an iron master, who leaves its victims no
avenue of escape, for the most depraved human being
loves liberty.

This terrific force is conditioned in our cruel
social and economic arrangement. I do not mean to
deny the biologic, physiologic, or psychologic factors
in creating crime; but there is hardly an advanced
criminologist who will not concede that the social and
economic influences are the most relentless, the most
poisonous germs of crime. Granted even that there
are innate criminal tendencies, it is none the less true
that these tendencies find rich nutrition in our social
environment.

There is close relation, says Havelock Ellis, between crimes against the person and the price of
alcohol, between crimes against property and the price
of wheat. He quotes Quetelet and Lacassagne, the

former looking upon society as the preparer of crime, and the criminals as instruments that execute them. The latter finds that "the social environment is the cultivation medium of criminality; that the criminal is the microbe, an element which only becomes important when it finds the medium which causes it to ferment; *every society has the criminals it deserves.*"*

The most "prosperous" industrial period makes it impossible for the worker to earn enough to keep up health and vigor. And as prosperity is, at best, an imaginary condition, thousands of people are constantly added to the host of the unemployed. From East to West, from South to North, this vast army tramps in search of work or food, and all they find is the workhouse or the slums. Those who have a spark of self-respect left, prefer open defiance, prefer crime to the emaciated, degraded position of poverty.

Edward Carpenter estimates that five-sixths of indictable crimes consist in some violation of property rights; but that is too low a figure. A thorough investigation would prove that nine crimes out of ten could be traced, directly or indirectly, to our economic and social iniquities, to our system of remorseless exploitation and robbery. There is no criminal so stupid but recognizes this terrible fact, though he may not be able to account for it.

A collection of criminal philosophy, which Havelock Ellis, Lombroso, and other eminent men have compiled, shows that the criminal feels only too

---

* *The Criminal.*

keenly that it is society that drives him to crime. A
Milanese thief said to Lombroso: "I do not rob, I
merely take from the rich their superfluities; besides,
do not advocates and merchants rob?" A murderer
wrote: "Knowing that three-fourths of the social
virtues are cowardly vices, I thought an open assault
on a rich man would be less ignoble than the cautious
combination of fraud." Another wrote: "I am imprisoned for stealing a half dozen eggs. Ministers
who rob millions are honored. Poor Italy!" An
educated convict said to Mr. Davitt: "The laws of
society are framed for the purpose of securing the
wealth of the world to power and calculation, thereby
depriving the larger portion of mankind of its rights
and chances. Why should they punish me for taking
by somewhat similar means from those who have
taken more than they had a right to?" The same
man added: "Religion robs the soul of its independence; patriotism is the stupid worship of the
world for which the well-being and the peace of the
inhabitants were sacrificed by those who profit by it,
while the laws of the land, in restraining natural
desires, were waging war on the manifest spirit of the
law of our beings. Compared with this," he concluded, "thieving is an honorable pursuit."*

Verily, there is greater truth in this philosophy
than in all the law-and-moral books of society.

The economic, political, moral, and physical factors being the microbes of crime, how does society
meet the situation?

---

* *The Criminal.*

The methods of coping with crime have no doubt undergone several changes, but mainly in a theoretic sense. In practice, society has retained the primitive motive in dealing with the offender; that is, revenge. It has also adopted the theologic idea; namely, punishment; while the legal and "civilized" methods consist of deterrence or terror, and reform. We shall presently see that all four modes have failed utterly, and that we are today no nearer a solution than in the dark ages.

The natural impulse of the primitive man to strike back, to avenge a wrong, is out of date. Instead, the civilized man, stripped of courage and daring, has delegated to an organized machinery the duty of avenging his wrongs, in the foolish belief that the State is justified in doing what he no longer has the manhood or consistency to do. The "majesty of the law" is a reasoning thing; it would not stoop to primitive instincts. Its mission is of a "higher" nature. True, it is still steeped in the theologic muddle, which proclaims punishment as a means of purification, or the vicarious atonement of sin. But legally and socially the statute exercises punishment, not merely as an infliction of pain upon the offender, but also for its terrifying effect upon others.

What is the real basis of punishment, however? The notion of a free will, the idea that man is at all times a free agent for good or evil; if he chooses the latter, he must be made to pay the price. Although this theory has long been exploded, and thrown upon the dustheap, it continues to be applied daily by the entire machinery of government, turning it into the

most cruel and brutal tormentor of human life. The
only reason for its continuance is the still more cruel
notion that the greater the terror punishment spreads,
the more certain its preventative effect.

Society is using the most drastic methods in dealing with the social offender. Why do they not deter?
Although in America a man is supposed to be considered innocent until proven guilty, the instruments
of law, the police, carry on a reign of terror, making
indiscriminate arrests, beating, clubbing, bullying
people, using the barbarous method of the "third
degree," subjecting their unfortunate victims to the
foul air of the station house, and the still fouler language of its guardians. Yet crimes are rapidly multiplying, and society is paying the price. On the other
hand, it is an open secret that when the unfortunate
citizen has been given the full "mercy" of the law,
and for the sake of safety is hidden in the worst of
hells, his real Calvary begins. Robbed of his rights as
a human being, degraded to a mere automaton without will or feeling, dependent entirely upon the mercy
of brutal keepers, he daily goes through a process of
dehumanization, compared with which savage revenge
was mere child's play.

There is not a single penal institution or reformatory in the United States where men are not tortured
"to be made good," by means of the black-jack, the
club, the strait-jacket, the water-cure, the "hum-
ming bird" (an electrical contrivance run along the
human body), the solitary, the bull-ring, and starvation diet. In these institutions his will is broken, his
soul degraded, his spirit subdued by the deadly mo-

notony and routine of prison life. In Ohio, Illinois, Pennsylvania, Missouri, and in the South, these horrors have become so flagrant as to reach the outside world, while in most other prisons the same Christian methods still prevail. But prison walls rarely allow the agonized shrieks of the victims to escape—prison walls are thick, they dull the sound. Society might with greater immunity abolish all prisons at once, than to hope for protection from these twentieth-century chambers of horrors.

Year after year the gates of prison hells return to the world an emaciated, deformed, will-less, shipwrecked crew of humanity, with the Cain mark on their foreheads, their hopes crushed, all their natural inclinations thwarted. With nothing but hunger and inhumanity to greet them, these victims soon sink back into crime as the only possibility of existence. It is not at all an unusual thing to find men and women who have spent half their lives—nay, almost their entire existence—in prison. I know a woman on Blackwell's Island, who had been in and out thirty-eight times; and through a friend I learn that a young boy of seventeen, whom he had nursed and cared for in the Pittsburg penitentiary, had never known the meaning of liberty. From the reformatory to the penitentiary had been the path of this boy's life, until, broken in body, he died a victim of social revenge. These personal experiences are substantiated by extensive data giving overwhelming proof of the utter futility of prisons as a means of deterrence or reform.

Well-meaning persons are now working for a new departure in the prison question,—reclamation, to

restore once more to the prisoner the possibility of
becoming a human being. Commendable as this is, I
fear it is impossible to hope for good results from
pouring good wine into a musty bottle. Nothing
short of a complete reconstruction of society will
deliver mankind from the cancer of crime. Still, if
the dull edge of our social conscience would be sharp-
ened, the penal institutions might be given a new coat
of varnish. But the first step to be taken is the
renovation of the social consciousness, which is in a
rather dilapidated condition. It is sadly in need to
be awakened to the fact that crime is a question of
degree, that we all have the rudiments of crime in us,
more or less, according to our mental, physical, and
social environment; and that the individual criminal
is merely a reflex of the tendencies of the aggregate.

With the social consciousness wakened, the average individual may learn to refuse the "honor" of
being the bloodhound of the law. He may cease to
persecute, despise, and mistrust the social offender,
and give him a chance to live and breathe among his
fellows. Institutions are, of course, harder to reach.
They are cold, impenetrable, and cruel; still, with the
social consciousness quickened, it might be possible to
free the prison victims from the brutality of prison
officials, guards, and keepers. Public opinion is a
powerful weapon; keepers of human prey, even, are
afraid of it. They may be taught a little humanity,
especially if they realize that their jobs depend upon it.

But the most important step is to demand for the
prisoner the right to work while in prison, with some
monetary recompense that would enable him to lay

aside a little for the day of his release, the beginning of a new life.

It is almost ridiculous to hope much from present society when we consider that workingmen, wage-slaves themselves, object to convict labor. I shall not go into the cruelty of this objection, but merely consider the impracticability of it. To begin with, the opposition so far raised by organized labor has been directed against windmills. Prisoners have always worked; only the State has been their exploiter, even as the individual employer has been the robber of organized labor. The States have either set the convicts to work for the government, or they have farmed convict labor to private individuals. Twenty-nine of the States pursue the latter plan. The Federal government and seventeen States have discarded it, as have the leading nations of Europe, since it leads to hideous overworking and abuse of prisoners, and to endless graft.

"Rhode Island, the State dominated by Aldrich, offers perhaps the worst example. Under a five-year contract, dated July 7th, 1906, and renewable for five years more at the option of private contractors, the labor of the inmates of the Rhode Island Penitentiary and the Providence County Jail is sold to the Reliance-Sterling Mfg. Co. at the rate of a trifle less than 25 cents a day per man. This Company is really a gigantic Prison Labor Trust, for it also leases the convict labor of Connecticut, Michigan, Indiana, Nebraska, and South Dakota penitentiaries, and the reformatories of New Jersey, Indiana, Illinois, and Wisconsin, eleven establishments in all.

"The enormity of the graft under the Rhode Island contract may be estimated from the fact that this same Company pays 62½ cents a day in Nebraska for the convict's labor, and that Tennessee, for example, gets $1.10 a day for a convict's work from the Gray-Dudley Hardware Co.; Missouri gets 70 cents a day from the Star Overall Mfg. Co.; West Virginia 65 cents a day from the Kraft Mfg. Co., and Maryland 55 cents a day from Oppenheim, Oberndorf & Co., shirt manufacturers. The very difference in prices points to enormous graft. For example, the Reliance-Sterling Mfg. Co. manufactures shirts, the cost by free labor being not less than $1.20 per dozen, while it pays Rhode Island thirty cents a dozen. Furthermore, the State charges this Trust no rent for the use of its huge factory, charges nothing for power, heat, light, or even drainage, and exacts no taxes. What graft!"*

It is estimated that more than twelve million dollars' worth of workingmen's shirts and overalls is produced annually in this country by prison labor. It is a woman's industry, and the first reflection that arises is that an immense amount of free female labor is thus displaced. The second consideration is that male convicts, who should be learning trades that would give them some chance of being self-supporting after their release, are kept at this work at which they can not possibly make a dollar. This is the more serious when we consider that much of this labor is done in reformatories, which so loudly profess to be training their inmates to become useful citizens.

---

* Quoted from the publications of the National Committee on Prison Labor.

The third, and most important, consideration is that the enormous profits thus wrung from convict labor are a constant incentive to the contractors to exact from their unhappy victims tasks altogether beyond their strength, and to punish them cruelly when their work does not come up to the excessive demands made.

Another word on the condemnation of convicts to tasks at which they cannot hope to make a living after release. Indiana, for example, is a State that has made a great splurge over being in the front rank of modern penological improvements. Yet, according to the report rendered in 1908 by the training school of its "reformatory," 135 were engaged in the manufacture of chains, 207 in that of shirts, and 255 in the foundry—a total of 597 in three occupations. But at this so-called reformatory 59 occupations were represented by the inmates, 39 of which were connected with country pursuits. Indiana, like other States, professes to be training the inmates of her reformatory to occupations by which they will be able to make their living when released. She actually sets them to work making chains, shirts, and brooms, the latter for the benefit of the Louisville Fancy Grocery Co. Broom-making is a trade largely monopolized by the blind, shirt-making is done by women, and there is only one free chain-factory in the State, and at that a released convict can not hope to get employment. The whole thing is a cruel farce.

If, then, the States can be instrumental in robbing their helpless victims of such tremendous profits is it not high time for organized labor to stop its idle howl;

and to insist on decent remuneration for the convict,
even as labor organizations claim for themselves? In
that way workingmen would kill the germ which
makes of the prisoner an enemy to the interests of
labor. I have said elsewhere that thousands of convicts, incompetent and without a trade, without means
of subsistence, are yearly turned back into the social
fold. These men and women must live, for even an
ex-convict has needs. Prison life has made them
anti-social beings, and the rigidly closed doors that
meet them on their release are not likely to decrease
their bitterness. The inevitable result is that they
form a favorable nucleus out of which scabs, black-
legs, detectives, and policemen are drawn, only too
willing to do the master's bidding. Thus organized
labor, by its foolish opposition to work in prison,
defeats its own ends. It helps to create poisonous
fumes that stifle every attempt for economic betterment. If the workingman wants to avoid these
effects, he should *insist* on the right of the convict to
work, he should meet him as a brother, take him into
his organization, and *with his aid turn against the system which grinds them both.*

Last, but not least, is the growing realization of
the barbarity and the inadequacy of the definite sentence. Those who believe in, and earnestly aim at, a
change are fast coming to the conclusion that man
must be given an opportunity to make good. And
how is he to do it with ten, fifteen, or twenty years'
imprisonment before him? The hope of liberty and
of opportunity is the only incentive to life, especially
the prisoner's life. Society has sinned so long against

him—it ought at least to leave him that. I am not very sanguine that it will, or that any real change in that direction can take place until the conditions that breed both the prisoner and the jailer will be forever abolished.

> Out of his mouth a red, red rose!
> Out of his heart a white!
> For who can say by what strange way
> Christ brings his will to light,
> Since the barren staff the pilgrim bore
> Bloomed in the great Pope's sight.

PATRIOTISM

A MENACE TO LIBERTY

WHAT is patriotism? Is it love of one's birthplace, the place of childhood's recollections and hopes, dreams and aspirations? Is it the place where, in childlike naivety, we would watch the fleeting clouds, and wonder why we, too, could not run so swiftly? The place where we would count the milliard glittering stars, terror-stricken lest each one "an eye should be," piercing the very depths of our little souls? Is it the place where we would listen to the music of the birds, and long to have wings to fly, even as they, to distant lands? Or the place where we would sit at mother's knee, enraptured by wonderful tales of great deeds and conquests? In short, is it love for the spot, every inch representing dear and precious recollections of a happy, joyous, and playful childhood?

If that were patriotism, few American men of today could be called upon to be patriotic, since the place of play has been turned into factory, mill, and mine, while deafening sounds of machinery have replaced the music of the birds. Nor can we longer hear the tales of great deeds, for the stories our mothers tell today are but those of sorrow, tears, and grief.

What, then, is patriotism? "Patriotism, sir, is the last resort of scoundrels," said Dr. Johnson. Leo Tolstoy, the greatest anti-patriot of our times, defines patriotism as the principle that will justify the training of wholesale murderers; a trade that requires better equipment for the exercise of man-killing than the making of such necessities of life as shoes, clothing, and houses; a trade that guarantees better returns and greater glory than that of the average workingman.

Gustave Hervé, another great anti-patriot, justly calls patriotism a superstition—one far more injurious, brutal, and inhumane than religion. The superstition of religion originated in man's inability to explain natural phenomena. That is, when primitive man heard thunder or saw the lightning, he could not account for either, and therefore concluded that back of them must be a force greater than himself. Similarly he saw a supernatural force in the rain, and in the various other changes in nature. Patriotism, on the other hand, is a superstition artificially created and maintained through a network of lies and falsehoods; a superstition that robs man of his self-respect and dignity, and increases his arrogance and conceit.

Indeed, conceit, arrogance, and egotism are the essentials of patriotism. Let me illustrate. Patriotism assumes that our globe is divided into little spots, each one surrounded by an iron gate. Those who have had the fortune of being born on some particular spot, consider themselves better, nobler, grander, more intelligent than the living beings inhabiting any other spot. It is, therefore, the duty of everyone

living on that chosen spot to fight, kill, and die in the
attempt to impose his superiority upon all the others.

The inhabitants of the other spots reason in like
manner, of course, with the result that, from early
infancy, the mind of the child is poisoned with blood-
curdling stories about the Germans, the French, the
Italians, Russians, etc. When the child has reached
manhood, he is thoroughly saturated with the belief
that he is chosen by the Lord himself to defend *his*
country against the attack or invasion of any foreigner. It is for that purpose that we are clamoring
for a greater army and navy, more battleships and
ammunition. It is for that purpose that America has
within a short time spent four hundred million dollars. Just think of it—four hundred million dollars
taken from the produce of *the people*. For surely it
is not the rich who contribute to patriotism. They
are cosmopolitans, perfectly at home in every land.
We in America know well the truth of this. Are not
our rich Americans Frenchmen in France, Germans in
Germany, or Englishmen in England? And do they
not squandor with cosmopolitan grace fortunes coined
by American factory children and cotton slaves? Yes,
theirs is the patriotism that will make it possible to
send messages of condolence to a despot like the Russian Tsar, when any mishap befalls him, as President
Roosevelt did in the name of *his* people, when Sergius
was punished by the Russian revolutionists.

It is a patriotism that will assist the arch-murderer,
Diaz, in destroying thousands of lives in Mexico, or
that will even aid in arresting Mexican revolutionists
on American soil and keep them incarcerated in

American prisons, without the slightest cause or reason.

But, then, patriotism is not for those who represent wealth and power. It is good enough for the people. It reminds one of the historic wisdom of Frederick the Great, the bosom friend of Voltaire, who said: "Religion is a fraud, but it must be maintained for the masses."

That patriotism is rather a costly institution, no one will doubt after considering the following statistics. The progressive increase of the expenditures for the leading armies and navies of the world during the last quarter of a century is a fact of such gravity as to startle every thoughtful student of economic problems. It may be briefly indicated by dividing the time from 1881 to 1905 into five-year periods, and noting the disbursements of several great nations for army and navy purposes during the first and last of those periods. From the first to the last of the periods noted the expenditures of Great Britain increased from $2,101,848,936 to $4,143,226,885, those of France from $3,324,500,000 to $3,455,109,900, those of Germany from $725,000,200 to $2,700,375,600, those of the United States from $1,275,500,750 to $2,650,900,450, those of Russia from $1,900,975,500 to $5,250,445,100, those of Italy from $1,600,975,750 to $1,755,500,100, and those of Japan from $182,900,500 to $700,925,475.

The military expenditures of each of the nations mentioned increased in each of the five-year periods under review. During the entire interval from 1881 to 1905 Great Britain's outlay for her army increased fourfold, that of the United States was tripled, Russia's was doubled, that of Germany increased 35 per cent., that of France about 15 per cent., and that of Japan nearly 500 per cent. If we compare the expenditures of these nations upon their armies with their total expenditures for all the twenty-five years ending with 1905, the proportion rose as follows:

In Great Britain from 20 per cent. to 37; in the United States from 15 to 23; in France from 16 to 18; in Italy from 12 to 15; in Japan from 12 to 14. On the other hand, it is interesting to note that the proportion in Germany decreased from about 58 per cent. to 25, the decrease being due to the enormous increase in the imperial expenditures for other purposes, the fact being that the army expenditures for the period of 1901-5 were higher than for any five-year period preceding. Statistics show that the countries in which army expenditures are greatest, in proportion to the total national revenues, are Great Britain, the United States, Japan, France, and Italy, in the order named.

The showing as to the cost of great navies is equally impressive. During the twenty-five years ending with 1905 naval expenditures increased approximately as follows: Great Britain, 300 per cent.; France 60 per cent.; Germany 600 per cent.; the United States 525 per cent.; Russia 300 per cent.; Italy 250 per cent.; and Japan, 700 per cent. With the exception of Great Britain, the United States spends more for naval purposes than any other nation, and this expenditure bears also a larger proportion to the entire national disbursements than that of any other power. In the period 1881-5, the expenditure for the United States navy was $6.20 out of each $100 appropriated for all national purposes; the amount rose to $6.60 for the next five-year period, to $8.10 for the next, to $11.70 for the next, and to $16.40 for 1901-5. It is morally certain that the outlay for the current period of five years will show a still further increase.

The rising cost of militarism may be still further illustrated by computing it as a per capita tax on population. From the first to the last of the five-year periods taken as the basis for the comparisons here given, it has risen as follows: In Great Britain, from $18.47 to $52.50; in France, from $19.66 to $23.62; in Germany, from $10.17 to $15.51; in the United States, from $5.62 to $13.64; in Russia, from $6.14 to $8.37; in Italy, from $9.59 to $11.24, and in Japan from 86 cents to $3.11.

It is in connection with this rough estimate of cost per capita that the economic burden of militarism is most appreciable. The irresistible conclusion from available data is that the increase of expenditure for army and navy purposes is rapidly surpassing the growth of population in each of the countries considered in the present calculation. In other words, a continuation of the increased demands of militarism threatens each of those nations with a progressive exhaustion both of men and resources.

The awful waste that patriotism necessitates ought to be sufficient to cure the man of even average intelligence from this disease. Yet patriotism demands still more. The people are urged to be patriotic and for that luxury they pay, not only by supporting their "defenders," but even by sacrificing their own children. Patriotism requires allegiance to the flag, which means obedience and readiness to kill father, mother, brother, sister.

The usual contention is that we need a standing army to protect the country from foreign invasion. Every intelligent man and woman knows, however, that this is a myth maintained to frighten and coerce the foolish. The governments of the world, knowing each other's interests, do not invade each other. They have learned that they can gain much more by international arbitration of disputes than by war and conquest. Indeed, as Carlyle said, "War is a quarrel between two thieves too cowardly to fight their own battle; therefore they take boys from one village and another village, stick them into uniforms, equip them with guns, and let them loose like wild beasts against each other."

It does not require much wisdom to trace every war back to a similar cause. Let us take our own Spanish-American war, supposedly a great and patriotic event in the history of the United States. How our hearts burned with indignation against the atrocious Spaniards! True, our indignation did not flare up spontaneously. It was nurtured by months of newspaper agitation, and long after Butcher Weyler had killed off many noble Cubans and outraged many Cuban women. Still, in justice to the American Nation be it said, it did grow indignant and was willing to fight, and that it fought bravely. But when the smoke was over, the dead buried, and the cost of the war came back to the people in an increase in the price of commodities and rent—that is, when we sobered up from our patriotic spree—it suddenly dawned on us that the cause of the Spanish-American war was the consideration of the price of sugar; or, to be more explicit, that the lives, blood, and money of the American people were used to protect the inter- ests of American capitalists, which were threatened by the Spanish government. That this is not an exaggeration, but is based on absolute facts and figures, is best proven by the attitude of the American government to Cuban labor. When Cuba was firmly in the clutches of the United States, the very soldiers sent to liberate Cuba were ordered to shoot Cuban workingmen during the great cigarmakers' strike, which took place shortly after the war.

Nor do we stand alone in waging war for such causes. The curtain is beginning to be lifted on the motives of the terrible Russo-Japanese war, which cost so much blood and tears. And we see again that back of the fierce Moloch of war stands the still fiercer god of Commercialism. Kuropatkin, the Russian Minister of War during the Russo-Japanese struggle, has revealed the true secret behind the latter. The Tsar and his Grand Dukes, having invested money in Corean concessions, the war was forced for the sole purpose of speedily accumulating large fortunes.

The contention that a standing army and navy is the best security of peace is about as logical as the claim that the most peaceful citizen is he who goes about heavily armed. The experience of every-day life fully proves that the armed individual is invari- ably anxious to try his strength. The same is historically true of governments. Really peaceful countries do not waste life and energy in war preparations, with the result that peace is maintained.

However, the clamor for an increased army and navy is not due to any foreign danger. It is owing to the dread of the growing discontent of the masses and of the international spirit among the workers. It is to meet the internal enemy that the Powers of various countries are preparing themselves; an enemy, who, once awakened to consciousness, will prove more dangerous than any foreign invader.

The powers that have for centuries been engaged in enslaving the masses have made a thorough study of their psychology. They know that the people at large are like children whose despair, sorrow, and tears can be turned into joy with a little toy. And the more gorgeously the toy is dressed, the louder the colors, the more it will appeal to the million-headed child.

An army and navy represents the people's toys. To make them more attractive and acceptable, hundreds and thousands of dollars are being spent for the display of these toys. That was the purpose of the American government in equipping a fleet and sending it along the Pacific coast, that every American citizen should be made to feel the pride and glory of the United States. The city of San Francisco spent one hundred thousand dollars for the entertainment of the fleet; Los Angeles, sixty thousand; Seattle and Tacoma, about one hundred thousand. To entertain the fleet, did I say? To dine and wine a few superior officers, while the "brave boys" had to mutiny to get sufficient food. Yes, two hundred and sixty thousand dollars were spent on fireworks, theatre parties, and revelries, at a time when men, women, and children through the breadth and length of the country were starving in the streets; when thousands of unemployed were ready to sell their labor at any price.

Two hundred and sixty thousand dollars! What could not have been accomplished with such an enormous sum? But instead of bread and shelter, the children of those cities were taken to see the fleet, that it may remain, as one of the newspapers said, "a lasting memory for the child."

A wonderful thing to remember, is it not? The implements of civilized slaughter. If the mind of the child is to be poisoned with such memories, what hope is there for a true realization of human brotherhood?

We Americans claim to be a peace-loving people. We hate bloodshed; we are opposed to violence. Yet we go into spasms of joy over the possibility of projecting dynamite bombs from flying machines upon helpless citizens. We are ready to hang, electrocute, or lynch anyone, who, from economic necessity, will risk his own life in the attempt upon that of some industrial magnate. Yet our hearts swell with pride at the thought that America is becoming the most powerful nation on earth, and that it will eventually plant her iron foot on the necks of all other nations.

Such is the logic of patriotism.

Considering the evil results that patriotism is fraught with for the average man, it is as nothing compared with the insult and injury that patriotism heaps upon the soldier himself,—that poor, deluded victim of superstition and ignorance. He, the savior of his country, the protector of his nation,—what has patriotism in store for him? A life of slavish submission, vice, and perversion, during peace; a life of danger, exposure, and death, during war.

While on a recent lecture tour in San Francisco, I visited the Presidio, the most beautiful spot overlooking the Bay and Golden Gate Park. Its purpose should have been playgrounds for children, gardens and music for the recreation of the weary. Instead it is made ugly, dull, and gray by barracks,—barracks wherein the rich would not allow their dogs to dwell. In these miserable shanties soldiers are herded like cattle; here they waste their young days, polishing the boots and brass buttons of their superior officers. Here, too, I saw the distinction of classes: sturdy sons of a free Republic, drawn up in line like convicts, saluting every passing shrimp of a lieutenant. American equality, degrading manhood and elevating the uniform!

Barrack life further tends to develop tendencies of sexual perversion. It is gradually producing along this line results similar to European military conditions. Havelock Ellis, the noted writer on sex psychology, has made a thorough study of the subject. I quote: "Some of the barracks are great centers of male prostitution. . . . The number of soldiers who prostitute themselves is greater than we are willing to believe. It is no exaggeration to say that in certain regiments the presumption is in favor of the venality of the majority of the men. . . . On summer even-

ings Hyde Park and the neighborhood of Albert Gate
are full of guardsmen and others plying a lively trade,
and with little disguise, in uniform or out. . . . In
most cases the proceeds form a comfortable addition
to Tommy Atkins' pocket money."

To what extent this perversion has eaten its way
into the army and navy can best be judged from the
fact that special houses exist for this form of prostitution. The practice is not limited to England; it
is universal. "Soldiers are no less sought after in
France than in England or in Germany, and special
houses for military prostitution exist both in Paris
and the garrison towns."

Had Mr. Havelock Ellis included America in his
investigation of sex perversion, he would have found
that the same conditions prevail in our army and
navy as in those of other countries. The growth of
the standing army inevitably adds to the spread of
sex perversion; the barracks are the incubators.

Aside from the sexual effects of barrack life, it
also tends to unfit the soldier for useful labor after
leaving the army. Men, skilled in a trade, seldom
enter the army or navy, but even they, after a military
experience, find themselves totally unfitted for their
former occupations. Having acquired habits of idleness and a taste for excitement and adventure, no
peaceful pursuit can content them. Released from
the army, they can turn to no useful work. But it is
usually the social riff-raff, discharged prisoners and
the like, whom either the struggle for life or their own
inclination drives into the ranks. These, their military
term over, again turn to their former life of crime,

more brutalized and degraded than before. It is a well-known fact that in our prisons there is a goodly number of ex-soldiers; while, on the other hand, the army and navy are to a great extent supplied with ex-convicts.

Of all the evil results I have just described none seems to me so detrimental to human integrity as the spirit patriotism has produced in the case of Private William Buwalda. Because he foolishly believed that one can be a soldier and exercise his rights as a man at the same time, the military authorities punished him severely. True, he had served his country fifteen years, during which time his record was unimpeachable. According to Gen. Funston, who reduced Buwalda's sentence to three years, "the first duty of an officer or an enlisted man is unquestioned obedience and loyalty to the government, and it makes no difference whether he approves of that government or not." Thus Funston stamps the true character of allegiance. According to him, entrance into the army abrogates the principles of the Declaration of Independence.

What a strange development of patriotism that turns a thinking being into a loyal machine!

In justification of this most outrageous sentence of Buwalda, Gen. Funston tells the American people that the soldier's action was "a serious crime equal to treason." Now, what did this "terrible crime" really consist of? Simply in this: William Buwalda was one of fifteen hundred people who attended a public meeting in San Francisco; and, oh, horrors, he shook hands with the speaker, Emma Goldman. A terrible crime, indeed, which the General calls "a great military offense, infinitely worse than desertion."

Can there be a greater indictment against patriotism than that it will thus brand a man a criminal, throw him into prison, and rob him of the results of fifteen years of faithful service?

Buwalda gave to his country the best years of his life and his very manhood. But all that was as nothing. Patriotism is inexorable and, like all insatiable monsters, demands all or nothing. It does not admit that a soldier is also a human being, who has a right to his own feelings and opinions, his own inclinations and ideas. No, patriotism can not admit of that. That is the lesson which Buwalda was made to learn; made to learn at a rather costly, though not at a useless price. When he returned to freedom, he had lost his position in the army, but he regained his self-respect. After all, that is worth three years of imprisonment.

A writer on the military conditions of America, in a recent article, commented on the power of the military man over the civilian in Germany. He said, among other things, that if our Republic had no other meaning than to guarantee all citizens equal rights, it would have just cause for existence. I am convinced that the writer was not in Colorado during the patriotic régime of General Bell. He probably would have changed his mind had he seen how, in the name of patriotism and the Republic, men were thrown into bull-pens, dragged about, driven across the border, and subjected to all kinds of indignities. Nor is that Colorado incident the only one in the growth of mili-

tary power in the United States. There is hardly a
strike where troops and militia do not come to the
rescue of those in power, and where they do not act as
arrogantly and brutally as do the men wearing the
Kaiser's uniform. Then, too, we have the Dick military law. Had the writer forgotten that?

A great misfortune with most of our writers is
that they are absolutely ignorant on current events, or
that, lacking honesty, they will not speak of these
matters. And so it has come to pass that the Dick
military law was rushed through Congress with little
discussion and still less publicity,—a law which gives
the President the power to turn a peaceful citizen into
a bloodthirsty man-killer, supposedly for the defense
of the country, in reality for the protection of the
interests of that particular party whose mouthpiece
the President happens to be.

Our writer claims that militarism can never
become such a power in America as abroad, since it is
voluntary with us, while compulsory in the Old World.
Two very important facts, however, the gentleman
forgets to consider. First, that conscription has
created in Europe a deep-seated hatred of militarism
among all classes of society. Thousands of young
recruits enlist under protest and, once in the army,
they will use every possible means to desert. Second,
that it is the compulsory feature of militarism which
has created a tremendous anti-militarist movement,
feared by European Powers far more than anything
else. After all, the greatest bulwark of capitalism is
militarism. The very moment the latter is undermined, capitalism will totter. True, we have no con-

scription; that is, men are not usually forced to enlist in the army, but we have developed a far more exacting and rigid force—necessity. Is it not a fact that during industrial depressions there is a tremendous increase in the number of enlistments? The trade of militarism may not be either lucrative or honorable, but it is better than tramping the country in search of work, standing in the bread line, or sleeping in municipal lodging houses. After all, it means thirteen dollars per month, three meals a day, and a place to sleep. Yet even necessity is not sufficiently strong a factor to bring into the army an element of character and manhood. No wonder our military authorities complain of the "poor material" enlisting in the army and navy. This admission is a very encouraging sign. It proves that there is still enough of the spirit of independence and love of liberty left in the average American to risk starvation rather than don the uniform.

Thinking men and women the world over are beginning to realize that patriotism is too narrow and limited a conception to meet the necessities of our time. The centralization of power has brought into being an international feeling of solidarity among the oppressed nations of the world; a solidarity which represents a greater harmony of interests between the workingman of America and his brothers abroad than between the American miner and his exploiting compatriot; a solidarity which fears not foreign invasion, because it is bringing all the workers to the point when they will say to their masters, "Go and do your own killing. We have done it long enough for you."

This solidarity is awakening the consciousness of

even the soldiers, they, too, being flesh of the flesh
of the great human family. A solidarity that has
proven infallible more than once during past struggles,
and which has been the impetus inducing the Parisian
soldiers, during the Commune of 1871, to refuse to
obey when ordered to shoot their brothers. It has
given courage to the men who mutinied on Russian
warships during recent years. It will eventually bring
about the uprising of all the oppressed and downtrodden against their international exploiters.

The proletariat of Europe has realized the great
force of that solidarity and has, as a result, inaugurated a war against patriotism and its bloody spectre,
militarism. Thousands of men fill the prisons of
France, Germany, Russia, and the Scandinavian
countries, because they dared to defy the ancient
superstition. Nor is the movement limited to the
working class; it has embraced representatives in all
stations of life, its chief exponents being men and
women prominent in art, science, and letters.

America will have to follow suit. The spirit of
militarism has already permeated all walks of life.
Indeed, I am convinced that militarism is growing a
greater danger here than anywhere else, because of
the many bribes capitalism holds out to those whom
it wishes to destroy.

The beginning has already been made in the
schools. Evidently the government holds to the
Jesuitical conception, "Give me the child mind, and
I will mould the man." Children are trained in military tactics, the glory of military achievements
extolled in the curriculum, and the youthful minds

perverted to suit the government. Further, the youth of the country is appealed to in glaring posters to join the army and navy. "A fine chance to see the world!" cries the governmental huckster. Thus innocent boys are morally shanghaied into patriotism, and the military Moloch strides conquering through the Nation.

The American workingman has suffered so much at the hands of the soldier, State and Federal, that he is quite justified in his disgust with, and his opposition to, the uniformed parasite. However, mere denunciation will not solve this great problem. What we need is a propaganda of education for the soldier: anti-patriotic literature that will enlighten him as to the real horrors of his trade, and that will awaken his consciousness to his true relation to the man to whose labor he owes his very existence.

It is precisely this that the authorities fear most. It is already high treason for a soldier to attend a radical meeting. No doubt they will also stamp it high treason for a soldier to read a radical pamphlet. But, then, has not authority from time immemorial stamped every step of progress as treasonable? Those, however, who earnestly strive for social reconstruction can well afford to face all that; for it is probably even more important to carry the truth into the barracks than into the factory. When we have undermined the patriotic lie, we shall have cleared the path for that great structure wherein all nationalities shall be united into a universal brotherhood,—a truly FREE SOCIETY.

Patriotism Brews racism!

FRANCISCO FERRER AND THE MODERN SCHOOL

EXPERIENCE has come to be considered the best school of life. The man or woman who does not learn some vital lesson in that school is looked upon as a dunce indeed. Yet strange to say, that though organized institutions continue perpetuating errors, though they learn nothing from experience, we acquiesce, as a matter of course.

There lived and worked in Barcelona a man by the name of Francisco Ferrer. A teacher of children he was, known and loved by his people. Outside of Spain only the cultured few knew of Francisco Ferrer's work. To the world at large this teacher was non-existent.

On the first of September, 1909, the Spanish government—at the behest of the Catholic Church—arrested Francisco Ferrer. On the thirteenth of October, after a mock trial, he was placed in the ditch at Montjuich prison, against the hideous wall of many sighs, and shot dead. Instantly Ferrer, the obscure teacher, became a universal figure, blazing forth the indignation and wrath of the whole civilized world against the wanton murder.

The killing of Francisco Ferrer was not the first crime committed by the Spanish government and the Catholic Church. The history of these institutions is one long stream of fire and blood. Still they have not learned through experience, nor yet come to realize that every frail being slain by Church and State grows and grows into a mighty giant, who will some day free humanity from their perilous hold.

Francisco Ferrer was born in 1859, of humble parents. They were Catholics, and therefore hoped to raise their son in the same faith. They did not know that the boy was to become the harbinger of a great truth, that his mind would refuse to travel in the old path. At an early age Ferrer began to question the faith of his fathers. He demanded to know how it is that the God who spoke to him of goodness and love would mar the sleep of the innocent child with dread and awe of tortures, of suffering, of hell. Alert and of a vivid and investigating mind, it did not take him long to discover the hideousness of that black monster, the Catholic Church. He would have none of it.

Francisco Ferrer was not only a doubter, a searcher for truth; he was also a rebel. His spirit would rise in just indignation against the iron régime of his country, and when a band of rebels, led by the brave patriot General Villacampa, under the banner of the Republican ideal, made an onslaught on that régime, none was more ardent a fighter than young Francisco Ferrer. The Republican ideal,—I hope no one will confound it with the Republicanism of this country. Whatever objection I, as an Anarchist, have to the Republicans of Latin countries, I know they tower high above that corrupt and reactionary party which, in America, is destroying every vestige of liberty and justice. One has but to think of the Mazzinis, the Garibaldis, the scores of others, to realize that their efforts were directed, not merely against the overthrow of despotism, but particularly against the Catholic Church, which from its very inception has been the enemy of all progress and liberalism.

In America it is just the reverse. Republicanism stands for vested rights, for imperialism, for graft, for the annihilation of every semblance of liberty. Its ideal is the oily, creepy respectability of a McKinley, and the brutal arrogance of a Roosevelt.

The Spanish republican rebels were subdued. It takes more than one brave effort to split the rock of ages, to cut off the head of that hydra monster, the Catholic Church and the Spanish throne. Arrest, persecution, and punishment followed the heroic attempt of the little band. Those who could escape the bloodhounds had to flee for safety to foreign shores. Francisco Ferrer was among the latter. He went to France.

How his soul must have expanded in the new land! France, the cradle of liberty, of ideas, of action. Paris, the ever young, intense Paris, with her pulsating life, after the gloom of his own belated country,—how she must have inspired him. What opportunities, what a glorious chance for a young idealist.

Francisco Ferrer lost no time. Like one famished

he threw himself into the various liberal movements, met all kinds of people, learned, absorbed, and grew. While there, he also saw in operation the Modern School, which was to play such an important and fatal part in his life.

The Modern School in France was founded long before Ferrer's time. Its originator, though on a small scale, was that sweet spirit Louise Michel. Whether consciously or unconsciously, our own great Louise felt long ago that the future belongs to the young generation; that unless the young be rescued from that mind and soul-destroying institution, the bourgeois school, social evils will continue to exist. Perhaps she thought, with Ibsen, that the atmosphere is saturated with ghosts, that the adult man and woman have so many superstitions to overcome. No sooner do they outgrow the deathlike grip of one spook, lo! they find themselves in the thraldom of ninety-nine other spooks. Thus but a few reach the mountain peak of complete regeneration.

The child, however, has no traditions to overcome. Its mind is not burdened with set ideas, its heart has not grown cold with class and caste distinctions. The child is to the teacher what clay is to the sculptor. Whether the world will receive a work of art or a wretched imitation, depends to a large extent on the creative power of the teacher.

Louise Michel was pre-eminently qualified to meet the child's soul cravings. Was she not herself of a childlike nature, so sweet and tender, unsophisticated and generous? The soul of Louise burned always at white heat over every social injustice. She was

invariably in the front ranks whenever the people
of Paris rebelled against some wrong. And as she
was made to suffer imprisonment for her great devotion to the oppressed, the little school on Mont-
martre was soon no more. But the seed was planted
and has since borne fruit in many cities of France.

The most important venture of a Modern School
was that of the great young old man Paul Robin.
Together with a few friends he established a large
school at Cempuis, a beautiful place near Paris. Paul
Robin aimed at a higher ideal than merely modern
ideas in education. He wanted to demonstrate by
actual facts that the burgeois conception of heredity
is but a mere pretext to exempt society from its
terrible crimes against the young. The contention
that the child must suffer for the sins of the fathers,
that it must continue in poverty and filth, that it must
grow up a drunkard or criminal, just because its
parents left it no other legacy, was too preposterous
to the beautiful spirit of Paul Robin. He believed
that whatever part heredity may play, there are other
factors equally great, if not greater, that may and
will eradicate or minimize the so-called first cause.
Proper economic and social environment, the breath
and freedom of nature, healthy exercise, love and
sympathy, and, above all, a deep understanding for
the needs of the child—these would destroy the cruel,
unjust, and criminal stigma imposed on the innocent
young.

Paul Robin did not select his children; he did
not go to the so-called best parents: he took his
material wherever he could find it. From the street,

the hovels, the orphan and foundling asylums, the reformatories, from all those gray and hideous places where a benevolent society hides its victims in order to pacify its guilty conscience. He gathered all the dirty, filthy, shivering little waifs his place would hold, and brought them to Cempuis. There, surrounded by nature's own glory, free and unrestrained, well fed, clean kept, deeply loved and understood, the little human plants began to grow, to blossom, to develop beyond even the expectations of their friend and teacher, Paul Robin.

The children grew and developed into self-reliant, liberty-loving men and women. What greater danger to the institutions that make the poor in order to perpetuate the poor? Cempuis was closed by the French government on the charge of co-education, which is prohibited in France. However, Cempuis had been in operation long enough to prove to all advanced educators its tremendous possibilities, and to serve as an impetus for modern methods of education, that are slowly but inevitably undermining the present system.

Cempuis was followed by a great number of other educational attempts,—among them, by Madelaine Vernet, a gifted writer and poet, author of *l'Amour Libre,* and Sebastian Faure, with his *La Ruche,** which I visited while in Paris, in 1907.

Several years ago Comrade Faure bought the land on which he built his *La Ruche*. In a comparatively short time he succeeded in transforming the former

---

* *The Beehive.*

wild, uncultivated country into a blooming spot, having all the appearance of a well-kept farm. A large, square court, enclosed by three buildings, and a broad path leading to the garden and orchards, greet the eye of the visitor. The garden, kept as only a Frenchman knows how, furnishes a large variety of vegetables for *La Ruche*.

Sebastian Faure is of the opinion that if the child is subjected to contradictory influences, its development suffers in consequence. Only when the material needs, the hygiene of the home, and intellectual environment are harmonious, can the child grow into a healthy, free being.

Referring to his school, Sebastian Faure has this to say:

"I have taken twenty-four children of both sexes, mostly orphans, or those whose parents are too poor to pay. They are clothed, housed, and educated at my expense. Till their twelfth year they will receive a sound elementary education. Between the age of twelve and fifteen—their studies still continuing—they are to be taught some trade, in keeping with their individual disposition and abilities. After that they are at liberty to leave *La Ruche* to begin life in the outside world, with the assurance that they may at any time return to *La Ruche,* where they will be received with open arms and welcomed as parents do their beloved children. Then, if they wish to work at our place, they may do so under the following conditions: One third of the product to cover his or her expenses of maintenance, another third to go towards the general fund set aside for accommodating new children, and the last third to be devoted to the personal use of the child, as he or she may see fit.

"The health of the children who are now in my care is perfect. Pure air, nutritious food, physical exercise in the open, long walks, observation of hygienic rules, the short and interesting method of instruction, and, above all, our affectionate understanding and care of the children, have produced admirable physical and mental results.

"It would be unjust to claim that our pupils have accomplished wonders; yet, considering that they belong to the average, having had no previous opportunities, the results are very gratifying indeed. The most important thing they have acquired—a rare trait with ordinary school children—is the love of study, the desire to know, to be informed. They have learned a new method of work, one that quickens the memory and stimulates the imagination. We make a particular effort to awaken the child's interest in his surroundings, to make him realize the importance of observation, investigation, and reflection, so that when the children reach maturity, they would not be deaf and blind to the things about them. Our children never accept anything in blind faith, without inquiry as to why and wherefore; nor do they feel satisfied until their questions are thoroughly answered. Thus their minds are free from doubts and fear resultant from incomplete or untruthful replies; it is the latter which warp the growth of the child, and create a lack of confidence in himself and those about him.

"It is surprising how frank and kind and affectionate our little ones are to each other. The harmony between themselves and the adults at *La Ruche* is highly encouraging. We should feel at fault if the children were to fear or honor us merely because we are their elders. We leave nothing undone to gain their confidence and love; that accomplished, understanding will replace duty'; confidence, fear; and affection, severity.

"No one has yet fully realized the wealth of sympathy, kindness, and generosity hidden in the soul of the child. The effort of every true educator should be to unlock that treasure—to stimulate the child's impulses, and call forth the best and noblest tendencies. What greater reward can there be for one whose life-work is to watch over the growth of the human plant, than to see its nature unfold its petals, and to observe it develop into a true individuality. My comrades at *La Ruche* look for no greater reward, and it is due to them and their efforts, even more than to my own, that our human garden promises to bear beautiful fruit."*

Regarding the subject of history and the prevailing old methods of instruction, Sebastian Faure said:

"We explain to our children that true history is yet to be written,—the story of those who have died, unknown, in the effort to aid humanity to greater achievement."†

Francisco Ferrer could not escape this great wave of Modern School attempts. He saw its possibilities, not merely in theoretic form, but in their practical application to every-day needs. He must have real-

---

* *Mother Earth*, 1907.
† *Ibid.*

ized that Spain, more than any other country, stands
in need of just such schools, if it is ever to throw
off the double yoke of priest and soldier.

When we consider that the entire system of education in Spain is in the hands of the Catholic Church,
and when we further remember the Catholic formula,
"To inculcate Catholicism in the mind of the child
until it is nine years of age is to ruin it forever for
any other idea," we will understand the tremendous
task of Ferrer in bringing the new light to his people.
Fate soon assisted him in realizing his great dream.

Mlle. Meunier, a pupil of Francisco Ferrer, and
a lady of wealth, became interested in the Modern
School project. When she died, she left Ferrer some
valuable property and twelve thousand francs yearly
income for the School.

It is said that mean souls can conceive of
naught but mean ideas. If so, the contemptible
methods of the Catholic Church to blackguard
Ferrer's character, in order to justify her own black
crime, can readily be explained. Thus the lie was
spread in American Catholic papers that Ferrer used
his intimacy with Mlle. Meunier to get possession of
her money.

Personally, I hold that the intimacy, of whatever nature, between a man and a woman, is their
own affair, their sacred own. I would therefore not
lose a word in referring to the matter, if it were
not one of the many dastardly lies circulated about
Ferrer. Of course, those who know the purity of
the Catholic clergy will understand the insinuation.
Have the Catholic priests ever looked upon woman

as anything but a sex commodity? The historical data regarding the discoveries in the cloisters and monasteries will bear me out in that. How, then, are they to understand the co-operation of a man and a woman, except on a sex basis?

As a matter of fact, Mlle. Meunier was considerably Ferrer's senior. Having spent her childhood and girlhood with a miserly father and a submissive mother, she could easily appreciate the necessity of love and joy in child life. She must have seen that Francisco Ferrer was a teacher, not college, machine, or diploma-made, but one endowed with genius for that calling.

Equipped with knowledge, with experience, and with the necessary means; above all, imbued with the divine fire of his mission, our Comrade came back to Spain, and there began his life's work. On the ninth of September, 1901, the first Modern School was opened. It was enthusiastically received by the people of Barcelona, who pledged their support. In a short address at the opening of the School, Ferrer submitted his program to his friends. He said: "I am not a speaker, not a propagandist, not a fighter. I am a teacher; I love children above everything. I think I understand them. I want my contribution to the cause of liberty to be a young generation ready to meet a new era."

He was cautioned by his friends to be careful in his opposition to the Catholic Church. They knew to what lengths she would go to dispose of an enemy. Ferrer, too, knew. But, like Brand, he believed in

all or nothing. He would not erect the Modern
School on the same old lie. He would be frank and
honest and open with the children.

Francisco Ferrer became a marked man. From
the very first day of the opening of the School, he
was shadowed. The school building was watched,
his little home in Mangat was watched. He was followed every step, even when he went to France or
England to confer with his colleagues. He was a
marked man, and it was only a question of time when
the lurking enemy would tighten the noose.

It succeeded, almost, in 1906, when Ferrer was
implicated in the attempt on the life of Alfonso. The
evidence exonerating him was too strong even for
the black crows;* they had to let him go—not for
good, however. They waited. Oh, they can wait,
when they have set themselves to trap a victim.

The moment came at last, during the anti-military
uprising in Spain, in July, 1909. One will have to
search in vain the annals of revolutionary history to
find a more remarkable protest against militarism.
Having been soldier-ridden for centuries, the people
of Spain could stand the yoke no longer. They
would refuse to participate in useless slaughter.
They saw no reason for aiding a despotic government
in subduing and oppressing a small people fighting
for their independence, as did the brave Riffs. No,
they would not bear arms against them.

For eighteen hundred years the Catholic Church
has preached the gospel of peace. Yet, when the
people actually wanted to make this gospel a living

* Black crows: The Catholic clergy.

reality, she urged the authorities to force them to bear arms. Thus the dynasty of Spain followed the murderous methods of the Russian dynasty,—the people were forced to the battlefield.

Then, and not until then, was their power of endurance at an end. Then, and not until then, did the workers of Spain turn against their masters, against those who, like leeches, had drained their strength, their very life-blood. Yes, they attacked the churches and the priests, but if the latter had a thousand lives, they could not possibly pay for the terrible outrages and crimes perpetrated upon the Spanish people.

Francisco Ferrer was arrested on the first of September, 1909. Until October first his friends and comrades did not even know what had become of him. On that day a letter was received by *L'Humanité* from which can be learned the whole mockery of the trial. And the next day his companion, Soledad Villafranca, received the following letter:

"No reason to worry; you know I am absolutely innocent. Today I am particularly hopeful and joyous. It is the first time I can write to you, and the first time since my arrest that I can bathe in the rays of the sun, streaming generously through my cell window. You, too, must be joyous."

How pathetic that Ferrer should have believed, as late as October fourth, that he would not be condemned to death. Even more pathetic that his friends and comrades should once more have made the blunder in crediting the enemy with a sense of justice. Time and again they had placed faith in the judicial powers, only to see their brothers killed before their very eyes. They made no preparation to rescue Ferrer, not even a protest of any extent; nothing. "Why, it is impossible to condemn Ferrer; he is innocent." But everything is possible with the Catholic Church. Is she not a practiced henchman, whose trials of her enemies are the worst mockery of justice?

On October fourth Ferrer sent the following letter to *L'Humanité:*

"The Prison Cell, Oct. 4, 1909.

"My dear Friends—Notwithstanding most absolute innocence, the prosecutor demands the death penalty, based on denunciations of the police, representing me as the chief of the world's Anarchists, directing the labor syndicates of France, and guilty of conspiracies and insurrections everywhere, and declaring that my voyages to London and Paris were undertaken with no other object.

"With such infamous lies they are trying to kill me.

"The messenger is about to depart and I have not time for more. All the evidence presented to the investigating judge by the police is nothing but a tissue of lies and calumnious insinuations. But no proofs against me, having done nothing at all.

"FERRER."

October thirteenth, 1909, Ferrer's heart, so brave, so staunch, so loyal, was stilled. Poor fools! The last agonized throb of that heart had barely died away when it began to beat a hundredfold in the hearts of the civilized world, until it grew into terrific thunder, hurling forth its malediction upon the instigators of the black crime.   Murderers of black garb and pious mien, to the bar of justice!

Did Francisco Ferrer participate in the anti-military uprising?   According to the first indictment, which appeared in a Catholic paper in Madrid, signed by the Bishop and all the prelates of Barcelona, he was not even accused of participation.   The indictment was to the effect that Francisco Ferrer was guilty of having organized godless schools, and having circulated godless literature.   But in the twentieth century men can not be burned merely for their godless beliefs.   Something else had to be devised; hence the charge of instigating the uprising.

In no authentic source so far investigated could a single proof be found to connect Ferrer with the uprising.   But then, no proofs were wanted, or accepted, by the authorities.   There were seventy-two witnesses, to be sure, but their testimony was taken on paper.   They never were confronted with Ferrer, or he with them.

Is it psychologically possible that Ferrer should have participated?   I do not believe it is, and here are my reasons.   Francisco Ferrer was not only a great teacher, but he was also undoubtedly a marvelous organizer.   In eight years, between 1901-1909, he had organized in Spain one hundred and nine schools, besides inducing the liberal element of his country to organize three hundred and eight other schools.

In connection with his own school work, Ferrer had
equipped a modern printing plant, organized a staff
of translators, and spread broadcast one hundred and
fifty thousand copies of modern scientific and so-
ciologic works, not to forget the large quantity of
rationalist text books. Surely none but the most
methodical and efficient organizer could have accomplished such a feat.

On the other hand, it was absolutely proven that
the anti-military uprising was not at all organized;
that it came as a surprise to the people themselves, like a great many revolutionary waves on
previous occasions. The people of Barcelona, for
instance, had the city in their control for four days,
and, according to the statement of tourists, greater
order and peace never prevailed. Of course, the
people were so little prepared that when the time
came, they did not know what to do. In this regard
they were like the people of Paris during the Commune of 1871. They, too, were unprepared. While
they were starving, they protected the warehouses
filled to the brim with provisions. They placed sen-
tinels to guard the Bank of France, where the bourgeoisie kept the stolen money. The workers of
Barcelona, too, watched over the spoils of their
masters.

How pathetic is the stupidity of the underdog;
how terribly tragic! But, then, have not his fetters
been forged so deeply into his flesh, that he would
not, even if he could, break them? The awe of
authority, of law, of private property, hundredfold

burned into his soul,—how is he to throw it off un-prepared, unexpectedly?

Can anyone assume for a moment that a man like Ferrer would affiliate himself with such a spon-taneous, unorganized effort? Would he not have known that it would result in a defeat, a disastrous defeat for the people? And is it not more likely that if he would have taken part, he, the experienced *entrepreneur*, would have thoroughly organized the attempt? If all other proofs were lacking, that one factor would be sufficient to exonerate Francisco Ferrer. But there are others equally convincing.

For the very date of the outbreak, July twenty-fifth, Ferrer had called a conference of his teachers and members of the League of Rational Education. It was to consider the autumn work, and particu-larly the publication of Elisée Reclus' great book, *L'Homme et la Terre,* and Peter Kropotkin's *Great French Revolution.* Is it at all likely, is it at all plausible that Ferrer, knowing of the uprising, being a party to it, would in cold blood invite his friends and colleagues to Barcelona for the day on which he realized their lives would be endangered? Surely, only the criminal, vicious mind of a Jesuit could credit such deliberate murder.

Francisco Ferrer had his life-work mapped out; he had everything to lose and nothing to gain, except ruin and disaster, were he to lend assistance to the outbreak. Not that he doubted the justice of the people's wrath; but his work, his hope, his very nature was directed toward another goal.

In vain are the frantic efforts of the Catholic

Church, her lies, falsehoods, calumnies. She stands condemned by the awakened human conscience of having once more repeated the foul crimes of the past.

Francisco Ferrer is accused of teaching the children the most blood-curdling ideas,—to hate God, for instance. Horrors! Francisco Ferrer did not believe in the existence of a God. Why teach the child to hate something which does not exist? Is it not more likely that he took the children out into the open, that he showed them the splendor of the sunset, the brilliancy of the starry heavens, the awe-inspiring wonder of the mountains and seas; that he explained to them in his simple, direct way the law of growth, of development, of the interrelation of all life? In so doing he made it forever impossible for the poisonous weeds of the Catholic Church to take root in the child's mind.

It has been stated that Ferrer prepared the children to destroy the rich. Ghost stories of old maids. Is it not more likely that he prepared them to succor the poor? That he taught them the humiliation, the degradation, the awfulness of poverty, which is a vice and not a virtue; that he taught the dignity and importance of all creative efforts, which alone sustain life and build character. Is it not the best and most effective way of bringing into the proper light the absolute uselessness and injury of parasitism?

Last, but not least, Ferrer is charged with undermining the army by inculcating anti-military ideas. Indeed? He must have believed with Tolstoy that war is legalized slaughter, that it perpetuates hatred and arrogance, that it eats away the heart of nations, and turns them into raving maniacs.

However, we have Ferrer's own word regarding his ideas of modern education:

"I would like to call the attention of my readers to this idea: All the value of education rests in the respect for the physical, intellectual, and moral will of the child. Just as in science no demonstration is possible save by facts, just so there is no real education save that which is exempt from all dogmatism, which leaves to the child itself the direction of its effort, and confines itself to the seconding of its effort. Now, there is nothing easier than to alter this purpose, and nothing harder than to respect it. Education is always imposing, violating, constraining; the real educator is he who can best protect the child against his (the teacher's) own ideas, his peculiar whims; he who can best appeal to the child's own energies.

"We are convinced that the education of the future will be of an entirely spontaneous nature; certainly we can not as yet realize it, but the evolution of methods in the direction of a wider comprehension of the phenomena of life, and the fact that all advances toward perfection mean the overcoming of restraint,—all this indicates that we are in the right when we hope for the deliverance of the child through science.

"Let us not fear to say that we want men capable of evolving without stopping, capable of destroying and renewing their environments without cessation, of renewing themselves also; men, whose intellectual independence will be their greatest force, who will attach themselves to nothing, always ready to accept what is best, happy in the triumph of new ideas, aspiring to live multiple lives in one life. Society fears such men; we therefore must not hope that it will ever want an education able to give them to us.

"We shall follow the labors of the scientists who study the child with the greatest attention, and we shall eagerly seek for means of applying their experience to the education which we want to build up, in the direction of an ever fuller liberation of the individual. But how can we attain our end? Shall it not be by putting ourselves directly to the work favoring the foundation of new schools, which shall be ruled as much as possible by this spirit of liberty, which we forefeel will dominate the entire work of education in the future?

"A trial has been made, which, for the present, has already given excellent results. We can destroy all which in the present school answers to the organization of constraint, the artificial surroundings by which children are separated from nature and life, the intellectual and moral discipline made use of to impose ready-made ideas upon them, beliefs which deprave and annihilate natural bent. Without fear of deceiving ourselves, we can restore the child to the environment which entices it, the environment of nature in which he will be in contact with all that he loves, and in which impressions of life will replace fastidious book-learning. If we did no more than that, we should already have prepared in great part the deliverance of the child.

"In such conditions we might already freely apply the data of science and labor most fruitfully.

"I know very well we could not thus realize all our hopes, that we should often be forced, for lack of knowledge, to employ undesirable methods; but a certitude would sustain us in our efforts—namely, that even without reaching our aim completely we should do more and better in our still imperfect work than the present school accomplishes. I like the free spontaneity of a child who knows nothing, better than the world-knowledge and intellectual deformity of a child who has been subjected to our present education."*

Had Ferrer actually organized the riots, had he fought on the barricades, had he hurled a hundred bombs, he could not have been so dangerous to the Catholic Church and to despotism, as with his opposition to discipline and restraint. Discipline and restraint—are they not back of all the evils in the world? Slavery, submission, poverty, all misery, all social iniquities result from discipline and restraint. Indeed, Ferrer was dangerous. Therefore he had to die, October thirteenth, 1909, in the ditch of Montjuich. Yet who dare say his death was in vain? In view of the tempestuous rise of universal indignation: Italy naming streets in memory of Francisco Ferrer, Belgium inaugurating a movement to erect a memorial; France calling to the front her most illustrious men to resume the heritage of the martyr; England being the first to issue a biography; all countries

---

* *Mother Earth,* December, 1909.

uniting in perpetuating the great work of Francisco Ferrer; America, even, tardy always in progressive ideas, giving birth to a Francisco Ferrer Association, its aim being to publish a complete life of Ferrer and to organize Modern Schools all over the country,—in the face of this international revolutionary wave, who is there to say Ferrer died in vain?

That death at Montjuich,—how wonderful, how dramatic it was, how it stirs the human soul. Proud and erect, the inner eye turned toward the light, Francisco Ferrer needed no lying priests to give him courage, nor did he upbraid a phantom for forsaking him. The consciousness that his executioners represented a dying age, and that his was the living truth, sustained him in the last heroic moments.

> A dying age and a living truth,
> The living burying the dead.

THE HYPOCRISY OF PURITANISM

SPEAKING of Puritanism in relation to American art, Mr. Gutzon Borglum said: "Puritanism has made us self-centered and hypocritical for so long, that sincerity and reverence for what is natural in our impulses have been fairly bred out of us, with the result that there can be neither truth nor individuality in our art."

Mr. Borglum might have added that Puritanism has made life itself impossible. More than art, more than estheticism, life represents beauty in a thousand variations; it is, indeed, a gigantic panorama of eternal change. Puritanism, on the other hand, rests on a fixed and immovable conception of life; it is based on the Calvinistic idea that life is a curse, imposed upon man by the wrath of God. In order to redeem himself man must do constant penance, must repudiate every natural and healthy impulse, and turn his back on joy and beauty.

Puritanism celebrated its reign of terror in England during the sixteenth and seventeenth centuries, destroying and crushing every manifestation of art and culture. It was the spirit of Puritanism which robbed Shelley of his children, because he would not bow to the dicta of religion. It was the same narrow spirit which alienated Byron from his native land, because that great genius rebelled against the monotony, dullness, and pettiness of his country. It was Puritanism, too, that forced some of England's freest women into the conventional lie of marriage: Mary Wollstonecraft and, later, George Eliot. And recently Puritanism has demanded another toll—the life of Oscar Wilde. In fact, Puritanism has never ceased to be the most pernicious factor in the domain of John Bull, acting as censor of the artistic expression of his people, and stamping its approval only on the dullness of middle-class respectability.

It is therefore sheer British jingoism which points to America as the country of Puritanic provincialism. It is quite true that our life is stunted by Puritanism, and that the latter is killing what is natural and healthy in our impulses. But it is equally true that it is to England that we are indebted for transplanting this spirit on American soil. It was bequeathed to us by the Pilgrim fathers. Fleeing from persecution and oppression, the Pilgrims of Mayflower fame established in the New World a reign of Puritanic tyranny and crime. The history of New England, and especially of Massachusetts, is full of the horrors that have turned life into gloom, joy and despair, naturalness into disease, honesty and truth into hideous lies and hypocrisies. The ducking-stool and whipping-post, as well as numerous other devices of torture, were the favorite English methods for American purification.

Boston, the city of culture, has gone down in the annals of Puritanism as the "Bloody Town." It rivaled Salem, even, in her cruel persecution of unauthorized religious opinions. On the now famous Common a half-naked woman, with a baby in her arms, was publicly whipped for the crime of free speech; and on the same spot Mary Dyer, another Quaker woman, was hanged in 1659. In fact, Boston has been the scene of more than one wanton crime committed by Puritanism. Salem, in the summer of 1692, killed eighteen people for witchcraft. Nor was Massachusetts alone in driving out the devil by fire and brimstone. As Canning justly said: "The Pilgrim fathers infested the New World to redress the balance of the Old." The horrors of that period have found their most supreme expression in the American classic, *The Scarlet Letter*.

Puritanism no longer employs the thumbscrew and lash; but it still has a most pernicious hold on the minds and feelings of the American people. Naught else can explain the power of a Comstock. Like the Torquemadas of ante-bellum days, Anthony Comstock is the autocrat of American morals; he dictates the standards of good and evil, of purity and vice. Like a thief in the night he sneaks into the private lives of the people, into their most intimate relations. The system of espionage established by this man Comstock puts to shame the infamous Third Division of the Russian secret police. Why does the public tolerate such an outrage on its liberties? Simply because Comstock is but the loud expression of the Puritanism bred in the Anglo-Saxon blood, and from whose thraldom even liberals have not succeeded in fully emancipating themselves. The visionless and leaden elements of the old Young Men's and Women's Christian Temperance Unions, Purity Leagues, American Sabbath Unions, and the Prohibition Party, with Anthony Comstock as their patron saint, are the grave diggers of American art and culture.

Europe can at least boast of a bold art and literature which delve deeply into the social and sexual problems of our time, exercising a severe critique of all our shams. As with a surgeon's knife every Puritanic carcass is dissected, and the way thus cleared for man's liberation from the dead weights of the past. But with Puritanism as the constant check upon American life, neither truth nor sincerity is possible. Nothing but gloom and mediocrity to dictate human conduct, curtail natural expression, and stifle our best impulses. Puritanism in this the twentieth century is as much the enemy of freedom and beauty as it was when it landed on Plymouth Rock. It repudiates, as something vile and sinful, our deepest feelings; but being absolutely ignorant as to the real functions of human emotions, Puritanism is itself the creator of the most unspeakable vices.

The entire history of asceticism proves this to be only too true. The Church, as well as Puritanism, has fought the flesh as something evil; it had to be subdued and hidden at all cost. The result of this vicious attitude is only now beginning to be recognized by modern thinkers and educators. They realize that "nakedness has a hygienic value as well as a spiritual significance, far beyond its influences in allaying the natural inquisitiveness of the young or acting as a preventative of morbid emotion. It is an inspiration to adults who have long outgrown any youthful curiosities. The vision of the essential and eternal human form, the nearest thing to us in all the world, with its vigor and its beauty and its grace, is one of the prime tonics of life."* But the spirit of purism has so perverted the human mind that it has lost the power to appreciate the beauty of nudity, forcing us to hide the natural form under the plea of chastity. Yet chastity itself is but an artificial imposition upon nature, expressive of a false shame of the human form. The modern idea of chastity, especially in reference to woman, its greatest victim, is but the sensuous exaggeration of our natural impulses. "Chastity varies with the amount of clothing," and hence Christians and purists forever hasten to cover the "heathen" with tatters, and thus convert him to goodness and chastity.

Puritanism, with its perversion of the significance and functions of the human body, especially in regard to woman, has condemned her to celibacy, or to the indiscriminate breeding of a diseased race, or to prostitution. The enormity of this crime against humanity is apparent when we consider the results. Absolute sexual continence is imposed upon the unmarried woman, under pain of being considered immoral or fallen, with the result of producing neurasthenia, impotence, depression, and a great variety of nervous

* *The Psychology of Sex.* Havelock Ellis.

complaints involving diminished power of work, limited enjoyment of life, sleeplessness, and preoccupation with sexual desires and imaginings. The arbitrary and pernicious dictum of total continence
probably also explains the mental inequality of the
sexes. Thus Freud believes that the intellectual inferiority of so many women is due to the inhibition
of thought imposed upon them for the purpose of
sexual repression. Having thus suppressed the natural sex desires of the unmarried woman, Puritanism, on the other hand, blesses her married sister
for incontinent fruitfulness in wedlock. Indeed, not
merely blesses her, but forces the woman, oversexed
by previous repression, to bear children, irrespective
of weakened physical condition or economic inability
to rear a large family. Prevention, even by scientific-
ally determined safe methods, is absolutely prohibited;
nay, the very mention of the subject is considered
criminal.

Thanks to this Puritanic tyranny, the majority of
women soon find themselves at the ebb of their physical resources. Ill and worn, they are utterly unable
to give their children even elementary care. That,
added to economic pressure, forces many women to
risk utmost danger rather than continue to bring forth
life. The custom of procuring abortions has reached
such vast proportions in America as to be almost
beyond belief. According to recent investigations
along this line, seventeen abortions are committed in
every hundred pregnancies. This fearful percentage
represents only cases which come to the knowledge of
physicians. Considering the secrecy in which this

practice is necessarily shrouded, and the consequent
professional inefficiency and neglect, Puritanism continuously exacts thousands of victims to its own
stupidity and hypocrisy.

Prostitution, although hounded, imprisoned, and
chained, is nevertheless the greatest triumph of Puritanism. It is its most cherished child, all hypocritical
sanctimoniousness notwithstanding. The prostitute is
the fury of our century, sweeping across the "civilized" countries like a hurricane, and leaving a trail of
disease and disaster. The only remedy Puritanism
offers for this ill-begotten child is greater repression
and more merciless persecution. The latest outrage
is represented by the Page Law, which imposes upon
the State of New York the terrible failure and crime
of Europe, namely, registration and identification of
the unfortunate victims of Puritanism. In equally
stupid manner purism seeks to check the terrible
scourge of its own creation—venereal diseases. Most
disheartening it is that this spirit of obtuse narrow-
mindedness has poisoned even our so-called liberals,
and has blinded them into joining the crusade against
the very things born of the hypocrisy of Puritanism—
prostitution and its results. In wilful blindness Puritanism refuses to see that the true method of prevention is the one which makes it clear to all that "venereal diseases are not a mysterious or terrible thing,
the penalty of the sin of the flesh, a sort of shameful
evil branded by purist malediction, but an ordinary
disease which may be treated and cured." By its methods of obscurity, disguise, and concealment, Puritanism has furnished favorable conditions for the growth

and spread of these diseases. Its bigotry is again most strikingly demonstrated by the senseless attitude in regard to the great discovery of Prof. Ehrlich, hypocrisy veiling the important cure for syphilis with vague allusions to a remedy for "a certain poison."

The almost limitless capacity of Puritanism for evil is due to its intrenchment behind the State and the law. Pretending to safeguard the people against "immorality," it has impregnated the machinery of government and added to its usurpation of moral guardianship the legal censorship of our views, feelings, and even of our conduct.

Art, literature, the drama, the privacy of the mails, in fact, our most intimate tastes, are at the mercy of this inexorable tyrant. Anthony Comstock, or some other equally ignorant policeman, has been given power to desecrate genius, to soil and mutilate the sublimest creation of nature—the human form. Books dealing with the most vital issues of our lives, and seeking to shed light upon dangerously obscured problems, are legaly treated as criminal offenses, and their helpless authors thrown into prison or driven to destruction and death.

Not even in the domain of the Tsar is personal liberty daily outraged to the extent it is in America, the stronghold of the Puritanic eunuchs. Here the only day of recreation left to the masses, Sunday, has been made hideous and utterly impossible. All writers on primitive customs and ancient civilization agree that the Sabbath was a day of festivities, free from care and duties, a day of general rejoicing and merrymaking. In every European country this tradition continues to bring some relief from the humdrum and stupidity of our Christian era. Everywhere concert halls, theaters, museums, and gardens are filled with men, women, and children, particularly workers with their families, full of life and joy, forgetful of the ordinary rules and conventions of their every-day existence. It is on that day that the masses demonstrate what life might really mean in a sane society, with work stripped of its profit-making, soul-destroying purpose.

Puritanism has robbed the people even of that one day. Naturally, only the workers are affected: our millionaires have their luxurious homes and elaborate clubs. The poor, however, are condemned to the monotony and dullness of the American Sunday. The sociability and fun of European outdoor life is here exchanged for the gloom of the church, the stuffy, germ-saturated country parlor, or the brutalizing atmosphere of the back-room saloon. In Prohibition States the people lack even the latter, unless they can invest their meager earnings in quantities of adulterated liquor. As to Prohibition, every one knows what a farce it really is. Like all other achievements of Puritanism it, too, has but driven the "devil" deeper into the human system. Nowhere else does one meet so many drunkards as in our Prohibition towns. But so long as one can use scented candy to abate the foul breath of hypocrisy, Puritanism is triumphant. Ostensibly Prohibition is opposed to liquor for reasons of health and economy, but the very spirit of Prohibition being itself abnormal, it succeeds but in creating an abnormal life.

Every stimulus which quickens the imagination and raises the spirits, is as necessary to our life as air. It invigorates the body, and deepens our vision of human fellowship. Without stimuli, in one form or another, creative work is impossible, nor indeed the spirit of kindliness and generosity. The fact that some great geniuses have seen their reflection in the goblet too frequently, does not justify Puritanism in attempting to fetter the whole gamut of human emotions. A Byron and a Poe have stirred humanity deeper than all the Puritans can ever hope to do. The former have given to life meaning and color; the latter are turning red blood into water, beauty into ugliness, variety into uniformity and decay. Puritanism, in whatever expression, is a poisonous germ. On the surface everything may look strong and vigorous; yet the poison works its way persistently, until the entire fabric is doomed. With Hippolyte Taine, every truly free spirit has come to realize that "Puritanism is the death of culture, philosophy, humoi, and good fellowship; its characteristics are dullness, monotony, and gloom."

THE TRAFFIC IN WOMEN

OUR REFORMERS have suddenly made a great discovery—the white slave traffic. The papers are full of these "unheard-of conditions," and lawmakers are already planning a new set of laws to check the horror.

It is significant that whenever the public mind is to be diverted from a great social wrong, a crusade is inaugurated against indecency, gambling, saloons, etc. And what is the result of such crusades? Gambling is increasing, saloons are doing a lively business through back entrances, prostitution is at its height, and the system of pimps and cadets is but aggravated.

How is it that an institution, known almost to every child, should have been discovered so suddenly? How is it that this evil, known to all sociologists, should now be made such an important issue?

To assume that the recent investigation of the white slave traffic (and, by the way, a very superficial investigation) has discovered anything new, is, to say the least, very foolish. Prostitution has been, and is, a widespread evil, yet mankind goes on its business, perfectly indifferent to the sufferings and distress of the victims of prostitution. As indifferent, indeed, as mankind has remained to our industrial system, or to economic prostitution.

Only when human sorrows are turned into a toy with glaring colors will baby people become interested —for a while at least. The people are a very fickle baby that must have new toys every day. The "righteous" cry against the white slave traffic is such a toy. It serves to amuse the people for a little while, and it will help to create a few more fat political jobs—parasites who stalk about the world as inspectors, investigators, detectives, and so forth.

What is really the cause of the trade in women? Not merely white women, but yellow and black women as well. Exploitation, of course; the merciless Moloch of capitalism that fattens on underpaid labor, thus driving thousands of women and girls into prostitution. With Mrs. Warren these girls feel, "Why waste your life working for a few shillings a week in a scullery, eighteen hours a day?"

Naturally our reformers say nothing about this cause. They know it well enough, but it doesn't pay to say anything about it. It is much more profitable to play the Pharisee, to pretend an outraged morality, than to go to the bottom of things.

However, there is one commendable exception among the young writers: Reginald Wright Kauffman, whose work *The House of Bondage* is the first earnest attempt to treat the social evil—not from a sentimental Philistine viewpoint. A journalist of wide experience, Mr. Kauffman proves that our in-

dustrial system leaves most women no alternative
except prostitution. The women portrayed in *The
House of Bondage* belong to the working class. Had
the author portrayed the life of women in other
spheres, he would have been confronted with the same
state of affairs.

Nowhere is woman treated according to the merit
of her work, but rather as a sex. It is therefore
almost inevitable that she should pay for her right
to exist, to keep a position in whatever line, with
sex favors. Thus it is merely a question of degree
whether she sells herself to one man, in or out of
marriage, or to many men. Whether our reformers
admit it or not, the economic and social inferiority
of woman is responsible for prostitution.

Just at present our good people are shocked by
the disclosures that in New York City alone one
out of every ten women works in a factory, that the
average wage received by women is six dollars per
week for forty-eight to sixty hours of work, and
that the majority of female wage workers face many
months of idleness which leaves the average wage
about $280 a year. In view of these economic hor-
rors, is it to be wondered at that prostitution and
the white slave trade have become such dominant
factors?

Lest the preceding figures be considered an exaggeration, it is well to examine what some authorities on prostitution have to say:

"A prolific cause of female depravity can be found
in the several tables, showing the description of the
employment pursued, and the wages received, by the

women previous to their fall, and it will be a question for the political economist to decide how far mere business consideration should be an apology on the part of employers for a reduction in their rates of remuneration, and whether the savings of a small percentage on wages is not more than counterbalanced by the enormous amount of taxation enforced on the public at large to defray the expenses incurred on account of a system of vice, *which is the direct result, in many cases, of insufficient compensation of honest labor."**

Our present-day reformers would do well to look into Dr. Sanger's book. There they will find that out of 2,000 cases under his observation, but few came from the middle classes, from well-ordered conditions, or pleasant homes. By far the largest majority were working girls and working women; some driven into prostitution through sheer want, others because of a cruel, wretched life at home, others again because of thwarted and crippled physical natures (of which I shall speak later on). Also it will do the maintainers of purity and morality good to learn that out of two thousand cases, 490 were married women, women who lived with their husbands. Evidently there was not much of a guaranty for their "safety and purity" in the sanctity of marriage.†

---

* Dr. Sanger, *The History of Prostitution.*

† It is a significant fact that Dr. Sanger's book has been excluded from the U. S. mails. Evidently the authorities are not anxious that the public be informed as to the true cause of prostitution.

Dr. Alfred Blaschko, in *Prostitution in the Nineteenth Century,* is even more emphatic in characterizing economic conditions as one of the most vital factors of prostitution.

"Although prostitution has existed in all ages, it was left to the nineteenth century to develop it into a gigantic social institution. The development of industry with vast masses of people in the competitive market, the growth and congestion of large cities, the insecurity and uncertainty of employment, has given prostitution an impetus never dreamed of at any period in human history."

And again Havelock Ellis, while not so absolute in dealing with the economic cause, is nevertheless compelled to admit that it is indirectly and directly the main cause. Thus he finds that a large percentage of prostitutes is recruited from the servant class, although the latter have less care and greater security. On the other hand, Mr. Ellis does not deny that the daily routine, the drudgery, the monotony of the servant girl's lot, and especially the fact that she may never partake of the companionship and joy of a home, is no mean factor in forcing her to seek recreation and forgetfulness in the gaiety and glimmer of prostitution. In other words, the servant girl, being treated as a drudge, never having the right to herself, and worn out by the caprices of her mistress, can find an outlet, like the factory or shopgirl, only in prostitution.

The most amusing side of the question now before the public is the indignation of our "good, respectable people," especially the various Christian

gentlemen, who are always to be found in the front
ranks of every crusade. Is it that they are absolutely ignorant of the history of religion, and especially of the Christian religion? Or is it that they
hope to blind the present generation to the part
played in the past by the Church in relation to prostitution? Whatever their reason, they should be the
last to cry out against the unfortunate victims of
today, since it is known to every intelligent student
that prostitution is of religious origin, maintained and
fostered for many centuries, not as a shame, but as a
virtue, hailed as such by the Gods themselves.

"It would seem that the origin of prostitution is
to be found primarily in a religious custom, religion,
the great conserver of social tradition, preserving in
a transformed shape a primitive freedom that was
passing out of the general social life. The typical
example is that recorded by Herodotus, in the fifth
century before Christ, at the Temple of Mylitta, the
Babylonian Venus, where every woman, once in her
life, had to come and give herself to the first stranger,
who threw a coin in her lap, to worship the goddess.
Very similar customs existed in other parts of western Asia, in North Africa, in Cyprus, and other
islands of the eastern Mediterranean, and also in
Greece, where the temple of Aphrodite on the fort at
Corinth possessed over a thousand hierodules, dedicated to the service of the goddess.

"The theory that religious prostitution developed,
as a general rule, out of the belief that the generative
activity of human beings possessed a mysterious and
sacred influence in promoting the fertility of Nature,

is maintained by all authoritative writers on the subject. Gradually, however, and when prostitution became an organized institution under priestly influence, religious prostitution developed utilitarian sides, thus helping to increase public revenue.

"The rise of Christianity to political power produced little change in policy. The leading fathers of the Church tolerated prostitution. Brothels under municipal protection are found in the thirteenth century. They constituted a sort of public service, the directors of them being considered almost as public servants."*

To this must be added the following from Dr. Sanger's work:

"Pope Clement II. issued a bull that prostitutes would be tolerated if they pay a certain amount of their earnings to the Church.

"Pope Sixtus IV. was more practical; from one single brothel, which he himself had built, he received an income of 20,000 ducats."

In modern times the Church is a little more careful in that direction. At least she does not openly demand tribute from prostitutes. She finds it much more profitable to go in for real estate, like Trinity Church, for instance, to rent out death traps at an exorbitant price to those who live off and by prostitution.

Much as I should like to, my space will not admit speaking of prostitution in Egypt, Greece, Rome, and during the Middle Ages. The conditions in the latter period are particularly interesting, inasmuch as pros-

* Havelock Ellis, *Sex and Society*.

titution was organized into guilds, presided over by a brothel queen. These guilds employed strikes as a medium of improving their condition and keeping a standard price. Certainly that is more practical a method than the one used by the modern wage-slave in society.

It would be one-sided and extremely superficial to maintain that the economic factor is the only cause of prostitution. There are others no less important and vital. That, too, our reformers know, but dare discuss even less than the institution that saps the very life out of both men and women. I refer to the sex question, the very mention of which causes most people moral spasms.

It is a conceded fact that woman is being reared as a sex commodity, and yet she is kept in absolute ignorance of the meaning and importance of sex. Everything dealing with that subject is suppressed, and persons who attempt to bring light into this terrible darkness are persecuted and thrown into prison. Yet it is nevertheless true that so long as a girl is not to know how to take care of herself, not to know the function of the most important part of her life, we need not be surprised if she becomes an easy prey to prostitution, or to any other form of a relationship which degrades her to the position of an object for mere sex gratification.

It is due to this ignorance that the entire life and nature of the girl is thwarted and crippled. We have long ago taken it as a self-evident fact that the boy may follow the call of the wild; that is to say, that the boy may, as soon as his sex nature asserts itself, satisfy that nature; but our moralists are scandalized at the very thought that the nature of a girl should assert itself. To the moralist prostitution does not consist so much in the fact that the woman sells her body, but rather that she sells it out of wedlock. That this is no mere statement is proved by the fact that marriage for monetary considerations is perfectly legitimate, sanctified by law and public opinion, while any other union is condemned and repudiated. Yet a prostitute, if properly defined, means nothing else than "any person for whom sexual relationships are subordinated to gain."*

"Those women are prostitutes who sell their bodies for the exercise of the sexual act and make of this a profession."†

In fact, Banger goes further; he maintains that the act of prostitution is "intrinsically equal to that of a man or woman who contracts a marriage for economic reasons."

Of course, marriage is the goal of every girl, but as thousands of girls cannot marry, our stupid social customs condemn them either to a life of celibacy or prostitution. Human nature asserts itself regardless of all laws, nor is there any plausible reason why nature should adapt itself to a perverted conception of morality.

Society considers the sex experiences of a man as attributes of his general development, while similar experiences in the life of a woman are looked upon as a terrible calamity, a loss of honor and of all that is

---

* Guyot, *La Prostitution.*
† Banger, *Criminalité et Condition Economique.*

good and noble in a human being. This double standard of morality has played no little part in the creation and perpetuation of prostitution. It involves the keeping of the young in absolute ignorance on sex matters, which alleged "innocence," together with an overwrought and stifled sex nature, helps to bring about a state of affairs that our Puritans are so anxious to avoid or prevent.

Not that the gratification of sex must needs lead to prostitution; it is the cruel, heartless, criminal persecution of those who dare divert from the beaten track, which is responsible for it.

Girls, mere children, work in crowded, overheated rooms ten to twelve hours daily at a machine, which tends to keep them in a constant over-excited sex state. Many of these girls have no home or comforts of any kind; therefore the street or some place of cheap amusement is the only means of forgetting their daily routine. This naturally brings them into close proximity with the other sex. It is hard to say which of the two factors brings the girl's over-sexed condition to a climax, but it is certainly the most natural thing that a climax should result. That is the first step toward prostitution. Nor is the girl to be held responsible for it. On the contrary, it is altogether the fault of society, the fault of our lack of understanding, of our lack of appreciation of life in the making; especially is it the criminal fault of our moralists, who condemn a girl for all eternity, because she has gone from the "path of virtue"; that is, because her first sex experience has taken place without the sanction of the Church.

The girl feels herself a complete outcast, with the doors of home and society closed in her face. Her entire training and tradition is such that the girl herself feels depraved and fallen, and therefore has no ground to stand upon, or any hold that will lift her up, instead of dragging her down. Thus society creates the victims that it afterwards vainly attempts to get rid of. The meanest, most depraved and decrepit man still considers himself too good to take as his wife the woman whose grace he was quite willing to buy, even though he might thereby save her from a life of horror. Nor can she turn to her own sister for help. In her stupidity the latter deems herself too pure and chaste, not realizing that her own position is in many respects even more deplorable than her sister's of the street.

"The wife who married for money, compared with the prostitute," says Havelock Ellis, "is the true scab. She is paid less, gives much more in return in labor and care, and is absolutely bound to her master. The prostitute never signs away the right over her own person, she retains her freedom and personal rights, nor is she always compelled to submit to man's embrace."

Nor does the better-than-thou woman realize the apologist claim of Lecky that "though she may be the supreme type of vice, she is also the most efficient guardian of virtue. But for her, happy homes would be polluted, unnatural and harmful practice would abound."

Moralists are ever ready to sacrifice one-half of the human race for the sake of some miserable institution which they can not outgrow. As a matter of fact, prostitution is no more a safeguard for the purity of the home than rigid laws are a safeguard against prostitution. Fully fifty per cent. of married men are patrons of brothels. It is through this virtuous element that the married women—nay, even the children—are infected with venereal diseases. Yet society has not a word of condemnation for the man, while no law is too monstrous to be set in motion against the helpless victim. She is not only preyed upon by those who use her, but she is also absolutely at the mercy of every policeman and miserable detective on the beat, the officials at the station house, the authorities in every prison.

In a recent book by a woman who was for twelve years the mistress of a "house," are to be found the following figures: "The authorities compelled me to pay every month fines between $14.70 to $29.70, the girls would pay from $5.70 to $9.70 to the police." Considering that the writer did her business in a small city, that the amounts she gives do not include extra bribes and fines, one can readily see the tremendous revenue the police department derives from the blood money of its victims, whom it will not even protect. Woe to those who refuse to pay their toll; they would be rounded up like cattle, "if only to make a favorable impression upon the good citizens of the city, or if the powers needed extra money on the side. For the warped mind who believes that a fallen woman is incapable of human emotion it would be impossible to realize the grief, the disgrace, the tears, the wounded pride that was ours every time we were pulled in."

Strange, isn't it, that a woman who has kept a "house" should be able to feel that way? But stranger still that a good Christian world should bleed and fleece such women, and give them nothing in return except obloquy and persecution. Oh, for the charity of a Christian world!

Much stress is laid on white slaves being imported into America. How would America ever retain her virtue if Europe did not help her out? I will not deny that this may be the case in some instances, any more than I will deny that there are emissaries of Germany and other countries luring economic slaves into America; but I absolutely deny that prostitution is recruited to any appreciable extent from Europe. It may be true that the majority of prostitutes of New York City are foreigners, but that is because the majority of the population is foreign. The moment we go to any other American city, to Chicago or the Middle West, we shall find that the number of foreign prostitutes is by far a minority.

Equally exaggerated is the belief that the majority of street girls in this city were engaged in this business before they came to America. Most of the girls speak excellent English, are Americanized in habits and appearance,—a thing absolutely impossible unless they had lived in this country many years. That is, they were driven into prostitution by American conditions, by the thoroughly American custom for excessive display of finery and clothes, which, of course, necessitates money,—money that cannot be earned in shops or factories.

In other words, there is no reason to believe that

any set of men would go to the risk and expense of
getting foreign products, when American conditions
are overflooding the market with thousands of girls.
On the other hand, there is sufficient evidence to prove
that the export of American girls for the purpose of
prostitution is by no means a small factor.

Thus Clifford G. Roe, ex-Assistant State Attorney
of Cook County, Ill., makes the open charge that New
England girls are shipped to Panama for the express
use of men in the employ of Uncle Sam. Mr. Roe
adds that "there seems to be an underground railroad
between Boston and Washington which many girls
travel." Is it not significant that the railroad should
lead to the very seat of Federal authority? That Mr.
Roe said more than was desired in certain quarters
is proved by the fact that he lost his position. It is
not practical for men in office to tell tales from school.

The excuse given for the conditions in Panama is
that there are no brothels in the Canal Zone. That is
the usual avenue of escape for a hypocritical world
that dares not face the truth. Not in the Canal Zone,
not in the city limits,—therefore prostitution does not
exist.

Next to Mr. Roe, there is James Bronson Reynolds, who has made a thorough study of the white
slave traffic in Asia. As a staunch American citizen
and friend of the future Napoleon of America, Theodore Roosevelt, he is surely the last to discredit the
virtue of his country. Yet we are informed by him
that in Hong Kong, Shanghai, and Yokohama, the
Augean stables of American vice are located. There
American prostitutes have made themselves so con-

spicuous that in the Orient "American girl" is synonymous with prostitute. Mr. Reynolds reminds his
countrymen that while Americans in China are under
the protection of our consular representatives, the
Chinese in America have no protection at all. Every
one who knows the brutal and barbarous persecution
Chinese and Japanese endure on the Pacific Coast,
will agree with Mr. Reynolds.

In view of the above facts it is rather absurd to
point to Europe as the swamp whence come all the
social diseases of America. Just as absurd is it to
proclaim the myth that the Jews furnish the largest
contingent of willing prey. I am sure that no one
will accuse me of nationalistic tendencies. I am glad
to say that I have developed out of them, as out of
many other prejudices. If, therefore, I resent the
statement that Jewish prostitutes are imported, it is
not because of any Judaistic sympathies, but because
of the facts inherent in the lives of these people. No
one but the most superficial will claim that Jewish
girls migrate to strange lands, unless they have some
tie or relation that brings them there. The Jewish
girl is not adventurous. Until recent years she had
never left home, not even so far as the next village or
town, except it were to visit some relative. Is it then
credible that Jewish girls would leave their parents or
families, travel thousands of miles to strange lands,
through the influence and promises of strange forces?
Go to any of the large incoming steamers and see for
yourself if these girls do not come either with their
parents, brothers, aunts, or other kinsfolk. There
may be exceptions, of course, but to state that large

numbers of Jewish girls are imported for prostitution, or any other purpose, is simply not to know Jewish psychology.

Those who sit in a glass house do wrong to throw stones about them; besides, the American glass house is rather thin, it will break easily, and the interior is anything but a gainly sight.

To ascribe the increase of prostitution to alleged importation, to the growth of the cadet system, or similar causes, is highly superficial. I have already referred to the former. As to the cadet system, abhorrent as it is, we must not ignore the fact that it is essentially a phase of modern prostitution,—a phase accentuated by suppression and graft, resulting from sporadic crusades against the social evil.

The procurer is no doubt a poor specimen of the human family, but in what manner is he more despicable than the policeman who takes the last cent from the street walker, and then locks her up in the station house? Why is the cadet more criminal, or a greater menace to society, than the owners of department stores and factories, who grow fat on the sweat of their victims, only to drive them to the streets? I make no plea for the cadet, but I fail to see why he should be mercilessly hounded, while the real perpetrators of all social iniquity enjoy immunity and respect. Then, too, it is well to remember that it is not the cadet who makes the prostitute. It is our sham and hypocrisy that create both the prostitute and the cadet.

Until 1894 very little was known in America of the procurer. Then we were attacked by an epidemic

of virtue. Vice was to be abolished, the country purified at all cost. The social cancer was therefore
driven out of sight, but deeper into the body. Keepers of brothels, as well as their unfortunate victims,
were turned over to the tender mercies of thè police.
The inevitable consequence of exorbitant bribes, and
the penitentiary, followed.

While comparatively protected in the brothels,
where they represented a certain monetary value, the
girls now found themselves on the street, absolutely
at the mercy of the graft-greedy police. Desperate,
needing protection and longing for affection, these
girls naturally proved an easy prey for cadets, themselves the result of the spirit of our commercial age.
Thus the cadet system was the direct outgrowth of
police persecution, graft, and attempted suppression
of prostitution. It were sheer folly to confound this
modern phase of the social evil with the causes of the
latter.

Mere suppression and barbaric enactments can
serve but to embitter, and further degrade, the unfortunate victims of ignorance and stupidity. The latter
has reached its highest expression in the proposed law
to make humane treatment of prostitutes a crime,
punishing any one sheltering a prostitute with five
years' imprisonment and $10,000 fine. Such an atti-
tude merely exposes the terrible lack of understanding
of the true causes of prostitution, as a social factor,
as well as manifesting the Puritanic spirit of the
Scarlet Letter days.

There is not a single modern writer on the subject
who does not refer to the utter futility of legislative

methods in coping with the issue. Thus Dr. Blaschko
finds that governmental suppression and moral crusades accomplish nothing save driving the evil into
secret channels, multiplying its dangers to society.
Havelock Ellis, the most thorough and humane student of prostitution, proves by a wealth of data that
the more stringent the methods of persecution the
worse the condition becomes. Among other data we
learn that in France, "in 1560, Charles IX. abolished
brothels through an edict, but the numbers of prostitutes were only increased, while many new brothels
appeared in unsuspected shapes, and were more dangerous. In spite of all such legislation, *or because of
it,* there has been no country in which prostitution has
played a more conspicuous part."*

An educated public opinion, freed from the legal
and moral hounding of the prostitute, can alone help
to ameliorate present conditions. Wilful shutting of
eyes and ignoring of the evil as a social factor of
modern life, can but aggravate matters. We must rise
above our foolish notions of "better than thou," and
learn to recognize in the prostitute a product of social
conditions. Such a realization will sweep away the
attitude of hypocrisy, and insure a greater understanding and more humane treatment. As to a thorough eradication of prostitution, nothing can accomplish that save a complete transvaluation of all
accepted values—especially the moral ones—coupled
with the abolition of industrial slavery.

---

* *Sex and Society.*

WOMAN SUFFRAGE

WE BOAST of the age of advancement, of science, and progress. Is it not strange, then, that we still believe in fetich worship? True, our fetiches have different form and substance, yet in their power over the human mind they are still as disastrous as were those of old.

Our modern fetich is universal suffrage. Those who have not yet achieved that goal fight bloody revolutions to obtain it, and those who have enjoyed its reign bring heavy sacrifice to the altar of this omnipotent diety. Woe to the heretic who dare question that divinity!

Woman, even more than man, is a fetich worshipper, and though her idols may change, she is ever on her knees, ever holding up her hands, ever blind to the fact that her god has feet of clay. Thus woman has been the greatest supporter of all deities from time immemorial. Thus, too, she has had to pay the price that only gods can exact,—her freedom, her heart's blood, her very life.

Nietzsche's memorable maxim, "When you go to woman, take the whip along," is considered very brutal, yet Nietzsche expressed in one sentence the attitude of woman towards her gods.

Religion, especially the Christian religion, has condemned woman to the life of an inferior, a slave. It has thwarted her nature and fettered her soul, yet the Christian religion has no greater supporter, none more devout, than woman. Indeed, it is safe to say that religion would have long ceased to be a factor in the lives of the people, if it were not for the support it receives from woman. The most ardent churchworkers, the most tireless missionaries the world over, are women, always sacrificing on the altar of the gods that have chained her spirit and enslaved her body.

The insatiable monster, war, robs woman of all that is dear and precious to her. It exacts her brothers, lovers, sons, and in return gives her a life of loneliness and despair. Yet the greatest supporter and worshiper of war is woman. She it is who instills the love of conquest and power into her children; she it is who whispers the glories of war into the ears of her little ones, and who rocks her baby to sleep with the tunes of trumpets and the noise of guns. It is woman, too, who crowns the victor on his return from the battlefield. Yes, it is woman who pays the highest price to that insatiable monster, war.

Then there is the home. What a terrible fetich it is! How it saps the very life-energy of woman,—this modern prison with golden bars. Its shining aspect blinds woman to the price she would have to pay as wife, mother, and housekeeper. Yet woman clings tenaciously to the home, to the power that holds her in bondage.

It may be said that because woman recognizes the awful toll she is made to pay to the Church, State, and the home, she wants suffrage to set herself free. That may be true of the few; the majority of suffragists repudiate utterly such blasphemy. On the contrary, they insist always that it is woman suffrage which will make her a better Christian and home-keeper, a staunch citizen of the State. Thus suffrage is only a means of strengthening the omnipotence of the very Gods that woman has served from time immemorial.

What wonder, then, that she should be just as devout, just as zealous, just as prostrate before the new idol, woman suffrage. As of old, she endures persecution, imprisonment, torture, and all forms of condemnation, with a smile on her face. As of old, the most enlightened, even, hope for a miracle from the twentieth-century deity,—suffrage. Life, happiness, joy, freedom, independence,—all that, and more, is to spring from suffrage. In her blind devotion woman does not see what people of intellect perceived fifty years ago: that suffrage is an evil, that it has only helped to enslave people, that it has but closed their eyes that they may not see how craftily they were made to submit.

Woman's demand for equal suffrage is based largely on the contention that woman must have the equal right in all affairs of society. No one could, possibly, refute that, if suffrage were a right. Alas, for the ignorance of the human mind, which can see a right in an imposition. Or is it not the most brutal imposition for one set of people to make laws that another set is coerced by force to obey? Yet woman clamors for that "golden opportunity" that has wrought so much misery in the world, and robbed man of his integrity and self-reliance; an imposition which has thoroughly corrupted the people, and made them absolute prey in the hands of unscrupulous politicians.

The poor, stupid, free American citizen! Free to starve, free to tramp the highways of this great country, he enjoys universal suffrage, and, by that right, he has forged chains about his limbs. The reward that he receives is stringent labor laws prohibiting the right of boycott, of picketing, in fact, of everything, except the right to be robbed of the fruits of his labor. Yet all these disastrous results of the twentieth-century fetich have taught woman nothing. But, then, woman will purify politics, we are assured.

Needless to say, I am not opposed to woman suffrage on the conventional ground that she is not equal to it. I see neither physical, psychological, nor mental reasons why woman should not have the equal right to vote with man. But that can not possibly blind me to the absurd notion that woman will accomplish that wherein man has failed. If she would not make things worse, she certainly could not make them better. To assume, therefore, that she would succeed in purifying something which is not susceptible of purification, is to credit her with supernatural powers. Since woman's greatest misfortune has been that she was looked upon as either angel or devil, her true salvation lies in being placed on earth; namely, in being considered human, and therefore subject to all human follies and mistakes. Are we, then, to believe that two errors will make a right? Are we to assume that the poison already inherent in politics will be decreased, if women were to enter the political arena? The most ardent suffragists would hardly maintain such a folly.

As a matter of fact, the most advanced students of universal suffrage have come to realize that all existing systems of political power are absurd, and are completely inadequate to meet the pressing issues of life. This view is also borne out by a statement of one who is herself an ardent believer in woman suffrage, Dr. Helen L. Sumner. In her able work on *Equal Suffrage,* she says: "In Colorado, we find that equal suffrage serves to show in the most striking way the essential rottenness and degrading character of the existing system." Of course, Dr. Sumner has in mind a particular system of voting, but the same applies with equal force to the entire machinery of the representative system. With such a basis, it is difficult to understand how woman, as a political factor, would benefit either herself or the rest of mankind.

But, say our suffrage devotees, look at the countries and States where female suffrage exists. See what woman has accomplished—in Australia, New Zealand, Finland, the Scandinavian countries, and in our own four States, Idaho, Colorado, Wyoming, and Utah. Distance lends enchantment—or, to quote a

Polish formula—"it is well where we are not." Thus one would assume that those countries and States are unlike other countries or States, that they have greater freedom, greater social and economic equality, a finer appreciation of human life, deeper understanding of the great social struggle, with all the vital questions it involves for the human race.

The women of Australia and New Zealand can vote, and help make the laws. Are the labor conditions better there than they are in England, where the suffragettes are making such a heroic struggle? Does there exist a greater motherhood, happier and freer children than in England? Is woman there no longer considered a mere sex commodity? Has she emancipated herself from the Puritanical double standard of morality for men and women? Certainly none but the ordinary female stump politician will dare answer these questions in the affirmative. If that be so, it seems ridiculous to point to Australia and New Zealand as the Mecca of equal suffrage accomplishments.

On the other hand, it is a fact to those who know the real political conditions in Australia, that politics have gagged labor by enacting the most stringent labor laws, making strikes without the sanction of an arbitration committee a crime equal to treason.

Not for a moment do I mean to imply that woman suffrage is responsible for this state of affairs. I do mean, however, that there is no reason to point to Australia as a wonder-worker of woman's accomplishment, since her influence has been unable to free labor from the thraldom of political bossism.

Finland has given woman equal suffrage; nay, even the right to sit in Parliament. Has that helped to develop a greater heroism, an intenser zeal than that of the women of Russia? Finland, like Russia, smarts under the terrible whip of the bloody Tsar. Where are the Finnish Perovskaias, Spiridonovas, Figners, Breshkovskaias? Where are the countless numbers of Finnish young girls who cheerfully go to Siberia for their cause? Finland is sadly in need of heroic liberators. Why has the ballot not created them? The only Finnish avenger of his people was a man, not a woman, and he used a more effective weapon than the ballot.

As to our own States where women vote, and which are constantly being pointed out as examples of marvels, what has been accomplished there through the ballot that women do not to a large extent enjoy in other States; or that they could not achieve through energetic efforts without the ballot?

True, in the suffrage States women are guaranteed equal rights to property; but of what avail is that right to the mass of women without property, the thousands of wage workers, who live from hand to mouth? That equal suffrage did not, and cannot, affect their condition is admitted even by Dr. Sumner, who certainly is in a position to know. As an ardent suffragist, and having been sent to Colorado by the Collegiate Equal Suffrage League of New York State to collect material in favor of suffrage, she would be the last to say anything derogatory; yet we are informed that "equal suffrage has but slightly affected the economic conditions of women. That women do not receive equal pay for equal work, and that, though woman in Colorado has enjoyed school suffrage since 1876, women teachers are paid less than in California." On the other hand, Miss Sumner fails to account for the fact that although women have had school suffrage for thirty-four years, and equal suffrage since 1894, the census in Denver alone a few months ago disclosed the fact of fifteen thousand defective school children. And that, too, with mostly women in the educational department, and also notwithstanding that women in Colorado have passed the "most stringent laws for child and animal protection." The women of Colorado "have taken great interest in the State institutions for the care of dependent, defective, and delinquent children." What a horrible indictment against woman's care and interest, if one city has fifteen thousand defective children. What about the glory of woman suffrage, since it has failed utterly in the most important social issue, the child? And where is the superior sense of justice that woman was to bring into the political field? Where was it in 1903, when the mine owners waged a guerilla war against the Western Miners' Union; when General Bell established a reign of terror, pulling men out of bed at night, kidnapping them across the border line, throwing them into bull pens, declaring "to hell with the Constitution, the club is the Constitution"? Where were the women politicians then, and why did they not exercise the power of their vote? But they did. They helped to defeat the most fair-minded and liberal man, Governor Waite. The latter had to make way for the tool of the mine kings, Governor Peabody, the enemy of labor, the Tsar of Colorado. "Certainly male suffrage could have done nothing worse." Granted. Wherein, then, are the advantages to woman and society from woman suffrage? The oft-repeated assertion that woman will purify politics is also but a myth. It is not borne out by the people who know the political conditions of Idaho, Colorado, Wyoming, and Utah.

Woman, essentially a purist, is naturally bigoted and relentless in her effort to make others as good as she thinks they ought to be. Thus, in Idaho, she has disfranchised her sister of the street, and declared all women of "lewd character" unfit to vote. "Lewd" not being interpreted, of course, as prostitution *in* marriage. It goes without saying that illegal prostitution and gambling have been prohibited. In this regard the law must needs be of feminine gender: it always prohibits. Therein all laws are wonderful. They go no further, but their very tendencies open all the floodgates of hell. Prostitution and gambling have never done a more flourishing business than since the law has been set against them.

In Colorado, the Puritanism of woman has expressed itself in a more drastic form. "Men of notoriously unclean lives, and men connected with saloons, have been dropped from politics since women have the vote."* Could Brother Comstock do more?

---

* *Equal Suffrage,* Dr. Helen Sumner.

Could all the Puritan fathers have done more? I
wonder how many women realize the gravity of this
would-be feat. I wonder if they understand that it
is the very thing which, instead of elevating woman,
has made her a political spy, a contemptible pry into
the private affairs of people, not so much for the
good of the cause, but because, as a Colorado woman
said, "they like to get into houses they have never
been in, and find out all they can, politically and
otherwise."* Yes, and into the human soul and its
minutest nooks and corners. For nothing satisfies
the craving of most women so much as scandal. And
when did she ever enjoy such opportunities as are
hers, the politician's?

"Notoriously unclean lives, and men connected
with the saloons." Certainly, the lady vote gatherers
can not be accused of much sense of proportion.
Granting even that these busybodies can decide whose
lives are clean enough for that eminently clean atmosphere, politics, must it follow that saloon-keepers
belong to the same category? Unless it be American
hypocrisy and bigotry, so manifest in the principle
of Prohibition, which sanctions the spread of drunkenness among men and women of the rich class, yet
keeps vigilant watch on the only place left to the
poor man. If no other reason, woman's narrow
and purist attitude toward life makes her a greater
danger to liberty wherever she has political power.
Man has long overcome the superstitions that still
engulf woman. In the economic competitive field,

---

* *Equal Suffrage.*

man has been compelled to exercise efficiency, judgment, ability, competency. He therefore had neither time nor inclination to measure everyone's morality with a Puritanic yardstick. In his political activities, too, he has not gone about blindfolded. He knows that quantity and not quality is the material for the political grinding mill, and, unless he is a sentimental reformer or an old fossil, he knows that politics can never be anything but a swamp.

Women who are at all conversant with the process of politics, know the nature of the beast, but in their self-sufficiency and egotism they make themselves believe that they have but to pet the beast, and he will become as gentle as a lamb, sweet and pure. As if women have not sold their votes, as if women politicians cannot be bought! If her body can be bought in return for material consideration, why not her vote? That it is being done in Colorado and in other States, is not denied even by those in favor of woman suffrage.

As I have said before, woman's narrow view of human affairs is not the only argument against her as a politician superior to man. There are others. Her life-long economic parasitism has utterly blurred her conception of the meaning of equality. She clamors for equal rights with man, yet we learn that "few women care to canvas in undesirable districts."* How little equality means to them compared with the Russian women, who face hell itself for their ideal!

Woman demands the same rights as man, yet

---

* Dr. Helen A. Sumner.

she is indignant that her presence does not strike him dead: he smokes, keeps his hat on, and does not jump from his seat like a flunkey. These may be trivial things, but they are nevertheless the key to the nature of American suffragists. To be sure, their English sisters have outgrown these silly notions. They have shown themselves equal to the greatest demands on their character and power of endurance. All honor to the heroism and sturdiness of the English suffragettes. Thanks to their energetic, aggressive methods, they have proved an inspiration to some of our own lifeless and spineless ladies. But after all, the suffragettes, too, are still lacking in appreciation of real equality. Else how is one to account for the tremendous, truly gigantic effort set in motion by those valiant fighters for a wretched little bill which will benefit a handful of propertied ladies, with absolutely no provision for the vast mass of working-women? True, as politicians they must be opportunists, must take half-measures if they can not get all. But as intelligent and liberal women they ought to realize that if the ballot is a weapon, the disinherited need it more than the economically superior class, and that the latter already enjoy too much power by virtue of their economic superiority.

The brilliant leader of the English suffragettes, Mrs. Emmeline Pankhurst, herself admitted, when on her American lecture tour, that there can be no equality between political superiors and inferiors. If so, how will the workingwomen of England, already inferior economically to the ladies who are benefited by the Shackleton bill,* be able to work with their political superiors, should the bill pass? Is it not probable that the class of Annie Keeney, so full of zeal, devotion, and martyrdom, will be compelled to carry on their backs their female political bosses, even as they are carrying their economic masters. They would still have to do it, were universal suffrage for men and women established in England. No matter what the workers do, they are made to pay, always. Still, those who believe in the power of the vote show little sense of justice when they concern themselves not at all with those whom, as they claim, it might serve most.

The American suffrage movement has been, until very recently, altogether a parlor affair, absolutely detached from the economic needs of the people. Thus Susan B. Anthony, no doubt an exceptional type of woman, was not only indifferent but antagonistic to labor; nor did she hesitate to manifest her antagonism when, in 1869, she advised women to take the places of striking printers in New York.† I do not know whether her attitude had changed before her death.

There are, of course, some suffragists who are affiliated with workingwomen—the Women's Trade Union League, for instance; but they are a small minority, and their activities are essentially economic. The rest look upon toil as a just provision of Provi-

---

* Mr. Shackleton was a labor leader. It is therefore self-evident that he should introduce a bill excluding his own constituents. The English Parliament is full of such Judases.

† *Equal Suffrage,* Dr. Helen A. Sumner.

dence. What would become of the rich, if not for
the poor? What would become of these idle, parasitic ladies, who squander more in a week than their
victims earn in a year, if not for the eighty million
wage-workers? Equality, who ever heard of such a
thing?

Few countries have produced such arrogance and
snobbishness as America. Particularly is this true of
the American woman of the middle class. She not
only considers herself the equal of man, but his superior, especially in her purity, goodness, and morality.
Small wonder that the American suffragist claims for
her vote the most miraculous powers. In her exalted
conceit she does not see how truly enslaved she is,
not so much by man, as by her own silly notions and
traditions. Suffrage can not ameliorate that sad
fact; it can only accentuate it, as indeed it does.

One of the great American women leaders claims
that woman is entitled not only to equal pay, but
that she ought to be legally entitled even to the pay
of her husband. Failing to support her, he should be
put in convict stripes, and his earnings in prison be
collected by his equal wife. Does not another brilliant exponent of the cause claim for woman that her
vote will abolish the social evil, which has been fought
in vain by the collective efforts of the most illustrious
minds the world over? It is indeed to be regretted
that the alleged creator of the universe has already
presented us with his wonderful scheme of things,
else woman suffrage would surely enable woman to
outdo him completely.

Nothing is so dangerous as the dissection of a

fetich. If we have outlived the time when such heresy was punishable by the stake, we have not outlived the narrow spirit of condemnation of those who dare differ with accepted notions. Therefore I shall probably be put down as an opponent of woman. But that can not deter me from looking the question squarely in the face. I repeat what I have said in the beginning: I do not believe that woman will make politics worse; nor can I believe that she could make it better. If, then, she cannot improve on man's mistakes, why perpetrate the latter?

History may be a compilation of lies; nevertheless, it contains a few truths, and they are the only guide we have for the future. The history of the political activities of men proves that they have given him absolutely nothing that he could not have achieved in a more direct, less costly, and more lasting manner. As a matter of fact, every inch of ground he has gained has been through a constant fight, a ceaseless struggle for self-assertion, and not through suffrage. There is no reason whatever to assume that woman, in her climb to emancipation, has been, or will be, helped by the ballot.

In the darkest of all countries, Russia, with her absolute despotism, woman has become man's equal, not through the ballot, but by her will to be and to do. Not only has she conquered for herself every avenue of learning and vocation, but she has won man's esteem, his respect, his comradeship; aye, even more than that: she has gained the admiration, the respect of the whole world. That, too, not through suffrage, but by her wonderful heroism, her fortitude,

her ability, willpower, and her endurance in her
struggle for liberty.   Where are the women in any
suffrage country or State that can lay claim to such
a victory?   When we consider the accomplishments
of woman in America, we find also that something
deeper and more powerful than suffrage has helped
her in the march to emancipation.

It is just sixty-two years ago since a handful of
women at the Seneca Falls Convention set forth a
few demands for their right to equal education with
men, and access to the various professions, trades,
etc.   What wonderful accomplishments, what wonderful triumphs!   Who but the most ignorant dare speak
of woman as a mere domestic drudge?   Who dare
suggest that this or that profession should not be
open to her?   For over sixty years she has molded
a new atmosphere and a new life for herself.   She
has become a world-power in every domain of human
thought and activity.   And all that without suffrage,
without the right to make laws, without the "privilege" of becoming a judge, a jailer, or an executioner.

Yes, I may be considered an enemy of woman;
but if I can help her see the light, I shall not complain.

The misfortune of woman is not that she is unable
to do the work of a man, but that she is wasting
her life-force to outdo him, with a tradition of centuries which has left her physically incapable of keeping pace with him.   Oh, I know some have succeeded,
but at what cost, at what terrific cost!   The import
is not the kind of work woman does, but rather the
quality of the work she furnishes.   She can give

suffrage or the ballot no new quality, nor can she receive anything from it that will enhance her own quality. Her development, her freedom, her independence, must come from and through herself. First, by asserting herself as a personality, and not as a sex commodity. Second, by refusing the right to anyone over her body; by refusing to bear children, unless she wants them; by refusing to be a servant to God, the State, society, the husband, the family, etc., by making her life simpler, but deeper and richer. That is, by trying to learn the meaning and substance of life in all its complexities, by freeing herself from the fear of public opinion and public condemnation. Only that, and not the ballot, will set woman free, will make her a force hitherto unknown in the world, a force for real love, for peace, for harmony; a force of divine fire, of life-giving; a creator of free men and women.

THE TRAGEDY OF WOMAN'S EMANCIPATION

I BEGIN with an admission: Regardless of all political and economic theories, treating of the fundamental differences between various groups within the human race, regardless of class and race distinctions, regardless of all artificial boundary lines between woman's rights and man's rights, I hold that there is a point where these differentiations may meet and grow into one perfect whole.

With this I do not mean to propose a peace treaty. The general social antagonism which has taken hold of our entire public life today, brought about through the force of opposing and contradictory interests, will crumble to pieces when the reorganization of our social life, based upon the principles of economic justice, shall have become a reality.

Peace or harmony between the sexes and individuals does not necessarily depend on a superficial equalization of human beings; nor does it call for the elimination of individual traits and peculiarities. The problem that confronts us today, and which the nearest future is to solve, is how to be one's self and yet in oneness with others, to feel deeply with all human beings and still retain one's own characteristic qualities. This seems to me to be the basis upon which the mass and the individual, the true democrat and the true individuality, man and woman, can meet without antagonism and opposition. The motto should not be: Forgive one another; rather, Understand one another. The oft-quoted sentence of Madame de Staël: "To understand everything means to forgive everything," has never particularly appealed to me; it has the odor of the confessional; to forgive one's fellow-being conveys the idea of pharisaical superiority. To understand one's fellow-being suffices. The admission partly represents the fundamental aspect of my views on the emancipation of woman and its effect upon the entire sex.

Emancipation should make it possible for woman to be human in the truest sense. Everything within her that craves assertion and activity should reach its fullest expression; all artificial barriers should be broken, and the road towards greater freedom cleared of every trace of centuries of submission and slavery.

This was the original aim of the movement for woman's emancipation. But the results so far achieved have isolated woman and have robbed her of the fountain springs of that happiness which is so essential to her. Merely external emancipation has made of the modern woman an artificial being, who reminds one of the products of French arboriculture with its arabesque trees and shrubs, pyramids, wheels, and wreaths; anything, except the forms which would be reached by the expression of her own inner quali-

ties. Such artificially grown plants of the female sex
are to be found in large numbers, especially in the
so-called intellectual sphere of our life.

Liberty and equality for woman! What hopes
and aspirations these words awakened when they
were first uttered by some of the noblest and bravest
souls of those days. The sun in all his light and
glory was to rise upon a new world; in this world
woman was to be free to direct her own destiny—
an aim certainly worthy of the great enthusiasm,
courage, perseverance, and ceaseless effort of the tremendous host of pioneer men and women, who staked
everything against a world of prejudice and ignorance.

My hopes also move towards that goal, but I hold
that the emancipation of woman, as interpreted and
practically applied today, has failed to reach that
great end. Now, woman is confronted with the
necessity of emancipating herself from emancipation,
if she really desires to be free. This may sound
paradoxical, but is, nevertheless, only too true.

What has she achieved through her emancipation?
Equal suffrage in a few States. Has that purified our
political life, as many well-meaning advocates predicted? Certainly not. Incidentally, it is really time
that persons with plain, sound judgment should cease
to talk about corruption in politics in a boarding-
school tone. Corruption of politics has nothing to do
with the morals, or the laxity of morals, of various
political personalities. Its cause is altogether a
material one. Politics is the reflex of the business and
industrial world, the mottos of which are: "To take
is more blessed than to give"; "buy cheap and sell

dear"; "one soiled hand washes the other." There is
no hope even that woman, with her right to vote, will
ever purify politics.

Emancipation has brought woman economic equality with man; that is, she can choose her own profession and trade; but as her past and present physical
training has not equipped her with the necessary
strength to compete with man, she is often compelled
to exhaust all her energy, use up her vitality, and
strain every nerve in order to reach the market value.
Very few ever succeed, for it is a fact that women
teachers, doctors, lawyers, architects, and engineers
are neither met with the same confidence as their
male colleagues, nor receive equal remuneration.
And those that do reach that enticing equality, generally do so at the expense of their physical and
psychical well-being. As to the great mass of working girls and women, how much independence is
gained if the narrowness and lack of freedom of the
home is exchanged for the narrowness and lack of
freedom of the factory, sweat-shop, department store,
or office? In addition is the burden which is laid on
many women of looking after a "home, sweet home"
—cold, dreary, disorderly, uninviting—after a day's
hard work. Glorious independence! No wonder that
hundreds of girls are so willing to accept the first offer
of marriage, sick and tired of their "independence"
behind the counter, at the sewing or typewriting
machine. They are just as ready to marry as girls of
the middle class, who long to throw off the yoke of
parental supremacy. A so-called independence which
leads only to earning the merest subsistence is not so

enticing, not so ideal, that one could expect woman to sacrifice everything for it. Our highly praised independence is, after all, but a slow process of dulling and stifling woman's nature, her love instinct, and her mother instinct.

Nevertheless, the position of the working girl is far more natural and human than that of her seemingly more fortunate sister in the more cultured professional walks of life—teachers, physicians, lawyers, engineers, etc., who have to make a dignified, proper appearance, while the inner life is growing empty and dead.

The narrowness of the existing conception of woman's independence and emancipation; the dread of love for a man who is not her social equal; the fear that love will rob her of her freedom and independence; the horror that love or the joy of motherhood will only hinder her in the full exercise of her profession—all these together make of the emancipated modern woman a compulsory vestal, before whom life, with its great clarifying sorrows and its deep, entrancing joys, rolls on without touching or gripping her soul.

Emancipation, as understood by the majority of its adherents and exponents, is of too narrow a scope to permit the boundless love and ecstasy contained in the deep emotion of the true woman, sweetheart, mother, in freedom.

The tragedy of the self-supporting or economically free woman does not lie in too many, but in too few experiences. True, she surpasses her sister of past generations in knowledge of the world and human nature; it is just because of this that she feels deeply the lack of life's essence, which alone can enrich the human soul, and without which the majority of women have become mere professional automatons.

That such a state of affairs was bound to come was foreseen by those who realized that, in the domain of ethics, there still remained many decaying ruins of the time of the undisputed superiority of man; ruins that are still considered useful. And, what is more important, a goodly number of the emancipated are unable to get along without them. Every movement that aims at the destruction of existing institutions and the replacement thereof with something more advanced, more perfect, has followers who in theory stand for the most radical ideas, but who, nevertheless, in their every-day practice, are like the average Philistine, feigning respectability and clamoring for the good opinion of their opponents. There are, for example, Socialists, and even Anarchists, who stand for the idea that property is robbery, yet who will grow indignant if anyone owe them the value of a half-dozen pins.

The same Philistine can be found in the movement for woman's emancipation. Yellow journalists and milk-and-water litterateurs have painted pictures of the emancipated woman that make the hair of the good citizen and his dull companion stand up on end. Every member of the woman's rights movement was pictured as a George Sand in her absolute disregard of morality. Nothing was sacred to her. She had no respect for the ideal relation between man and woman. In short, emancipation stood only for a reckless life of lust and sin; regardless of society, religion, and morality. The exponents of woman's rights were highly indignant at such misrepresentation, and, lacking humor, they exerted all their energy to prove that they were not at all as bad as they were painted, but the very reverse. Of course, as long as woman was the slave of man, she could not be good and pure, but now that she was free and independent she would prove how good she could be and that her influence would have a purifying effect on all institutions in society. True, the movement for woman's rights has broken many old fetters, but it has also forged new ones. The great movement of *true* emancipation has not met with a great race of women who could look liberty in the face. Their narrow, Puritanical vision banished man, as a disturber and doubtful character, out of their emotional life. Man was not to be tolerated at any price, except perhaps as the father of a child, since a child could not very well come to life without a father. Fortunately, the most rigid Puritans never will be strong enough to kill the innate craving for motherhood. But woman's freedom is closely allied with man's freedom, and many of my so-called emancipated sisters seem to overlook the fact that a child born in freedom needs the love and devotion of each human being about him, man as well as woman. Unfortunately, it is this narrow conception of human relations that has brought about a great tragedy in the lives of the modern man and woman.

About fifteen years ago appeared a work from the pen of the brilliant Norwegian Laura Marholm, called *Woman, a Character Study.* She was one of the first to call attention to the emptiness and narrowness of the existing conception of woman's emancipation, and its tragic effect upon the inner life of woman. In her work Laura Marholm speaks of the fate of several gifted women of international fame: the genius Eleonora Duse; the great mathematician and writer Sonya Kovalevskaia; the artist and poet-nature Marie Bashkirtzeff, who died so young. Through each description of the lives of these women of such extraordinary mentality runs a marked trail of unsatisfied craving for a full, rounded, complete, and beautiful life, and the unrest and loneliness resulting from the lack of it. Through these masterly psychological sketches one cannot help but see that the higher the mental development of woman, the less possible it is for her to meet a congenial mate who will see in her, not only sex, but also the human being, the friend, the comrade and strong individuality, who cannot and ought not lose a single trait of her character.

The average man with his self-sufficiency, his ridiculously superior airs of patronage towards the female sex, is an impossibility for woman as depicted in the *Character Study* by Laura Marholm. Equally impossible for her is the man who can see in her nothing more than her mentality and her genius, and who fails to awaken her woman nature.

A rich intellect and a fine soul are usually considered necessary attributes of a deep and beautiful personality. In the case of the modern woman, these attributes serve as a hindrance to the complete assertion of her being. For over a hundred years the old form of marriage, based on the Bible, "till death doth part," has been denounced as an institution that stands for the sovereignty of the man over the woman, of her complete submission to his whims and commands, and absolute dependence on his name and support. Time and again it has been conclusively proved that the old matrimonial relation restricted woman to the function of man's servant and the bearer of his children. And yet we find many emancipated women who prefer marriage, with all its deficiencies, to the narrowness of an unmarried life; narrow and unendurable because of the chains of moral and social prejudice that cramp and bind her nature.

The explanation of such inconsistency on the part of many advanced women is to be found in the fact that they never truly understood the meaning of emancipation. They thought that all that was needed was independence from external tyrannies; the internal tyrants, far more harmful to life and growth—ethical and social conventions—were left to take care of themselves; and they have taken care of themselves. They seem to get along as beautifully in the heads and hearts of the most active exponents of woman's emancipation, as in the heads and hearts of our grandmothers.

These internal tyrants, whether they be in the form of public opinion or what will mother say, or brother, father, aunt, or relative of any sort; what will Mrs. Grundy, Mr. Comstock, the employer, the Board of Education say? All these busybodies, moral detectives, jailers of the human spirit, what

will they say? Until woman has learned to defy them
all, to stand firmly on her own ground and to insist
upon her own unrestricted freedom, to listen to the
voice of her nature, whether it call for life's greatest
treasure, love for a man, or her most glorious privilege, the right to give birth to a child, she cannot call
herself emancipated. How many emancipated women
are brave enough to acknowledge that the voice of
love is calling, wildly beating against their breasts,
demanding to be heard, to be satisfied.

The French writer Jean Reibrach, in one of his
novels, *New Beauty,* attempts to picture the ideal,
beautiful, emancipated woman. This ideal is embodied in a young girl, a physician. She talks very
cleverly and wisely of how to feed infants; she is
kind, and administers medicines free to poor mothers.
She converses with a young man of her acquaintance
about the sanitary conditions of the future, and how
various bacilli and germs shall be exterminated by
the use of stone walls and floors, and by the doing
away with rugs and hangings. She is, of course, very
plainly and practically dressed, mostly in black. The
young man, who, at their first meeting, was overawed
by the wisdom of his emancipated friend, gradually
learns to understand her, and recognizes one fine
day that he loves her. They are young, and she is
kind and beautiful, and though always in rigid attire,
her appearance is softened by a spotlessly clean white
collar and cuffs. One would expect that he would
tell her of his love, but he is not one to commit
romantic absurdities. Poetry and the enthusiasm of
love cover their blushing faces before the pure beauty

of the lady. He silences the voice of his nature, and remains correct. She, too, is always exact, always rational, always well behaved. I fear if they had formed a union, the young man would have risked freezing to death. I must confess that I can see nothing beautiful in this new beauty, who is as cold as the stone walls and floors she dreams of. Rather would I have the love songs of romantic ages, rather Don Juan and Madame Venus, rather an elopement by ladder and rope on a moonlight night, followed by the father's curse, mother's moans, and the moral comments of neighbors, than correctness and propriety measured by yardsticks. If love does not know how to give and take without restrictions, it is not love, but a transaction that never fails to lay stress on a plus and a minus.

The greatest shortcoming of the emancipation of the present day lies in its artificial stiffness and its narrow respectabilities, which produce an emptiness in woman's soul that will not let her drink from the fountain of life. I once remarked that there seemed to be a deeper relationship between the old-fashioned mother and hostess, ever on the alert for the happiness of her little ones and the comfort of those she loved, and the truly new woman, than between the latter and her average emancipated sister. The disciples of emancipation pure and simple declared me a heathen, fit only for the stake. Their blind zeal did not let them see that my comparison between the old and the new was merely to prove that a goodly number of our grandmothers had more blood in their veins, far more humor and wit, and certainly a greater amount of naturalness, kind-heartedness, and simplicity, than the majority of our emancipated professional women who fill the colleges, halls of learning, and various offices. This does not mean a wish to return to the past, nor does it condemn woman to her old sphere, the kitchen and the nursery.

Salvation lies in an energetic march onward towards a brighter and clearer future. We are in need of unhampered growth out of old traditions and habits. The movement for woman's emancipation has so far made but the first step in that direction. It is to be hoped that it will gather strength to make another. The right to vote, or equal civil rights, may be good demands, but true emancipation begins neither at the polls nor in courts. It begins in woman's soul. History tells us that every oppressed class gained true liberation from its masters through its own efforts. It is necessary that woman learn that lesson, that she realize that her freedom will reach as far as her power to achieve her freedom reaches. It is, therefore, far more important for her to begin with her inner regeneration, to cut loose from the weight of prejudices, traditions, and customs. The demand for equal rights in every vocation of life is just and fair; but, after all, the most vital right is the right to love and be loved. Indeed, if partial emancipation is to become a complete and true emancipation of woman, it will have to do away with the ridiculous notion that to be loved, to be sweetheart and mother, is synonymous with being slave or subordinate. It will have to do away with the absurd notion of the dualism of the sexes, or that man and woman represent two antagonistic worlds.

Pettiness separates; breadth unites. Let us be broad and big. Let us not overlook vital things because of the bulk of trifles confronting us. A true conception of the relation of the sexes will not admit of conqueror and conquered; it knows of but one great thing: to give of one's self boundlessly, in order to find one's self richer, deeper, better. That alone can fill the emptiness, and transform the tragedy of woman's emancipation into joy, limitless joy.

MARRIAGE AND LOVE

THE popular notion about marriage and love is that they are synonymous, that they spring from the same motives, and cover the same human needs. Like most popular notions this also rests not on actual facts, but on superstition.

Marriage and love have nothing in common; they are as far apart as the poles; are, in fact, antagonistic to each other. No doubt some marriages have been the result of love. Not, however, because love could assert itself only in marriage; much rather is it because few people can completely outgrow a convention. There are to-day large numbers of men and women to whom marriage is naught but a farce, but who submit to it for the sake of public opinion. At any rate, while it is true that some marriages are based on love, and while it is equally true that in some cases love continues in married life, I maintain that it does so regardless of marriage, and not because of it.

On the other hand, it is utterly false that love results from marriage. On rare occasions one does hear of a miraculous case of a married couple falling in love after marriage, but on close examination it will be found that it is a mere adjustment to the inevitable. Certainly the growing-used to each other is far away from the spontaneity, the intensity, and beauty of love, without which the intimacy of marriage must prove degrading to both the woman and the man.

Marriage is primarily an economic arrangement, an insurance pact. It differs from the ordinary life insurance agreement only in that it is more binding, more exacting. Its returns are insignificantly small compared with the investments. In taking out an insurance policy one pays for it in dollars and cents, always at liberty to discontinue payments. If, however, woman's premium is a husband, she pays for it with her name, her privacy, her self-respect, her very life, "until death doth part." Moreover, the marriage insurance condemns her to life-long dependency, to parasitism, to complete uselessness, individual as well as social. Man, too, pays his toll, but as his sphere is wider, marriage does not limit him as much as woman. He feels his chains more in an economic sense.

Thus Dante's motto over Inferno applies with equal force to marriage: "Ye who enter here leave all hope behind."

That marriage is a failure none but the very stupid will deny. One has but to glance over the statistics of divorce to realize how bitter a failure marriage really is. Nor will the stereotyped Philistine argument that the laxity of divorce laws and the growing looseness of woman account for the fact that: first, every twelfth marriage ends in divorce; second, that since 1870 divorces have increased from

28 to 73 for every hundred thousand population; third, that adultery, since 1867, as ground for divorce, has increased 270.8 per cent.; fourth, that desertion increased 369.8 per cent.

Added to these startling figures is a vast amount of material, dramatic and literary, further elucidating this subject. Robert Herrick, in *Together;* Pinero, in *Mid-Channel;* Eugene Walter, in *Paid in Full,* and scores of other writers are discussing the barrenness, the monotony, the sordidness, the inadequacy of marriage as a factor for harmony and understanding.

The thoughtful social student will not content himself with the popular superficial excuse for this phenomenon. He will have to dig down deeper into the very life of the sexes to know why marriage proves so disastrous.

Edward Carpenter says that behind every marriage stands the life-long environment of the two sexes; an environment so different from each other that man and woman must remain strangers. Separated by an insurmountable wall of superstition, custom, and habit, marriage has not the potentiality of developing knowledge of, and respect for, each other, without which every union is doomed to failure.

Henrik Ibsen, the hater of all social shams, was probably the first to realize this great truth. Nora leaves her husband, not—as the stupid critic would have it—because she is tired of her responsibilities or feels the need of woman's rights, but because she has come to know that for eight years she had lived with a stranger and borne him children. Can there be anything more humiliating, more degrading than a life-long proximity between two strangers? No need for the woman to know anything of the man, save his income. As to the knowledge of the woman—what is there to know except that she has a pleasing appearance? We have not yet outgrown the theologic myth that woman has no soul, that she is a mere appendix to man, made out of his rib just for the convenience of the gentleman who was so strong that he was afraid of his own shadow.

Perchance the poor quality of the material whence woman comes is responsible for her inferiority. At any rate, woman has no soul—what is there to know about her? Besides, the less soul a woman has the greater her asset as a wife, the more readily will she absorb herself in her husband. It is this slavish acquiescence to man's superiority that has kept the marriage institution seemingly intact for so long a period. Now that woman is coming into her own, now that she is actually growing aware of herself as a being outside of the master's grace, the sacred institution of marriage is gradually being undermined, and no amount of sentimental lamentation can stay it.

From infancy, almost, the average girl is told that marriage is her ultimate goal; therefore her training and education must be directed towards that end. Like the mute beast fattened for slaughter, she is prepared for that. Yet, strange to say, she is allowed to know much less about her function as wife and mother than the ordinary artisan of his trade. It is indecent and filthy for a respectable girl to know anything of the marital relation. Oh, for the inconsistency of respectability, that needs the marriage vow

to turn something which is filthy into the purest and
most sacred arrangement that none dare question or
criticize. Yet that is exactly the attitude of the average upholder of marriage. The prospective wife and
mother is kept in complete ignorance of her only
asset in the competitive field—sex. Thus she enters
into life-long relations with a man only to find herself shocked, repelled, outraged beyond measure by
the most natural and healthy instinct, sex. It is safe
to say that a large percentage of the unhappiness,
misery, distress, and physical suffering of matrimony
is due to the criminal ignorance in sex matters that is
being extolled as a great virtue. Nor is it at all an
exaggeration when I say that more than one home has
been broken up because of this deplorable fact.

If, however, woman is free and big enough to
learn the mystery of sex without the sanction of
State or Church, she will stand condemned as utterly
unfit to become the wife of a "good" man, his goodness consisting of an empty head and plenty of
money. Can there be anything more outrageous than
the idea that a healthy, grown woman, full of life and
passion, must deny nature's demand, must subdue
her most intense craving, undermine her health and
break her spirit, must stunt her vision, abstain from
the depth and glory of sex experience until a "good"
man comes along to take her unto himself as a wife?
That is precisely what marriage means. How can
such an arrangement end except in failure? This is
one, though not the least important, factor of marriage, which differentiates it from love.

Ours is a practical age. The time when Romeo and Juliet risked the wrath of their fathers for love, when Gretchen exposed herself to the gossip of her neighbors for love, is no more. If, on rare occasions, young pople allow themselves the luxury of romance, they are taken in care by the elders, drilled and pounded until they become "sensible."

The moral lesson instilled in the girl is not whether the man has aroused her love, but rather is it, "How much?" The important and only God of practical American life: Can the man make a living? Can he support a wife? That is the only thing that justifies marriage. Gradually this saturates every thought of the girl; her dreams are not of moonlight and kisses, of laughter and tears; she dreams of shopping tours and bargain counters. This soul-poverty and sordidness are the elements inherent in the marriage institution. The State and the Church approve of no other ideal, simply because it is the one that necessitates the State and Church control of men and women.

Doubtless there are people who continue to consider love above dollars and cents. Particularly is this true of that class whom economic necessity has forced to become self-supporting. The tremendous change in woman's position, wrought by that mighty factor, is' indeed phenomenal when we reflect that it is but a short time since she has entered the industrial arena. Six million women wage-earners; six million women, who have the equal right with men to be exploited, to be robbed, to go on strike; aye, to starve even. Anything more, my lord? Yes, six million wage-workers in every walk of life, from the highest brain work to the most difficult menial labor in the mines and on the railroad tracks; yes, even detectives and policemen. Surely the emancipation is complete.

Yet with all that, but a very small number of the vast army of women wage-workers look upon work as a permanent issue, in the same light as does man. No matter how decrepit the latter, he has been taught to be independent, self-supporting. Oh, I know that no one is really independent in our economic treadmill; still, the poorest specimen of a man hates to be a parasite; to be known as such, at any rate.

The woman considers her position as worker transitory, to be thrown aside for the first bidder. That is why it is infinitely harder to organize women than men. "Why should I join a union? I am going to get married, to have a home." Has she not been taught from infancy to look upon that as her ultimate calling? She learns soon enough that the home, though not so large a prison as the factory, has more solid doors and bars. It has a keeper so faithful that naught can escape him. The most tragic part, however, is that the home no longer frees her from wage-slavery; it only increases her task.

According to the latest statistics submitted before a Committee "on labor and wages, and congestion of population," ten per cent. of the wage workers in New York City alone are married, yet they must continue to work at the most poorly paid labor in the world. Add to this horrible aspect the drudgery of housework, and what remains of the protection and glory of the home? As a matter of fact, even the middle-class girl in marriage can not speak of her home, since it is the man who creates her sphere. It is not important whether the husband is a brute or a darling. What I wish to prove is that marriage guarantees woman a home only by the grace of her husband. There she moves about in *his* home, year after year, until her aspect of life and human affairs becomes as flat, narrow, and drab as her surroundings. Small wonder if she becomes a nag, petty, quarrelsome, gossipy, unbearable, thus driving the man from the house. She could not go, if she wanted to; there is no place to go. Besides, a short period of married life, of complete surrender of all faculties, absolutely incapacitates the average woman for the outside world. She becomes reckless in appearance, clumsy in her movements, dependent in her decisions, cowardly in her judgment, a weight and a bore, which most men grow to hate and despise. Wonderfully inspiring atmosphere for the bearing of life, is it not?

But the child, how is it to be protected, if not for marriage? After all, is not that the most important consideration? The sham, the hypocrisy of it! Marriage protecting the child, yet thousands of children destitute and homeless. Marriage protecting the child, yet orphan asylums and reformatories overcrowded, the Society for the Prevention of Cruelty to Children keeping busy in rescuing the little victims from "loving" parents, to place them under more loving care, the Gerry Society. Oh, the mockery of it!

Marriage may have the power to "bring the horse to water," but has it ever made him drink? The law will place the father under arrest, and put him in con-

vict's clothes; but has that ever stilled the hunger of
the child? If the parent has no work, or if he hides
his identity, what does marriage do then? It invokes
the law to bring the man to "justice," to put him
safely behind closed doors; his labor, however, goes
not to the child, but to the State. The child receives
but a blighted memory of its father's stripes.

As to the protection of the woman,—therein lies
the curse of marriage. Not that it really protects her,
but the very idea is so revolting, such an outrage and
insult on life, so degrading to human dignity, as to
forever condemn this parasitic institution.

It is like that other paternal arrangement—capitalism. It robs man of his birthright, stunts his growth,
poisons his body, keeps him in ignorance, in poverty
and dependence, and then institutes charities that
thrive on the last vestige of man's self-respect.

The institution of marriage makes a parasite of
woman, an absolute dependent. It incapacitates her
for life's struggle, annihilates her social consciousness,
paralyzes her imagination, and then imposes its gra-
cious protection, which is in reality a snare, a travesty
on human character.

If motherhood is the highest fulfillment of
woman's nature, what other protection does it need
save love and freedom? Marriage but defiles, outrages, and corrupts her fulfillment. Does it not say to
woman, Only when you follow me shall you bring
forth life? Does it not condemn her to the block,
does it not degrade and shame her if she refuses to
buy her right to motherhood by selling herself? Does
not marriage only sanction motherhood, even though

conceived in hatred, in compulsion? Yet, if motherhood be of free choice, of love, of ecstasy, of defiant
passion, does it not place a crown of thorns upon an
innocent head and carve in letters of blood the hideous
epithet, Bastard? Were marriage to contain all the
virtues claimed for it, its crimes against motherhood
would exclude it forever from the realm of love.

Love, the strongest and deepest element in all life,
the harbinger of hope, of joy, of ecstasy; love, the
defier of all laws, of all conventions; love, the freest,
the most powerful moulder of human destiny; how
can such an all-compelling force be synonymous with
that poor little State and Church-begotten weed,
marriage?

Free love? As if love is anything but free! Man
has bought brains, but all the millions in the world
have failed to buy love. Man has subdued bodies, but
all the power on earth has been unable to subdue love.
Man has conquered whole nations, but all his armies
could not conquer love. Man has chained and fettered the spirit, but he has been utterly helpless before
love. High on a throne, with all the splendor and
pomp his gold can command, man is yet poor and
desolate, if love passes him by. And if it stays, the
poorest hovel is radiant with warmth, with life and
color. Thus love has the magic power to make of a
beggar a king. Yes, love is free; it can dwell in no
other atmosphere. In freedom it gives itself un-
reservedly, abundantly, completely. All the laws on
the statutes, all the courts in the universe, cannot tear
it from the soil, once love has taken root. If, however, the soil is sterile, how can marriage make it bear

fruit? It is like the last desperate struggle of fleeting
life against death.

Love needs no protection; it is its own protection.
So long as love begets life no child is deserted, or
hungry, or famished for the want of affection.   I
know this to be true.   I know women who became
mothers in freedom by the men they loved.   Few
children in wedlock enjoy the care, the protection,
the devotion free motherhood is capable of bestowing.

The defenders of authority dread the advent of a
free motherhood, lest it will rob them of their prey.
Who would fight wars?   Who would create wealth?
Who would make the policeman, the jailer, if woman
were to refuse the indiscriminate breeding of children?   The race, the race! shouts the king, the president, the capitalist, the priest.   The race must be preserved, though woman be degraded to a mere machine,
—and the marriage institution is our only safety valve
against the pernicious sex-awakening of woman.   But
in vain these frantic efforts to maintain a state of
bondage.   In vain, too, the edicts of the Church, the
mad attacks of rulers, in vain even the arm of the
law.   Woman no longer wants to be a party to the
production of a race of sickly, feeble, decrepit,
wretched human beings, who have neither the strength
nor moral courage to throw off the yoke of poverty
and slavery.   Instead she desires fewer and better
children, begotten and reared in love and through free
choice; not by compulsion, as marriage imposes.   Our
pseudo-moralists have yet to learn the deep sense of
responsibility toward the child, that love in freedom
has awakened in the breast of woman.   Rather would

she forego forever the glory of motherhood than bring forth life in an atmosphere that breathes only destruction and death. And if she does become a mother, it is to give to the child the deepest and best her being can yield. To grow with the child is her motto; she knows that in that manner alone can she help build true manhood and womanhood.

Ibsen must have had a vision of a free mother, when, with a master stroke, he portrayed Mrs. Alving. She was the ideal mother because she had outgrown marriage and all its horrors, because she had broken her chains, and set her spirit free to soar until it returned a personality, regenerated and strong. Alas, it was too late to rescue her life's joy, her Oswald; but not too late to realize that love in freedom is the only condition of a beautiful life. Those who, like Mrs. Alving, have paid with blood and tears for their spiritual awakening, repudiate marriage as an imposition, a shallow, empty mockery. They know, whether love last but one brief span of time or for eternity, it is the only creative, inspiring, elevating basis for a new race, a new world.

In our present pygmy state love is indeed a stranger to most people. Misunderstood and shunned, it rarely takes root; or if it does, it soon withers and dies. Its delicate fiber can not endure the stress and strain of the daily grind. Its soul is too complex to adjust itself to the slimy woof of our social fabric. It weeps and moans and suffers with those who have need of it, yet lack the capacity to rise to love's summit.

Some day, some day men and women will rise, they will reach the mountain peak, they will meet big and strong and free, ready to receive, to partake, and to bask in the golden rays of love. What fancy, what imagination, what poetic genius can foresee even approximately the potentialities of such a force in the life of men and women. If the world is ever to give birth to true companionship and oneness, not marriage, but love will be the parent.

THE MODERN DRAMA

A POWERFUL DISSEMINATOR OF RADICAL THOUGHT

So LONG as discontent and unrest make themselves but dumbly felt within a limited social class, the powers of reaction may often succeed in suppressing such manifestations. But when the dumb unrest grows into conscious expression and becomes almost universal, it necessarily affects all phases of human thought and action, and seeks its individual and social expression in the gradual transvaluation of existing values.

An adequate appreciation of the tremendous spread of the modern, conscious social unrest cannot be gained from merely propagandistic literature. Rather must we become conversant with the larger phases of human expression manifest in art, literature, and, above all, the modern drama—the strongest and most far-reaching interpreter of our deep-felt dissatisfaction.

What a tremendous factor for the awakening of conscious discontent are the simple canvasses of a Millet! The figures of his peasants—what terrific indictment against our social wrongs; wrongs that condemn the Man With the Hoe to hopeless drudgery, himself excluded from Nature's bounty.

The vision of a Meunier conceives the growing solidarity and defiance of labor in the group of miners carrying their maimed brother to safety. His genius thus powerfully portrays the interrelation of the seething unrest among those slaving in the bowels of the earth, and the spiritual revolt that seeks artistic expression.

No less important is the factor for rebellious awakening in modern literature—Turgeniev, Dostoyevsky, Tolstoy, Andreiev, Gorki, Whitman, Emerson, and scores of others embodying the spirit of universal ferment and the longing for social change.

Still more far-reaching is the modern drama, as the leaven of radical thought and the disseminator of new values.

It might seem an exaggeration to ascribe to the modern drama such an important rôle. But a study of the development of modern ideas in most countries will prove that the drama has succeeded in driving home great social truths, truths generally ignored when presented in other forms. No doubt there are exceptions, as Russia and France.

Russia, with its terrible political pressure, has made people think and has awakened their social sympathies, because of the tremendous contrast which exists between the intellectual life of the people and the despotic régime that is trying to crush that life. Yet while the great dramatic works of Tolstoy, Tchechov, Gorki, and Andreiev closely mirror the life and the struggle, the hopes and aspirations of the Russian people, they did not influence radical thought to the extent the drama has done in other countries.

Who can deny, however, the tremendous influence exerted by *The Power of Darkness* or *Night Lodging*. Tolstoy, the real, true Christian, is yet the greatest enemy of organized Christianity. With a master hand he portrays the destructive effects upon the human mind of the power of darkness, the superstitions of the Christian Church.

What other medium could express, with such dramatic force, the responsibility of the Church for crimes committed by its deluded victims; what other medium could, in consequence, rouse the indignation of man's conscience?

Similarly direct and powerful is the indictment contained in Gorki's *Night Lodging*. The social pariahs, forced into poverty and crime, yet desperately clutch at the last vestiges of hope and aspiration. Lost existences these, blighted and crushed by cruel, unsocial environment.

France, on the other hand, with her continuous struggle for liberty, is indeed the cradle of radical thought; as such she, too, did not need the drama as a means of awakening. And yet the works of Brieux —as *Robe Rouge,* portraying the terrible corruption of the judiciary—and Mirbeau's *Les Affaires sont les Affaires*—picturing the destructive influence of wealth on the human soul—have undoubtedly reached wider circles than most of the articles and books which have been written in France on the social question.

In countries like Germany, Scandinavia, England, and even in America—though in a lesser degree—the drama is the vehicle which is really making history, disseminating radical thought in ranks not otherwise to be reached.

Let us take Germany, for instance. For nearly a quarter of a century men of brains, of ideas, and of the greatest integrity, made it their life-work to spread the truth of human brotherhood, of justice, among the oppressed and downtrodden. Socialism, that tremendous revolutionary wave, was to the victims of a merciless and inhumane system like water to the parched lips of the desert traveler. Alas! The cultured people remained absolutely indifferent; to them that revolutionary tide was but the murmur of dissatisfied, discontented men, dangerous, illiterate trouble-makers, whose proper place was behind prison bars.

Self-satisfied as the "cultured" usually are, they could not understand why one should fuss about the fact that thousands of people were starving, though they contributed towards the wealth of the world. Surrounded by beauty and luxury, they could not believe that side by side with them lived human beings degraded to a position lower than a beast's, shelterless and ragged, without hope or ambition.

This condition of affairs was particularly pronounced in Germany after the Franco-German war. Full to the bursting point with its victory, Germany thrived on a sentimental, patriotic literature, thereby poisoning the minds of the country's youth by the glory of conquest and bloodshed.

Intellectual Germany had to take refuge in the literature of other countries, in the works of Ibsen, Zola, Daudet, Maupassant, and especially in the great

works of Dostoyevsky, Tolstoy, and Turgeniev. But
as no country can long maintain a standard of culture
without a literature and drama related to its own soil,
so Germany gradually began to develop a drama
reflecting the life and the struggles of its own people.

Arno Holz, one of the youngest dramatists of that
period, startled the Philistines out of their ease and
comfort with his *Familie Selicke*. The play deals
with society's refuse, men and women of the alleys,
whose only subsistence consists of what they can pick
out of the garbage barrels. A gruesome subject, is it
not? And yet what other method is there to break
through the hard shell of the minds and souls of
people who have never known want, and who therefore assume that all is well in the world?

Needless to say, the play aroused tremendous
indignation. The truth is bitter, and the people living
on the Fifth Avenue of Berlin hated to be confronted
with the truth.

Not that *Familie Selicke* represented anything that
had not been written about for years without any
seeming result. But the dramatic genius of Holz, together with the powerful interpretation of the play,
necessarily made inroads into the widest circles, and
forced people to think about the terrible inequalities
around them.

Sudermann's *Ehre** and *Heimat*† deal with vital
subjects. I have already referred to the sentimental
patriotism so completely turning the head of the average German as to create a perverted conception of

* *Honor.*
† *Magda.*

honor. Duelling became an every-day affair, costing innumerable lives. A great cry was raised against the fad by a number of leading writers. But nothing acted as such a clarifier and exposer of that national disease as the *Ehre*.

Not that the play merely deals with duelling; it analyzes the real meaning of honor, proving that it is not a fixed, inborn feeling, but that it varies with every people and every epoch, depending particularly on one's economic and social station in life. We realize from this play that the man in the brownstone mansion will necessarily define honor differently from his victims.

The family Heinecke enjoys the charity of the millionaire Mühling, being permitted to occupy a dilapidated shanty on his premises in the absence of their son, Robert. The latter, as Mühling's representative, is making a vast fortune for his employer in India. On his return Robert discovers that his sister had been seduced by young Mühling, whose father graciously offers to straighten matters with a check for 40,000 marks. Robert, outraged and indignant, resents the insult to his family's honor, and is forthwith dismissed from his position for impudence. Robert finally throws this accusation into the face of the philanthropist millionaire:

"We slave for you, we sacrifice our heart's blood for you, while you seduce our daughters and sisters and kindly pay for their disgrace with the gold we have earned for you. That is what you call honor."

An incidental side-light upon the conception of honor is given by Count Trast, the principal character

in the *Ehre,* a man widely conversant with the customs
of various climes, who relates that in his many travels
he chanced across a savage tribe whose honor he mor-
tally offended by refusing the hospitality which
offered him the charms of the chieftain's wife.

The theme of *Heimat* treates of the struggle
between the old and the young generations. It holds
a permanent and important place in dramatic literature.

Magda, the daughter of Lieutenant-Colonel
Schwartz, has committed an unpardonable sin: she
refused the suitor selected by her father. For daring
to disobey the parental commands she is driven from
home. Magda, full of life and the spirit of liberty,
goes out into the world to return to her native town,
twelve years later, a celebrated singer. She consents
to visit her parents on condition that they respect the
privacy of her past. But her martinet father immediately begins to question her, insisting on his
"paternal rights." Magda is indignant, but gradually
his persistence brings to light the tragedy of her life.
He learns that the respected Councillor von Keller
had in his student days been Magda's lover, while she
was battling for her economic and social independence. The consequence of the fleeting romance was a
child, deserted by the man even before birth. The
rigid military father of Magda demands as retribution
from Councillor von Keller that he legalize the love
affair. In view of Magda's social and professional
success, Keller willingly consents, but on condition
that she forsake the stage, and place the child in an
institution. The struggle between the Old and the

New culminates in Magda's defiant words of the woman grown to conscious independence of thought and action: ". . . I'll say what I think of you—of you and your respectable society. Why should I be worse than you that I must prolong my existence among you by a lie! Why should this gold upon my body, and the lustre which surrounds my name, only increase my infamy? Have I not worked early and late for ten long years? Have I not woven this dress with sleepless nights? Have I not built up my career step by step, like thousands of my kind? Why should I blush before anyone? I am myself, and through myself I have become what I am."

The general theme of *Heimat*—the struggle between the old and young generations—was not original. It had been previously treated by a master hand in *Fathers and Sons,* portraying the awakening of an age. But though artistically far inferior to Turgeniev's work, *Heimat*—depicting the awakening of a sex—proved a powerful revolutionizing factor, mainly because of its dramatic expression.

The dramatist who not only disseminated radicalism, but literally revolutionized the thoughtful Germans, is Gerhardt Hauptmann. His first play, *Vor Sonnenaufgang,** refused by every leading German threatre, but finally performed in the independent Lessing Theatre, acted like a stroke of lightning, illuminating the entire social horizon. Its subject matter deals with the life of an extensive land-owner, ignorant, illiterate, and brutalized, and his economic

---

* *Before Sunrise.*

slaves of the same mental calibre. The influence of
wealth, both on the victims who created it and the
possessor thereof, is shown in the most vivid colors,
as resulting in drunkenness, idiocy, and decay. But
the most striking feature of *Vor Sonnenaufgang,* the
one which brought a shower of abuse on Hauptmann's
head, was the question as to the indiscriminate breeding of children by unfit parents.

During the second performance of the play a leading Berlin surgeon almost caused a panic in the
theatre by swinging a pair of forceps over his head
and screaming at the top of his voice: "The decency
and morality of Germany are at stake if childbirth is
to be discussed openly from the stage." The surgeon
is forgotten, and Hauptmann stands a colossal figure
before the world.

When *Die Weber** first saw the light, pande-
monium broke out in the land of thinkers and poets.
"What," cried the moralists, "workingmen, dirty,
filthy slaves, to be put on the stage! Poverty in all
its horrors and ugliness to be dished out as an after-
dinner amusement? That is too much!"

Indeed, it was too much for the fat and greasy
bourgeoisie to be brought face to face with the horrors
of the weaver's existence. It was too much because
of the truth and reality that rang like thunder in the
deaf ears of self-satisfied society, *J'accuse!*

Of course, it was generally known even before the
appearance of this drama that capital can not get fat
unless it devours labor, that wealth can not be hoarded

---

* *The Weavers.*

except through the channels of poverty, hunger, and cold; but such things are better kept in the dark, lest the victims awaken to a realization of their position. But it is the purpose of the modern drama to rouse the consciousness of the oppressed; and that, indeed, was the purpose of Gerhardt Hauptmann in depicting to the world the conditions of the weavers in Silesia. Human beings working eighteen hours daily, yet not earning enough for bread and fuel; human beings living in broken, wretched huts half covered with snow, and nothing but tatters to protect them from the cold; infants covered with scurvy from hunger and exposure; pregnant women in the last stages of consumption. Victims of a benevolent Christian era, without life, without hope, without warmth. Ah, yes, it was too much!

Hauptmann's dramatic versatility deals with every stratum of social life. Besides portraying the grinding effect of economic conditions, he also treats of the struggle of the individual for his mental and spiritual liberation from the slavery of convention and tradition. Thus Heinrich, the bell-forger, in the dramatic prose-poem *Die Versunkene Glocke*,* fails to reach the mountain peaks of liberty because, as Rautendelein said, he had lived in the valley too long. Similarly Dr. Vockerath and Anna Maar remain lonely souls because they, too, lack the strength to defy venerated traditions. Yet their very failure must awaken the rebellious spirit against a world forever hindering individual and social emancipation.

---

* *The Sunken Bell.*

Max Halbe's *Jugend** and Wedekind's *Frühling's Erwachen†* are dramas which have disseminated radical thought in an altogether different direction. They treat of the child and the dense ignorance and narrow Puritanism that meet the awakening of nature. Particularly is this true of *Frühling's Erwachen.* Young girls and boys sacrificed on the altar of false education and of our sickening morality that prohibits the enlightenment of youth as to questions so imperative to the health and well-being of society,— the origin of life, and its functions. It shows how a mother—and a truly good mother, at that—keeps her fourteen-year-old daughter in absolute ignorance as to all matters of sex, and when finally the young girl falls a victim to her ignorance, the same mother sees her child killed by quack medicines. The inscription on her grave states that she died of anaemia, and morality is satisfied.

The fatality of our Puritanic hypocrisy in these matters is especially illumined by Wedekind in so far as our most promising children fall victims to sex ignorance and the utter lack of appreciation on the part of the teachers of the child's awakening.

Wendla, unusually developed and alert for her age, pleads with her mother to explain the mystery of life:

"I have a sister who has been married for two and a half years. I myself have been made an aunt for the third time, and I haven't the least idea how it all comes about. . . . Don't be cross, Mother, dear! Whom in the world should I ask but you? Don't

---

* *Youth.*
† *The Awakening of Spring.*

scold me for asking about it.   Give me an answer.—
How does it happen?—You cannot really deceive
yourself that I, who am fourteen years old, still
believe in the stork."

Were her mother herself not a victim of false
notions of morality, an affectionate and sensible
explanation might have saved her daughter.   But the
conventional mother seeks to hide her "moral" shame
and embarrassment in this evasive reply:

"In order to have a child—one must love—the
man—to whom one is married. . . . One must love
him, Wendla, as you at your age are still unable to
love.—Now you know it!"

How much Wendla "knew" the mother realized
too late.   The pregnant girl imagines herself ill with
dropsy.   And when her mother cries in desperation,
"You haven't the dropsy, you have a child, girl," the
agonized Wendla exclaims in bewilderment: "But it's
not possible, Mother, I am not married yet. . . . Oh,
Mother, why didn't you tell me everything?"

With equal stupidity the boy Morris is driven to
suicide because he fails in his school examinations
And Melchior, the youthful father of Wendla's unborn
child, is sent to the House of Correction, his early
sexual awakening stamping him a degenerate in the
eyes of teachers and parents.

For years thoughtful men and women in Germany
had advocated the compelling necessity of sex enlightenment.   *Mutterschutz,* a publication specially devoted
to frank and intelligent discussion of the sex problem,
has been carrying on its agitation for a considerable
time.   But it remained for the dramatic genius of

Wedekind to influence radical thought to the extent of forcing the introduction of sex physiology in many schools of Germany.

Scandinavia, like Germany, was advanced through the drama much more than through any other channel. Long before Ibsen appeared on the scene, Björnson, the great essayist, thundered against the inequalities and injustice prevalent in those countries. But his was a voice in the wilderness, reaching but the few. Not so with Ibsen. His *Brand, Doll's House, Pillars of Society, Ghosts,* and *An Enemy of the People* have considerably undermined the old conceptions, and replaced them by a modern and real view of life. One has but to read *Brand* to realize the modern conception, let us say, of religion,—religion, as an ideal to be achieved on earth; religion as a principle of human brotherhood, of solidarity, and kindness.

Ibsen, the supreme hater of all social shams, has torn the veil of hypocrisy from their faces. His greatest onslaught, however, is on the four cardinal points supporting the flimsy network of society. First, the lie upon which rests the life of today; second, the futility of sacrifice as preached by our moral codes; third, petty material consideration, which is the only god the majority worships; and fourth, the deadening influence of provincialism. These four recur as the *Leitmotiv* in most of Ibsen's plays, but particularly in *Pillars of Society, Doll's House, Ghosts,* and *An Enemy of the People.*

Pillars of Society! What a tremendous indictment against the social structure that rests on rotten and decayed pillars,—pillars nicely gilded and apparently intact, yet merely hiding their true condition. And what are these pillars?

Consul Bernick, at the very height of his social and financial career, the benefactor of his town and the strongest pillar of the community, has reached the summit through the channel of lies, deception, and fraud. He has robbed his bosom friend Johann of his good name, and has betrayed Lona Hessel, the woman he loved, to marry her stepsister for the sake of her money. He has enriched himself by shady transactions, under cover of "the community's good," and finally even goes to the extent of endangering human life by preparing the *Indian Girl,* a rotten and dangerous vessel, to go to sea.

But the return of Lona brings him the realization of the emptiness and meanness of his narrow life. He seeks to placate the waking conscience by the hope that he has cleared the ground for the better life of his son, of the new generation. But even this last hope soon falls to the ground, as he realizes that truth cannot be built on a lie. At the very moment when the whole town is prepared to celebrate the great benefactor of the community with banquet praise, he himself, now grown to full spiritual manhood, confesses to the assembled townspeople:

"I have no right to this homage—. . . My fellow-citizens must know me to the core. Then let everyone examine himself, and let us realize the prediction that from this event we begin a new time. The old, with its tinsel, its hypocrisy, its hollowness, its lying propriety, and its pitiful cowardice, shall lie behind us like a museum, open for instruction."

With a *Doll's House* Ibsen has paved the way for woman's emancipation. Nora awakens from her doll's rôle to the realization of the injustice done her by her father and her husband, Helmer Torvald.

"While I was at home with father, he used to tell me all his opinions, and I held the same opinions. If I had others I concealed them, because he would not have approved. He used to call me his doll child, and play with me as I played with my dolls. Then I came to live in your house. You settled everything according to your taste, and I got the same taste as you, or I pretended to. When I look back on it now, I seem to have been living like a beggar, from hand to mouth. I lived by performing tricks for you, Torvald, but you would, have it so. You and father have done me a great wrong."

In vain Helmer uses the old philistine arguments of wifely duty and social obligations. Nora has grown out of her doll's dress into full stature of conscious womanhood. She is determined to think and judge for herself. She has realized that, before all else, she is a human being, owing the first duty to herself. She is undaunted even by the possibility of social ostracism. She has become sceptical of the justice of the law, the wisdom of the constituted. Her rebelling soul rises in protest against the existing. In her own words: "I must make up my mind which is right, society or I."

In her childlike faith in her husband she had hoped for the great miracle. But it was not the disappointed hope that opened her vision to the falsehoods of marriage. It was rather the smug contentment of Helmer with a safe lie—one that would remain hidden and not endanger his social standing.

When Nora closed behind her the door of her gilded cage and went out into the world a new, regenerated personality, she opened the gate of freedom and truth for her own sex and the race to come.

More than any other play, *Ghosts* has acted like a bomb explosion, shaking the social structure to its very foundations.

In *Doll's House* the justification of the union between Nora and Helmer rested at least on the husband's conception of integrity and rigid adherence to our social morality. Indeed, he was the conventional ideal husband and devoted father. Not so in *Ghosts*. Mrs. Alving married Captain Alving only to find that he was a physical and mental wreck, and that life with him would mean utter degradation and be fatal to possible offspring. In her despair she turned to her youth's companion, young Pastor Manders who, as the true savior of souls for heaven, must needs be indifferent to earthly necessities. He sent her back to shame and degradation,—to her duties to husband and home. Indeed, happiness—to him—was but the unholy manifestation of a rebellious spirit, and a wife's duty was not to judge, but "to bear with humility the cross which a higher power had for your own good laid upon you."

Mrs. Alving bore the cross for twenty-six long years. Not for the sake of the higher power, but for her little son Oswald, whom she longed to save from the poisonous atmosphere of her husband's home.

It was also for the sake of the beloved son that

she supported the lie of his father's goodness, in super-
stitious awe of "duty and decency." She learned—
alas, too late—that the sacrifice of her entire life had
been in vain, and that her son Oswald was visited by
the sins of his father, that he was irrevocably doomed.
This, too, she learned, that "we are all of us ghosts.
It is not only what we have inherited from our father
and mother that walks in us. It is all sorts of dead
ideas and lifeless old beliefs. They have no vitality,
but they cling to us all the same and we can't get rid
of them. . . . And then we are, one and all, so piti-
fully afraid of light. When you forced me under the
yoke you called Duty and Obligation; when you
praised as right and proper what my whole soul
rebelled against as something loathsome, it was then
that I began to look into the seams of your doctrine. I
only wished to pick at a single knot, but when I had
got that undone, the whole thing ravelled out. And
then I understood that it was all machine-sewn."

How could a society machine-sewn, fathom the
seething depths whence issued the great masterpiece
of Henrik Ibsen? It could not understand, and therefore it poured the vials of abuse and venom upon its
greatest benefactor. That Ibsen was not daunted he
has proved by his reply in *An Enemy of the People*.

In that great drama Ibsen performs the last funeral
rites over a decaying and dying social system. Out
of its ashes rises the regenerated individual, the bold
and daring rebel. Dr. Stockman, an idealist, full of
social sympathy and solidarity, is called to his native
town as the physician of the baths. He soon discovers that the latter are built on a swamp, and that

instead of finding relief the patients, who flock to the place, are being poisoned.

An honest man, of strong convictions, the doctor considers it his duty to make his discovery known. But he soon learns that dividends and profits are concerned neither with health nor priniciples. Even the reformers of the town, represented in the *People's Messenger,* always ready to prate of their devotion to the people, withdraw their support from the "reckless" idealist, the moment they learn that the doctor's discovery may bring the town into disrepute, and thus injure their pockets.

But Doctor Stockman continues in the faith he entertains for his townsmen. They would hear him. But here, too, he soon finds himself alone. He cannot even secure a place to proclaim his great truth. And when he finally succeeds, he is overwhelmed by abuse and ridicule as the enemy of the people. The doctor, so enthusiastic of his townspeople's assistance to eradicate the evil, is soon driven to a solitary position. The announcement of his discovery would result in a pecuniary loss to the town, and that consideration induces the officials, the good citizens, and soul reformers, to stifle the voice of truth. He finds them all a compact majority, unscrupulous enough to be willing to build up the prosperity of the town on a quagmire of lies and fraud. He is accused of trying to ruin the community. But to his mind "it does not matter if a lying community is ruined. It must be levelled to the ground. All men who live upon lies must be exterminated like vermin. You'll bring it to such a pass that the whole country will deserve to perish."

Doctor Stockman is not a practical politician. A free man, he thinks, must not behave like a blackguard. "He must not so act that he would spit in his own face." For only cowards permit "considerations" of pretended general welfare or of party to override truth and ideals. "Party programmes wring the necks of all young, living truths; and considerations of expediency turn morality and righteousness upside down, until life is simply hideous."

These plays of Ibsen—*The Pillars of Society, A Doll's House, Ghosts,* and *An Enemy of the People*—constitute a dynamic force which is gradually dissipating the ghosts walking the social burying ground called civilization. Nay, more; Ibsen's destructive effects are at the same time supremely constructive, for he not merely undermines existing pillars; indeed, he builds with sure strokes the foundation of a healthier, ideal future, based on the sovereignty of the individual within a sympathetic social environment.

England with her great pioneers of radical thought, the intellectual pilgrims like Godwin, Robert Owen, Darwin, Spencer, William Morris, and scores of others; with her wonderful larks of liberty—Shelley, Byron, Keats—is another example of the influence of dramatic art. Within comparatively a few years the dramatic works of Shaw, Pinero, Galsworthy, Rann Kennedy, have carried radical thought to the ears formerly deaf even to Great Britain's wondrous poets. Thus a public which will remain indifferent reading an essay by Robert Owen on poverty, or ignore Bernard Shaw's Socialistic tracts, was made to think by *Major Barbara,* wherein poverty is

described as the greatest crime of Christian civilization. "Poverty makes people weak, slavish, puny;
poverty creates disease, crime, prostitution; in fine,
poverty is responsible for all the ills and evils of the
world." Poverty also necessitates dependency, chari-
table organizations, institutions that thrive off the very
thing they are trying to destroy. The Salvation
Army, for instance, as shown in *Major Barbara,*
fights drunkenness; yet one of its greatest contributors
is Badger, a whiskey distiller, who furnishes yearly
thousands of pounds to do away with the very source
of his wealth. Bernard Shaw therefore concludes
that the only real benefactor of society is a man like
Undershaft, Barbara's father, a cannon manufacturer,
whose theory of life is that powder is stronger than
words.

"The worst of crimes," says Undershaft, "is poverty. All the other crimes are virtues beside it; all
the other dishonors are chivalry itself by comparison.
Poverty blights whole cities; spreads horrible pesti-
lences; strikes dead the very soul of all who come
within sight, sound, or smell of it. What you call
crime is nothing; a murder here, a theft there, a blow
now and a curse there: what do they matter? They
are only the accidents and illnesses of life; there are
not fifty genuine professional criminals in London.
But there are millions of poor people, abject people,
dirty people, ill-fed, ill-clothed people. They poison
us morally and physically; they kill the happiness of
society; they force us to do away with our own liberties and to organize unnatural cruelties for fear they
should rise against us and drag us down into their

abyss. . . . Poverty and slavery have stood up for
centuries to your sermons and leading articles; they
will not stand up to my machine guns. Don't preach
at them; don't reason with them. Kill them. . . .
It is the final test of conviction, the only lever strong
enough to overturn a social system. . . . Vote! Bah!
When you vote, you only change the name of the
cabinet. When you shoot, you pull down governments, inaugurate new epochs, abolish old orders, and
set up new."

No wonder people cared little to read Mr. Shaw's
Socialistic tracts. In no other way but in the drama
could he deliver such forcible, historic truths. And
therefore it is only through the drama that Mr. Shaw
is a revolutionary factor in the dissemination of radical ideas.

After Hauptmann's *Die Weber, Strife,* by Galsworthy, is the most important labor drama.

The theme of *Strife* is a strike with two dominant
factors: Anthony, the president of the company, rigid,
uncompromising, unwilling to make the slightest con-
cession, although the men held out for months and are
in a condition of semi-starvation; and David Roberts,
an uncompromising revolutionist, whose devotion to
the workingmen and the cause of freedom is at white
heat. Between them the strikers are worn and weary
with the terrible struggle, and are harassed and
driven by the awful sight of poverty and want in their
families.

The most marvelous and brilliant piece of work in
Strife is Galsworthy's portrayal of the mob in its
fickleness and lack of backbone. One moment they

applaud old Thomas, who speaks of the power of God and religion and admonishes the men against rebellion; the next instant they are carried away by a walking delegate, who pleads the cause of the union,—the union that always stands for compromise, and which forsakes the workingmen whenever they dare to strike for independent demands; again they are aglow with the earnestness, the spirit, and the intensity of David Roberts—all these people willing to go in whatever direction the wind blows. It is the curse of the working class that they always follow like sheep led to slaughter.

Consistency is the greatest crime of our commercial age. No matter how intense the spirit or how important the man, the moment he will not allow himself to be used or sell his principles, he is thrown on the dustheap. Such was the fate of the president of the company, Anthony, and of David Roberts. To be sure they represented opposite poles—poles antagonistic to each other, poles divided by a terrible gap that can never be bridged over. Yet they shared a common fate. Anthony is the embodiment of conservatism, of old ideas, of iron methods:

"I have been chairman of this company thirty-two years. I have fought the men four times. I have never been defeated. It has been said that times have changed. If they have, I have not changed with them. It has been said that masters and men are equal. Cant. There can be only one master in a house. It has been said that Capital and Labor have the same interests. Cant. Their interests are as wide asunder as the poles. There is only one way of treating men—

with the iron rod. Masters are masters. Men are men."

We may not like this adherence to old, reactionary notions, and yet there is something admirable in the courage and consistency of this man, nor is he half as dangerous to the interests of the oppressed, as our sentimental and soft reformers who rob with nine fingers, and give libraries with the tenth; who grind human beings like Russell Sage, and then spend millions of dollars in social research work; who turn beautiful young plants into faded old women, and then give them a few paltry dollars or found a Home for Working Girls. Anthony is a worthy foe; and to fight such a foe, one must learn to meet him in open battle.

David Roberts has all the mental and moral attributes of his adversary, coupled with the spirit of revolt and the depth of modern ideas. He, too, is consistent, and wants nothing for his class short of complete victory.

"It is not for this little moment of time we are fighting, not for our own little bodies and their warmth: it is for all those who come after, for all times. Oh, men, for the love of them don't turn up another stone on their heads, don't help to blacken the sky. If we can shake that white-faced monster with the bloody lips that has sucked the lives out of ourselves, our wives, and children, since the world began, if we have not the hearts of men to stand against it, breast to breast and eye to eye, and force it backward till it cry for mercy, it will go on sucking life, and we shall stay forever where we are, less than the very dogs."

It is inevitable that compromise and petty interest should pass on and leave two such giants behind. Inevitable, until the mass will reach the stature of a David Roberts. Will it ever? Prophecy is not the vocation of the dramatist, yet the moral lesson is evident. One cannot help realizing that the workingmen will have to use methods hitherto unfamiliar to them; that they will have to discard all those elements in their midst that are forever ready to reconcile the irreconcilable, namely Capital and Labor. They will have to learn that characters like David Roberts are the very forces that have revolutionized the world and thus paved the way for emancipation out of the clutches of that "white-faced monster with bloody lips," towards a brighter horizon, a freer life, and a deeper recognition of human values.

No subject of equal social import has received such extensive consideration within the last few years as the question of prison and punishment.

Hardly any magazine of consequence that has not devoted its columns to the discussion of this vital theme. A number of books by able writers, both in America and abroad, have discussed this topic from the historic, psychologic, and social standpoint, all agreeing that present penal institutions and our mode of coping with crime have in every respect proved inadequate as well as wasteful. One would expect that something very radical should result from the cumulative literary indictment of the social crimes perpetrated upon the prisoner. Yet with the exception of a few minor and comparatively insignificant reforms in some of our prisons, absolutely nothing has been accomplished. But at last this grave social wrong has found dramatic interpretation in Galsworthy's *Justice*.

The play opens in the office of James How and Sons, Solicitors. The senior clerk, Robert Cokeson, discovers that a check he had issued for nine pounds has been forged to ninety. By elimination, suspicion falls upon William Falder, the junior office clerk. The latter is in love with a married woman, the abused, ill-treated wife of a brutal drunkard. Pressed by his employer, a severe yet not unkindly man, Falder confesses the forgery, pleading the dire necessity of his sweetheart, Ruth Honeywill, with whom he had planned to escape to save her from the unbearable brutality of her husband. Notwithstanding the entreaties of young Walter, who is touched by modern ideas, his father, a moral and law-respecting citizen, turns Falder over to the police.

The second act, in the court-room, shows Justice in the very process of manufacture. The scene equals in dramatic power and psychologic verity the great court scene in *Resurrection*. Young Falder, a nervous and rather weakly youth of twenty-three, stands before the bar. Ruth, his married sweetheart, full of love and devotion, burns with anxiety to save the youth whose affection brought about his present predicament. The young man is defended by Lawyer Frome, whose speech to the jury is a masterpiece of deep social philosophy wreathed with the tendrils of human understanding and sympathy. He does not attempt to dispute the mere fact of Falder having altered the check; and though he pleads temporary aberration in defense of his client, that plea is based upon a social consciousness as deep and all-embracing as the roots of our social ills—"the background of life, that palpitating life which always lies behind the commission of a crime." He shows Falder to have faced the alternative of seeing the beloved woman murdered by her brutal husband, whom she cannot divorce; or of taking the law into his own hands. The defence pleads with the jury not to turn the weak young man into a criminal by condemning him to prison, for "justice is a machine that, when someone has given it a starting push, rolls on of itself. . . . Is this young man to be ground to pieces under this machine for an act which, at the worst, was one of weakness? Is he to become a member of the luckless crews that man those dark, ill-starred ships called prisons? . . . I urge you, gentlemen, do not ruin this young man. For as a result of those four minutes, ruin, utter and irretrievable, stares him in the face. . . . The rolling of the chariot wheels of Justice over this boy began when it was decided to prosecute him."

But the chariot of Justice rolls mercilessly on, for—as the learned Judge says—"the law is what it is—a majestic edifice, sheltering all of us, each stone of which rests on another."

Falder is sentenced to three years' penal servitude.

In prison, the young, inexperienced convict soon finds himself the victim of the terrible "system." The authorities admit that young Falder is mentally and physically "in bad shape," but nothing can be done in the matter: many others are in a similar position, and "the quarters are inadequate."

The third scene of the third act is heart-gripping in its silent force. The whole scene is a pantomime, taking place in Falder's prison cell.

"In fast-falling daylight, Falder, in his stockings, is seen standing motionless, with his head inclined towards the door, listening. He moves a little closer to the door, his stockinged feet making no noise. He stops at the door. He is trying harder and harder to hear something, any little thing that is going on outside. He springs suddenly upright—as if at a sound —and remains perfectly motionless. Then, with a heavy sigh, he moves to his work, and stands looking at it, with his head down; he does a stitch or two, having the air of a man so lost in sadness that each stitch is, as it were, a coming to life. Then, turning abruptly, he begins pacing his cell, moving his head, like an animal pacing its cage. He stops again at the door, listens, and, placing the palms of his hands against it with his fingers spread out, leans his forehead against the iron. Turning from it, presently, he moves slowly back towards the window, holding his head, as if he felt that it were going to burst, and stops under the window. But since he cannot see out of it he leaves off looking, and, picking up the lid of one of the tins, peers into it, as if trying to make a companion of his own face. It has grown very nearly dark. Suddenly the lid falls out of his hand with a clatter—the only sound that has broken the silence —and he stands staring intently at the wall where the stuff of the shirt is hanging rather white in the darkness—he seems to be seeing somebody or something there. There is a sharp tap and click; the cell light behind the glass screen has been turned up. The cell is brightly lighted. Falder is seen gasping for breath.

"A sound from far away, as of distant, dull beating on thick metal, is suddenly audible. Falder shrinks back, not able to bear this sudden clamor. But the sound grows, as though some great tumbril were rolling towards the cell. And gradually it seems to hypnotize him. He begins creeping inch by inch nearer to the door. The banging sound, traveling from cell to cell, draws closer and closer; Falder's hands are seen moving as if his spirit had already joined in this beating, and the sound swells till it seems to have entered the very cell. He suddenly raises his clenched fists. Panting violently, he flings himself at his door, and beats on it."

Finally Falder leaves the prison, a broken ticket-of-leave man, the stamp of the convict upon his brow, the iron of misery in his soul. Thanks to Ruth's pleading, the firm of James How and Son is willing to take Falder back in their employ, on condition that he give up Ruth. It is then that Falder learns the awful news that the woman he loves had been driven by the merciless economic Moloch to sell herself. She "tried making skirts . . . cheap things. . . . I never made more than ten shillings a week, buying my own cotton, and working all day. I hardly ever got to bed till past twelve. . . . And then . . . my employer happened—he's happened ever since." At this terrible psychologic moment the police appear to drag him back to prison for failing to report himself as ticket-of-leave man. Completely overcome by the inexorability of his environment, young Falder seeks and finds peace, greater than human justice, by throwing himself down to death, as the detectives are taking him back to prison.

It would be impossible to estimate the effect produced by this play. Perhaps some conception can be gained from the very unusual circumstance that it had proved so powerful as to induce the Home Secretary of Great Britain to undertake extensive prison reforms in England. A very encouraging sign this, of the influence exerted by the modern drama. It is to be hoped that the thundering indictment of Mr. Galsworthy will not remain without similar effect upon the public sentiment and prison conditions of America. At any rate it is certain that no other modern play has borne such direct and immediate fruit in wakening the social conscience.

Another modern play, *The Servant in the House*, strikes a vital key in our social life. The hero of Mr. Kennedy's masterpiece is Robert, a coarse, filthy drunkard, whom respectable society has repudiated. Robert, the sewer cleaner, is the real hero of the play; nay, its true and only savior. It is he who volunteers to go down into the dangerous sewer, so that his comrades "can 'ave light and air." After all, has he not sacrificed his life always, so that others may have light and air?

The thought that labor is the redeemer of social well-being has been cried from the housetops in every tongue and every clime. Yet the simple words of

Robert express the significance of labor and its mission with far greater potency.

America is still in its dramatic infancy. Most of the attempts along this line to mirror life, have been wretched failures. Still, there are hopeful signs in the attitude of the intelligent public toward modern plays, even if they be from foreign soil.

The only real drama America has so far produced is *The Easiest Way*, by Eugene Walter.

It is supposed to represent a "peculiar phase" of New York life. If that were all, it would be of minor significance. That which gives the play its real importance and value lies much deeper. It lies, first, in the fundamental current of our social fabric which drives us all, even stronger characters than Laura, into the easiest way—a way so very destructive of integrity, truth, and justice. Secondly, the cruel, senseless fatalism conditioned in Laura's sex. These two features put the universal stamp upon the play, and characterize it as one of the strongest dramatic indictments against society.

The criminal waste of human energy, in economic and social conditions, drives Laura as it drives the average girl to marry any man for a "home"; or as it drives men to endure the worst indignities for a miserable pittance.

Then there is that other respectable institution, the fatalism of Laura's sex. The inevitability of that force is summed up in the following words: "Don't you know that we count no more in the life of these men than tamed animals? It's a game, and if we don't play our cards well, we lose." Woman in the

battle with life has but one weapon, one commodity—
sex. That alone serves as a trump card in the game
of life.

This blind fatalism has made of woman a parasite,
an inert thing. Why then expect perseverance or
energy of Laura? The easiest way is the path mapped
out for her from time immemorial. She could follow
no other.

A number of other plays could be quoted as characteristic of the growing rôle of the drama as a disseminator of radical thought. Suffice it to mention
The Third Degree, by Charles Klein; *The Fourth
Estate*, by Medill Patterson; *A Man's World*, by Ida
Croutchers,—all pointing to the dawn of dramatic art
in America, an art which is discovering to the people
the terrible diseases of our social body.

It has been said of old, all roads lead to Rome. In
paraphrased application to the tendencies of our day,
it may truly be said that all roads lead to the great
social reconstruction. The economic awakening of the
workingman, and his realization of the necessity for
concerted industrial action; the tendencies of modern
education, especially in their application to the free
development of the child; the spirit of growing unrest
expressed through, and cultivated by, art and literature, all pave the way to the Open Road. Above all,
the modern drama, operating through the double channel of dramatist and interpreter, affecting as it does
both mind and heart, is the strongest force in developing social discontent, swelling the powerful tide of
unrest that sweeps onward and over the dam of ignorance, prejudice, and superstition.

A CATALOG OF SELECTED
DOVER BOOKS
IN ALL FIELDS OF INTEREST

DRAWINGS OF REMBRANDT, edited by Seymour Slive. Updated Lippmann, Hofstede de Groot edition, with definitive scholarly apparatus. All portraits, biblical sketches, landscapes, nudes. Oriental figures, classical studies, together with selection of work by followers. 550 illustrations. Total of 630pp. 9⅛ × 12¼.
21485-0, 21486-9 Pa., Two-vol. set $29.90

GHOST AND HORROR STORIES OF AMBROSE BIERCE, Ambrose Bierce. 24 tales vividly imagined, strangely prophetic, and decades ahead of their time in technical skill: "The Damned Thing," "An Inhabitant of Carcosa," "The Eyes of the Panther," "Moxon's Master," and 20 more. 199pp. 5⅜ × 8½. 20767-6 Pa. $4.95

ETHICAL WRITINGS OF MAIMONIDES, Maimonides. Most significant ethical works of great medieval sage, newly translated for utmost precision, readability. Laws Concerning Character Traits, Eight Chapters, more. 192pp. 5⅜ × 8½.
24522-5 Pa. $5.95

THE EXPLORATION OF THE COLORADO RIVER AND ITS CANYONS, J. W. Powell. Full text of Powell's 1,000-mile expedition down the fabled Colorado in 1869. Superb account of terrain, geology, vegetation, Indians, famine, mutiny, treacherous rapids, mighty canyons, during exploration of last unknown part of continental U.S. 400pp. 5⅜ × 8½. 20094-9 Pa. $7.95

HISTORY OF PHILOSOPHY, Julián Marías. Clearest one-volume history on the market. Every major philosopher and dozens of others, to Existentialism and later. 505pp. 5⅜ × 8½. 21739-6 Pa. $9.95

ALL ABOUT LIGHTNING, Martin A. Uman. Highly readable nontechnical survey of nature and causes of lightning, thunderstorms, ball lightning, St. Elmo's Fire, much more. Illustrated. 192pp. 5⅜ × 8½. 25237-X Pa. $5.95

SAILING ALONE AROUND THE WORLD, Captain Joshua Slocum. First man to sail around the world, alone, in small boat. One of great feats of seamanship told in delightful manner. 67 illustrations. 294pp. 5⅜ × 8½. 20326-3 Pa. $4.95

LETTERS AND NOTES ON THE MANNERS, CUSTOMS AND CONDITIONS OF THE NORTH AMERICAN INDIANS, George Catlin. Classic account of life among Plains Indians: ceremonies, hunt, warfare, etc. 312 plates. 572pp. of text. 6⅛ × 9¼. 22118-0, 22119-9, Pa., Two-vol. set $17.90

THE SECRET LIFE OF SALVADOR DALÍ, Salvador Dalí. Outrageous but fascinating autobiography through Dalí's thirties with scores of drawings and sketches and 80 photographs. A must for lovers of 20th-century art. 432pp. 6½ × 9¼. (Available in U.S. only) 27454-3 Pa. $9.95

THE BOOK OF BEASTS: Being a Translation from a Latin Bestiary of the Twelfth Century, T. H. White. Wonderful catalog of real and fanciful beasts: manticore, griffin, phoenix, amphivius, jaculus, many more. White's witty erudite commentary on scientific, historical aspects enhances fascinating glimpse of medieval mind. Illustrated. 296pp. 5⅜ × 8¼. (Available in U.S. only) 24609-4 Pa. $7.95

FRANK LLOYD WRIGHT: Architecture and Nature with 160 Illustrations, Donald Hoffmann. Profusely illustrated study of influence of nature—especially prairie—on Wright's designs for Fallingwater, Robie House, Guggenheim Museum, other masterpieces. 96pp. 9¼ × 10¾. 25098-9 Pa. $8.95

FRANK LLOYD WRIGHT'S FALLINGWATER, Donald Hoffmann. Wright's famous waterfall house: planning and construction of organic idea. History of site, owners, Wright's personal involvement. Photographs of various stages of building. Preface by Edgar Kaufmann, Jr. 100 illustrations. 112pp. 9¼ × 10. 23671-4 Pa. $8.95

YEARS WITH FRANK LLOYD WRIGHT: Apprentice to Genius, Edgar Tafel. Insightful memoir by a former apprentice presents a revealing portrait of Wright the man, the inspired teacher, the greatest American architect. 372 black-and-white illustrations. Preface. Index. vi + 228pp. 8¼ × 11. 24801-1 Pa. $10.95

THE STORY OF KING ARTHUR AND HIS KNIGHTS, Howard Pyle. Enchanting version of King Arthur fable has delighted generations with imaginative narratives of exciting adventures and unforgettable illustrations by the author. 41 illustrations. xviii + 313pp. 6⅛ × 9¼. 21445-1 Pa. $6.95

THE GODS OF THE EGYPTIANS, E. A. Wallis Budge. Thorough coverage of numerous gods of ancient Egypt by foremost Egyptologist. Information on evolution of cults, rites and gods; the cult of Osiris; the Book of the Dead and its rites; the sacred animals and birds; Heaven and Hell; and more. 956pp. 6⅛ × 9¼. 22055-9, 22056-7 Pa., Two-vol. set $21.90

A THEOLOGICO-POLITICAL TREATISE, Benedict Spinoza. Also contains unfinished *Political Treatise*. Great classic on religious liberty, theory of government on common consent. R. Elwes translation. Total of 421pp. 5⅜ × 8½. 20249-6 Pa. $7.95

INCIDENTS OF TRAVEL IN CENTRAL AMERICA, CHIAPAS, AND YUCATAN, John L. Stephens. Almost single-handed discovery of Maya culture; exploration of ruined cities, monuments, temples; customs of Indians. 115 drawings. 892pp. 5⅜ × 8½. 22404-X, 22405-8 Pa., Two-vol. set $17.90

LOS CAPRICHOS, Francisco Goya. 80 plates of wild, grotesque monsters and caricatures. Prado manuscript included. 183pp. 6⅝ × 9⅝. 22384-1 Pa. $6.95

AUTOBIOGRAPHY: The Story of My Experiments with Truth, Mohandas K. Gandhi. Not hagiography, but Gandhi in his own words. Boyhood, legal studies, purification, the growth of the Satyagraha (nonviolent protest) movement. Critical, inspiring work of the man who freed India. 480pp. 5⅜ × 8½. (Available in U.S. only) 24593-4 Pa. $6.95

ILLUSTRATED DICTIONARY OF HISTORIC ARCHITECTURE, edited by Cyril M. Harris. Extraordinary compendium of clear, concise definitions for over 5,000 important architectural terms complemented by over 2,000 line drawings. Covers full spectrum of architecture from ancient ruins to 20th-century Modernism. Preface. 592pp. 7½ × 9⅜. 24444-X Pa. $15.95

THE NIGHT BEFORE CHRISTMAS, Clement Moore. Full text, and woodcuts from original 1848 book. Also critical, historical material. 19 illustrations. 40pp. 4⅝ × 6. 22797-9 Pa. $2.50

THE LESSON OF JAPANESE ARCHITECTURE: 165 Photographs, Jiro Harada. Memorable gallery of 165 photographs taken in the 1930's of exquisite Japanese homes of the well-to-do and historic buildings. 13 line diagrams. 192pp. 8⅜ × 11¼. 24778-3 Pa. $10.95

THE AUTOBIOGRAPHY OF CHARLES DARWIN AND SELECTED LETTERS, edited by Francis Darwin. The fascinating life of eccentric genius composed of an intimate memoir by Darwin (intended for his children); commentary by his son, Francis; hundreds of fragments from notebooks, journals, papers; and letters to and from Lyell, Hooker, Huxley, Wallace and Henslow. xi + 365pp. 5⅜ × 8. 20479-0 Pa. $6.95

WONDERS OF THE SKY: Observing Rainbows, Comets, Eclipses, the Stars and Other Phenomena, Fred Schaaf. Charming, easy-to-read poetic guide to all manner of celestial events visible to the naked eye. Mock suns, glories, Belt of Venus, more. Illustrated. 299pp. 5¼ × 8¼. 24402-4 Pa. $7.95

BURNHAM'S CELESTIAL HANDBOOK, Robert Burnham, Jr. Thorough guide to the stars beyond our solar system. Exhaustive treatment. Alphabetical by constellation: Andromeda to Cetus in Vol. 1; Chamaeleon to Orion in Vol. 2; and Pavo to Vulpecula in Vol. 3. Hundreds of illustrations. Index in Vol. 3. 2,000pp. 6⅛ × 9¼. 23567-X, 23568-8, 23673-0 Pa., Three-vol. set $41.85

STAR NAMES: Their Lore and Meaning, Richard Hinckley Allen. Fascinating history of names various cultures have given to constellations and literary and folkloristic uses that have been made of stars. Indexes to subjects. Arabic and Greek names. Biblical references. Bibliography. 563pp. 5⅜ × 8½. 21079-0 Pa. $8.95

THIRTY YEARS THAT SHOOK PHYSICS: The Story of Quantum Theory, George Gamow. Lucid, accessible introduction to influential theory of energy and matter. Careful explanations of Dirac's anti-particles, Bohr's model of the atom, much more. 12 plates. Numerous drawings. 240pp. 5⅜ × 8½. 24895-X Pa. $5.95

CHINESE DOMESTIC FURNITURE IN PHOTOGRAPHS AND MEASURED DRAWINGS, Gustav Ecke. A rare volume, now affordably priced for antique collectors, furniture buffs and art historians. Detailed review of styles ranging from early Shang to late Ming. Unabridged republication. 161 black-and-white drawings, photos. Total of 224pp. 8⅜ × 11¼. (Available in U.S. only) 25171-3 Pa. $13.95

VINCENT VAN GOGH: A Biography, Julius Meier-Graefe. Dynamic, penetrating study of artist's life, relationship with brother, Theo, painting techniques, travels, more. Readable, engrossing. 160pp. 5⅜ × 8½. (Available in U.S. only) 25253-1 Pa. $4.95

HOW TO WRITE, Gertrude Stein. Gertrude Stein claimed anyone could understand her unconventional writing—here are clues to help. Fascinating improvisations, language experiments, explanations illuminate Stein's craft and the art of writing. Total of 414pp. 4⅝ × 6⅜. 23144-5 Pa. $6.95

ADVENTURES AT SEA IN THE GREAT AGE OF SAIL: Five Firsthand Narratives, edited by Elliot Snow. Rare true accounts of exploration, whaling, shipwreck, fierce natives, trade, shipboard life, more. 33 illustrations. Introduction. 353pp. 5⅜ × 8½. 25177-2 Pa. $8.95

THE HERBAL OR GENERAL HISTORY OF PLANTS, John Gerard. Classic descriptions of about 2,850 plants—with over 2,700 illustrations—includes Latin and English names, physical descriptions, varieties, time and place of growth, more. 2,706 illustrations. xlv + 1,678pp. 8½ × 12¼. 23147-X Cloth. $75.00

DOROTHY AND THE WIZARD IN OZ, L. Frank Baum. Dorothy and the Wizard visit the center of the Earth, where people are vegetables, glass houses grow and Oz characters reappear. Classic sequel to *Wizard of Oz*. 256pp. 5⅜ × 8. 24714-7 Pa. $5.95

SONGS OF EXPERIENCE: Facsimile Reproduction with 26 Plates in Full Color, William Blake. This facsimile of Blake's original "Illuminated Book" reproduces 26 full-color plates from a rare 1826 edition. Includes "The Tyger," "London," "Holy Thursday," and other immortal poems. 26 color plates. Printed text of poems. 48pp. 5¼ × 7. 24636-1 Pa. $3.95

SONGS OF INNOCENCE, William Blake. The first and most popular of Blake's famous "Illuminated Books," in a facsimile edition reproducing all 31 brightly colored plates. Additional printed text of each poem. 64pp. 5¼ × 7. 22764-2 Pa. $3.95

PRECIOUS STONES, Max Bauer. Classic, thorough study of diamonds, rubies, emeralds, garnets, etc.: physical character, occurrence, properties, use, similar topics. 20 plates, 8 in color. 94 figures. 659pp. 6⅛ × 9¼. 21910-0, 21911-9 Pa., Two-vol. set $15.90

ENCYCLOPEDIA OF VICTORIAN NEEDLEWORK, S. F. A. Caulfeild and Blanche Saward. Full, precise descriptions of stitches, techniques for dozens of needlecrafts—most exhaustive reference of its kind. Over 800 figures. Total of 679pp. 8⅛ × 11. Two volumes. Vol. 1 22800-2 Pa. $11.95
Vol. 2 22801-0 Pa. $11.95

THE MARVELOUS LAND OF OZ, L. Frank Baum. Second Oz book, the Scarecrow and Tin Woodman are back with hero named Tip, Oz magic. 136 illustrations. 287pp. 5⅜ × 8½. 20692-0 Pa. $5.95

WILD FOWL DECOYS, Joel Barber. Basic book on the subject, by foremost authority and collector. Reveals history of decoy making and rigging, place in American culture, different kinds of decoys, how to make them, and how to use them. 140 plates. 156pp. 7⅞ × 10¾. 20011-6 Pa. $8.95

HISTORY OF LACE, Mrs. Bury Palliser. Definitive, profusely illustrated chronicle of lace from earliest times to late 19th century. Laces of Italy, Greece, England, France, Belgium, etc. Landmark of needlework scholarship. 266 illustrations. 672pp. 6⅛ × 9¼. 24742-2 Pa. $14.95

ILLUSTRATED GUIDE TO SHAKER FURNITURE, Robert Meader. All furniture and appurtenances, with much on unknown local styles. 235 photos. 146pp. 9 × 12. 22819-3 Pa. $8.95

WHALE SHIPS AND WHALING: A Pictorial Survey, George Francis Dow. Over 200 vintage engravings, drawings, photographs of barks, brigs, cutters, other vessels. Also harpoons, lances, whaling guns, many other artifacts. Comprehensive text by foremost authority. 207 black-and-white illustrations. 288pp. 6 × 9. 24808-9 Pa. $9.95

THE BERTRAMS, Anthony Trollope. Powerful portrayal of blind self-will and thwarted ambition includes one of Trollope's most heartrending love stories. 497pp. 5⅜ × 8½. 25119-5 Pa. $9.95

ADVENTURES WITH A HAND LENS, Richard Headstrom. Clearly written guide to observing and studying flowers and grasses, fish scales, moth and insect wings, egg cases, buds, feathers, seeds, leaf scars, moss, molds, ferns, common crystals, etc.—all with an ordinary, inexpensive magnifying glass. 209 exact line drawings aid in your discoveries. 220pp. 5⅜ × 8½. 23330-8 Pa. $4.95

RODIN ON ART AND ARTISTS, Auguste Rodin. Great sculptor's candid, wide-ranging comments on meaning of art; great artists; relation of sculpture to poetry, painting, music; philosophy of life, more. 76 superb black-and-white illustrations of Rodin's sculpture, drawings and prints. 119pp. 8⅜ × 11¼. 24487-3 Pa. $7.95

FIFTY CLASSIC FRENCH FILMS, 1912–1982: A Pictorial Record, Anthony Slide. Memorable stills from Grand Illusion, Beauty and the Beast, Hiroshima, Mon Amour, many more. Credits, plot synopses, reviews, etc. 160pp. 8¼ × 11. 25256-6 Pa. $11.95

THE PRINCIPLES OF PSYCHOLOGY, William James. Famous long course complete, unabridged. Stream of thought, time perception, memory, experimental methods; great work decades ahead of its time. 94 figures. 1,391pp. 5⅜ × 8½. 20381-6, 20382-4 Pa., Two-vol. set $23.90

BODIES IN A BOOKSHOP, R. T. Campbell. Challenging mystery of blackmail and murder with ingenious plot and superbly drawn characters. In the best tradition of British suspense fiction. 192pp. 5⅜ × 8½. 24720-1 Pa. $4.95

CALLAS: PORTRAIT OF A PRIMA DONNA, George Jellinek. Renowned commentator on the musical scene chronicles incredible career and life of the most controversial, fascinating, influential operatic personality of our time. 64 black-and-white photographs. 416pp. 5⅜ × 8¼. 25047-4 Pa. $8.95

GEOMETRY, RELATIVITY AND THE FOURTH DIMENSION, Rudolph Rucker. Exposition of fourth dimension, concepts of relativity as Flatland characters continue adventures. Popular, easily followed yet accurate, profound. 141 illustrations. 133pp. 5⅜ × 8½. 23400-2 Pa. $4.95

HOUSEHOLD STORIES BY THE BROTHERS GRIMM, with pictures by Walter Crane. 53 classic stories—Rumpelstiltskin, Rapunzel, Hansel and Gretel, the Fisherman and his Wife, Snow White, Tom Thumb, Sleeping Beauty, Cinderella, and so much more—lavishly illustrated with original 19th century drawings. 114 illustrations. x + 269pp. 5⅜ × 8½. 21080-4 Pa. $4.95

SUNDIALS, Albert Waugh. Far and away the best, most thorough coverage of ideas, mathematics concerned, types, construction, adjusting anywhere. Over 100 illustrations. 230pp. 5⅜ × 8½. 22947-5 Pa. $5.95

PICTURE HISTORY OF THE NORMANDIE: With 190 Illustrations, Frank O. Braynard. Full story of legendary French ocean liner: Art Deco interiors, design innovations, furnishings, celebrities, maiden voyage, tragic fire, much more. Extensive text. 144pp. 8⅞ × 11¾. 25257-4 Pa. $10.95

THE FIRST AMERICAN COOKBOOK: A Facsimile of "American Cookery," 1796, Amelia Simmons. Facsimile of the first American-written cookbook published in the United States contains authentic recipes for colonial favorites—pumpkin pudding, winter squash pudding, spruce beer, Indian slapjacks, and more. Introductory Essay and Glossary of colonial cooking terms. 80pp. 5⅜ × 8½. 24710-4 Pa. $3.50

101 PUZZLES IN THOUGHT AND LOGIC, C. R. Wylie, Jr. Solve murders and robberies, find out which fishermen are liars, how a blind man could possibly identify a color—purely by your own reasoning! 107pp. 5⅜ × 8½. 20367-0 Pa. $2.95

ANCIENT EGYPTIAN MYTHS AND LEGENDS, Lewis Spence. Examines animism, totemism, fetishism, creation myths, deities, alchemy, art and magic, other topics. Over 50 illustrations. 432pp. 5⅜ × 8½. 26525-0 Pa. $8.95

ANTHROPOLOGY AND MODERN LIFE, Franz Boas. Great anthropologist's classic treatise on race and culture. Introduction by Ruth Bunzel. Only inexpensive paperback edition. 255pp. 5⅜ × 8½. 25245-0 Pa. $7.95

THE TALE OF PETER RABBIT, Beatrix Potter. The inimitable Peter's terrifying adventure in Mr. McGregor's garden, with all 27 wonderful, full-color Potter illustrations. 55pp. 4¼ × 5½. (Available in U.S. only) 22827-4 Pa. $1.75

THREE PROPHETIC SCIENCE FICTION NOVELS, H. G. Wells. *When the Sleeper Wakes, A Story of the Days to Come* and *The Time Machine* (full version). 335pp. 5⅜ × 8½. (Available in U.S. only) 20605-X Pa. $8.95

APICIUS COOKERY AND DINING IN IMPERIAL ROME, edited and translated by Joseph Dommers Vehling. Oldest known cookbook in existence offers readers a clear picture of what foods Romans ate, how they prepared them, etc. 49 illustrations. 301pp. 6⅛ × 9¼. 23563-7 Pa. $7.95

SHAKESPEARE LEXICON AND QUOTATION DICTIONARY, Alexander Schmidt. Full definitions, locations, shades of meaning of every word in plays and poems. More than 50,000 exact quotations. 1,485pp. 6½ × 9¼. 22726-X, 22727-8 Pa., Two-vol. set $31.90

THE WORLD'S GREAT SPEECHES, edited by Lewis Copeland and Lawrence W. Lamm. Vast collection of 278 speeches from Greeks to 1970. Powerful and effective models; unique look at history. 842pp. 5⅜ × 8½. 20468-5 Pa. $12.95

THE BLUE FAIRY BOOK, Andrew Lang. The first, most famous collection, with many familiar tales: Little Red Riding Hood, Aladdin and the Wonderful Lamp, Puss in Boots, Sleeping Beauty, Hansel and Gretel, Rumpelstiltskin; 37 in all. 138 illustrations. 390pp. 5⅜ × 8½. 21437-0 Pa. $6.95

THE STORY OF THE CHAMPIONS OF THE ROUND TABLE, Howard Pyle. Sir Launcelot, Sir Tristram and Sir Percival in spirited adventures of love and triumph retold in Pyle's inimitable style. 50 drawings, 31 full-page. xviii + 329pp. 6½ × 9¼. 21883-X Pa. $7.95

THE MYTHS OF THE NORTH AMERICAN INDIANS, Lewis Spence. Myths and legends of the Algonquins, Iroquois, Pawnees and Sioux with comprehensive historical and ethnological commentary. 36 illustrations. 5⅜ × 8½. 25967-6 Pa. $8.95

GREAT DINOSAUR HUNTERS AND THEIR DISCOVERIES, Edwin H. Colbert. Fascinating, lavishly illustrated chronicle of dinosaur research, 1820s to 1960. Achievements of Cope, Marsh, Brown, Buckland, Mantell, Huxley, many others. 384pp. 5¼ × 8¼. 24701-5 Pa. $7.95

THE TASTEMAKERS, Russell Lynes. Informal, illustrated social history of American taste 1850s–1950s. First popularized categories Highbrow, Lowbrow, Middlebrow. 129 illustrations. New (1979) afterword. 384pp. 6 × 9. 23993-4 Pa. $8.95

DOUBLE CROSS PURPOSES, Ronald A. Knox. A treasure hunt in the Scottish Highlands, an old map, unidentified corpse, surprise discoveries keep reader guessing in this cleverly intricate tale of financial skullduggery. 2 black-and-white maps. 320pp. 5⅜ × 8½. (Available in U.S. only) 25032-6 Pa. $6.95

AUTHENTIC VICTORIAN DECORATION AND ORNAMENTATION IN FULL COLOR: 46 Plates from "Studies in Design," Christopher Dresser. Superb full-color lithographs reproduced from rare original portfolio of a major Victorian designer. 48pp. 9¼ × 12¼. 25083-0 Pa. $7.95

PRIMITIVE ART, Franz Boas. Remains the best text ever prepared on subject, thoroughly discussing Indian, African, Asian, Australian, and, especially, Northern American primitive art. Over 950 illustrations show ceramics, masks, totem poles, weapons, textiles, paintings, much more. 376pp. 5⅜ × 8. 20025-6 Pa. $7.95

SIDELIGHTS ON RELATIVITY, Albert Einstein. Unabridged republication of two lectures delivered by the great physicist in 1920–21. *Ether and Relativity* and *Geometry and Experience*. Elegant ideas in nonmathematical form, accessible to intelligent layman. vi + 56pp. 5⅜ × 8½. 24511-X Pa. $3.95

THE WIT AND HUMOR OF OSCAR WILDE, edited by Alvin Redman. More than 1,000 ripostes, paradoxes, wisecracks: Work is the curse of the drinking classes, I can resist everything except temptation, etc. 258pp. 5⅜ × 8½. 20602-5 Pa. $4.95

ADVENTURES WITH A MICROSCOPE, Richard Headstrom. 59 adventures with clothing fibers, protozoa, ferns and lichens, roots and leaves, much more. 142 illustrations. 232pp. 5⅜ × 8½. 23471-1 Pa. $4.95

PLANTS OF THE BIBLE, Harold N. Moldenke and Alma L. Moldenke. Standard reference to all 230 plants mentioned in Scriptures. Latin name, biblical reference, uses, modern identity, much more. Unsurpassed encyclopedic resource for scholars, botanists, nature lovers, students of Bible. Bibliography. Indexes. 123 black-and-white illustrations. 384pp. 6 × 9. 25069-5 Pa. $8.95

FAMOUS AMERICAN WOMEN: A Biographical Dictionary from Colonial Times to the Present, Robert McHenry, ed. From Pocahontas to Rosa Parks, 1,035 distinguished American women documented in separate biographical entries. Accurate, up-to-date data, numerous categories, spans 400 years. Indices. 493pp. 6½ × 9¼. 24523-3 Pa. $10.95

THE FABULOUS INTERIORS OF THE GREAT OCEAN LINERS IN HISTORIC PHOTOGRAPHS, William H. Miller, Jr. Some 200 superb photographs capture exquisite interiors of world's great "floating palaces"—1890s to 1980s: *Titanic, Ile de France, Queen Elizabeth, United States, Europa,* more. Approx. 200 black-and-white photographs. Captions. Text. Introduction. 160pp. 8⅞ × 11¾. 24756-2 Pa. $9.95

THE GREAT LUXURY LINERS, 1927–1954: A Photographic Record, William H. Miller, Jr. Nostalgic tribute to heyday of ocean liners. 186 photos of *Ile de France, Normandie, Leviathan, Queen Elizabeth, United States,* many others. Interior and exterior views. Introduction. Captions. 160pp. 9 × 12. 24056-8 Pa. $12.95

A NATURAL HISTORY OF THE DUCKS, John Charles Phillips. Great landmark of ornithology offers complete detailed coverage of nearly 200 species and subspecies of ducks: gadwall, sheldrake, merganser, pintail, many more. 74 full-color plates, 102 black-and-white. Bibliography. Total of 1,920pp. 8⅝ × 11¼. 25141-1, 25142-X Cloth., Two-vol. set $100.00

THE SEAWEED HANDBOOK: An Illustrated Guide to Seaweeds from North Carolina to Canada, Thomas F. Lee. Concise reference covers 78 species. Scientific and common names, habitat, distribution, more. Finding keys for easy identification. 224pp. 5⅜ × 8½. 25215-9 Pa. $6.95

THE TEN BOOKS OF ARCHITECTURE: The 1755 Leoni Edition, Leon Battista Alberti. Rare classic helped introduce the glories of ancient architecture to the Renaissance. 68 black-and-white plates. 336pp. 8⅜ × 11¼. 25239-6 Pa. $14.95

MISS MACKENZIE, Anthony Trollope. Minor masterpieces by Victorian master unmasks many truths about life in 19th-century England. First inexpensive edition in years. 392pp. 5⅜ × 8½. 25201-9 Pa. $8.95

THE RIME OF THE ANCIENT MARINER, Gustave Doré, Samuel Taylor Coleridge. Dramatic engravings considered by many to be his greatest work. The terrifying space of the open sea, the storms and whirlpools of an unknown ocean, the ice of Antarctica, more—all rendered in a powerful, chilling manner. Full text. 38 plates. 77pp. 9¼ × 12. 22305-1 Pa. $4.95

THE EXPEDITIONS OF ZEBULON MONTGOMERY PIKE, Zebulon Montgomery Pike. Fascinating firsthand accounts (1805–6) of exploration of Mississippi River, Indian wars, capture by Spanish dragoons, much more. 1,088pp. 5⅜ × 8½. 25254-X, 25255-8 Pa., Two-vol. set $25.90

CATALOG OF DOVER BOOKS

A CONCISE HISTORY OF PHOTOGRAPHY: Third Revised Edition, Helmut Gernsheim. Best one-volume history—camera obscura, photochemistry, daguerreotypes, evolution of cameras, film, more. Also artistic aspects—landscape, portraits, fine art, etc. 281 black-and-white photographs. 26 in color. 176pp. 8⅜ × 11¼.
25128-4 Pa. $14.95

THE DORÉ BIBLE ILLUSTRATIONS, Gustave Doré. 241 detailed plates from the Bible: the Creation scenes, Adam and Eve, Flood, Babylon, battle sequences, life of Jesus, etc. Each plate is accompanied by the verses from the King James version of the Bible. 241pp. 9 × 12. 23004-X Pa. $9.95

WANDERINGS IN WEST AFRICA, Richard F. Burton. Great Victorian scholar/adventurer's invaluable descriptions of African tribal rituals, fetishism, culture, art, much more. Fascinating 19th-century account. 624pp. 5⅜ × 8½. 26890-X Pa. $12.95

HISTORIC HOMES OF THE AMERICAN PRESIDENTS, Second Revised Edition, Irvin Haas. Guide to homes occupied by every president from Washington to Bush. Visiting hours, travel routes, more. 175 photos. 160pp. 8¼ × 11.
26751-2 Pa. $9.95

THE HISTORY OF THE LEWIS AND CLARK EXPEDITION, Meriwether Lewis and William Clark, edited by Elliott Coues. Classic edition of Lewis and Clark's day-by-day journals that later became the basis for U.S. claims to Oregon and the West. Accurate and invaluable geographical, botanical, biological, meteorological and anthropological material. Total of 1,508pp. 5⅜ × 8½.
21268-8, 21269-6, 21270-X Pa., Three-vol. set $29.85

LANGUAGE, TRUTH AND LOGIC, Alfred J. Ayer. Famous, clear introduction to Vienna, Cambridge schools of Logical Positivism. Role of philosophy, elimination of metaphysics, nature of analysis, etc. 160pp. 5⅜ × 8½. (Available in U.S. and Canada only) 20010-8 Pa. $3.95

MATHEMATICS FOR THE NONMATHEMATICIAN, Morris Kline. Detailed, college-level treatment of mathematics in cultural and historical context, with numerous exercises. For liberal arts students. Preface. Recommended Reading Lists. Tables. Index. Numerous black-and-white figures. xvi + 641pp. 5⅜ × 8½.
24823-2 Pa. $11.95

HANDBOOK OF PICTORIAL SYMBOLS, Rudolph Modley. 3,250 signs and symbols, many systems in full; official or heavy commercial use. Arranged by subject. Most in Pictorial Archive series. 143pp. 8⅛ × 11. 23357-X Pa. $7.95

INCIDENTS OF TRAVEL IN YUCATAN, John L. Stephens. Classic (1843) exploration of jungles of Yucatan, looking for evidences of Maya civilization. Travel adventures, Mexican and Indian culture, etc. Total of 669pp. 5⅜ × 8½.
20926-1, 20927-X Pa., Two-vol. set $13.90

CATALOG OF DOVER BOOKS

DEGAS: An Intimate Portrait, Ambroise Vollard. Charming, anecdotal memoir by famous art dealer of one of the greatest 19th-century French painters. 14 black-and-white illustrations. Introduction by Harold L. Van Doren. 96pp. 5⅜ × 8½.
25131-4 Pa. $4.95

PERSONAL NARRATIVE OF A PILGRIMAGE TO AL-MADINAH AND MECCAH, Richard F. Burton. Great travel classic by remarkably colorful personality. Burton, disguised as a Moroccan, visited sacred shrines of Islam, narrowly escaping death. 47 illustrations. 959pp. 5⅜ × 8½.
21217-3, 21218-1 Pa., Two-vol. set $19.90

PHRASE AND WORD ORIGINS, A. H. Holt. Entertaining, reliable, modern study of more than 1,200 colorful words, phrases, origins and histories. Much unexpected information. 254pp. 5⅜ × 8½.
20758-7 Pa. $5.95

THE RED THUMB MARK, R. Austin Freeman. In this first Dr. Thorndyke case, the great scientific detective draws fascinating conclusions from the nature of a single fingerprint. Exciting story, authentic science. 320pp. 5⅜ × 8½. (Available in U.S. only)
25210-8 Pa. $6.95

AN EGYPTIAN HIEROGLYPHIC DICTIONARY, E. A. Wallis Budge. Monumental work containing about 25,000 words or terms that occur in texts ranging from 3000 B.C. to 600 A.D. Each entry consists of a transliteration of the word, the word in hieroglyphs, and the meaning in English. 1,314pp. 6⅜ × 10.
23615-3, 23616-1 Pa., Two-vol. set $35.90

THE COMPLEAT STRATEGYST: Being a Primer on the Theory of Games of Strategy, J. D. Williams. Highly entertaining classic describes, with many illustrated examples, how to select best strategies in conflict situations. Prefaces. Appendices. xvi + 268pp. 5⅜ × 8½.
25101-2 Pa. $6.95

THE ROAD TO OZ, L. Frank Baum. Dorothy meets the Shaggy Man, little Button-Bright and the Rainbow's beautiful daughter in this delightful trip to the magical Land of Oz. 272pp. 5⅜ × 8.
25208-6 Pa. $5.95

POINT AND LINE TO PLANE, Wassily Kandinsky. Seminal exposition of role of point, line, other elements in nonobjective painting. Essential to understanding 20th-century art. 127 illustrations. 192pp. 6½ × 9¼.
23808-3 Pa. $5.95

LADY ANNA, Anthony Trollope. Moving chronicle of Countess Lovel's bitter struggle to win for herself and daughter Anna their rightful rank and fortune—perhaps at cost of sanity itself. 384pp. 5⅜ × 8½.
24669-8 Pa. $8.95

EGYPTIAN MAGIC, E. A. Wallis Budge. Sums up all that is known about magic in Ancient Egypt: the role of magic in controlling the gods, powerful amulets that warded off evil spirits, scarabs of immortality, use of wax images, formulas and spells, the secret name, much more. 253pp. 5⅜ × 8½.
22681-6 Pa. $4.95

THE DANCE OF SIVA, Ananda Coomaraswamy. Preeminent authority unfolds the vast metaphysic of India: the revelation of her art, conception of the universe, social organization, etc. 27 reproductions of art masterpieces. 192pp. 5⅜ × 8½.
24817-8 Pa. $6.95

CHRISTMAS CUSTOMS AND TRADITIONS, Clement A. Miles. Origin, evolution, significance of religious, secular practices. Caroling, gifts, yule logs, much more. Full, scholarly yet fascinating; non-sectarian. 400pp. 5⅜ × 8½.
23354-5 Pa. $7.95

THE HUMAN FIGURE IN MOTION, Eadweard Muybridge. More than 4,500 stopped-action photos, in action series, showing undraped men, women, children jumping, lying down, throwing, sitting, wrestling, carrying, etc. 390pp. 7⅞ × 10⅝.
20204-6 Cloth. $24.95

THE MAN WHO WAS THURSDAY, Gilbert Keith Chesterton. Witty, fast-paced novel about a club of anarchists in turn-of-the-century London. Brilliant social, religious, philosophical speculations. 128pp. 5⅜ × 8½. 25121-7 Pa. $3.95

A CÉZANNE SKETCHBOOK: Figures, Portraits, Landscapes and Still Lifes, Paul Cézanne. Great artist experiments with tonal effects, light, mass, other qualities in over 100 drawings. A revealing view of developing master painter, precursor of Cubism. 102 black-and-white illustrations. 144pp. 8¾ × 6⅜. 24790-2 Pa. $6.95

AN ENCYCLOPEDIA OF BATTLES: Accounts of Over 1,560 Battles from 1479 B.C. to the Present, David Eggenberger. Presents essential details of every major battle in recorded history, from the first battle of Megiddo in 1479 B.C. to Grenada in 1984. List of Battle Maps. New Appendix covering the years 1967–1984. Index. 99 illustrations. 544pp. 6½ × 9¼. 24913-1 Pa. $14.95

AN ETYMOLOGICAL DICTIONARY OF MODERN ENGLISH, Ernest Weekley. Richest, fullest work, by foremost British lexicographer. Detailed word histories. Inexhaustible. Total of 856pp. 6½ × 9¼.
21873-2, 21874-0 Pa., Two-vol. set $19.90

WEBSTER'S AMERICAN MILITARY BIOGRAPHIES, edited by Robert McHenry. Over 1,000 figures who shaped 3 centuries of American military history. Detailed biographies of Nathan Hale, Douglas MacArthur, Mary Hallaren, others. Chronologies of engagements, more. Introduction. Addenda. 1,033 entries in alphabetical order. xi + 548pp. 6½ × 9¼. (Available in U.S. only)
24758-9 Pa. $13.95

LIFE IN ANCIENT EGYPT, Adolf Erman. Detailed older account, with much not in more recent books: domestic life, religion, magic, medicine, commerce, and whatever else needed for complete picture. Many illustrations. 597pp. 5⅜ × 8½.
22632-8 Pa. $9.95

HISTORIC COSTUME IN PICTURES, Braun & Schneider. Over 1,450 costumed figures shown, covering a wide variety of peoples: kings, emperors, nobles, priests, servants, soldiers, scholars, townsfolk, peasants, merchants, courtiers, cavaliers, and more. 256pp. 8⅜ × 11¼. 23150-X Pa. $9.95

THE NOTEBOOKS OF LEONARDO DA VINCI, edited by J. P. Richter. Extracts from manuscripts reveal great genius; on painting, sculpture, anatomy, sciences, geography, etc. Both Italian and English. 186 ms. pages reproduced, plus 500 additional drawings, including studies for *Last Supper, Sforza* monument, etc. 860pp. 7⅞ × 10¾. (Available in U.S. only) 22572-0, 22573-9 Pa., Two-vol. set $35.90

THE ART NOUVEAU STYLE BOOK OF ALPHONSE MUCHA: All 72 Plates from "Documents Decoratifs" in Original Color, Alphonse Mucha. Rare copyright-free design portfolio by high priest of Art Nouveau. Jewelry, wallpaper, stained glass, furniture, figure studies, plant and animal motifs, etc. Only complete one-volume edition. 80pp. 9⅜ × 12¼. 24044-4 Pa. $9.95

ANIMALS: 1,419 COPYRIGHT-FREE ILLUSTRATIONS OF MAMMALS, BIRDS, FISH, INSECTS, ETC., edited by Jim Harter. Clear wood engravings present, in extremely lifelike poses, over 1,000 species of animals. One of the most extensive pictorial sourcebooks of its kind. Captions. Index. 284pp. 9 × 12.
23766-4 Pa. $9.95

OBELISTS FLY HIGH, C. Daly King. Masterpiece of American detective fiction, long out of print, involves murder on a 1935 transcontinental flight—"a very thrilling story"—NY Times. Unabridged and unaltered republication of the edition published by William Collins Sons & Co. Ltd., London, 1935. 288pp. 5⅜ × 8½. (Available in U.S. only) 25036-9 Pa. $5.95

VICTORIAN AND EDWARDIAN FASHION: A Photographic Survey, Alison Gernsheim. First fashion history completely illustrated by contemporary photographs. Full text plus 235 photos, 1840-1914, in which many celebrities appear. 240pp. 6½ × 9¼. 24205-6 Pa. $8.95

THE ART OF THE FRENCH ILLUSTRATED BOOK, 1700-1914, Gordon N. Ray. Over 630 superb book illustrations by Fragonard, Delacroix, Daumier, Doré, Grandville, Manet, Mucha, Steinlen, Toulouse-Lautrec and many others. Preface. Introduction. 633 halftones. Indices of artists, authors & titles, binders and provenances. Appendices. Bibliography. 608pp. 8⅜ × 11¼. 25086-5 Pa. $24.95

THE WONDERFUL WIZARD OF OZ, L. Frank Baum. Facsimile in full color of America's finest children's classic. 143 illustrations by W. W. Denslow. 267pp. 5⅜ × 8½. 20691-2 Pa. $7.95

FOLLOWING THE EQUATOR: A Journey Around the World, Mark Twain. Great writer's 1897 account of circumnavigating the globe by steamship. Ironic humor, keen observations, vivid and fascinating descriptions of exotic places. 197 illustrations. 720pp. 5⅜ × 8½. 26113-1 Pa. $15.95

THE FRIENDLY STARS, Martha Evans Martin & Donald Howard Menzel. Classic text marshalls the stars together in an engaging, non-technical survey, presenting them as sources of beauty in night sky. 23 illustrations. Foreword. 2 star charts. Index. 147pp. 5⅜ × 8½. 21099-5 Pa. $3.95

FADS AND FALLACIES IN THE NAME OF SCIENCE, Martin Gardner. Fair, witty appraisal of cranks, quacks, and quackeries of science and pseudoscience: hollow earth, Velikovsky, orgone energy, Dianetics, flying saucers, Bridey Murphy, food and medical fads, etc. Revised, expanded In the Name of Science. "A very able and even-tempered presentation."—The New Yorker. 363pp. 5⅜ × 8.
20394-8 Pa. $6.95

ANCIENT EGYPT: ITS CULTURE AND HISTORY, J. E Manchip White. From pre-dynastics through Ptolemies: society, history, political structure, religion, daily life, literature, cultural heritage. 48 plates. 217pp. 5⅜ × 8½. 22548-8 Pa. $5.95

SIR HARRY HOTSPUR OF HUMBLETHWAITE, Anthony Trollope. Incisive, unconventional psychological study of a conflict between a wealthy baronet, his idealistic daughter, and their scapegrace cousin. The 1870 novel in its first inexpensive edition in years. 250pp. 5⅜ × 8½. 24953-0 Pa. $6.95

LASERS AND HOLOGRAPHY, Winston E. Kock. Sound introduction to burgeoning field, expanded (1981) for second edition. Wave patterns, coherence, lasers, diffraction, zone plates, properties of holograms, recent advances. 84 illustrations. 160pp. 5⅜ × 8¼. (Except in United Kingdom) 24041-X Pa. $3.95

INTRODUCTION TO ARTIFICIAL INTELLIGENCE: Second, Enlarged Edition, Philip C. Jackson, Jr. Comprehensive survey of artificial intelligence—the study of how machines (computers) can be made to act intelligently. Includes introductory and advanced material. Extensive notes updating the main text. 132 black-and-white illustrations. 512pp. 5⅜ × 8½. 24864-X Pa. $10.95

HISTORY OF INDIAN AND INDONESIAN ART, Ananda K. Coomaraswamy. Over 400 illustrations illuminate classic study of Indian art from earliest Harappa finds to early 20th century. Provides philosophical, religious and social insights. 304pp. 6⅜ × 9⅜. 25005-9 Pa. $11.95

THE GOLEM, Gustav Meyrink. Most famous supernatural novel in modern European literature, set in Ghetto of Old Prague around 1890. Compelling story of mystical experiences, strange transformations, profound terror. 13 black-and-white illustrations. 224pp. 5⅜ × 8½. (Available in U.S. only) 25025-3 Pa. $6.95

PICTORIAL ENCYCLOPEDIA OF HISTORIC ARCHITECTURAL PLANS, DETAILS AND ELEMENTS: With 1,880 Line Drawings of Arches, Domes, Doorways, Facades, Gables, Windows, etc., John Theodore Haneman. Sourcebook of inspiration for architects, designers, others. Bibliography. Captions. 141pp. 9 × 12. 24605-1 Pa. $8.95

BENCHLEY LOST AND FOUND, Robert Benchley. Finest humor from early 30s, about pet peeves, child psychologists, post office and others. Mostly unavailable elsewhere. 73 illustrations by Peter Arno and others. 183pp. 5⅜ × 8½. 22410-4 Pa. $4.95

ERTÉ GRAPHICS, Erté. Collection of striking color graphics: *Seasons, Alphabet, Numerals, Aces* and *Precious Stones*. 50 plates, including 4 on covers. 48pp. 9⅜ × 12¼. 23580-7 Pa. $7.95

THE JOURNAL OF HENRY D. THOREAU, edited by Bradford Torrey, F. H. Allen. Complete reprinting of 14 volumes, 1837–61, over two million words; the sourcebooks for *Walden*, etc. Definitive. All original sketches, plus 75 photographs. 1,804pp. 8½ × 12¼. 20312-3, 20313-1 Cloth., Two-vol. set $130.00

CASTLES: Their Construction and History, Sidney Toy. Traces castle development from ancient roots. Nearly 200 photographs and drawings illustrate moats, keeps, baileys, many other features. Caernarvon, Dover Castles, Hadrian's Wall, Tower of London, dozens more. 256pp. 5⅜ × 8¼. 24898-4 Pa. $7.95

CATALOG OF DOVER BOOKS

AMERICAN CLIPPER SHIPS: 1833–1858, Octavius T. Howe & Frederick C. Matthews. Fully-illustrated, encyclopedic review of 352 clipper ships from the period of America's greatest maritime supremacy. Introduction. 109 halftones. 5 black-and-white line illustrations. Index. Total of 928pp. 5⅜ × 8½.
25115-2, 25116-0 Pa., Two-vol. set $17.90

TOWARDS A NEW ARCHITECTURE, Le Corbusier. Pioneering manifesto by great architect, near legendary founder of "International School." Technical and aesthetic theories, views on industry, economics, relation of form to function, "mass-production spirit," much more. Profusely illustrated. Unabridged translation of 13th French edition. Introduction by Frederick Etchells. 320pp. 6⅛ × 9¼. (Available in U.S. only) 25023-7 Pa. $8.95

THE BOOK OF KELLS, edited by Blanche Cirker. Inexpensive collection of 32 full-color, full-page plates from the greatest illuminated manuscript of the Middle Ages, painstakingly reproduced from rare facsimile edition. Publisher's Note. Captions. 32pp. 9⅜ × 12¼. (Available in U.S. only) 24345-1 Pa. $5.95

BEST SCIENCE FICTION STORIES OF H. G. WELLS, H. G. Wells. Full novel *The Invisible Man,* plus 17 short stories: "The Crystal Egg," "Aepyornis Island," "The Strange Orchid," etc. 303pp. 5⅜ × 8½. (Available in U.S. only)
21531-8 Pa. $6.95

AMERICAN SAILING SHIPS: Their Plans and History, Charles G. Davis. Photos, construction details of schooners, frigates, clippers, other sailcraft of 18th to early 20th centuries—plus entertaining discourse on design, rigging, nautical lore, much more. 137 black-and-white illustrations. 240pp. 6⅛ × 9¼.
24658-2 Pa. $6.95

ENTERTAINING MATHEMATICAL PUZZLES, Martin Gardner. Selection of author's favorite conundrums involving arithmetic, money, speed, etc., with lively commentary. Complete solutions. 112pp. 5⅜ × 8½. 25211-6 Pa. $3.50

THE WILL TO BELIEVE, HUMAN IMMORTALITY, William James. Two books bound together. Effect of irrational on logical, and arguments for human immortality. 402pp. 5⅜ × 8½. 20291-7 Pa. $8.95

THE HAUNTED MONASTERY and THE CHINESE MAZE MURDERS, Robert Van Gulik. 2 full novels by Van Gulik continue adventures of Judge Dee and his companions. An evil Taoist monastery, seemingly supernatural events; overgrown topiary maze that hides strange crimes. Set in 7th-century China. 27 illustrations. 328pp. 5⅜ × 8½. 23502-5 Pa. $6.95

CELEBRATED CASES OF JUDGE DEE (DEE GOONG AN), translated by Robert Van Gulik. Authentic 18th-century Chinese detective novel; Dee and associates solve three interlocked cases. Led to Van Gulik's own stories with same characters. Extensive introduction. 9 illustrations. 237pp. 5⅜ × 8½.
23337-5 Pa. $5.95

Prices subject to change without notice.

Available at your book dealer or write for free catalog to Dept. GI, Dover Publications, Inc., 31 East 2nd St., Mineola, N.Y. 11501. Dover publishes more than 175 books each year on science, elementary and advanced mathematics, biology, music, art, literary history, social sciences and other areas.

E S O *

How You and Your Lover Can Give Each Other Hours of
*EXTENDED SEXUAL ORGASM

ALAN P. BRAUER, M.D., AND
DONNA J. BRAUER

WARNER BOOKS

A Time Warner Company

PUBLISHER'S NOTE: The information, advice, and programs herein are not intended to replace the services of trained health professionals, or be a substitute for medical advice. You are advised to consult with your health care professional with regard to matters relating to your health, and in particular regarding matters that may require diagnosis or medical attention.

Copyright © 1983, 2001 by Alan P. Brauer
All rights reserved.

Warner Books, Inc., 1271 Avenue of the Americas, New York, NY 10020
Visit our Web site at www.twbookmark.com

 A Time Warner Company

Printed in the United States of America
First Printing: April 2001
10 9 8 7 6 5 4 3 2

Library of Congress Cataloging-in-Publication Data

Brauer, Alan P.
    ESO: how you and your lover can give each other hours of extended sexual orgasm / Alan P. Brauer and Donna J. Brauer.— [Updated and rev. ed.].
        p. cm.
    Includes bibliographical references and index.
    ISBN 0-446-67762-0
    1. Sex instruction. 2. Orgasm. I. Brauer, Donna. II. Title

HQ31 .B772 2001
613.9'6—dc21   00-047742

Book design and text composition by L&G McRee

This book is dedicated to the many pioneer sexual researchers whose work has influenced and helped to provide much of the information on which the ESO program is based. We thank the many thousands of people who attended our weekend workshops or participated in relationship training at our medical center, who helped to validate our teaching methods.

Contents

Illustrations

1

The Promise of Pleasure

The purpose of this book is to help you improve the quality and strength of your intimate relationship, to increase your sexual pleasure, and to experience enhanced orgasm if you choose to do so.

The information presented here is based primarily on our experience and feedback from the several thousand couples who have applied the methods we and others have developed. More than half a million people have bought previous editions of this book and its sequel, *The ESO Ecstasy Program*. Many have generously shared with us dramatic testimonials about the life-changing experiences that resulted from reading and practicing the ESO* program. Our readers represent not just the sexually adventurous underground, but people from a wide range of educational, economic, and social backgrounds. We have been surprised by the number of conservative couples who have responded with enthusiasm to *ESO*, as well as by the huge age range the book has attracted—men and women

*Pronounced Eee-Ess-Oh, like ESP or IBM.

in their seventies and eighties as well as young people in their twenties. The promise of increasing sexual pleasure seems to tap a basic human instinct inhibited by centuries of negative social, cultural, and religious training.

Helping couples to find more satisfaction and sexual pleasure together basically means helping them enjoy more of the experiences that brought them together in the first place: fun, romance, and sex.

It takes more than a willing body for optimum sexual experiences. The popular saying, "The mind is the most important sex organ in the body," is true, but few books address how to use your mind to enhance sexual pleasure. Exercises in this book will teach you proven mental and physical skills. The physical skills are embodied in specific techniques, while the mental exercises help you focus on pleasurable thoughts and sensations and cancel thoughts that block arousal. You will also learn the power of focusing your full attention on your partner's sexual nervous system.

This is a "what's possible" and how-to book. But how-to instructions don't have to be boring or mechanical. They can be an adventure, like trying a new recipe, but more fun and potentially life-changing. Embark on our program with an open mind and a sense of adventure, and we're confident you'll be glad you did.

At the beginning of a relationship, most couples are passionate. Stimulated by novelty and lust, each partner experiences high natural levels of sexual arousal. So most couples initially enjoy relatively good sex. It's rare, however, for the passion enjoyed early in relationships to persist for more than a few years. The novelty wears off. Other demands devour the couple's time and attention. Habit lulls them into failing to learn new techniques. Doing so may seem like too much trouble, or new techniques may seem threatening, implying that the usual ways aren't good enough. For these and other reasons, married sex too often means routine or even boring sex.

Even if you have never had thrilling sex, or if you once did but have lost excitement, you can learn to significantly increase your levels of sexual pleasure. Learning ESO techniques of sexual enhancement with a partner requires a willingness to create the conditions for intimacy: making time for sexual "dates," practicing honest communication, and being deliberate about creating romance even if you have been together for decades. Doing so is worth the time and trouble, because the rewards are incalculable in personal self-confidence, enhanced passion, and greater levels of intimacy with your partner than you have ever known— even in the early days of your relationship.

People without partners can benefit as well from expanding their sensual and orgasmic repertoire. Their increased self-knowledge and skill will improve their capacity for intimacy in future relationships.

When we published the first edition of this book in 1983, many people reacted with skepticism or even humor to the idea of extending the orgasmic experience in men and women by half an hour or more. Sexual expectations have changed in the intervening years, however, and more people—especially women—have come to believe that full sexual pleasure is part of their birthright. While some people still doubt the possibility of extending the orgasmic response, any number of sexual studies, books, and teaching videos focused on enhancing orgasm have followed in the wake of our pioneering work. In the twenty-first century, sexual ecstasy with a committed partner has come to seem more attainable.

The ESO program consists of three major elements:

1. **Prerequisites for Sexual Pleasure.** For couples this element includes learning and practicing romance, improving sexual and nonsexual communication, making

and keeping agreements, building trust, scheduling sex, and practicing sexual hygiene. Individuals learn how to train their attention to reduce anxiety and tension and increase pleasurable sensation.
2. **Basic Sexuality.** The essentials of learning how to operate your own and your partner's sexual nervous system.
3. **Advanced Sexual Techniques; ESO.** Methodology and training for the sexually curious or adventurous.

About two-thirds of readers practice and report benefits from the first two elements of the program. About one-third of readers go on to experiment with the advanced techniques.

What Is ESO?

In 1975 we heard from a married couple doing sex research that they had discovered how to make climax—sexual orgasm—last much longer than anyone has ever thought possible. Not seconds longer or minutes longer. *Hours* longer, they said.

They were willing to allow us to observe them making love, which we did, in a structured teaching situation. We saw all the signs of orgasmic response, extended on that particular occasion for almost an hour. Afterward we listened to the couple's explanation of how they learned by trial and error to extend their orgasms. We went home and practiced. Over the next several months we taught ourselves.

We were convinced then from personal experience that vastly extended climax is possible and can be learned. Until the early 1960s, medical science taught, and almost everyone believed, that human beings could not voluntarily control their heartbeat, their blood pressure, the temperature of their hands, their response to pain. We now know that people can be trained very simply to control all those responses and many more. The discovery came as a surprise, late in the history of mankind. The training is now called biofeedback, and it's used every day. We use it routinely in our medical practice. If we can learn to influence so many different kinds of bodily responses, why not the orgasmic response too? We set out to develop ways to teach others to extend orgasm in a step-by-step, safely structured system in a therapeutic program.

FEMALE ESO

William H. Masters and Virginia E. Johnson, the pioneering sex researchers, clocked female orgasm in their experimental subjects at an average of four to twelve seconds per climax. Dr. Seymour Fisher, in his thorough 1973 study *The Female Orgasm*, discovered a similar average—six to twelve seconds. Both Masters and Johnson and Fisher have noted that a few exceptional women experience unusually intense orgasms that last longer than twenty seconds. Male orgasm has been reported to average about the same few seconds as female.

In the literature of sex therapy, there were early references to something like extended orgasm in women. Dr. Irene Kassorla, in *Nice Girls Do*, discusses a "maxi orgasm," which she describes as "feeling deeper, more concentrated, more intense." Alice Kahn Ladas, Beverly Whipple, and John D. Perry, in *The G Spot*, mention some women who have "'multiple ejaculatory orgasms,' sometimes lasting up to an hour or more." Isolated reports exist in scientific journals of men who have multiple orgasms without ejaculation. Nonetheless, very little detailed information has been available on these intensely pleasurable states, and hardly any step-by-step program for achieving them. *ESO* offers explanation and a step-by-step learning program for you to practice. We hope it can help you find your way to greater pleasure.

It is important to note that ESO is not merely extended foreplay. It is not simply "multiple orgasm." Nor is it some ancient system of subtle spiritual discipline. *At its ultimate level, for women, ESO is deep, continuous orgasm of ever-increasing arousal lasting thirty minutes to an hour or more.* The woman experiences intense, measurable, continuous muscular contractions of two types—superficial and deep. *For men, ESO at its ultimate level is first-stage orgasm, that momentary peak of intense pleasure just before a man feels he is going to ejaculate, extended in time for thirty minutes to an hour or more.* There is hard erection and copious secretion of clear fluid.

The foundation for female ESO usually begins with clenching vaginal contractions like those of ordinary, brief orgasm but continuing without any pause or rest between contractions for one minute or more. Each contraction is short, lasting about one second.

The start of female ESO is characterized by longer, rhythmic cycles of deep pelvic muscle push-outs. Each push-out can last ten seconds or more. It is followed immediately by another push-out or by one or more clenching vaginal contractions lasting several seconds each. We identify this state of mixed deep and shallow contractions as Phase I. It may continue for fifteen minutes or longer. Women experience it subjectively as continuous orgasmic pleasure—rising and leveling but never dropping away. Women in this phase of ESO are aware that they must deliberately reach for sensation and let go of mental resistance to climb higher and avoid dropping away.

At the highest level of female ESO, which we call Phase II, continuous slow waves of push-outs of the deep pelvic muscles replace the mixed contractions of Phase I. Each contraction lasts up to thirty seconds, and there are no rest periods between. Women experience this phase subjectively as a continuous orgasmic increase. They feel as if they are on a smoothly ascending orgasmic track and they don't have to work to stay there. They can drop their level of arousal and stop their ESO experience whenever they or their partners decide. They can very quickly reenter ESO within the next twenty-four hours or so, whenever they and their partners choose. This quick reentry into ESO we call the Rapid Orgasmic Response.

Like other sexologists, we categorize types of orgasms, but it's important to recognize that orgasms are unique experiences, different each time even for the same woman. From one woman to another, the difference can be enormous. Two researchers, William Hartman and Marilyn Fithian, have proposed that each woman's orgasm is so unique it should be called "orgasmic fingerprinting." In fact, women who have learned ESO have a wider range of orgasmic possibilities that they may express during any particular experience.

Since women are usually less genitally focused than men, it's easier for them to experience a total body orgasm than it is for a man.

ESO is an art form, an intensely personal act of creation. Every experience is different. Surprise commingled with familiarity is part of the pleasure.

MALE ESO

ESO is a range of experiences for men as well. Male orgasm ordinarily consists of two phases: an emission phase lasting three to five seconds, followed by a sense of ejaculatory urgency and then an ejaculation phase of approximately ten contractions lasting about ten seconds. In Phase I ESO the emission phase is extended—to one minute, ten minutes, or more—followed by an intense but not necessarily extended ejaculation phase. Men experience this phase subjectively as sustained orgasmic pleasure. They are aware that they must deliberately concentrate on control techniques to avoid cresting over into ejaculation. That feels like climbing to increased arousal, leveling, climbing higher, and leveling again.

At the highest level of male ESO, Phase II, a man finds himself in a continuous state of orgasmic emission for thirty minutes or more. Small quantities of clear pre-ejaculate fluid issue almost continuously, drop by drop, from his penis. His anal sphincter is relaxed and open. As with female ESO, he feels as if he is on an orgasmic track, continuously climbing, where he no longer needs to concentrate on holding back his ejaculation. Whenever he or his partner decides, he can ejaculate. The ejaculation phase may involve twenty or more intense contractions and last twenty seconds or more.

If he and his partner wish, a man experienced in Phase II ESO may then, with continued stimulation, maintain full or partial erection and reenter an emission state of orgasm in a very short time after ejaculating—within minutes, even within seconds.

Most people, even some sexologists, think that ejaculation is orgasm. If ejaculation were orgasm, then orgasm would be exclusively a male experience. In fact, of course, women have orgasm too.

Professor Herant Katchadourian of Stanford University has noted that this idea of men experiencing multiple orgasms by delaying or even withholding ejaculation is not new. The Chinese Taoists described methods for the male to achieve multiple orgasms more than 3,000 years ago. Dr. Katchadourian writes in *Fundamentals of Human Sexuality* that "some men are able to inhibit the emission of semen while they experience the orgasmic contractions: in other words, they have non-ejaculatory orgasms. Such orgasms do not seem to be followed by a loss of erection, thereby allowing these men to have consecutive or multiple orgasms." Alfred Kinsey noted that prepubescent boys, whose sexual physiology is still immature, are capable of experiencing repeated orgasms, sometimes five or more; this ability sharply declines when ejaculatory orgasms begin in puberty. Mantak Chia and Douglas Abrams Arava theorize in *The Multi-Orgasmic Man* that "the experience of ejaculating, when it happens, is so overwhelming that it eclipses the experience of orgasm and causes men to lose the ability to distinguish between the two. To become multi-orgasmic, you must learn (or possibly relearn) to separate the different sensations of arousal and to revel in orgasm without cresting over into ejaculation."

As with female ESO, early reports in the scientific literature (Robbins and Jensen 1978, for example) documented cases of men who have multiple orgasms without ejaculation. Hartman and Fithian studied hundreds of males in their laboratory, and found that twelve percent of the men they studied were multiply orgasmic. Chia and Arava describe how to separate orgasm and ejaculation, allowing the momentary release of ejaculation to be transformed into multiple peaks of whole-body orgasms.

In the fifty years since Kinsey found that about fourteen percent of women were multiply orgasmic, knowledge of the possibility has increased that proportion to about fifty percent. Fifty percent of women, that is, now report at least occasional multiple orgasms. As more men learn about their orgasmic potential, perhaps multiple orgasms will become as common for them as for their partners.

The Taoists learned long ago that experiencing orgasm without ejaculation improves health and even lengthens life. They attributed these effects to reduced fatigue and depletion; we might point instead to increased production of endorphins. But whatever the cause, thousands of men who have followed the program in this book have learned how to enjoy extended orgasm, and many have reported health benefits—particularly improved mood and reduced discomfort from chronic physical symptoms.

• • •

The discovery that both male and female orgasm can be extended for long periods of time was more than a surprise. It was a shock. You may find it hard to believe. But you don't have to take our word for it. You can experience it for yourself—by learning ESO. The most intense physical pleasure that human beings ever feel can be extended. With training, you can extend your experience of continuous orgasm to a minute or five minutes or half an hour or more. You need a willing partner, a developing sense of trust, and time.

This book tells how.

2

Creating the Conditions for Pleasure

For Couples

We assume at the outset that you are reading this book because you want to improve your relationship and increase your sexual pleasure. We will offer a variety of programs and exercises to help you do so. They've been tried by thousands of other men and women, and they work.

You and your partner may decide to follow the program we describe here to extend your orgasms. We hope you will. It's important to start out with realistic expectations. A realistic first goal for most couples would be to extend your orgasms to double or triple their present length. That may mean twenty seconds instead of ten. It may mean a full minute or even two.

Once you've established that new level of experience, you might reasonably consider a more ambitious program of moving toward five to ten minutes of continuous orgasm. From that level you might decide to move toward having ESO for a full half hour, which is what many couples agree is a delightful and suitable ultimate goal. You may spend several months of pleasurable practice before achieving this level of orgasm.

Experiencing ESO for an hour or more may require more months of practice. Not everyone will be sufficiently persistent to achieve it. In our experience, couples who achieve this level of ESO communicate exceptionally well and have large reserves of trust and love.

If you extend your orgasms from six seconds to even one full minute, you will already have increased your time of maximum pleasure by tenfold. That should be cause for celebration. At that point you can, if you wish, decide together to aim for still longer orgasmic experience. After the first major step, you'll find it easier to go on to experience longer periods of ESO.

Most of the basic skills that prepare you for extended orgasm can be learned by self-stimulation. Some men and women have occasionally experienced a low level of ESO alone. But for higher levels of ESO you will need a partner. You need someone you trust who is willing to give you full attention—and then accept your full attention in return. The essence of ESO is both partners giving full attention to one sexual nervous system at a time. This book is written, then, for couples: man and woman, husband and wife, lovers of the same or opposite sex.* Both partners should read it carefully from beginning to end and then discuss it and arrive at agreement on their goals. They may then go back and begin to follow our directions to achieve whatever level of training they've planned.

Many couples find it useful to go through ESO training for the pleasure of the process and not necessarily to extend their orgasms. Other couples may choose to read the entire book and then practice only part of its program—chapter 3, "Developing Skills," for example, or chapter 4, "Getting Together"—without working on ESO at all.

---

*Single men and women can train themselves in ESO skills to share when they find a partner. ESO is entirely possible for same-sex couples, male or female, as well. Wherever we discuss a partner of the opposite gender, same-sex couples should read in the appropriate modifications of direction for their gender.

We can't stress enough the importance of discussing with each other fully beforehand how you feel about deciding to expand your sexual experience. Many men and women believe that they would like to experience greater sexual pleasure. But most of us have fears of doing so and hidden doubts. You and your partner must arrive at clear agreement on the principle of increasing your sexuality together. You must also agree on exactly how you wish to accomplish that increase, and you need to share your doubts and hesitations about doing so.

Sometimes one partner attempts to coerce or intimidate the other into agreement. That won't work. Unless you *both* honestly share an equal interest in sexual enhancement, you are likely to encounter problems in achieving improvement.

If you don't honestly want to pursue extended orgasm, don't agree with your partner to do so. Without honest agreement you'll end up sabotaging your partner's goal. Then he or she, not understanding the sabotage, will feel guilt and blame.

You might agree instead to any number of pleasurable but less ambitious goals we suggest along the way. For example, you might agree simply to do, at a specific time, one of the many exercises we describe. It could even be one of the communication exercises rather than something more specifically sexual. Or you might agree to work with your partner on improving a sexual problem that either of you perceives you have. Limited agreements like these can lay the groundwork for broader agreements in the future. There's much valuable information in this book that you can incorporate into your current lovemaking without pursuing extended orgasm. You can derive significant sexual benefit without making major changes in your sexual commitment. Remember, all of the programs and exercises we suggest are meant to be *fun*. Don't turn them into work.

Our purpose in presenting new information on extended orgasm is not to create new pressures for sexual performance. Rather, we want to open up pleasurable possibilities for adventurous people. Participation is definitely *voluntary*.

Reasons for ESO

Some people, when they hear of ESO, ask why they should bother. For those who need reasons, there are a number of very good ones.

One is that better sex is better for your health. It's good exercise. It stimulates the central nervous system, releases tension, and relieves stress. It stimulates the hormone system to help both men and women stay healthy and young.

A second reason is that ESO improves your mood. An extended orgasm is better than a tranquilizer or antidepressant medication. When you practice ESO with the regularity we suggest in this book, these physical and emotional improvements continue.

Another reason is that people who experience frequent high-quality sex function more efficiently in their other activities. They have more energy to devote to their work, to their family, and to friends.

Still another reason is that better sex strengthens a relationship. Couples who are happier in bed are more likely to be happy together when they're out of bed. Better sex by itself won't save a failing marriage, but it definitely can help. Sex is an important form of communication, and better communication will improve any relationship.

ESO helps make a couple's relationship more secure. They learn to depend on the superior sexual experiences and excellent sexual communication they have achieved. When they attain ESO together, or significantly improve their sexual experiences, they know they are dedicated to pleasing each other and value each other that much more. They're less likely to seek other partners. They don't want to lose what they've gained.

The most obvious reason for learning ESO is that orgasm is pleasurable. Ask any number of people what experience they have that is intrinsically good. The only experience everyone is likely to agree on is sexual orgasm. Sex is more than orgasm, certainly. But the point of sex is pleasure for yourself and the gift of pleasure to your partner. Orgasm is that pleasure focused most intensely.

Yet the average orgasm is only ten seconds long. The average frequency of intercourse is once or twice a week. That's twenty seconds a week, about one and a half minutes a month, about eighteen minutes a year. In fifty years, that's about fifteen hours. For fifteen hours of ecstasy we devote how many thousands and thousands of hours to thinking about sex, worrying about sex, daydreaming about sex, wishing for sex, planning for sex?

With ESO you can spend more of those hours actually *having* sex. Intensely. You have pleasure and the gift of pleasure to win. You have nothing to lose and much to gain. Some men, when they hear of ESO, immediately feel threatened. They think of how much they struggle to retard ejaculation or to maintain an erection, how hard they work to give their partners pleasure. They visualize that process going on for an hour or more and they panic.

It deserves to be said up front: partners *take turns*— equal and equally pleasurable turns—giving each other ESO, and their primary instruments of stimulation are their hands.

Men and women think and communicate differently, which leads to confusion and misinterpretation both ways. ESO makes sex, at least, less confusing, because partners share similar goals in being deliberate about pleasure. A man learns to understand a woman's sexual needs and to satisfy them fully. As a result, his sexual self-confidence skyrockets. Whatever his age, whatever his previous experience, he learns that he can give his partner enormous pleasure whenever she wants. "The feeling of power is unbelievable," one of our clients told us when his wife began having ESO. "I never knew what I was missing!"

Similarly, men begin paying attention to their own pleasure, not only to what they can do for their partner. When Fred, a shy accountant, married to Carol for eight years, learned ESO, he told us, "Sometimes I get an erection just thinking about our lovemaking now."

Men who come to us reporting problems maintaining erection are delighted to discover that they can thoroughly satisfy their partners with ESO *without erection*. Since that's a less demanding situation, and since their partners' passion is highly erotic to them, their erections usually return.

Some women, when they hear of ESO, worry that it will be too strenuous. It would be if the extended state were as athletically extreme as familiar, brief orgasm. We find instead that after a woman moves into the extended state, her blood pressure, heart rate, and respiration rate drop from their initial peaks, even though she continues intensely in orgasm. The body balances and relaxes, much as it does with meditation, although none of these physical measures drops all the way to the resting rate until after ESO ends. Both men and women then feel relaxed and peaceful.

Women who have felt frustration and bitterness in their relationships with their partners become much less angry, and more content and loving, when they regularly experience ESO. They learn that deep sexual pleasure is their birthright and they learn to assert themselves to have it. Barbara, a client who was hostile to her husband and drifting toward divorce until they worked together to learn ESO, described the change to us. "I used to pick on Hal for everything," she said. "Nothing he did anymore was right. Now he's wonderful, he's my wonderful lover—even though I know he's still doing a lot of the same things that used to make me mad."

Some men and women resist learning ESO because they fear their partners will somehow become insatiable, find other partners, have affairs. It's a myth that unleashing your sexual desires will result in your losing control and having sex with people outside your relationship. These betrayals don't happen in relationships with adequate levels of commitment and trust. Couples who learn ESO together almost always become closer, more loving, and more secure. They are grateful to each other; they've learned to depend on each other; they're much less inclined to look elsewhere for sexual excitement. They know how difficult it would be to achieve such excellent communication and such intense satisfaction with a stranger.

Men and women whose have lived together for years, couples whose lives have become routine, even report falling in love again when they learn ESO. Bonnie, in her seventh year of marriage, told us about the results of one memorable night of ESO: "I was sitting in a sales meeting the next day. I thought back to our lovemaking the night before and suddenly I was turned on. I felt so *connected* to Phil. It was wonderful. I was already looking forward to seeing him again, and it was only ten in the morning."

Discovering *by experience* that vastly more pleasure is possible for you than you ever imagined, even in fantasy, can have an enormous impact on your life. The men and women we know who have learned ESO are more confident, more optimistic, and happier than they have ever been.

Emotional Risks of Practicing ESO

The main emotional risks of attempting ESO training are:

- Frustration with trying to let go of your negative thoughts and mental resistances.
- A consequent sense of failure and inadequacy.
- Anger or disappointment with a partner who chooses not to work on sexual enhancement. An angry or disappointed partner may then look outside the relationship. This consequence isn't common, but it's more likely in people less restrained by rules and within relationships with insufficient levels of commitment and trust. ESO practice alone isn't likely to result in such an outcome. An interest in seeking sexual opportunities outside a committed relationship may in fact be reduced by learning ESO.

Reasons to Postpone ESO

There are conditions when some people should postpone learning ESO. Men and women who have serious heart disease, have suffered a recent stroke, or have acute injuries or a serious, chronic illness may want to talk to their doctors first. A guideline: anyone who is able to perform moderate physical exercise should be able to practice ESO.

Couples on the verge of breaking up, couples with serious problems, may need counseling first. If working toward ESO makes your relationship worse rather than better, that's a sign that you need outside help.

Individuals with severe sexual problems may want to seek counseling for those problems before learning ESO. (If you're worried that you qualify, see "Defining Sexual Problems," page 221, for identification of problem areas and guidance on what to do.)

Otherwise, ESO is a delight to young and old.

Creating Trust

The most important single precondition for ESO is trust. You don't even have to love your partner (it helps), but he or she must be someone you trust. Otherwise you won't allow yourself to become a passive receiver of the pleasure your partner is giving you. You won't be willing to let go.

You create trust with good communication, communication without fear. (For detailed suggestions to help you and your partner communicate, see "More Communication," page 247.) What you trust your partner to do is to care about your well-being and not deliberately hurt you, physically or emotionally.

Trust is an important asset in any relationship. It should be valued accordingly and taken seriously. Once it's lost, it's hard to regain. If someone lies to you, you don't easily believe him or her again. If someone ridicules you, you don't easily put yourself again in his or her hands.

How can you create trust? Make trust a goal and say so: "I want to trust you. I want you to trust me." Start with simple agreements in nonsexual areas. Work into more serious problem areas from there.

One of the couples we see in therapy, for example, came to us unhappy with how far they had grown apart. They were both involved in their work and didn't spend much time together. Bob's personality is severely analytic, Ellen's extremely emotional.* Potentially they complement each

---

*We're not using real names, and we've changed some details to protect our clients' privacy. That will be true throughout this book. Remember also that most of the men and women we see come to us initially with problems. Even people with problems are able to achieve ESO. Their stories are valuable for identifying and dramatizing ways to improve sexual functioning. Take from them what is useful to you.

other, but at that time they clashed. Lack of trust was basic
to their disagreement.

Ellen, for example, never knew when Bob would be
home for dinner. It infuriated her. She fixed dinner, Bob
was late, and dinner was ruined. Bob didn't call to let Ellen
know when he would be late, it turned out, because in the
past, when he had called, she had argued with him and
pressured him to match his work schedule to her dinner
plans.

We asked Bob and Ellen to make an agreement: he
would call her when he expected to be late; she wouldn't
pressure him when he called. A small detail, but a way
of building trust. They've kept the agreement, and in
this area at least, both of them trust each other more.
As a result, they have begun to talk about other areas of
conflict. Ellen is moderating her emotionalism. Bob is
warming up and talking more about his feelings. They'll
need to make other agreements. Equally important,
they'll need to keep them. That's how learning to trust
each other works.

The Question of Time

Look at the following list of ways people spend time. As
you scan it, jot down how many minutes or hours you give
each week to each activity:

Working	Talking to your sexual partner
Eating	Shopping
Sleeping	Talking on the telephone
Taking care of children	Visiting friends
Watching television	Going to movies/concerts/
Cleaning house	plays
Playing a sport	Reading books

Computer activities   Listening to music
Practicing a hobby   Making love

You may be surprised to see how little time you spend in sexual intimacy compared to other activities. You're an exceptional lover if you devote as much as two hours a week to making love. Most people give far more time to watching television (the national average is more than six hours a day per person) than they do to lovemaking. They leave sex unscheduled and catch it when they can.

They do so partly because they believe sex should be "spontaneous." If it's deliberate, they think, then it must be forced. If it's forced, then it must be a burden and a duty rather than an expression of love.

No one learns to dance, swim, or ski "spontaneously," nor does anyone maintain those skills without scheduling time to perform them. Why should an equally subtle, complex skill like sexual pleasuring be different? And why shouldn't deliberately allowing time for intimacy with your partner be counted as an expression of love? It was when you were dating.

In fact, better lovemaking is possible only by giving sex priority in your life. Look again at the weekly activity list. We all have to work, eat, sleep, take care of ourselves and our children. But after those necessities, which activity feels best? Which makes you happiest and makes your partner happiest? Wouldn't you rather enjoy good lovemaking than watch TV or stare at a computer screen?

Scheduling ESO

For ESO, moderate blocks of time must be set aside every week, especially while you are learning. You'll need a major period of time during the weekend, a minimum of an hour and a half, and two shorter periods during the

week of at least thirty minutes each. All these times are
minimums. If you can find more time, you should. Every
day isn't too often.

The idea of giving sex priority and scheduling it is new
enough and scary enough to most people that they resist
doing so. We'll talk about resistance in more detail later.
Right now we only want to mention that failing to find time
for ESO is the most universal resistance we've encountered. We often have to ask couples to bring their desk cal-
endars or appointment books into our office so they can
agree then and there on times for ESO training and write
those times into their schedules. If you and your partner
can't arrange a schedule verbally, get out your calendar or
electronic scheduler, appoint times to be together, and
write them down.

You'll find that some times are better for you than
others, of course. Setting aside several hours on a weekend
isn't usually a problem. Finding time on weekdays can be.
Couples we work with usually schedule evening times
during the week. Those times should not be the half hours
just before sleep, because most people are too sleepy then
to give pleasuring their full attention. Leave yourself time
after intimacy to do the things you do to get ready to sleep.
If you regularly begin sleep at 10 P.M., schedule your ESO
practice time to end at 9:30.

You will probably have to limit or even give up some of
your other activities to learn ESO. You'd do that to learn
any new skill. Except for the time involved, ESO is free.
You need invest only moderate time and a dash of courage.
It's worth the time, we promise you!

TIMES TO AVOID

There will inevitably be times when your or your partner's
emotional or physical energy is too high or too low to allow

you to shift attention to pleasurable experience. Sexual interest can vary greatly, and such variation is not always predictable. When emotions or energy are flat, or when there's high nervous or emotional tension, it may be best to agree to reschedule planned sexual "dates," or to modulate high or low levels of emotion before beginning sexual interaction. Emotional modulation is usually more important for women than men because women's hormone levels are generally more variable.

Unreleased, unused sexual energy itself can build to the point of finding discharge in emotional responses expressed in seemingly unrelated ways: restlessness, irritability, anger, depression, fatigue, unreasonable criticism, or general dissatisfaction with one's quality of life. Such negative emotional states are not always due to unreleased sexual energy, though. They may be due to a variety of other influences. Whatever the cause, couples seeking to move toward higher levels of sexual pleasure must learn to recognize and deal with these extremes of emotional variation. (See "Appreciations and Resentments," page 86, and "More Communication," page 247.)

ESO SKILLS IMPROVE WITH PRACTICE

Week by week as you follow the program to learn ESO you will experience increasing pleasure in sexual intimacy. The gain is immediate and increasing. Within several months, depending on where you start from, you should find yourself skilled at creating and maintaining orgasm longer than you do now. ESO is open-ended. You can keep on refining your skills. We've seen no limit to the levels of pleasure possible with continued experience. But ESO can be maintained as a skill, once learned, with sessions of an hour or two once a week. Weekly sessions are necessary to keep muscular- and reflex-control skills tuned. They probably also maintain hormone production at suitably high levels.

With such weekly renewal it's also possible to have good *brief* sex at other times during the week. A woman experienced in ESO usually begins extended orgasm with brief sex almost as soon as her partner's penis enters her vagina. Her partner's state of arousal will also be higher; he will feel more pleasure more quickly and his orgasm will last longer because her strong, continuous contractions stimulate his penis. Five-minute sex under these conditions can satisfy both partners. The "quickie" and the "nooner" come into their own.

INTERRUPTIONS

There are unavoidable interruptions in every couple's sexual life. Holiday activities, visiting relatives, sick children, business travel, personal illness, even the subtle cycles of individual sexual intensity, may interrupt your learning. What you have learned won't be lost, any more than the ability to ski or sail or ride a bicycle is lost when it isn't practiced. Your skills will come back to you when you begin again. You may be wobbly at first. You can pick up and go on.

Discuss your schedule with your partner and agree on ample time for learning ESO: two or more half-hour sessions during the week and at least an hour and a half on weekends.

Creating Romance

If sex is scheduled, what happens to romance? You need to learn to create it deliberately.

(A word here about being deliberate. This applies to

scheduling lovemaking. It applies to creating romance. It applies to ESO training itself: you may feel silly at first, learning all these new structures. Awkward. Self-conscious. Like an actor in a new role who hasn't yet mastered his lines. You feel that way because you're acquiring new skills. You acquire any new skill by working through the procedure deliberately until it begins to be automatic—"natural," as we say. When you're doing something deliberately, you're watching yourself. And watching yourself means, literally, being self-conscious. It's normal. It's necessary to learning. The way to deal with it is to laugh at yourself. Accept the awkwardness and enjoy a temporary vacation from life's burden of dignity. Be supportive of your partner's awkwardness—laugh *with* your partner. There's room for laughter in bed. You're there, after all, to have fun.)

Romance. Some men won't know what that is. Most women will. We wish men and women were equally knowledgeable, but they aren't. That's been our experience as therapists. Perhaps someday they will be. For now, by default, women have volunteered to be the keepers of romance. Men usually undervalue it. They've been taught to ignore it and get the job done. In recent years, though, women have become more assertive, and some men have also begun to wish for romance.

Romance is setting and mood. It's positive attention to each other rather than to outside matters. It's positive feelings and talk rather than negative. It's taking a positive inventory of your partner—discovering, rediscovering, and enjoying your partner's attractive qualities and ignoring for the moment your critical thoughts. It's compliments, looking at one another with appreciation, listening, touching, hugging, holding hands. It's a formal way into intimacy, an arrangement of symbols and cues.

Romance is also—and this may be why so many men distrust it—a tacit request for reassurance. "Before I allow

you access to my body, I would like to know that you value
me. I would like you to tell me so. I would like you to show
me by giving me your attention, even by praising me and
declaring your love, if only for this moment. You will lose
yourself in pleasure with the gift of my body and my
mouth and my hands; is reassurance too much to ask?"

If you think romance is a waste of time, think again.
Paying attention to romance will win your romantic
partner's warm attention in return. Isn't that what you
want?

Creating romance is a social skill. People who are good at
it weren't born that way. They learned. So can you.

Romance is important to ESO training. You're acquiring
new skills, but they aren't merely mechanical. They're an
enlarging of your experience of intimacy with your
partner. They depend on trust and caring. You don't send
your genitals alone into the bedroom. All of you is there.
All of you must be considered, and all of your partner. So
communication, setting, and mood are important when
you're learning ESO, just as they are at other intimate
times. Without them, one or both of you will be distracted
or feel used. Neither state is conducive to pleasure.

The way to find out what your partner considers romantic is to ask. The way to let your partner know is to
speak up.

We give our clients that advice, and they mention mind
reading: "He should already know." In fact, the conditions
that encourage someone to feel warm and sexy are as individually specific as most other human preferences. A fire
may seem romantic to one person and boring to another.
Tastes in music vary across an enormous range.

One of our clients, Alex, couldn't decide what to give his
wife for their sixth wedding anniversary. The year before,
he'd taken her out for an expensive dinner. Instead of
pleasing her, that had made her cold and withdrawn. We

suggested that Alex give Helen a single red rose this time. He was skeptical. We encouraged him, and he bought the rose and took it home. The next time we saw Alex, he raved. "It's amazing. I gave Helen one rose and she was warm all evening." Helen simply wanted to know that Alex thought of her apart from the normal routines of the day. Alex took *clients* out to dinner. The rose was only for her. That was romantic to Helen, then.

If neither of you is quite sure what you find romantic, think back to when you were dating. People in the early stages of courtship usually pay more attention to romance. Did you take walks together? Hold hands? Talk—share experiences, make each other laugh? Compliment each other more than you do now? Discuss restoring some of these pleasures to your lives.

Longing for romance—for close, loving attention—and sexual frustration can be mixed up together, especially in women. When women are sexually frustrated and miss the positive romantic attention they feel they need, we've found they become withdrawn, depressed, or angry. In a word, irritable. This reaction, which is often unconscious, may lead them to start arguments over issues that are seemingly unrelated. That sounds irrational, but it operates by the logic of frustration: at least their arguing makes their partners pay attention, and better angry attention than none at all.

Partners, especially men, need to be alert enough to read such responses accurately. When a man finds his partner deliberately picking a fight, he should try to give her his positive, romantic, undivided attention and work *slowly* toward lovemaking. Often it's not until after satisfactory sex that a woman (or a man, although we find this syndrome more frequently in women) will recognize the real source of her hostility for what it is—pent-up sexual frustration and a hunger for loving attention. She may not acknowledge those motives, but her partner will still find

her to be calmer, less irritable, and ultimately more loving
if he pays attention.

Incorporate romance into your daily living. Start in the
morning, not ten minutes before you have sex.

Paying Attention

Most romantic arrangements have in common a space of
time and a partner's full positive attention. Attention first
of all. Call your partner during the day. Let each other
know you care. When you come home from work, after
you've allowed yourself half an hour or so for practical
matters, sit down and talk. Sit down and listen. Pay more
attention to what your partner is saying than to what you
want to reply. "What did you do today?" Listen support-
ively while your partner clears away the day's debris. Until
the debris is cleared away, you can't come together emotionally. (For exercises to guide you, see "More Communication," page 247.)

At such times both of you should emphasize positives,
set aside negatives, and postpone discussing problems, unless there's an emergency. You can find other times for
criticism, worries, complaints. (Some people don't believe
they can control their feelings deliberately. They can. We
all do, whenever we're in social situations where anger, for
example, is inappropriate. With bosses, for example, or in
church. If it's possible to control your feelings among
strangers, it's equally possible with the man or woman you
love.) Imagine you're beginning an evening or weekend
date. Compliment each other. Joke. Tease. Kid. Touch.
Have fun together. Lighten your heart. *Care.* Tonight's the
night!

Sit down to a romantic dinner. That may mean candle-
light and a bottle of wine. It may mean a sandwich out
under a tree. It may mean no more—but no less—than

husband and wife smiling at each other across a table of children. Eating is a pleasure of its own, one we have shaped to a way of sharing. Eat for the pleasure of the food and pay attention to the partner you're sharing it with.

After dinner you may have to interrupt this pleasant performance you've arranged. Discuss what needs to be done to clear the decks: children put to bed, a telephone call made, a favorite TV show watched, the dog walked. Agree when you'll get back together. Then go ahead and do what you need to do to make possible your space of private, uninterrupted time.

Romantics don't like interruptions. The evening would be smoother without them. But intimacy won't be lost if you both agree to them and know that after they're dealt with, you'll pick up where you left off, and that the goal you're both working toward is clearing time together in privacy to give each other pleasure.

Arranging a Place

We approach the bedroom door (or the living-room floor, or whatever other comfortable space of privacy you've chosen). The room you choose for lovemaking deserves attention.

It ought to be warm enough for nakedness. If turning up the furnace isn't possible, consider buying a space heater that you can use during lovemaking and afterward put it away.

Unless you live alone, the room should have a door and the door should have a privacy lock. If it doesn't, install one. Nothing is harder on lovemaking than the sudden appearance in the room of a child who wonders why you're wrestling or a grandmother looking for something to read.

For mood as well as for privacy, you'll probably want a source of pleasant sound. Uninterrupted music is best. A stereo is nice. A radio will serve. Some people like to leave on their TV. That's less satisfactory because picture and sound can distract you from giving your partner your undivided attention.

Sounds that screen may be important to you as you learn ESO, because one of the skills you'll work on is vocalizing your pleasure, and you may feel inhibited if you think other people can hear. We encourage couples to moan. If they don't know how, we teach them. They start by practicing deliberately at times when they're not making love. They blush and giggle about it. We teach vocalizing because silence during lovemaking is a learned control that limits pleasure. If you're thinking about not making noise, you're not completely letting go. ESO involves learning to let go completely, learning to abandon yourself to sensation. Silence also often means you're holding your breath. That interferes with reaching orgasm and moving above orgasm to ESO. (For further discussion about vocalizing, see "Learning to Vocalize," page 260.)

Most people make love on a bed. You may want to provide a special sheet for ESO to protect your sleeping sheets from the lubricants you will use. You don't have to change the sheets. Just put the special sheet on top. There's nothing wrong with making love on the floor, on pillows. Create a nest, a comfortable place. Be deliberate about it.

Be deliberate about light levels, candles, incense if you like incense, and any other special arrangements you enjoy—erotic media such as videos, for example. If deliberation still seems foolish, think about the last party you gave. You sent invitations, cleaned house, bought food and drink. You probably showered beforehand and dressed in special clothes you don't wear every day. You adjusted lights, stacked your favorite CDs on your stereo, set out your better glasses and china and tableware. Your guests arrived. No one mentioned the special preparations other than to compliment you on them. You forgot about them to have fun. You do the same thing when you create a special setting for lovemaking.

LIGHTING

Light levels can be a problem if partners disagree. Low, warm light is better than darkness for ESO. Observing each other passionately naked is erotic. And whoever is pleasuring needs to see what he's doing. The eyes of the pleasured partner won't always be open, but the eyes of the partner giving pleasure probably will be. If either of you prefers total darkness during lovemaking, you should both discuss why. Often the reason is self-consciousness about your body. Talk it out. Your partner may not feel the same way you do: "I'm embarrassed about my stretch marks." "I'm glad you told me. I'm not even aware of them. I love your body."

(If you want to work toward adding light comfortably to your lovemaking, you can. See "Adding Light," page 259.)

SUPPLIES

You should arrange ahead of time any equipment or supplies you want in the room you've chosen for lovemaking—perhaps towels, bathrobes, a carafe of juice or wine or a favorite beverage.

One supply you'll need is a good lubricant. It must be oil-based, not water-based. You will need a lubricant for ESO because you'll be stroking delicate tissue for long periods of time. Natural lubrication, even for women who naturally lubricate extensively during sex, isn't adequate. Neither is saliva. Neither are lotions, creams, jellies, nor any other water-based substances. Oil-based lubricants

damage latex products, including condoms, but as you'll
see, stimulation to ESO is primarily (and can be exclusively) accomplished manually and orally. That means you
can enjoy ESO using effective lubrication, then take a moment to remove that lubrication before proceeding to intercourse using a condom or a diaphragm. If disease
protection is an issue throughout sexual contact, you can
confine yourself to manual stimulation. (For more discussion of this issue, see "Lubrication," page 257.)

We have found two commercial lubricants that serve
well for ESO. One is petrolatum, also known as petroleum
jelly. The best-known brand of petrolatum is Vaseline. It's
a long-lasting lubricant, but it's extremely difficult to wash
off and many people find it too greasy. It isn't our first
choice, but it will serve.

Unscented Albolene Liquifying Cleaner, a makeup re-
mover, is the best lubricant for ESO. It feels better than
petrolatum. Our experience with many hundreds of
clients confirms that it is definitely the most sensuous,
long-lasting lubricant available. It isn't widely distributed,
but if you can possibly find it in your local drugstore, do
not substitute any other type of lubricant. In contact with
skin, it melts to the consistency of natural sexual lubrication but is longer-lasting. It is also completely tasteless,
for those times when you proceed from manual to oral
stimulation. Even people who at first resist using a lubricant find that the experience of using Albolene usually
changes their doubts into appreciation. Albolene comes
in eight-ounce jars. We recommend that you transfer a
portion into a smaller container for lovemaking, to reduce
the small risk of inadvertently contaminating your supply
from one lovemaking session to another with bacteria
from your fingers.

If Albolene isn't available, one practical solution is to
make your own lubricant. Use the following basic recipe.

20 tablespoons mineral oil
4 tablespoons melted paraffin
2 tablespoons melted petrolatum

Heat to boiling an inch of water in a large saucepan. Set petrolatum in its store container in the boiling water to melt and measure 2 tablespoons into a small saucepan. Melt chunks of paraffin in a second small saucepan or bowl set in the boiling water and measure into the saucepan that contains the measured petrolatum. Set the saucepan with the paraffin/petrolatum mixture into the boiling water and add the mineral oil. Stir to thoroughly mix. While liquid, pour mixture into decorative container. Container should have a lid. Allow to cool.

You can scent and flavor this lubricant—or petrolatum or Albolene, for that matter—by adding flavoring oils while it's still liquid. Almond, coconut, lemon, banana, and vanilla are possible flavorings. Be sure the flavoring you use is an oil, not an extract. Extracts are made with alcohol and won't mix. Two or three drops of flavoring oil are enough. Adding oil of cloves produces a slight warming effect that some people enjoy.

(If you're uncomfortable using a lubricant and for alternative lubricant suggestions, see "Lubrication," page 257.)

Fingernails

For ESO, nails need to be trimmed very short and with the corners rounded. It's a minor but important point, a sub-sub-sub-issue under the heading of trust. Unless your nails are short, you'll cause your partner pain. Women who enjoy long fingernails will be sorry to sacrifice them, but short nails are a necessity. At the very least, one finger on a woman's dominant hand must be short-nailed. Two or three short-nailed fingers are preferable. Life is compromise. The benefit in this case is pleasure.

Bathing

Allow time to bathe or shower together before ESO. Our experience as physician and sex therapist confirms that nothing inhibits good sex more than poor hygiene. You've read in other guidebooks that the smells of the beloved are wonderful, and if they're fresh, they may be. But most Americans are conditioned to thorough cleanliness, especially for oral sex. The way to assure each other that you are clean is to bathe together.

By bathing together, what could be an interruption becomes a sensual pleasure of its own. Wash each other's genitals—that helps you to know them. Dry each other afterward and enjoy that pleasure too. Women who have a persistent problem with odor or discharge should rely on their gynecologist's advice.

An alternative to bathing together is washing your partner's genitals with a cloth as a prelude to lovemaking. You can use a soapy washcloth to clean, a wet one to rinse, and a towel to dry. You can then place the towel under your partner to protect the bed sheets, carpet, or upholstery from lubricants and sexual fluids.

Alcohol

Some people find that alcohol enhances mood and promotes relaxation. Use it, if you both agree, in moderation. Alcohol is an anesthetic, like ether or chloroform. It also causes depression and emotional instability. A man who drinks too much will have serious trouble achieving and maintaining an erection. More than two glasses of wine or beer or two cocktails during any three-hour period before or during lovemaking is probably too much. Don't delude yourself about alcohol. You'd be surprised how many people do.

Marijuana

Marijuana alters the perception of time. For some users, time seems to pass more slowly than usual. Pleasurable feelings may seem prolonged. Marijuana also helps some people focus their attention on feelings rather than thoughts.

On the other hand, frequent—daily—marijuana use has been proven in authoritative scientific studies to lower androgens, which are the main hormones determining the level of sex drive—libido—in both men and women. Low androgens in men not only diminish interest in sex, they also adversely affect erection and ejaculation. Daily marijuana use—even two joints a day—appears to produce as much lung damage as a pack of cigarettes. Also, among some users, marijuana can cause anxiety and paranoia.

Finally, although vast numbers of people have sampled it, marijuana is illegal.

You will have to decide if the benefits of using marijuana outweigh the serious disadvantages. If you decide for marijuana, don't use it every time you have sex. *ESO produces a natural high that is far better than any drug-induced high.* A prolonged state of orgasm stimulates your production of sex hormones. It also seems to increase the pleasurable levels of your body's own natural narcotic, endorphin.

Anger

One final caution: as you enter the bedroom, leave anger outside. Even if you're angry. If you've agreed to come together with your partner for lovemaking, give up anger while you do. Lovemaking isn't a time for criticism, for complaint, for nagging, least of all for anger. If you're feeling angry, imagine gathering your anger together and stuffing it into a plastic garbage bag. Close the bag with a twist tie. Set it outside the bedroom door. You can pick it up in half an hour. Maybe the garbage man will tiptoe up to the door while you're inside, giving and taking pleasure, and carry your garbage away. (If anger continues to be a problem, see "More Communication," page 247.)

The scene is set. You'll soon forget the props. You're ready to begin. The seventeenth-century English poet John Donne knew how miraculous that beginning can feel:

> *And now good morrow to our waking souls,*
> *Which watch not one another out of fear;*
> *For love, all love of other sights controls,*
> *And makes one little room, an everywhere.*

3
Developing Skills

What You Should Know
About Anatomy

To give pleasure, you need to understand your partner's sexual anatomy. To take pleasure, you need to understand your own. We also want to identify the parts and responses we'll be talking about later. Some you'll know. Others may not be familiar. Here's a brief review.

Female Anatomy

We'll discuss the female anatomy first.

The major labia normally rest closed over the other parts of the female genitals, protecting them. *Labia* means "lips." That's more or less what they look like under their protective padding of hair. When a woman becomes sexually excited, her major labia expand and flatten against her groin, opening her genitals and exposing their sensitive inner structures.

The minor labia also normally rest closed. With sexual excitement they lengthen and thicken until they protrude

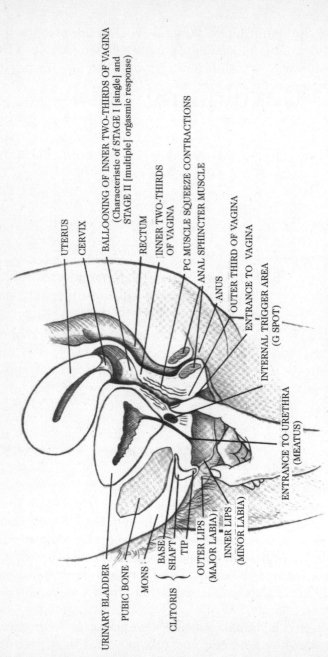

URINARY BLADDER

PUBIC BONE

MONS

CLITORIS
    BASE
    SHAFT
    TIP

OUTER LIPS
(MAJOR LABIA)

INNER LIPS
(MINOR LABIA)

ENTRANCE TO URETHRA
(MEATUS)

UTERUS

CERVIX

BALLOONING OF INNER TWO-THIRDS OF VAGINA
(Characteristic of STAGE I [single] and
STAGE II [multiple] orgasmic response)

RECTUM

INNER TWO-THIRDS
OF VAGINA

PC MUSCLE SQUEEZE CONTRACTIONS

ANAL SPHINCTER MUSCLE

ANUS

OUTER THIRD OF VAGINA

ENTRANCE TO VAGINA

INTERNAL TRIGGER AREA
(G SPOT)

1 FEMALE ANATOMY

well past the major labia. When a woman approaches orgasm, the minor labia change color, depending on skin color and how many children a woman has had, to bright red or even to a deep wine.

The clitoris, with its glans, its hood, and its shaft, appears at the upper junction of the minor labia. When a woman is sexually stimulated, the glans clitoris enlarges at least enough to smooth out the wrinkles in its covering of skin. In a minority of women the glans may enlarge up to double its normal size. However little or much it swells, its changes follow along with the changes in the length and thickness of the minor labia. As a woman reaches a high level of sexual arousal and approaches orgasm, the entire body of the clitoris—glans and shaft—retracts inward and down toward the vagina, until the glans is entirely hidden under the clitoral hood. If arousal then decreases, the clitoris reappears. If arousal increases again, the clitoris retracts again.

Downward from the clitoris and within the shelter of the major and minor labia is the small opening of the urethra. The urethra is the tube that leads outward from the bladder and carries away urine.

Downward from the urethral opening is the opening of the vagina. The vagina serves for sexual intercourse and for birth. Normally the vagina is collapsed upon itself so that its walls are touching all along its length. A woman's first physical response to sexual stimulation is vaginal lubrication. The walls of the vagina produce lubricating fluid by a process similar to sweating.

With continuing arousal the vagina opens and lengthens. It produces more lubrication. The uterus—the womb—elevates inside the body, making a tentlike space above the bottom of the vaginal barrel. At the same time the outer third of the vaginal barrel becomes congested with blood and actually closes down smaller than its previous opening, which allows it to hold and to feel a penis of any size, from very small to very large.

With the beginning of brief Stage I orgasm the outer third of the vagina pulses in rhythmic contraction. This pulsing is the work of a sling of muscle, the pubococcygeus (*pyub*-oh-cock-sih-*gee*-us), that attaches to the pubic bone in front and the coccyx or tailbone in back. The PC muscle surrounds the opening of the urethra and the vagina. It's an important muscle to get to know. We'll discuss it after we describe the male's sexual anatomy.

Research by W. B. Cutler et al. has demonstrated that the cervix, generally thought to be insensitive to pain or pleasure, is an orgasmic trigger in 35 percent of women studied. One method of cervix stimulation is called "cervical tapping"; it's described in the section on intercourse on page 170.

It's probably significant that female genital structures are controlled by different nerves. There is evidence that the pudendal nerve causes the PC muscle to contract in the outer part of the vagina. The deeper vaginal structures, including the G-spot area and the cervix, are controlled by the pelvic nerve and hypogastric plexus. This may explain why there seem to be several types of orgasmic responses.

LOCATING THE INNER TRIGGER—THE G SPOT

An important and still mildly controversial feature of female anatomy is an area in the vagina that in many women can help function as an orgasmic trigger. It's not usually sensitive nor even palpable except at high levels of sexual excitement. Some sexually experimental couples have known for years of an inner trigger area, but it was first mentioned in the professional literature more than fifty years ago by a gynecologist, Dr. Ernest Grafenberg. And only in the past several decades have sex therapists appreciated the important role this area can serve in the orgasmic process.

It's variously called "the twelve o'clock spot," the "inner trigger," the "Grafenberg spot," or the "G spot." It's an area of tissue in the upper front wall of the vagina, varying in size from shirt-button to coat-button, just behind the pubic bone, which is the bone you can feel above and toward the front of the vagina. The G-spot trigger area is located on the vaginal wall about one and a half to two inches in depth at the twelve o'clock position. Sometimes it's more toward the eleven or one o'clock position.

It normally can't be easily felt. The best time to locate it is immediately after a woman has had orgasm. It is then already somewhat enlarged and sensitive. If a partner presses the G-spot trigger area with one or two fingers and strokes it at a rate of about once a second, a woman mentally open to the experience will usually become more sexually aroused, sometimes explosively so. Experiment with alternating lighter and firmer pressure. Be guided by your partner's response.

The next-best time to locate the G spot is when a woman is near orgasm. If her partner continues clitoral stimulation manually or orally, when he identifies and strokes the G spot she may crest over into orgasm.

Pressure on the G spot may feel uncomfortable at first. It may produce an urge to urinate. That's not a sign that a partner should stop stimulating the area. He should simply lighten his stroke. After a minute or so of continued pressure and stroking, discomfort usually gives way to pleasure.

With continued stroking, the G spot increases in size, hardens—much as the clitoris and penis do—and is then easier to locate.

What exactly is this inner trigger area? There are several theories. It may be sensitive because nerves from the clitoris pass through it on their way to the spinal cord. It may be an area surrounding the female urethra that contains a vestigial prostate gland. Gynecologists and pathologists agree that the area does contain some paraurethral ducts that are similar to the male prostate, and as we will discuss later, stimulating the male prostate helps to trigger a deeper male orgasm in many men.

Alice Kahn Ladas, Beverly Whipple, and John D. Perry in 1982 were the first to report that stimulation of this spot in some women caused them to ejaculate a fluid similar to seminal fluid. Since then, other researchers have confirmed the Ladas findings. In 1995, with the assistance of a urologist, Gary Schubach inserted catheters in women who were able to ejaculate and found that while some of the ejaculatory fluid came from the bladder, some indeed came from the prostate-like paraurethral glands.

The controversy that erupted in the 1980s regarding the existence of the G spot appears resolved. Most sexologists agree that there is an area in the front wall of the vagina that can be identified in many, but not all, women. Because the size, shape, and location vary from one woman to another, a more accurate name might be the "G-spot area." With proper stimulation, most but not all women will find stimulating this area highly pleasurable. G-spot stimulation will sometimes cause some women to "ejaculate" a watery fluid, reportedly not urine, which comes from the urethra. Produced by paraurethral glands, which are similar to the male's prostate gland, this fluid is analogous to the pre-ejaculatory fluid men produced when their Cowper's gland is stimulated by light pressure on the penile bulb. Some women prefer a clitorally induced orgasm first, then G-spot stimulation. Others prefer a period of clitoral arousal, followed by simultaneous stimulation of clitoris and G spot to produce a "blended" orgasm, which is the beginning stage of ESO.

Regardless of whether or not females ejaculate, locating the internal trigger area at about the twelve o'clock position in the upper wall of the vagina is important for women who wish to experience ESO. Later on we'll explain how to do so.*

A woman who is unable to locate the G spot will still very possibly discover an area in her vagina that is especially sensitive. Usually this area is located along the front wall of the vagina, but sensitivity may occur instead at other positions. Careful attention to the sex exploration exercises we will be discussing—both partners' attention—can help with identifying a vaginal area or areas that respond pleasurably to stimulation. Later, when we talk about stimulating the G spot, women who have located other areas of vaginal sensitivity should direct stimulation there instead.

Male Anatomy

Next, look at the male sexual anatomy.

The male penis in its unaroused state is a short, soft tube of spongy tissue that provides a channel for emptying the bladder of urine. The male urethra runs along the length of the underside of the penis. The penis itself is not a muscle and contains no muscles, nor any bones. Two to three inches of it is rooted inside the body in the pubococcygeus musculature. Specific exercises can strengthen that musculature and thus help make erections harder. (See page 73, "Advanced Techniques.")

In males who haven't been circumcised, the head of the penis—the glans—is covered by a loose tube of skin called

*Very occasionally we have encountered women who develop a bladder infection called cystitis when they are beginning to learn about G-spot stimulation. This is easily treated with antibiotics and usually does not occur again. It may be like "honeymoon cystitis," which occurs once or twice in some brides and other women who begin sexual activity after a period of sexual inactivity. It can be annoying, but it is not dangerous.

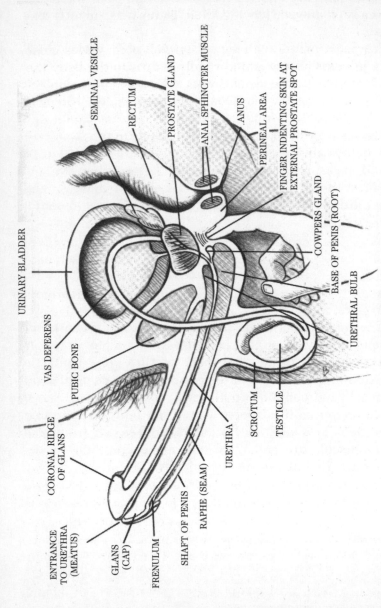

URINARY BLADDER

SEMINAL VESICLE

RECTUM

PROSTATE GLAND

ANAL SPHINCTER MUSCLE

ANUS

PERINEAL AREA

FINGER INDENTING SKIN AT
EXTERNAL PROSTATE SPOT

COWPERS GLAND

BASE OF PENIS (ROOT)

URETHRAL BULB

VAS DEFERENS

PUBIC BONE

SCROTUM

TESTICLE

URETHRA

CORONAL RIDGE
OF GLANS

ENTRANCE
TO URETHRA
(MEATUS)

GLANS
(CAP)

FRENULUM

SHAFT OF PENIS

RAPHE (SEAM)

2 MALE ANATOMY

the foreskin. Circumcised males have had their foreskins surgically removed, leaving their glans permanently exposed.

The penis erects with sexual stimulation. Valves close down in veins that would normally return to the body the blood carried to the penis by its arteries. The organ increases in length and thickness as its spongy tissue fills with blood.

With increasing arousal the glans swells to several times its unaroused state and sometimes darkens in color. Erection occurs in newborn baby boys as well as in men ninety years old. It occurs a number of times every night during sleep in every healthy male. Erection is a man's first physical response to sexual stimulation, as lubrication is a woman's. At ejaculation, semen spurts from the urethral opening in the penis with enough force to propel itself outward several inches, sometimes a foot or more.

Aroused or unaroused, different penises vary greatly in thickness and length. The size differences are largely hereditary. They don't correlate with body size. A large man may have a small penis; a small man may have a large penis. Penises do tend to withdraw into the body with lack of sexual use, as some sexually inactive older men have discovered. Some men experienced in ESO have reported some long-lasting if not permanent increase in the length of their penises—up to an inch. This increase may come from a stretching of the ligaments that support the penile bulb rooted inside the body. Frequent, prolonged, and maximum erection, all part of ESO, stimulate the penis over a period of months to enlarge to its maximum length and thickness. Further stimulation comes from the exercises we'll be recommending to strengthen the PC muscle and muscles at the penile base and from the stimulation techniques of ESO itself, which push the deep penile bulb forward. A man can track changes in penile length during ESO training by measuring his erect penis along the top, from pubic bone to tip. If penis size is a concern of yours or of your partner's, this increase could be a fringe benefit of learning ESO.

In our experience, most men overemphasize the value of a large penis. The great majority of women count many other qualities in a man more important than the size of his penis. And couples who regularly experience ESO, in particular, enjoy such high levels of sexual satisfaction and such correspondingly high levels of sexual self-confidence that any concern they may once have had about penis size becomes minimal.

Below and behind the penis is the scrotum. The scrotum is a sac of skin that contains the testicles, the two walnut-size glands where sperm are nurtured. The scrotum, and the two cords that support the testicles, raise and lower the testicles against and away from the body to regulate their temperature. Sperm die if they're kept at body temperature for very long, which is why the wives of men who wear tight undershorts sometimes have difficulty getting pregnant.

With sexual arousal a man's testicles swell, sometimes doubling or even tripling in size. Along with the thickened, engorged scrotum, they draw up against his body as he approaches orgasm. Men usually can't ejaculate until their testicles are fully drawn up against their bodies.[*]

Behind the scrotum, toward the anus, and inside the body are two glands: the prostate and the Cowper's (named for the English anatomist who first identified it and also known as the bulbo-urethral). The Cowper's gland is located at the base of the penis, behind the scrotum; there is no equivalent organ in women. It supplies the clear, thready, slippery fluid that men secrete during

---

[*]Men under fifty. Men over fifty may not experience full elevation of both testicles. Some men with low-hanging testicles find that although their scrotum lifts, it never actually pulls the testicles against the body.

sexual arousal prior to ejaculation, the preseminal fluid that heralds the approach of the emission phase of orgasm. The prostate is a little farther behind the scrotum and deeper inside the body than the Cowper's. It surrounds the male urethra in front of the urinary bladder and supplies part of the fluid that bathes the swimming sperm produced by the testicles and expelled from the body at ejaculation.

With erection and a moderate level of sexual arousal, external stimulation of the Cowper's can be highly pleasurable. You or your partner can identify the Cowper's gland area by locating the underside of the erect penis behind the scrotum with a finger and then with light to moderate pressure running the finger back to the bulb at the base of the penis. Pressing forward at the base of the penis should feel arousing. Because some men find the sensation unusual, stimulating this area to enhance pleasure may take some practice, but it's worth it.

The prostate in the male, like the G spot in the female, is often highly sensitive to stimulation, especially when there is already excitement with erection. A man's sexual arousal can be increased simply by massaging his prostate with a finger inserted through the anus into the rectum. The prostate can also be stimulated less directly—but more easily and comfortably—by applying pressure behind the scrotum to the area between the back of the scrotum and the anus, in the valley of skin known as the perineum (pear-ih-*nee*-um). We call this important pressure point the *external prostate spot*. There is some evidence that men who go through life with a low frequency of orgasm are more likely to suffer from prostate enlargement and prostatic cancer than men who are sexually more active. Not every man finds this stimulation arousing at first. The closer a man is to orgasm, the more likely he is to find prostate stimulation pleasurable.

Certain Taoists called the external prostate spot (in approximate translation) the "million-dollar point," referring to the price of having a Taoist master demonstrate its location. Stimulation of these areas is one requirement for males learning to experience ESO. The entire area between the scrotum and the anus needs to be carefully explored to find and develop new erotic pleasure zones. The anus itself, which has a high concentration of nerves, can be pleasurably stimulated—lightly on the exterior or with a partly inserted finger—during sexual arousal. Hygienic caution should be observed following insertion.

THE FOUR ERECTION STAGES

According to both Taoist practitioners and modern Western medicine, there are four stages of male erection.

1. Latent (filling): Engorgement begins. The penis stirs and becomes slightly erect.
2. Tumescent (swelling): The penis becomes firm but is not yet rigid enough for penetration.
3. Full erection: The penis is erect and hard. This is the desirable phase for practicing avoiding ejaculation, lasting longer, and ESO training.
4. Rigid erection: The penis is stiff, throbbing, hot, ready to burst, close to ejaculation. The scrotum contracts, drawing the testicles against the body.

Some men move from flaccidity to ejaculation so rapidly that they and their partners fail to realize that erection progresses through distinct stages. To extend orgasmic response, you will have to slow down the progress of erection enough so that you and your partner can learn to recognize the staging process. We'll discuss how to do that.

Although most men who learn to experience ESO do so with some level of erection, it isn't necessary to have an erection for ESO. The reflexes of orgasm are mediated by

the sympathetic branch of the nervous system, whereas
erection is controlled by the parasympathetic branch; the
two branches don't necessarily act in concert.

Similarities

Male and female sexual anatomy look dramatically different, and they are—one is almost the reverse of the
other—but in terms of how the genitals develop, they're
very much alike. The male and female genitals evolve from
the same tissues in the developing fetus. Look at the illustration "Comparable Male-Female Structures," which
shows the male and female genitals side by side.

3 COMPARABLE MALE-FEMALE STRUCTURES

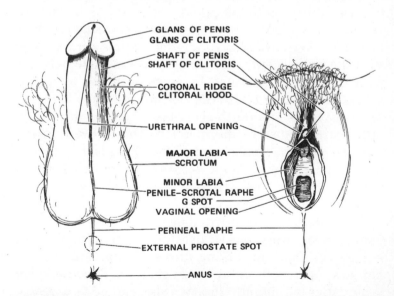

GLANS OF PENIS
GLANS OF CLITORIS

SHAFT OF PENIS
SHAFT OF CLITORIS

CORONAL RIDGE
CLITORAL HOOD

URETHRAL OPENING

MAJOR LABIA
SCROTUM

MINOR LABIA
PENILE–SCROTAL RAPHE
G SPOT
VAGINAL OPENING

PERINEAL RAPHE

EXTERNAL PROSTATE SPOT

ANUS

The male scrotum and the female major labia develop from
the same fetal tissue. The shaft of the penis and the shaft

of the clitoris correspond. So, most importantly, do the glans penis and the glans clitoris. Remember these similarities when you stimulate your partner. They'll help you understand where your partner is sensitive and how that sensitivity feels.

The similarity between the glans penis and the glans clitoris partly explains why many women don't have orgasm during ordinary intercourse. When a man's penis is thrusting in a woman's vagina, he's directly stimulating his most sensitive organ but only indirectly stimulating hers. Only about one woman in three is orgasmic with intercourse. That's another reason why ESO, which involves direct clitoral stimulation (and direct penile stimulation), is more pleasurable than intercourse alone.

The importance of clitoral stimulation cannot be underestimated. Jeff, the boyfriend of one of our clients, learned that the hard way. Angie almost moved out. They're thirty-five and thirty-three years old. Angie works in an office, Jeff in construction. Angie came to see us because she expected to be transferred to another state soon and wasn't sure she wanted Jeff to go along. She was extremely angry with him, partly because he wasted all his money and some of hers on drugs, partly because he made love to her vigorously but inattentively. She'd been orgasmic with other partners before she met Jeff. They'd been orgasmic together at first. Now she rarely had orgasm. She would passively lie back without actively participating in intercourse. She felt that Jeff had stopped caring about her pleasure and was concerned only about his own.

We worked to improve their whole relationship. Included in that work was straightforward training in manual stimulation and in taking turns giving and receiving pleasure. Within three weeks Angie started having orgasm again. After ten therapy sessions she learned to extend her orgasm to three minutes at a time. Jeff also learned to extend his orgasm. The quality of their intercourse changed wonderfully. For that and other reasons their entire relationship improved. When Angie's job transfer came through, she enthusiastically encouraged Jeff to join her. He did. Angie wrote us later that she has had some orgasms with Jeff that have lasted five to ten minutes.

Differences

One more comment about anatomy: each of us is different, from our unique fingerprints and the unique sizes and responses of our genitals to our unique patterns of orgasm. "There is nothing more characteristic of the sexual response," the pioneer sex researcher Alfred Kinsey concluded after interviewing thousands of men and women, "than the fact that it is not the same in any two individuals." That's because the body's central organ of sexual response is the brain.

Some women can stimulate themselves to orgasm by caressing only their breasts; others cannot. Some men and women experience a red, rashlike flush on their upper bodies with orgasm; others do not. Some men stop thrusting at the onset of orgasm; others continue thrusting until orgasm is concluded. There are patterns common to all, and there is much of sensation and pleasure that can be learned. It's worth remembering always that your partner is first of all an individual, is first of all a human being, and is more like you than different—concerning problems as well as pleasures.

The Chemistry of Sex

Although many people believe that sex is inherently mystical, studies continue to demonstrate the fundamentally biological nature of the sexual response. Specific hormones have been found in the brain and the genitals that can facilitate or disrupt sexual response.

People who have taken antidepressants such as Prozac, Zoloft, or Paxil have discovered that an immediate and sometimes dramatic decrease in orgasmic response is a common side effect. Sexual response returns rapidly when the medication is discontinued. This interruption appears to be related to alterations in brain serotonin metabolism, although the exact mechanism is not fully understood.

Another nervous system chemical, nitric oxide, was only recently discovered, and has been found to play an essential role in erections in men and perhaps arousal in women. The much-discussed drug Viagra increases nitric oxide concentration in the penis, which is why it's prescribed for erectile dysfunction. A variety of other hormones and peptides are being studied for their effect on sexual functioning.

Men who notice a persistent decline in sexual interest or response should consider having their testosterone levels checked. Even younger men may experience declines. Women also produce testosterone, although at lower levels than men. Lower testosterone production in women probably explains why women on the average have lower levels of sexual interest compared to men—they fantasize less about sex, for example. But female testosterone levels are just as important to libido. Women who notice a decline in libido or sexual response (which may accompany menopause) are advised to ask their doctor about having their testosterone level checked. For both men and women, two levels are important: "total" and "free." If "free" levels in particular are below the norm for their age and sex, both men and women should discuss hormone replacement therapy. Male hormone replacement therapy can be administered via injection, patch, or topical gel. Women need lower doses, best supplied via prescription gel or a custom-formulated cream. Ask your doctor.

Adrenaline (epinephrine) produced by sympathetic nervous system arousal increases heart rate, muscle tension, and blood pressure; it also increases sexual excitement. Novelty, adventure, risk, and surprise all stimulate adrenaline production and therefore sexual arousal. So pushing beyond your usual habits and boundaries by trying new sexual techniques or having sex at unaccustomed times can recharge your lovemaking.

Also, frequency helps. In *Love Cycles*, Winifred Cutler reports that couples who had regular weekly intercourse had synchronous increases in their respective estrogen and testosterone levels.

Medical research will continue to elucidate the molecular chemistry of sex and may bring improvements, but developing maximum sexual potential will still require careful attention to your own and your partner's mental and physical responses. Think of yourselves as a team of sexual investigators, and you are most likely to make the discoveries that will allow you to experience sexual breakthroughs.

Learn to Control Your Mind

20–0 COUNTDOWN

Sexual pleasure is an experience controlled partly by physical and partly by mental stimulation. The two systems of control overlap and to some extent duplicate each other. A man may have an erection, for example, while doing no more than thinking about a sexual situation. He may also have an erection while unconscious—on the operating table, for example, under anesthesia, when his genital area is being washed to prepare him for surgery. A woman may similarly feel the female equivalent of erection—vaginal lubrication and engorgement—while thinking sexual thoughts. She is equally capable of arousal under purely physical stimulation, such as when a partner gently stimulates her genitals while she's asleep and she lubricates without awakening.

Extending sexual response involves training both physical and mental control systems. For increasing mental control, the 20–0 Countdown is an extremely simple yet remarkably effective exercise. Mental control—learning to concentrate—by narrowing the focus of attention, more specifically to screen out unwanted thoughts, is important to helping to learn to experience extended orgasm. You do not have to be a victim of your destructive or counterproductive thoughts.

Our thoughts, a background of noise like static on the radio, constantly distract us. To see for yourself, close your eyes. Become aware of your breathing. Counting backward from 20, count your exhaled breaths silently to yourself. Whenever you're distracted by a thought, continue your countdown with the last number you remember. Try to notice how many times you're distracted. If you're like most of us, you didn't get very far down the list of numbers before a thought intervened. It probably took you several tries before you were able to count all the way down to 0. Most people are victims of their thoughts. A thought comes in and continues its development in your mind unless you have the skills to stop that thought and restructure it.

You're born with the ability to visualize. You can visualize many things simultaneously. Language doesn't work the same way. It's linear; you can only say one word to yourself at a time. Try to say yes and no to yourself simultaneously. You can't do it. You can say half of one word and half of another, but you can't say both at the same time. One way to block thoughts, then, is to repeat a word over and over to yourself. That's the basis for some traditional systems of meditation.

We counseled a stockbroker recently who had a

problem achieving erection. Like many businessmen, he was a type A personality—intense, driven, high-achieving, and impatient. We assigned him the 20–0 Countdown exercise. He tried it. We asked him how far he got before his first distracting thought intruded. He grinned when he answered. "Twenty," he said.

Like our stockbroker, many people have trouble counting down past 19 or 18 before an intrusive thought appears. Such thoughts come in many forms. Physical needs intrude: "I have to go to the bathroom." "I'm hungry." "A beer would taste good about now." "My nose itches." Doubts intrude: "Why am I doing this?" "Will this really help?" Environmental distractions occur: "Is that dog ever going to stop barking?" "I think I hear the kids fighting." "Was that the door?" There seems to be a continual background of thinking going on just below consciousness; thoughts rise to the surface like bubbles. You may even find yourself thinking about the fact that you're not supposed to be thinking. The sheer quantity of thoughts that the mind manufactures every minute can be overwhelming. The mind doesn't like to be controlled. It likes to think whatever it chooses. The important point to remember, though, is that once any particular thought becomes conscious, your conscious mind can control or change it if you decide to do so.

The 20–0 Countdown exercise is not only a valuable way of measuring the relative quiet (or noise) going on in your head. It's also a way to achieve a measure of control over that constant stream of thoughts. After a few weeks of practicing this exercise, you should find that your concentration has improved significantly. The nice thing about the countdown is that you can continually monitor your improvement.

The technical term for deliberately stopping thoughts and controlling the flow of conscious thoughts is "cognitive restructuring." Cognitive restructuring isn't mumbo jumbo. It's a commonplace method in psychology, and it works. In some ways it's similar to the techniques used in some forms of Eastern meditation, and the goals are the same: control of the flow of thoughts passing through the conscious mind.

The 20–0 Countdown may be your first deliberate attempt to focus your concentration and take control of your thoughts. Doing this brief, deceptively simple exercise is a way to begin learning to relax. Relaxation is a key to improving your physical and emotional well-being. In sexual training we've found daily practice of the 20–0 Countdown invaluable for reducing the stress and distraction that interfere with intimacy and sexual pleasure.

THE EXERCISE

Begin by making yourself comfortable. Sit in a comfortable chair with your back straight, your neck relaxed, and your chin resting on your chest or your head against a headrest. Position your feet flat on the floor. Rest your hands comfortably on your thighs. Then close your eyes, clear your mind of intrusive thoughts, and become aware of your breathing. Focus your attention (concentrate) on the feeling of the cool air coming in through your nostrils and the warm air going out. Begin counting down silently from 20 to 0. Say the number to yourself. Count down one number at each exhalation, imagining the number being written on a blackboard. Keep repeating the same number silently to yourself over and over until the next exhalation, then change numbers.

If you find your attention diverted by a thought or a sound, remind yourself to return your attention to the number, repeating it and again visualizing it. If you have trouble visualizing the number, imagine writing it. Twenty, for example: imagine the 2 being written first and then the

0. Continue counting until you reach 0, then open your eyes.

Review when your attention was diverted. At what number did an intrusive thought appear? Keep track of how long you kept your attention focused on the countdown before you were distracted by an intrusive thought. Your progress in concentration training can be measured in part by the gradual lowering of this number.

Do a countdown *four times a day*. Do it before you get out of bed as your first waking act, at lunchtime, at the end of the workday, and last of all at night lying down before you go to sleep. This schedule will give you practice stopping thoughts during the active and less active parts of your day, preparing you to control your thoughts during your sexual interactions. Try in each case to find a quiet location where you won't be disturbed. The full exercise will take about three minutes each time you do it, for a total of twelve minutes a day.

Sex Muscle (Kegel) Exercises

Even knowledgeable men and women who have heard of the great value of developing the special sex muscles usually have not bothered to train them. For increased sexual pleasure we strongly advise all our clients to develop their sexual muscles (the pubococcygeus or PC muscles). You may not know that you do, but you probably use your PC muscle to increase sexual arousal during intercourse. The stronger your PC, the more control you have over its action. The better exercised it is, the greater the flow of stimulating blood in the genitals. Weight lifters find pleasure "pumping up" their muscles by exercising them at the beginning of a workout, causing them to enlarge and fill with blood. Working your PC similarly adds pleasure during sexual stimulation.

PC exercise is extremely important to successful ESO.
Back in the late 1940s a gynecologist named Dr. Arnold
Kegel (pronounced *Kay*-gill) developed a good, basic program of PC exercises to help women who have problems
controlling their bladders. It's clear now that "Kegel exercises" work equally well for men and condition the PC for
sexual arousal.

Here's how a woman can identify her PC muscle:

Sit on a toilet. Spread your legs apart. See if you can
stop and start the flow of urine without moving your legs.
The muscle you use to do that, the one that turns the flow
on and off, is your PC muscle. If you don't find it the first
time, don't give up. Try again the next time you have to
urinate.

And here's how a man can identify his PC:

Try to stop the flow of urine during urination. The
muscle you use is your PC. You may feel a tightening
around your anus as well. You also use your PC to force out
the last drops of urine.

Kegel exercises are simple three-part exercises:

Slow clenches: Squeeze and clench the PC muscle
as you did to stop the flow of urine. Take a deep
breath. Hold your breath and clench your muscle for
ten seconds. Then relax your muscle and exhale for
ten seconds. Relax. Exhale. When alone, you can
make an "ahhh" sound when you breathe out.

Flutters: Clench and relax the PC once per second.
Breathe slowly and regularly.

Clench push-outs: This is similar to the slow
clench, except instead of relaxing your muscle after
contracting it, you actively bear down or push out.
Women: bear down moderately as if trying to have a
bowel movement or as if in labor. Men: bear down
moderately as if you're forcing out urine or a bowel
movement. Men and women: this exercise will use a

number of stomach (abdominal) muscles as well as the PC muscle. You'll also feel your anus tightening and relaxing. Clench and inhale for a count of ten. Then push out and exhale for ten seconds.

Begin training your PC by doing ten slow clenches, ten flutters, and ten push-outs (that's one *set*) five times every day.

After a week, add five slow clenches, five flutters, and five push-outs to each set and continue doing five sets a day.

After another week, add five more of each exercise and continue doing five sets a day.

Add five of each exercise each week until a set includes thirty of each exercise. Then continue doing at least five sets a day every day to maintain muscle tone. Sex muscle exercises should become a daily lifetime practice.

You can do Kegel exercises almost anywhere—when you're driving, walking, watching TV, doing dishes, sitting at a desk, lying in bed.

When you start exercising, you may find that your PC doesn't want to stay tightened during slow clenches. You may not be able to do flutters very quickly or evenly. That's because the muscle is weak. Control improves with practice.

If your PC feels tired in the middle of a set, give it a few seconds' rest and then continue.

To feel the contractions of her PC muscle and check on its increasing strength, a woman can insert one or two lubricated fingers into her vagina while exercising. Holding an object in her vagina during PC exercise can speed progress toward strength and control. Other than fingers, a woman may use a penis-shaped vibrator. Switching on the vibrator can add pleasurable sensations to the exercise.

Kegel exercises help men develop stronger erections. Learning to tighten, to relax, and to push out the PC muscle allows a man to control his sexual system the way he controls a car. *Tightening* is the accelerator, increasing arousal. *Pushing out* is the brake—it can help stop ejaculation.

Remember to breathe in evenly to a count of ten and out to a count of ten while you're doing Kegel exercises. Do one hundred to two hundred contractions (when you've trained yourself up to that level) faithfully every day. They'll help you with ESO.

Breathing

Conscious, deliberate, slow deep breathing is an essential skill for learning ESO. Breathing is a good way to work through resistance. Concentrating on deep, regular breathing from the diaphragm, with the stomach rising and falling rather than just the chest, helps bring you back from thought to sensation, to attention to your body. It also helps because many people hold their breath when they're reaching for increased sexual arousal, tightening their muscles and reducing the oxygen supply to the body and the brain.

Breathing also helps because the breathing reflex is complex and many bodily systems involved in sexual arousal are interconnected with it. Breathing produces relaxation by changing the state of the body's autonomic nervous system. There's anxiety behind each and every one of your resistances, and relaxation reduces anxiety.

Testicle Elevations

These more advanced exercises are obviously for men. It isn't crucial to learn these techniques to achieve ESO, but they help. We'll address men directly in this section.

We said earlier that men can't ejaculate until their testicles are elevated close against their bodies. Cocking a gun is a good analogy. The gun won't go off unless the hammer is pulled back. Similarly, unless your testicles elevate, you don't ejaculate. If you learn to elevate and to lower your testicles voluntarily, you gain control over an important automatic function. That control increases your erection strength and degree of arousal. Alternatively, it delays ejaculation. Learning to delay ejaculation is a crucial part of learning male ESO.

Voluntary elevation of the testicles may seem difficult at first. It takes time to learn to identify the specific muscles involved. Initially you'll need to tighten all the lower abdominal muscles to raise your testicles. Later, with practice, you'll be able to raise them using only the appropriate pelvic muscles without tensing the abdominal muscles at all.

It's also difficult at first to feel the testicles moving up and down. Use a mirror to help you see what's happening. Even better, ring your scrotum above your testicles with thumb and middle finger and gently pull down. Then you'll be able to feel a slight movement of your testicles when you correctly contract and relax the internal muscles that control their elevation.

Once you locate the right muscles, practice raising and lowering your testicles until you can quickly do so one hundred times in succession. Practice this exercise either sitting at the edge of a chair or standing with your feet spaced about eighteen inches apart. Practice elevating your testicles both with and without an erection, while you are stimulating yourself and while you are being stimulated by your partner.

The scrotal pull technique, described later in this chapter, helps with ejaculatory control by using your or your partner's hand to gently pull down on the scrotum.

Physical Exercise

ESO is energetic, but it isn't strenuous. You don't have to be an athlete to learn it and to do it well. On the other hand, better physical conditioning will improve your ability to give your partner pleasure and to take pleasure yourself.

So, besides Kegel exercises and other specifically sexual exercises, we recommend that both men and women follow a regular program of at least moderate overall physical conditioning. Depending upon your age, your present condition, and your general health, such a program may include jogging, bicycling, walking, jumping rope, doing push-ups, sit-ups, calisthenics, group or individual exercise, or swimming.

If physical exercise is to be of any value to you, you must do it regularly—at least three times a week. But exercise sessions don't have to be long. Even five or ten minutes of moderate calisthenics or exercise against resistance can make a large difference in your physical stamina and sense of well-being within a month or two.

A study by James White of the University of California at San Diego compared middle-aged men who followed a prescribed exercise program three hours a week for nine months with a group of similar men who didn't exercise. The exercise group had significantly more sexual drive, arousal, and orgasms.

Note that upper-body exercises, particularly arm exercises that work the bicep and tricep muscles, can give a man more endurance for prolonged manual stimulation of his partner's clitoris and vagina. So, too, a woman in better physical condition will find it easier and more comfortable to stimulate her partner at length and vigorously.

You don't have to become a bodybuilder. You don't have to pump iron. But you'll feel better and have more pleasure sexually if you practice at least moderate physical conditioning for at least ninety minutes a week.

Self-Stimulation

Training in self-stimulation is a basic preparation for ESO. You may know self-stimulation by another name. The old medical term, derived from an obscure Latin word, is *masturbation*. Recognizing the value of this practice for promoting sexual improvement, the Taoists call it "self-cultivation."

Self-stimulation doesn't cause insanity, warts, acne, blindness, criminality, homosexuality, ulcers, epilepsy, addiction, or hairy palms. The Victorians thought that female self-stimulation was a disease, one they sometimes "cured," horribly, by surgically removing the clitoris. Equally mistakenly, the Victorians believed that each man had only a finite amount of semen and could "spend" himself to exhaustion and premature senility—a theory long since laid to rest. In fact, semen is a renewable resource. The more stimulation and the greater the number of ejaculations, the more total semen a man produces in his lifetime. The glands that contribute their fluids to the ejaculate, the prostate gland in particular, work much like the salivary glands. If no food is at hand, human beings produce less saliva. If no sexual stimulation is at hand, men produce less seminal fluid. It's true that the total number of sperm present in the body at birth as germ cells is finite. But sperm only accounts for about two percent of the ejaculate volume, and men start life with so many billions of sperm cells that they don't need to worry about running out.

In short, self-stimulation not only isn't bad for you, it can in fact be sexually beneficial in a variety of ways. It can help women learn how to achieve easier and better orgasms, and men, ejaculatory control. It's a major sexual

learning tool because it puts you completely in charge of
your stimulation. You can find out what feels good without
worrying about your partner at the same time. Even if you
have a good sexual relationship with a loving partner, you
will benefit from going back to basics, and so will he or she.

Some men and women feel strongly inhibited from self-
stimulation because of religious training. For discussion of
that problem, see "Religious Prohibitions," page 196, in
chapter 8, "Overcoming Resistances."

We treat clients with many different sexual problems.
Self-stimulation training is important to that treatment.
Even though our clients come to us for help, they often resist stimulating themselves when we advise it. Fear blocks
the way.

Bruce was a thirty-four-year-old salesman who complained he wasn't interested in sex. He drank too much
and spent too much time in bed—alone, unfortunately. He
didn't have a girlfriend. He didn't have many other friends
either. He hadn't self-stimulated in more than three years.

He protested the self-stimulation training we assigned
him. He said it was silly. We insisted. He didn't even have
to have an erection, we told him. He only had to self-stimulate thirty minutes a day, three days a week.

For two weeks Bruce complained that the self-stimulation wasn't working. When it didn't work, he said, he
stopped doing it: what was the point? That was Bruce's
way of sabotaging his progress, but we continued to insist
that he follow our program and report his accomplishments.

Three weeks in, Bruce began having erections with self-
stimulation. We suggested Kegel exercises, encouraged
him to talk about his fantasies, and taught him ways to
relax. By the seventh week of treatment he was self-stimulating to orgasm every day. He was drinking less. His energy was returning.

Bruce stopped therapy after three months. By then he

was having successful sexual encounters with women. He returned two months later with a girlfriend he was serious about. He wanted to learn ESO. Five months before, Bruce had claimed he didn't even think about sex. Self-stimulation training precipitated the dramatic change.

Anna, the forty-seven-year-old wife of a computer company executive, had an equally dramatic success with self-stimulation. Her husband, Gary, convinced her to see us after a suicide gesture (she'd taken several sleeping pills, but not a lethal dose). We learned that she had suffered periodic depressions for many years that long-term psychotherapy had only marginally improved and that antidepressant drugs didn't budge. We also learned that she had never been orgasmic and didn't practice self-stimulation. She and Gary made love several times a month, two or three minutes at a time.

Anna thought very little of herself. We worked to improve her self-esteem. We also started her self-stimulating. Like Bruce, but for different reasons, she resisted. Bruce was afraid of failing. Anna didn't like herself. We asked her to begin simply by looking at herself in a mirror and finding her good points. We asked her to start a program of Kegel exercises.

Eventually Anna learned to have orgasm with self-stimulation, using her hand. "I never thought I could," she told us. "I'm actually beginning to look forward to my private sex time."

Self-stimulation was only a beginning for Anna and Gary. We worked with both of them to help them learn longer and more pleasurable lovemaking. Five months after starting therapy, Anna was no longer depressed. She is now reliably orgasmic with intercourse and with oral and manual stimulation. She occasionally self-stimulates to orgasm. She and Gary make love once or twice a week, and sometimes Anna initiates that lovemaking. We noticed especially an outward change that mirrored Anna's inward improvement. Before therapy, she wore dark colors and matronly clothes. Now she dresses stylishly in colors as cheerful as she has come to feel.

Taking Pleasure for Yourself

Once you decide to begin ESO training, plan to set aside at least the first two weeks of additional time for concentrating on self-stimulation. During that time you may also continue lovemaking with your partner. You may need to devote more than two weeks to self-stimulation exercises, depending on what you learn about your response. If so, continue your usual lovemaking through that period as well.

Three times during these first two weeks, set aside at least thirty minutes of private time—not secret, private— for self-stimulation. Let your partner know, but spend this time alone. Your purpose is to learn to give yourself pleasure or to improve your skills. Then you'll know how to teach your partner.

Pamper yourself. Take a sensuous shower or bath and notice the pleasant feeling of warm water on your skin. Afterward spend some time looking at your body and appreciating its good features. Be as positive and friendly with yourself as you try to be with your partner when you're creating a mood of romance.

Touch your body. Explore it for pleasure—kneading muscles, massaging scalp, caressing skin. Men especially may feel embarrassed caressing themselves. Do it anyway to learn what feels good, even if you think you already know. Many men are almost entirely focused on genital stimulation. They can increase their levels of pleasure enormously by widening their focus to include their entire bodies—scalp, head, face, neck, arms, hands, nipples, chest, back, belly, buttocks, thighs, calves, and feet.

At some point during this time of touching and self-exploration, move to a comfortable place where you can sit or lie down—on a chair, on pillows on the floor, or lying in bed. When you've touched your body for pleasure for at least five minutes, start to explore your genitals. Even if you're familiar with self-stimulation, approach your genitals as if you're doing so for the first time. Don't fall immediately into a practiced pattern. Really *notice* what you're doing, what you're discovering, and how it feels.

After a while, add lubrication and notice the difference between dry stimulation and stimulation with a lubricant.

Now we'll discuss men and women separately. However, both of you should read both discussions.

Self-Stimulation for Men

BASIC TECHNIQUES

The basic requirements for effective self-stimulation are (1) ample time, (2) PC and pelvic muscle strengthening and control, and (3) paying attention to sensation.

Begin, then, by lubricating not only your penis but also your scrotum and perineum. (If you're uncomfortable using a lubricant, see "Lubrication," page 257.) Now proceed to stimulate yourself to erection. If this is difficult, try forming a ring with the thumb and index finger of your left hand wrapped as tightly as you find comfortable around the base of your penis while you stimulate the shaft and glans with your right hand. Erection rings of rubber or other materials are sold for this purpose. Some erection rings work better than others. Those for the medical market are available in various sizes and work best (see "Products and Where to Find Them," page 269). If you are unable to achieve at least a moderate erection despite allowing yourself relaxed time, using a lubricant and incor-

porating visually stimulating materials—and especially if
you also do not have early-morning sleep erections—you
may have a physical problem and may wish to consult a
physician. (See also "Sexual Problems," page 221.)

Once you stimulate yourself to erection, see if you can
keep that erection with self-stimulation and without ejaculation for at least thirty minutes. You are aiming to maintain a stage 3 erection—full, but not the maximal
throbbing erection of stage 4, ready to explode. During
that thirty minutes, see if you can bring yourself close to
orgasm at least six times. Stop your stroking or reduce
speed and pressure each time you near the "point of no return" (ejaculatory inevitability). The process of repeatedly
stopping stimulation for ten or more seconds and then re-
suming stimulation is called "peaking."

If at any time you lose control and ejaculate, enjoy the
orgasm, wait awhile, then begin stimulation again. You'll
find control easier with sexual tension reduced.

If you're used to quick self-stimulation, you may find
that sustaining an erection without orgasm for thirty minutes is difficult at first. You may want to start with only
that goal. Then at later sessions add progressively more
near-orgasm peaks during the thirty minutes.

Experiment with different kinds of strokes. Most men
stimulate themselves with a basic up-and-down stroke of
one hand. Some men stimulate themselves by rolling
their penis in two hands. Your hand can be turned
thumb-up or thumb-down; you can make a ring of your
thumb and forefinger; you can concentrate stimulation on
the shaft or the glans; you can use both hands and stroke
from mid-shaft outward in both directions at once, toward the glans and toward the base; you can press your
penis against your belly and rub its underside with the
flat of your palm; you can change hands; and these are
only a few of the many possible variations. Each time you
stimulate yourself is a new experience, because you have

added your previous experience to the total of what you know and feel. Your goal is not to ejaculate but to *feel more*—to enjoy the process. If you pay attention to sensation, you won't be bored. Boredom is a form of resistance. If self-stimulation is boring, see chapter 8, "Overcoming Resistances."

We once treated an athletic young man named Patrick who stimulated himself by hanging from a chinning bar and banging his erect penis against a door frame. Having conditioned himself to such violent sensations, Patrick wasn't able to enjoy orgasm any other way. That didn't bother him so long as he was unattached, but then he met a girl. Jenny wasn't anything at all like a door frame. Patrick and Jenny had a problem. We helped them solve it by developing a program of gradual deconditioning. Patrick went back to subtler sensations. First we instructed him to use his own hands vigorously and have an ejaculation. Then Jenny added her hand to his. Then he learned to have orgasm and ejaculate with the stimulation of Jenny's hands alone. Then Patrick learned to insert himself into Jenny's vagina just before ejaculation. Before long he was able to enjoy normal intercourse.

When you have achieved hard erection and sustained it for at least five minutes, continue stroking your penis while stimulating your external prostate spot and controlling ejaculation with the scrotal pull technique, which we will explain shortly.

Prostate stimulation involves pressing upward firmly on the perineum, between the anus and the back of the scrotum, with one or more fingers. See illustration 2, "Male Anatomy," page 44. You may not be familiar with the sensation. Explore it with an open mind. The first stage of orgasm, the emission phase, involves automatic contractions of the prostate. Firm, rhythmic pressure on the prostate, even from outside the body, partly duplicates these sensations of first-stage orgasm. But because you aren't stimulating the ejaculatory reflex, the orgasmic contractions proceed without ejaculation.

If you find it awkward to stimulate your external prostate spot with your left hand (assuming you are right-handed and have been using your dominant hand to stimulate your penis), switch hands and stroke your penis with your left hand while you search out and rhythmically press your external prostate spot with your right. Because this spot is located behind the base of the penis, which is buried inside the body, pressing on it firmly pushes extra blood into your penis, which then should swell and pleasurably throb.

When you find yourself approaching orgasm, one good way to control ejaculation is simply to stop stroking. Use this "stop-start" method first to see how it works. Alternatively, you can press firmly on the external prostate spot, which can help reduce the ejaculatory reflex and which many men also find pleasurable.

Still another way to achieve ejaculatory control is scrotal pulling. Pulling your testicles away from your body prevents you from ejaculating. Try it.

To apply the scrotal pull, grasp the scrotum above your testicles with the thumb and forefinger of your left hand. When you're near orgasm, pull firmly down. It is not painful as you are squeezing the scrotal sac *above* the testicles, not the testicles themselves. Also, you are applying *gradual* pressure. At other times, for stimulation, pull lightly in rhythm as you stroke. Become thoroughly familiar with the scrotal pull (see illustration 11 on page 149 for a partner-assisted version of the scrotal pull). You'll need to teach it to your partner for ESO.

We sometimes have a man use an adjustable cloth or leather snap ring around his scrotum above his testicles to help him learn the effects of scrotal pulling. Such a ring applies constant pressure, which many men find arousing, and can aid in controlling ejaculation. It should never be adjusted so tightly that it cuts off circulation completely. After thirty to forty-five minutes, loosen the ring. (See "Products and Where to Find Them," page 269.)

As part of your self-stimulation exercises, you should practice voluntary testicle elevation and lowering, which we discussed earlier. Nearing ejaculation, deliberately relax the muscles that hold your testicles close to your body and notice the effect. You may find the muscular control difficult at first, and the effect may seem too subtle to notice. Keep practicing. After the ejaculatory urge has subsided somewhat, resume stimulating your penis with your hand and at the same time deliberately elevate your testicles. Notice the subtle effect of increasing arousal.

Put it all together with the Whole Penis Stimulation exercise. Use your dominant hand to stroke your penis head and shaft. Your lower hand massages the entire buried penile shaft and the deeper area behind it, the external prostate spot. The basic stroke is a milking action from back to front, resulting in maximum engorgement.

When you've trained yourself to maintain hard, pleasurable erection without orgasm for at least fifteen minutes, go on to half an hour. Once you can sustain erection for thirty minutes without ejaculating, you will be able to sustain it for as long as you want. Thirty minutes is a necessary minimum to build up the muscular tension and vasocongestion that is essential for ESO. (If you have trouble delaying ejaculation, see "Early Ejaculation," page 233.)

It may take you longer than two weeks to learn how to prolong erection without ejaculation. If so, continue self-stimulation exercises until you do before going on to ESO training with your partner. *At minimum you should be able to delay ejaculation with self-stimulation for at least thirty minutes before you begin ESO training with your partner.* If you haven't learned to maintain ejaculatory control yourself, how can you teach someone else to do it for you?

Devices

Using a vibrator is another good form of stimulation to add. A convenient method is to grasp the base of your penis with your left forefinger and thumb, palm cupping your scrotum and middle finger on your external prostate spot. Holding the vibrator in your right hand, place the vibrator head on the underside of the head of your penis, sandwiching the penis against the back of your left hand. (We know this sounds contortionist. It's easier to do than to describe. Try it. You'll see how everything arranges itself.) Vibrators can also be very effective for applying stimulation externally to the prostate. (For further discussion, see "Vibrators," page 266.)

Various kinds of self-stimulation devices, some with built-in vibrators, are available. For men interested in high-tech equipment, an automated, adjustable stroking sleeve called Venus II is the most sophisticated. (See "Products and Where to Find Them," page 269.)

If you usually use erotic media—magazines, the Internet, videotapes—during self-stimulation, continue to do so now. If you've never done so, you may want to try, to see if they add to arousal.

You may not notice any improvement in your sexual experience the first time you add something new. You need time to become comfortable with new procedures, new sensations, and new props. If you find a vibrator disappointing the first time you use it, for instance, don't give it up. Try it again—try it several more times—experimenting with it at leisure before you pass judgment on its value.

Occasionally, when you've stimulated yourself to a high

level of arousal, wipe the lubricant off the head of your penis and see if you're secreting clear fluid. Male ESO is marked by such secretions, sometimes in considerable volume—a teaspoon or more. If you produce a few drops during self-stimulation, then you can judge that you're near the beginning of ESO. Notice what you did to get there. Note that while it's possible to learn ESO solo, it's easier with a motivated, committed partner.

ADVANCED TECHNIQUES

1. *Erection exercises.* Sit on the edge of a chair with your legs spread apart. While you are fully erect, locate the muscles that make your penis throb—that is, that make it get fuller. Locate the muscles that make your penis move up and down, side to side, and back and forth.

Practice moving your penis in these different directions. Practice with your knees together. Practice while squatting and while lying down on your back. You've already begun exercising the muscles involved in making your penis move. They're the PC muscles, the abdominal muscles, the buttocks, and the thighs. Notice the effects that contracting single sets and combinations of these muscles have on your penis's movement and on your sensations of pleasure.

Practicing these exercises will increase the strength and hardness of your erection. You can develop further strength by hanging a towel on your erect penis and lifting it. Start with a small face towel and work up to larger, heavier bath towels.

These exercises not only develop extra muscle strength, but also increase the supply of blood to your genitals.

2. *Repeated ejaculation.* Stimulate yourself without ejaculation for thirty minutes, reward yourself with ejaculation,

but then immediately resume stimulating your penis. Strongly contract your sex muscles and focus intently on your genital sensations. Instead of becoming soft, your penis will remain relatively hard. As you continue stimulating it, it will gradually become more erect. You may need to increase the amount of stimulation significantly the second time. Be sure to provide vigorous stimulation and milking pressure to your external prostate spot and penile bulb.

Continue to stimulate yourself for at least another ten minutes. You may experience another ejaculation, with the volume of your ejaculate somewhat reduced. Each time you approach ejaculation, instead of distracting yourself by thinking of other things, pay attention to your penis and to the sensations in your genitals.

3. *Non-emission ejaculation: seminal fluid retention (holding it in).* This exercise is a variation of the repeated-ejaculation exercise. Stimulate yourself without ejaculation for thirty minutes, then increase stimulation. When you feel yourself just beginning to ejaculate, stop stimulating your penis with your right hand but press hard on your external prostate spot with your left hand. Hold your breath. Squeeze your PC muscles and your other sexual muscles as tightly as you can. Your goal is to stop completely the ejaculatory fluid from squirting out. If you have trained your PC and other sexual muscles, you'll discover that you can retain most of your ejaculate. Surprisingly, though, your orgasm will continue and may even feel stronger.

After your contractions have ceased, resume stimulating yourself. Your erection will probably continue and your arousal will return to a high level. Since you have retained most of your semen, you probably won't have to wait as long as usual before you can have another ejaculation. You may find you can ejaculate again within several minutes. When you decide on a final ejaculation, let go of all tension as completely as you can. Relax or push out your sex muscles. Breathe deeply, emphasizing exhaling completely. Your second ejaculation may be as strong as or stronger than your first.

Notice the amount of fluid you produce in each modified ejaculation. Count the number of internal contractions you experience each time. The initial contractions are the strongest; subsequent contractions are more subtle but should be included in your count. Compare the number of contractions in your usual orgasm with the number of contractions you experience during these modified procedures.

As you strengthen your sexual muscles and develop control, you may be able to enjoy three or more—possibly even up to ten—separate and distinct orgasms with ejaculation during a single session of self-stimulating. Since you reestablish muscular and vascular tension almost immediately after each modified ejaculation, the cumulative effect is additive: each ejaculation feels a little stronger than the one before. You certainly don't have to try for ten, by the way. Whenever you think you're ready for the final big orgasm, simply let go and enjoy it without holding back any semen.

4. *Stretching orgasm.* After you've practiced your Kegel and other sexual-muscle exercises for three to four weeks, you'll be ready to begin stretching your orgasms.

Notice how many contractions you feel during a usual ejaculation—normally between three and eight. Once your muscles are toned, you should be able at least to double that number and to reverse their order of intensity. Instead of the strongest contractions coming at the beginning, you can learn to space them further apart and to save the best for the end.

Begin as you began the two preceding exercises, with thirty minutes of stimulation. This time, however, as you

approach ejaculation, tighten your muscles as you did to
hold your ejaculate in, but instead of completely stopping
all stimulation, continue stimulating your penis very
slowly throughout ejaculation, pushing the sensation on
and on, stretching it out for as long as you can sustain it.
Allow the sensations in your genitals to expand outward to
all parts of your body.

Self-Stimulation for Women

BASIC TECHNIQUES

As a woman, you need to realize first of all that self-
stimulation is good for you. It's not a substitute but a supplement. It's healthy. It feels good. It allows you to learn
how you like to be pleasured so that you can teach your
partner. Best of all, it adds to your orgasmic capacity. The
more orgasms you experience, the more you can have.

*Every healthy human female is potentially multi-
orgasmic and is potentially capable of learning to experience ESO.* That's your birthright. Why shouldn't you claim
it? And the most reliable preparation for ESO is self-stimulation.

Your goal during this preliminary two weeks or more of
self-stimulation is different from a man's. He's discovering
what feels good and how to spread arousal throughout his
body. He's also learning to delay orgasm—learning how to
hold back. You're discovering what feels good. But you're
also learning to *have* orgasm—learning how to let go. Most
nonorgasmic women can learn to have orgasms with a
partner. It helps if they are willing to train themselves to
have an orgasm with self-stimulation first and then teach
an attentive, willing partner how they like to do it. If you
already know how to have orgasm reliably with self-stimu-

lation, you're learning to extend your capacity, to have several orgasms in a row.

When you've touched your body for pleasure, then, and begun genital exploration, lubricate yourself thoroughly. (If you're uncomfortable using a lubricant, see "Lubrication," page 257.) Lubricate your major and minor labia, your clitoris, the opening into your vagina, and even a little inside. Lubricate your perineum—the valley of skin between the lower margin of your labia and your anus.

Begin to explore the touch and the stroking you like. First find areas of your genitals that feel good to touch. Then begin touching and stroking those areas for arousal.

If you aren't used to self-stimulation, you may want to pleasure yourself for one or more sessions without trying to achieve orgasm. Later, when you feel you're ready, you can go all the way.

If you're used to self-stimulation, you might spend some time exploring new strokes and touches and pressures. Then go on through orgasm and see if you can give yourself several orgasms in a row. Allow yourself to have any fantasies that you find exciting.

The object of these self-stimulation exercises is to bring yourself to the point where you can have several orgasms on your own, using only your hands. When you reach that point, you're ready to go on to ESO training with your partner. It may well take more than two weeks. That's fine. You need to learn how to pleasure yourself so you can teach your partner.

Many women today have taught themselves to have orgasm with a vibrator. Vibrators are a godsend, especially in learning about orgasm for the first time, but you can ultimately get more pleasure without a vibrator than with one. If you only self-stimulate with a vibrator, use this preliminary time period to teach yourself to have orgasm by hand.

If you find that you can't achieve orgasm using only your hands, you've encountered a resistance. The way through the resistance is by deconditioning. Give yourself one or more orgasms using your vibrator. Then put it aside and continue to have more orgasms with your hands. At later sessions, put the vibrator aside just before orgasm and use your hands for orgasm itself. Eventually you should be able to stimulate yourself to orgasm without the vibrator. You may still want to use it at other times as a variation you enjoy.

When you can stimulate yourself by hand to several orgasms, then you're ready to begin training with your partner for ESO. (If you are unable to have orgasm with self-stimulation, see "Preorgasmia," page 238.)

ADVANCED TECHNIQUES

1. *Clitoral stimulation.* Women don't need to worry about delaying orgasm, of course; their aim can be to improve the ease, intensity, number, and duration of their orgasms. Breathing, bearing down, pushing out, and pressing the clitoris against the pubic bone without moving your hands or body during orgasm can extend orgasmic contractions by a minute or more. The main problem women will face in learning to extend orgasm is mental resistances; to deal with those, review our discussion of that problem beginning on page 119. This is where the skills you've learned doing 20–0 Countdowns (see page 53) come in; the better you are at concentration, the more success you'll have with directing your thoughts where you want them and countering intrusive thoughts.

Often one area of the clitoris is somewhat more sensitive and responsive than another. Discover if this is true for you by first stimulating one side, pausing for a few seconds to allow arousal to drop a bit, and then stimulating the other side with the same number of strokes and approximately the same pressure and in the same location.

For instance, stimulate the right side of the shaft of your clitoris with your right forefinger, up and down at about one stroke per second for thirty seconds, then pause for ten or fifteen seconds and stimulate the other side of the clitoris with the same finger at the same rate and same pressure for thirty strokes. Notice which type of stimulation felt better. If you aren't sure, repeat the process several times.

Hold the shaft of your clitoris between your index and middle fingers and rub up and down and from side to side at about one stroke per second. Vary the rate and pressure of this up-and-down movement, noticing what effect it has on your arousal. You need to become an expert on the subtlety and great variety of methods of stroking and stimulating your clitoris.

Now try using a circular motion on your clitoris, applying firm pressure with your index and middle fingers over the entire clitoral area as if you're massaging a muscle under the skin. Circle one way, clockwise, and then the opposite way. Start with a rate of about one cycle per second for at least fifteen seconds, and then change direction. Experiment with faster and slower stroking. You may want to increase the rate of your stroking to two or possibly three strokes per second. It's possible to move your hand very rapidly for short distances. Often the alternation of very fast with very slow and very firm with very light strokes, both in predictable and in teasing, unpredictable patterns, can be an effective way of rapidly increasing your arousal levels.

Try another method. Place two or three fingers over your clitoral area and vibrate your hand as fast as you can, as if you were duplicating a vibrator at slow speed for a short period of time. Also try brushing your fingers rapidly side to side across your clitoris. Remember that the more effectively you can learn to stimulate yourself, the better able you will be to teach a partner to do the same. The more you understand the subtleties of stroking and the variety of methods, the better able you will be to train a man to do the same or even better. Men are likely to be more receptive to learning how to stimulate you if you can analyze some of the basic components, such as the different types of clitoral strokes, and break down the learning process into separate steps. After some practice, the separate steps can be combined into a smooth, flowing, spontaneous process, and you both benefit.

Be sure to experiment with fantasy. Many women require more mental stimulation than men (hence their need for romance and foreplay). Read sexually arousing material as you stimulate yourself or imagine yourself a scriptwriter. Create a sexual scenario in words and pictures. Try several different fantasies as you stimulate yourself with predictable, steady rhythm. As your mental story increases in excitement, speed up your stimulation to match it. Stretch out your fantasy to allow sexual tension to build. Avoid culminating your fantasy too quickly. Physical stimulation should keep pace with your mental images, increasing muscle tension in the genital region.

Practice a complete set of your three sex muscle/breathing exercises at the same time you stimulate your clitoris. Use a relatively steady clitoral stroke pattern to allow you to observe the effects of repetitively contracting and relaxing, pushing out separately and also in synchrony with breathing.

After about thirty minutes of stimulating yourself in this way, reward yourself with an orgasm. Deliberately try to stretch it out in time and intensity. You don't have to leave better orgasms to chance. Stop moving your hand as you slide down the other side of orgasm, cup your hand and press it firmly against your clitoris and pubic bone. Remember to breathe and do deliberate push-outs. Eventually, as your knowledge of this process improves, you'll be able to teach and guide your partner to providing the most effective strokes, pressure, and timing, while you supply the fantasy.

2. *Discovering your G-spot area.* Stimulating your G-spot area yourself using your hand alone requires considerable dexterity. Not all women will want or need to do so. If you're adventurous, it's much easier to explore G-spot stimulation with a device constructed for this purpose that extends your reach. Dildos with a curved head, with or without batteries, are useful. A product called the Crystal Wand is elegant and easy to use. "G Spotter" attachments for plug-in vibrators are available. (See "Products and Where to Find Them," page 269.)

Once you have obtained a G-spot stimulator, experiment with using it just before, during, and after your clitoral orgasm. Try stimulating your G-spot area while you simultaneously stimulate your clitoris. Also stimulate your G-spot area without clitoral stimulation. What areas do you most like stimulated? What are your favorite sequences and types of pressure?

Deliberately push out your PC muscles and breathe deeply while you stimulate your G spot. Making *aaaaaH-HHHaaaa* sounds with your mouth open may help to increase sensation.

Mirroring Your Partner

After you've both learned effective self-stimulation, you should move on to sexual communication. You each need to learn how the other likes to be pleasured. The way to do that is first to watch each other and then to teach each other.

We'd suggest you spend at least one session taking turns watching each other self-stimulate. Watch without touching. You can talk or ask questions if you like, but not help.

Then, at the next session, you should take turns mimicking exactly what you saw the other do. Keep that up in additional sessions until you can effectively stimulate your partner, letting your partner be the judge. That may take one session. It may take five or ten. You want to learn at least to equal what your partner can do alone—to equal, at minimum, the best your partner can do with self-stimulation.

This training is instruction. You should each tell each other what's happening and if it's being done right. Guide your partner's hands. Be assertive if you're the one teaching and be accepting if you're the one being taught. Leave anger out of it. Drop your ego. Your partner is the expert, the teacher; you're the novice, the student.

People who have known each other for years, long-married couples, may feel their egos bruising when they accept the student position. They may be surprised to learn that they haven't known what their partners really enjoy. Take the lesson for what it is—a chance to give and receive more pleasure than you were giving and receiving before. You'll be loved that much more for accepting the emotional discomfort.

We saw that result with our clients Chris and Myrna, husband and wife for twenty-five years. Chris was a rugged, silent man, a restaurant owner who worked hard. Myrna had to drag him in to see us. He wasn't interested in sex, she said. Chris admitted it. He had trouble achieving erection. "I don't feel like a man," he told us. When they were younger they'd made love two or three times a week; they'd found affection, trust, and friendship together. Now that closeness was fading. Chris accepted the change silently, but Myrna missed what they had shared.

There was hidden anger between Chris and Myrna. There were communication problems, and an escape into work made easier by the challenge of operating their own business. We concentrated on those problems. But we also helped Chris and Myrna learn to pleasure each other. That's where the surprises came. Chris discovered that Myrna was much happier and more responsive when he was gentle with her—when he massaged her and stroked her for long, pleasant minutes before initiating intercourse. Myrna discovered that Chris sometimes wished for oral sex but was too inhibited to ask.

They learned and changed. They're much closer now than they were. Chris has strong erections that he sustains in lovemaking for up to half an hour. Myrna is sometimes able to extend orgasm. Their major limiting factor is time—that restaurant still makes its demands.

Men who feel they should automatically know how to stimulate a woman might remember that women don't automatically know how to stimulate them. Neither sex is born with magic fingers or magic organs. Both have to learn by observation or by being taught. Direct teaching is best.

After each practice session of watching your partner self-stimulate and then mirroring what you saw, talk about what you experienced and what you learned. Say what you liked about watching each other. Say what surprised you. Say what you didn't like and would do differently next time. *Spend at least five minutes after each session debriefing.* That can be painful, too, but it's crucially important. Talk about your feelings. Use the Appreciations and Resentments exercise we describe in the next chapter.

When you know sexual anatomy, when you're regularly doing Kegel exercises, when you've learned well how to pleasure yourselves and each other, and when you can easily communicate your sexual feelings, you may be ready to get together for ESO.

In the section on communicating, in chapter 10, "Solving Problems," we describe more structures for teaching each other pleasure. Look at "Getting to Know You"(page 251) and "Pleasure Turns"(page 252). "An Hour of Pleasure"(page 252) and "Sensory Focus"(page 253) can also be useful and fun.

4
Getting Together

Talking About Feelings

By now you should know yourself and your partner better than you did before you began reading this book. Simple exercises and physical exploration reach beyond the physical into the emotional. We'd be surprised if you haven't discovered strong feelings about some of what you've learned.

We hope you have. We hope you've talked about them. And we hope talking hasn't deteriorated into argument. It's easy, especially where sex is concerned, to hurt each other's feelings. It's easy to misunderstand. We advise couples we work with to practice a daily communication exercise that helps clear the air. We recommend it equally to you. You may find yourselves resisting it at first, for the usual reason: because it can feel silly. But it's a good basic format for communicating. Many of our client couples tell us that communication exercises soon become second nature to them, part of their normal, day-to-day conversation.

Appreciations and Resentments

RATIONALE

This exercise is one of the most important in the ESO program! Read it several times. When you begin communicating in this safe, structured way, your relationship is likely to improve. Ask your partner's agreement to do the exercise and start doing it immediately, every day, even if you "don't have time," even if "it seems silly," even if you "can't think of anything to say."

Expressing yourself to your partner is not the same as communicating with your partner. Communication requires feedback—communication in return—or at least acknowledgment of receipt. Merely talking to your partner doesn't mean that he/she understands you or agrees with you or even that he/she heard what you said. When attention is focused elsewhere, a person simply may not be processing what you're saying. Even if the words are being processed, your intent might not be clearly understood. An essential first step in communication is determining if you have your partner's attention. That means that when you start a communication process, your partner needs to give an observable indication of listening early in the process. Similarly, your partner needs to acknowledge at the conclusion of the communication process that he/she heard and understands what you said.

To help you communicate more effectively, we offer here an exercise designed to foster good communication. *Appreciations* and *resentments* are little thoughts and feelings that too often in a relationship remain unspoken, or are spoken in such a way that your partner filters them out. From doubt or fear or simply from preoccupation with other activities, we hold many feelings inside us, frequently delaying expressing them past the time when doing so would be appropriate.

You may think in the morning, "Jane is certainly considerate, marshaling the kids off to school while I enjoy the morning paper." But you may not tell your partner how much you appreciate those few quiet minutes to yourself that she makes possible.

Or you may think, "I hate the way Don flirts at parties." But to avoid starting an argument, you may avoid telling your partner of the hurt you feel and what specific behavior initiated that feeling.

The Appreciations and Resentments exercise is one of the most important exercises in this book. You have to like each other and be able to talk to each other if you're going to enjoy adequate lovemaking regularly and for the long term. Appreciations and Resentments is a safe way we've devised to allow you to share information that you would like your partner to know.

Some of that information will be uncomfortable to share and to hear. But if it exists in your partner's mind, it's part of reality, and it's better to know that reality. Unspoken, it will accumulate in a mental file labeled "Negative experiences of my partner," and when that file is loaded, some otherwise innocuous act will set it off. Then you'll find out about all the contents of the file, all at once, in a manner that's likely to be considerably more uncomfortable than if you'd learned of it in smaller segments as the feelings occurred. Generally speaking, what you don't know about your partner's feelings is more damaging to a relationship than what you do know. Knowledge, even of negative conditions, can at least be worked with and usually worked through.

Some of the information you'll be sharing—expressions of appreciation you may not have made before or often enough—will give you pleasure. No one tires of being appreciated. Everyone likes approval and honest compliments. Six months ago you may have told your partner how much you enjoy her sense of humor or how much you admire his strength, but all of us love to hear those things more often. In the beginning, when you were dating, you complimented one another a lot, didn't you? Appreciation warmly, honestly, and openly expressed binds a relationship together, and we never really outgrow our need for it.

Resentments can be harder to express, but unexpressed, they fester. They accumulate into major arguments. They sabotage agreement and poison trust. They need to be communicated regularly and honestly so that your partner knows how you feel. No one can read your mind. You have to communicate to be understood. The Appreciations and Resentments exercise encourages that communication by enforcing regularity and providing a context designed deliberately to be as neutral as possible.

In therapy we find that many couples resist practicing this exercise. It requires discipline and hard work. It may open what looks at first to be a can of worms. But if there are worms, they need to be looked at; otherwise, they'll grow and become even more unattractive and difficult to deal with later. Based on our extensive experience as counselors, we assure you that you will find it extremely difficult to improve your sexual relationship unless you improve communication across your entire relationship. You can expect such improvements if you practice Appreciations and Resentments. Doing this exercise exactly as described, without any deviation—*ever*—is like having a therapist on hand to help you full-time.

THE COMMUNICATION EXERCISE

The Script

Appreciation:
You say: "[Your partner's name], there's something I'd like to tell you."

Your partner responds: "Okay, I'm listening."
You state an appreciation.
Your partner responds: "Thank you."

Resentment:
You say: "[Your partner's name], there's something I'd like to tell you."
Your partner responds: "Okay, I'm listening."
You state a resentment.
Your partner responds: "Thank you."

An appreciation must include:
Objective report—a brief, factual description about the matter or situation:

a. when it occurred;
b. what you observed and/or heard, i.e., your perceptions;
c. your positive feelings.

A resentment must include:
Objective report—a short, specific, factual description about the matter or situation:

a. when it occurred;
b. what you observed and/or heard, i.e., your perceptions;
c. your negative feelings;
d. how you would have preferred your partner to have acted or how the situation might have been handled differently or better.

If you want to discuss any appreciations or resentments you must wait at least thirty minutes and then ask your partner for explicit agreement to do so. You may not circumvent this rule by expressing an appreciation or resentment on a subject or situation about which your partner has expressed one within the past twenty-four hours.

Face your partner. Make and keep eye contact. Avoid excessive body movements and facial expressions, such as rolling your eyes, sighing, grimacing, shaking your head.

Use "I" statements about your feelings rather than "you" statements. Avoid using the words "always" and "never." Make only statements: don't ask questions. Be specific and brief.

Use a neutral tone of voice. Avoid detectable emotions such as anger, judgment, or sarcasm. Feelings should be conveyed only by the words themselves.

Beltline rule: Some issues are intrinsically unresolvable or destructive to verbalize. If you discover such an issue, agree to avoid bringing it up.

Follow this format and these rules exactly, with no deviations.

Subject matter should start, preferably, with current concerns: things that happened today, yesterday, or within the last week. You may, however, bring up matters from any time in the past (unless they fall under the "beltline rule" you have both agreed to). Or you may choose to mention a general pattern you've observed in your partner. It's preferable, but not essential, that a particular resentment have some connection with, or relationship to, the preceding appreciation.

Here's an example of a complete round of Appreciations and Resentments.

You might begin by mentioning small things:
You say: "Susan, there's something I'd like to tell you."
"Okay, I'm listening."
"When we were watching TV last night, you were playful

and a little silly. You were fun, and I love it when you show that positive, emotional side."

"Thank you."

That's an appreciation. Follow it with a resentment:

"Susan, there's something I'd like to tell you."

"Okay, I'm listening."

"This evening I was late and forgot to stop at the grocery store. You attacked me with accusations of never listening to you, being lazy, selfish, and acting like my father. You raised your voice and you brought up three or four situations from the past that had nothing to do with getting the groceries. The more I tried to reason with you, the angrier you became. When negative emotion controls you, I close off and nothing gets accomplished. I felt you were being unfair, emotional, and illogical. What I'd like you to be willing to do in the future when you're feeling upset is to tell me in a more logical way and stick to the subject."

"Thank you."

More general problems can be good subjects for Appreciations and Resentments:

"Tom, there's something I'd like to tell you."

"Okay, I'm listening."

"Yesterday we went to your parents' house for the holiday. I like your parents and enjoy being with them and with you."

"Thank you."

"Tom, there's something I'd like to tell you."

"Okay, I'm listening."

"When we spent the entire holiday with your family, I felt my family was left out. They've told me more than once that they'd like us to spend more holiday time with them. I felt disappointed and annoyed with you for not arranging more fairly to distribute the holidays between our families. I'd like you to be willing to alternate or split those days more equally in the future. I'd like to discuss this problem at our business meeting next week."

"Thank you."

Resentments may include things you've observed, things you've heard, feelings you've felt, things you would prefer had happened differently. Be sure to state your appreciations and resentments in a *neutral,* not an emotional, angry, nagging, or sarcastic tone of voice. Express your emotions in words, not in nuances. That way your partner will hear the *content* of your message clearly and won't be distracted by the tone.

An important guideline for the resentments part of the exercise is to use "I" statements when you're describing your feelings, rather than "you" statements. Stick to talking about a behavior you didn't like, rather than condemning your partner's entire personality. Rather than stating, "You're a stupid idiot," say, "When you sped through that stop light, I was shocked at your poor judgment." Avoid the words "always" and "never." An example of a resentment pattern to avoid is: "You *never* put the top back on the toothpaste tube." Such statements will immediately put your partner on the defensive and will probably start an argument. He may rebut with times he has capped the tube and attack you for some irritating habit of your own.

Don't hit below the belt. For example: "I resented having to give up my education so that you could attend law school." "I've never felt the same about you since I found out about your affair with X." However you feel about such resentments, if you have agreed despite your feelings to do the Appreciations and Resentments exercise, then you should avoid bringing them up in that context. If your relationship is to be healthy, such questions will someday have to be resolved. A structured exercise isn't the time, though the increased trust and intimacy this form of communication engenders may make it possible to confront them at a later time.

You may, however, bring up issues that allow some possibility of improvement and do not carry with them purely destructive connotations:

"Bob, there's something I'd like to tell you."

"Okay, I'm listening."

"The party tonight was certainly lively. That new couple we met might be fun to see again. I was glad you encouraged us to go."

"Thank you."

"Bob, there's something I'd like to tell you."

"Okay, I'm listening."

"At the party you were talking to that cute blonde on the patio for a long time. When I came over, you seemed to ignore me and continued talking to her without including me. In the future in a situation like that I'd like to have you put your arm around me or take my hand, introduce me, and include me in the conversation."

"Thank you."

The point of Appreciations and Resentments is safe communication. It's safe because you've agreed in advance to listen and to acknowledge but not to argue. It also builds trust. We've seen too many couples communicate only their resentments. They hardly ever compliment each other.

Choose a neutral time to practice the Appreciations and Resentments exercise. Schedule a specific time of day and stick to it. Working couples often discover that after dinner is a comfortable time for them to practice Appreciations and Resentments. But any time of day that's mutually acceptable will do. We suggest you schedule at least two complete rounds a day, every day. They'll take about five

minutes each for a total of ten minutes per day, seventy
minutes per week.

Appreciations and Resentments often brings up important and powerful subject matter that merits further discussion. To preserve the emotional safety and trust that go
along with communicating in this structured way and to
allow the exercise to become a "safety valve" for the
stresses your relationship inevitably experiences, you and
your partner must agree to delay that further discussion. If
you wish to discuss a particular appreciation or resentment, please agree: (1) to wait at least thirty minutes, (2)
to ask your partner's permission, and (3) to respect absolutely your partner's right to refuse to discuss at that moment what they've told you. At least thirty minutes later, if
you wish, you can ask again.

Appreciations and Resentments is not only a powerful
tool for communication between partners, it's also valuable to each of you personally, because it encourages you
to acknowledge and formulate feelings you may only partly
have realized you feel. People often have trouble talking
about their feelings. They tend to be vague. Appreciations
and Resentments can help you to be more specific about
your needs and desires, which helps you understand yourself as well as communicate with your partner. After a few
weeks you'll discover how powerful this exercise is.

You're likely to encounter resistance to doing Appreciations and Resentments. "This is ridiculous," your partner
will say to you. "I don't know why we have to go through
this charade. We communicate fine." Or you'll find yourself thinking, "I don't have any resentments today." Such
resistance is common.

People claim, for example, that they have nothing to
say. But even people who have known each other for only
a few minutes can usually find qualities they like or don't
like about each other. Couples who have been together
months and years have a vast stockpile of appreciations

and resentments available—thousands of past experiences to draw from, plus all of the new feelings that come up each and every day.

Similarly, some people resist doing the exercise by claiming they already communicate well with their partners. But Appreciations and Resentments is different from even exceptionally open informal communication because it is structured. It compels candor even as it holds anger and estrangement temporarily at bay. So there's great value in doing it, even for partners who already communicate well. Even if doing the Appreciations and Resentments exercise seems embarrassing and valueless at first, please practice it for at least four weeks before you pass judgment. We are convinced that the resulting openness and the new information you acquire about your partner will surprise you.

Ideally, you and your partner should take turns initiating this exercise so that each of you gets used to being both giver and receiver. One of you—often the woman— will tend to be more enthusiastic about it. To counterbalance that tendency, take turns initiating it. Women sometimes feel that men don't communicate well enough with them and care enough about improving their relationship. If this is the case, a woman will probably appreciate the exercise even more if her partner initiates it. We encourage you to experiment with a full month of Appreciations and Resentments, initiated the majority of the time by the man, and watch what happens.

More About Trust

We said earlier that trust is vital to ESO. We'd like to say more about that now.

ESO requires *both* partners to give their full attention to one of their sexual systems at a time. That double attention greatly increases the pleasure. If you are the passive, receiving partner, you concentrate on your own feelings while the active partner *also* concentrates on your feelings. You give up control to the active partner. That's where the trust comes in—trust that you won't be hurt, trust that your partner will learn what to do to stimulate you in a way that will allow you to let go of your resistances to pleasure.

Only by your teaching, verbal and nonverbal, can your partner learn to stimulate you effectively. *You are the only final authority on your own sexual response.* People often believe that they should know instinctively how to satisfy their partners. But every human being's response to sexual stimulation is different. So no one, man or woman, can know your response in advance. They have to be taught.

That teaching requires trust. If, when you say, "That feels uncomfortable. Try a lighter touch," your partner gets mad and says, "Oh, the hell with you. If I'm not doing it right, do it yourself. This is stupid," then no one is going to learn. Instead, each of you needs to put your ego aside, say "Thank you," and follow directions.

Sex is a skill. No one is automatically an expert. Each of you is responsible only for understanding your own response. Your partner's response you'll have to learn from the only living expert—your partner. You'll learn more quickly by following the guidelines in this book.

Saying Yes to Sex

One of the most effective ways we know to build trust in a relationship is to make an agreement with your partner always to say yes to sex. There are very few valid reasons for refusing. If lovemaking is inconvenient at the time your partner asks you, you can offer an alternative time. "I'd like to finish what I'm doing right now, but I'd love for us to have sex about an hour after dinner tonight." You *must* keep that agreement. Otherwise your partner will learn not to trust you.

The idea of never denying sex to their partners frightens some people. They use sex as a weapon and don't want to disarm. But using sex as a weapon creates enormous distrust and resentment in the victim. So the weapon eventually turns back emotional injury to the user. No one wins that war.

Others fear that sex is somehow addictive. Without denial, they think, it will spiral out of control. If denial has been a part of your relationship, your partner is likely to ask to make love more often when denial is set aside. Partly that's a way of testing a newfound agreement. Partly it's a way of establishing a new pattern of lovemaking free of control. Partly it's a response to the novelty of the arrangement.

But sex isn't addictive. To the contrary, the problem for most sexually active couples—even couples skilled at ESO—is finding time for regular sex in the midst of all their other activities.

Sometimes we prescribe an orgasm a day for clients we treat in therapy. That's a healthy goal to have. It ought to be a pleasant prescription, more fun than its predecessor, an apple a day, but our clients complain about the time it takes. After ESO training, that attitude changes. Even a "quickie" finds both partners in enthusiastic agreement.

We should add that we also sometimes find it useful to prescribe, for a few weeks or months, for couples in severe conflict, no sex at all. Wonderful as it is, routine sex obviously doesn't cure every ill. We prescribe thoughtfulness and other demonstrations of affection—holding hands, hugging, kissing, romantic attention—as substitutes.

Finally, some people fear saying yes because they don't

enjoy sex. Once a week, once a month, is more than enough for them. Since sex is a skill, that's a vicious circle. You can't improve—or even maintain what you have—without practice. Neither can your partner.

Agreeing to sex builds trust by freeing each other of rejection. You accept your partner's sexual needs as your responsibility; your partner accepts yours. Women in particular learn the pleasure of asking for lovemaking when they want it. That's something many women don't trust their partners enough to do.

Men who believe they're sexual failures if they don't anticipate all their partner's needs find mutual sexual responsibility frees them from that pressure. When they grow beyond feeling threatened, they discover that it's flattering to be asked.

Connecting

Before you begin touching or stimulating each other, it's important to connect mentally. One way to do that is to talk about pleasant times and experiences, past or imagined. Keep your talk light and positive. It's the wrong time to bring up balancing your checkbook or handling your mother-in-law.

Silent eye contact can help you connect. Sitting or lying down, facing each other, look at one of your partner's eyes or at the forehead center. Resist any tendency to talk or giggle. Allow yourself to be comfortable and relaxed with yourself and your partner. Think peaceful, positive thoughts. Imagine being absorbed by your partner's eyes.

Dancing Hands is another useful exercise. Sitting facing one another, making solid eye contact, hold your hands at chest level with palms toward your partner while your partner does the same. Your palms should almost—but not quite—touch. One of you leads by moving your hands up, down, sideways, and around at varying speed. The other follows intuitively. After about two minutes, leader becomes follower for two minutes. Continue to alternate silently until you feel connected.

Kissing

Kissing is reputed to be the world's most powerful aphrodisiac. Its reputation is deserved. The *Kamasutra,* the great Sanskrit love poem of ancient India, lists no fewer than eighteen different kinds of kisses, arranged according to their potential for arousal. Other Oriental love manuals classify different kisses by descriptive names: "tea blossom," for example, "rose hip," "summer squall."

Kissing is not simply one among many techniques of lovemaking. Kissing is a world in itself, a communication that stimulates and mirrors the entire range of actions and experiences involved in intimate sexual expression. Not surprisingly, in our training we spend a lot of time with the simple (and not so simple) kiss. Kissing is an excellent way of establishing emotional, physical, and mental connections with your partner.

Sadly, many couples have neglected the kiss as an instrument of communicating affection and arousal. "He doesn't like to kiss" is one of the more common complaints we hear from women in counseling. Women also frequently say, "He used to kiss more when we were dating. Now it's very brief at best. He just doesn't seem interested anymore." They sense that kissing is communication and feel unprepared for further intimacy without it. Kissing is a loving way to change the focus of your attention from other responsibilities to each other. It demonstrates caring and loving, which is a very helpful transition for lovemaking. It also helps eliminate intrusive thoughts.

At first, kissing as an exercise may seem silly. Partners

who have been together for a long time will naturally resist being told how to kiss. Kissing is something most of us learned in junior high school. What could there possibly be to learn?

More than you might imagine. Doing the Kissing exercise can deepen your physical and emotional understanding of each other and foster wonderful intimacy. Most people do not realize how important a communication a kiss is. A kiss isn't just two lips touching. There's a message behind that touch, complex and important. Whether you close your eyes when you kiss, or look at the person you love in intimate closeness, the kiss itself communicates what you're thinking and feeling to your partner.

THE EXERCISE

Practice the Kissing exercise four times a week, fifteen minutes at a time, for a total of one hour. Put this book near you when you begin and consult it as you go. Don't stop to look at your watch—approximate the time.

1. *A touch of romance.* Sit together comfortably on a couch, fully clothed, with the lights low, with music playing softly in the background.
2. *Say how you like it.* The man begins by telling his partner how he likes ideally to be kissed (without expecting that he will necessarily be kissed that way) (thirty seconds).
3. *Show how you like it.* The woman then kisses the man the way *she herself* likes to be kissed, incorporating any of the man's earlier suggestions only if she wishes to do so (thirty to forty-five seconds).
4. *Puckering with a peck.* With soft and slightly puckered lips, she slowly and gently pecks around his lips from one side of his mouth to the other, circling or criss-

crossing. Sometimes she may concentrate more on the top lip, sometimes on the bottom lip (thirty to forty-five seconds).

5. *Nibbling.* She then gently nibbles on his lips with her own, taking some of his lower lip between her lips, beginning at one side and moving to the other, then nibbling the top lip from one side to the other circling or crisscrossing in the same way (thirty to forty-five seconds).

6. *Nibble and a peck, dry.* She next alternates pecking and nibbling (one minute).

7. *Nibble and a peck, moist.* The woman then moistens her lips and tongue and runs her tongue over her partner's lips, occasionally remoistening her lips while alternating this kiss with light, puckered kisses and nibbles (one minute).

8. *French and review.* She then begins to insert her tongue in his mouth intermittently, circling his tongue, alternating so-called French kissing with kisses from the previous steps—nibbling, puckered kisses, licking (one minute).

9. *Free theme.* Finally, the woman chooses whatever kisses she enjoys most, using the techniques we've described or others of her own devising, as she likes (one minute).

After the woman's part of the exercise is completed, you should reverse roles. Go through each of the kissing movements exactly as before, but the *woman* begins by telling her partner how *she* likes to be kissed. The man then kisses her as *he* likes to be kissed, incorporating his partner's wishes to the degree that he desires. The man then proceeds to the subsequent steps of the exercise.

When you've both taken turns, spend a few moments discussing what you liked most about the exercise, what you liked least, how you felt about doing it, and what you learned. Alternate who starts the Kissing exercise.

Sexual Exploration

Sexual Exploration is an exercise in teaching each other
where you're sensitive to pleasure. It's best done at home,
in bed, when you've both bathed and have a space of private time together.

You'll take turns. Decide who's first. Get a hand mirror.
Refer to the drawings of the male and female genitals. See
illustrations 5 and 12 (pages 113 and 151) for body positions.

First take turns pointing out and naming all the pelvic
and genital structures. Find the glans penis, the glans clitoris, and so on.

Then apply a lubricant and explore your partner's genitals, using strokes of different lengths and pressures. Your
partner should experience each stroke and rate it on a
scale of –10 to +10, the minus numbers indicating discomfort, the plus numbers indicating comfort and
pleasure.

Spend a minimum of ten minutes per person in this exploration and go over each of the genital structures in turn.
The man should insert a finger into the woman's vagina to
explore the sensations in different areas. A way to describe
the areas is by reference to the hours on a clock face:
twelve o'clock, upward toward the navel; one o'clock,
moving right; three o'clock, halfway down; and so on. The
woman should try squeezing the penis in both its soft and
its hard states until the man indicates discomfort, so she
can learn how much pressure the penis can take. Both
partners should explore, in the course of several sessions,
until they learn their partner's anatomy and unique areas
of sensitivity well.

Afterward, spend a few minutes discussing what you
were thinking and feeling and what you learned. Please
practice Sexual Exploration at least once even if you think
you have done something similar or if it seems elementary.

Everyone, including sexually experienced couples who have been together for a long time, can benefit from practicing this exercise once in a while. Physical responses change. So do psychological needs. It's a way of staying in touch.

Sexual Communication

Talking during sex can distract from arousal, but verbal feedback from your partner is important at times for information on preferences and technique. When doing any of the ESO exercises, it's useful periodically to ask short, simple questions that can be answered "yes" or "no."

To learn where best to stimulate, with what pressure, and how rapidly, ask your partner, "Harder? Softer? Faster? Slower? Here? Is this good?" Be prepared and willing to change your stroking in either subtle or major ways. Or ask your partner to show you using their own hands on themselves or guiding yours, a powerful way to learn what your partner prefers. Telling your partner what you are going to do just before you do it is a valuable method of sexual communication. The anticipation you produce by announcing what's coming helps focus and build your partner's attention on sensation.

Foreplay

Foreplay is as necessary a preliminary to ESO as it is to ordinary lovemaking. It follows naturally from bathing together and drying each other off. When you're naked together, when you've lain down together, begin by touching each other for pleasure. Explore each other's body. Tease. Giggle. Have fun!

Women especially tend to resent immediate genital stimulation. They feel used. Don't emphasize the genitals at first. Kiss and caress. Enjoy the warmth of skin, the weight and texture of muscle and flesh. The skin is the body's largest sense organ. Human beings need to be touched.

FOCUS ON SENSATION

Directing your attention outward or inward is a skill you will use for ESO. You can improve it during foreplay. When you touch your partner to *give* pleasure, you're directing your attention outward. It's possible then to shift that attention and direct it inward—to notice how touching your partner feels to *you*. Then a sense of your partner's body— the sexiness of her curves, of his muscles—flows back through your fingertips. Your touch is creating heat and electrical energy that is actually transferred to your hands and into your own nervous system. Focus your attention on this subtle process. As you become aware of it, the amount and transfer of the energy to and from your partner may even increase.

We're not speaking poetically. Directing your attention is mental, but it's real. We all do it. If you're watching a favorite show, concentrating on reading the newspaper, or daydreaming, you may not hear what someone in the room says. Your attention is elsewhere. Couples can use this skill of directing attention for pleasure.

You can easily shift your attention back and forth from outward to inward. Pleasure builds if you do. In ESO training you'll use this skill to help clear away distractions and work through mental resistance. Foreplay is a good time to practice.

There's another kind of shifting attention that gives

pleasure. It happens when you touch your partner for pleasure and your partner responds to that touch with increased arousal. Then you in turn are aroused by your partner's response. When you take turns pleasuring each other to ESO, you'll find that your partner's arousal stimulates your own.

Taoists teach that the body's most basic energy, *chi*, moves toward where you focus your mind's attention. Although forty-nine cultures have a word for *chi*, it's notable that the West does not. The closest English equivalent is "life energy." *Chi* is integral to the acupuncture system, which proposes that energy flows in defined channels or paths, called meridians. Meridians have been verified by a variety of electronic methods. Western biofeedback research in turn has repeatedly demonstrated that focusing your attention on an area of the body can cause increased blood, nervous, and muscle activity.

You may prefer to think of the process as looking with your mind's eye, or swinging a searchlight or a laser beam around to illuminate a specific part of your body. What do you see, however dimly? What kind of sensations are you feeling, however faint? If that body area could speak, what would it be saying? When you become aware of *chi*, it often feels tingling, warm, light prickling, buzzing.

The idea of shifting *chi* to a region of your body may seem improbable. Even if you are dubious or skeptical, at least pretend with us for a while that you have the ability to feel more from any part of your body onto which you direct your focused, quiet attention. The stronger your mind's focus, the stronger the flow of *chi*.

The sensory focus exercises in the ESO program will be the first opportunity you will have to practice the power of moving *chi* and becoming aware of *chi* moving throughout your body. The sexual exercises will have you concentrating your attention on your genitals and pelvic area.

The best training for learning to focus your attention on a particular area is meditation. You don't need expensive or time-consuming formal instruction to learn and practice the basics. The 20–0 Countdown (see page 53) is an easy and effective meditative procedure.

MASSAGE

Massage can be a part of foreplay, but it's optional. You might casually spend several minutes massaging your partner's face, hands, feet, back. You might offer a full-body massage. Reach an agreement before you begin on longer massages:

"For the next ten minutes I'd like to give you a massage."

"Okay."

That relieves the receiver of guilt. Your partner knows what to expect and can relax and enjoy the experience. If you pay some attention to the pleasure coming back to you from massaging, you'll enjoy the experience too.

Several good books have been published about massage. You may want to refer to the bibliography at the end of this book to locate one to learn the details of technique.

SENSORY FOCUS

Sensory Focus is an excellent way to move from day-to-day thoughts and worries into sensuality. It slows down the unromantic rush of hopping into bed and diving for the genitals. Especially if you are concerned about your or your partner's sexual functioning, you should practice this graduated set of exercises frequently. We describe Sensory Focus in full detail on page 253.

Mutual Stimulation

With this exercise you can improve sexual communication and increase trust while you build mutual sexual arousal.

Both partners lie on their sides, man on his right side, woman on her right side, resting on their elbows, facing each other's genitals (see illustration number 4 for position). The woman's left hand stimulates the shaft and glans of the penis. Her right hand is free to stimulate the scrotum and external prostate spot. The man stimulates the clitoris with his left hand and the vagina with his right. Both partners should use lubrication.

Stimulate each other simultaneously for at least thirty minutes. While you're doing so, talk to each other about your feelings and reactions. Tell your partner what feels good, what doesn't, what you'd like done differently.

If one of you becomes bored or loses excitement, say so. Your partner can give you suggestions for redirecting your attention to increasing pleasure and can alter the stimulation you're getting.

Note that each partner is free to provide oral stimulation. Keep it brief for now; oral stimulation limits talk.

Do this exercise at least three times a week for at least one week. You'll find it useful to repeat from time to time as a way of staying in touch.

4 MUTUAL SIMULTANEOUS STIMULATION:
COMMUNICATION POSITION

*Man and woman both lie on sides, resting on an elbow,
facing partner's genitals. Woman has one hand on penis,
other on scrotum or external prostate spot. Man has one
hand on clitoris, other on G spot. Full manual/oral stimulation possible. Allows for teaching and learning at
same time. Couple may alternate between verbal and
noverbal communication, noticing differences. Good initial position, creating sexual arousal and interest in both
partners and establishing equality in relationship. Easy
transition to being either giver or receiver (taking turns).*

Taking Turns

In this step-by-step progression toward ESO another preliminary is to agree on who will first be the active pleasure giver and who will first be the receiver.

Taking turns pleasuring is vital to achieving ESO. It allows the partner being pleasured to let go of outward attention and concentrate on inward feelings. The pleasured partner needs to be completely free of concern about what to do next, what comes next, how the other person feels— actively experiencing, but allowing the partner to take charge. That's why trust is crucial to success.

Besides the pleasure itself, receiving pleasure offers the receiver a chance to develop a sense of surrender. Learning to allow your partner to take control of your pleasure is an important prerequisite to relaxing sufficiently to experience ESO. Men who are used to controlling and being in control may find relinquishing control especially unfamiliar and challenging.

We advise couples learning ESO to begin with the man pleasuring and the woman being pleasured. If a man has orgasm with ejaculation, he's not as likely to give his partner his full attention afterward. A woman is potentially capable of many orgasms. If, taking her pleasure first, she has an orgasm, that only adds to the experience; it doesn't end it. A woman needs to feel cared for. She may not trust her partner to give her the pleasure she requires. Once her partner has pleasured her to orgasm she will trust him more and thus more easily let go of resistance. It's a wise man who takes care of his partner first. Her enthusiasm to stimulate him when his turn comes will be his delightful reward.

Later, when you've learned ESO, you can vary the sequence. While you're learning, the rule is, Women first. It works better that way.

Are You Ready for ESO?

You're ready to begin practicing to experience ESO when:

1. You and your partner both agree that you understand each other's anatomy.
2. Men: you can stimulate yourself to a reliable erection within five minutes and peak yourself—stopping just short of ejaculation—at least six times in a thirty-minute period.
3. Women: you can have orgasm reliably with self-stimulation, using only your hands, without a vibrator.
4. Men: you can reliably stimulate your partner to an orgasm within twenty minutes, using your hands, your mouth, or both.
5. Women: you can stimulate your partner with your hands, your mouth, or both to a reliable erection and can peak him, stopping just short of ejaculation, at least six times in a thirty-minute period.
6. You can both comfortably express and hear your sexual appreciations and resentments.

If you have difficulty with number 1, review the anatomy descriptions in this book with your partner and then review your partner's anatomy, using the Sexual Exploration exercise (page 102).

If you have difficulty with numbers 2 or 3, review the discussion of self-stimulation in this book and keep practicing.

If you have difficulty with numbers 4 or 5, turn to chapter 3, "Developing Skills," to the section called "Mirroring Your Partner" (page 81). Review and practice Sensory Focus steps 3 and 4. Include in your review the exercise Taking Charge on page 252.

If you have difficulty with number 6, review and continue to practice the exercises in this chapter. Do Appreciations and Resentments faithfully every day.

If you continue to have difficulty, read chapter 10, "Solving Problems." If you fit any of these problem categories, follow the advice we give there.

After you've solved any difficulties, proceed to the next chapter. You're ready to begin practicing to experience ESO!

5

Female ESO:
How to Stimulate
a Woman

Teasing Her Genitals

This chapter will tell you, the man, how to stimulate your female partner to ESO.* "You" here will mean the active, stimulating partner. Both partners should read this chapter carefully before going on. Much that we'll have to say applies equally to men and women.

After a time of pleasant foreplay, the woman finds a comfortable position lying on her back. She props her head on a pillow if she likes. She separates her legs. She can flex them, knees raised, or extend them. Comfort with access is the key.

You may kneel (see illustration 5 on page 113), sit cross-legged, lie on your stomach, lie beside your partner or between her legs, arranging yourself so that you can see and easily touch her genitals. You may locate yourself on her left side so that your right hand has access to her clitoris and your left hand to her vagina. Or you may prefer to be on her right so that you can use your right hand for vaginal

_____

*These directions apply equally to same-sex couples where female stimulates female.

stimulation. Be comfortable. Use your hands as they work best for you.

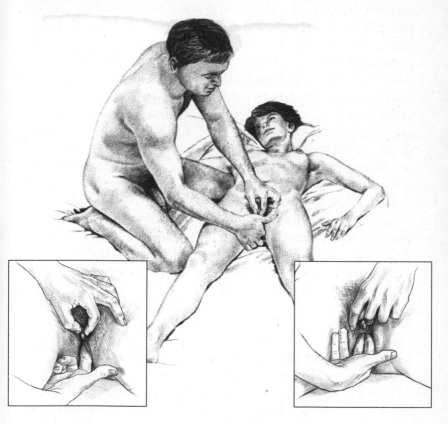

5 MALE STIMULATING FEMALE: KNEELING

Easy access to genitals with both hands. Good for intimate eye contact and expressions of love. Easy transition to kneeling-over position.

Left inset shows basic two-fingered manual stroke.

Right inset shows (three-fingered) thumb anchor stroke variation.

Now carefully apply lubricant—warming it first in your hand—to your partner's entire genital area: major labia, minor labia, the clitoris and its structures, the opening of the vagina, a little way into the vagina itself, and down along the perineum. The external anal area responds pleasurably to stimulation. If your partner likes stimulation there, lubricate the anal area too.

Too much lubricant is better than too little. Be generous. Even though it's nonabsorbent, some of it will melt away or be absorbed by the skin. Remember that a woman's genital lubrication comes from the inner walls of her vagina. The clitoris produces no natural lubricant of its own.

Begin now lightly stimulating the external genitals—the pubic hair, the major labia. Lightly brushing the pubic hair, gently pulling it, creates arousal, because all the structures in the area are connected. What you're doing is a localized version of foreplay, gradually approaching the sensitive areas enclosed within the major and minor labia. Just as you did in foreplay, you're following the principle of general stimulation before localized stimulation. When women pleasure themselves, they usually do the same thing, caressing the overall genital area before concentrating on the clitoris.

In a sense, you're teasing. Teasing creates arousal. You circle the clitoris, slowly closing in. Press lightly with the palm of your hand or several fingers together on the major labia and the pubic hair. Then, over a period of a minute or two, gradually make teasing circles closer to the clitoris. Brush the clitoris sometimes as your hand circles.

Stroking the Clitoris

When you approach the clitoris itself, touch it only lightly at first. All the nerve endings found in the glans penis are concentrated into the clitoris's small area. It's extremely sensitive.

Every woman's preference for clitoral stimulation is unique. Some women like a very light touch. Some prefer the clitoral shaft stroked rather than the glans. Others don't want the clitoris touched directly at all. Often the clitoris is more sensitive on the right side; sometimes it is more sensitive on the left. You need to get to know your partner's clitoris well. You and your partner's clitoris need to become intimate friends.

You began that friendship with sexual communication training in chapter 4. You saw the clitoris change shape, color, and position with sexual arousal. Now you need to extend your knowledge by giving your partner's clitoris your close, full attention. Your goal at this point is to stimulate your partner to orgasm with your hand. (You may already have found successful ways to do that. Read this section through anyway to learn about their application to ESO.)

No single stroke will work reliably for all women. You'll have to proceed by trial and error. Your partner showed you what felt good to her during sexual communication training. Apply that information now.

Many women complain that their men don't experiment enough with different kinds of strokes. Or that the experimenting happens too fast, the man moving from one stroke to another before the woman has had time to relax with it and see how it feels.

To find a stroke that your partner likes, try different areas of the clitoris and different pressures on the clitoris. Change strokes only gradually. Watch your partner's response. If her genitals are becoming more engorged, you're doing fine. The best way to approach the clitoris is with thumb and forefinger. Your thumb at the top of the clitoris—toward the stomach—anchors it. Your forefinger strokes it lower down. (See illustration number 6 on page

117.) You stroke one side for a while, the top, the other side. The motion can be up and down or circling, and the thumb can rock. Or roll the clitoris lightly between forefinger and thumb. (See illustration number 5 on page 113.) Try these variations; make up others as you go.

Your basic stroke should be slow and steady, about one cycle per second.

Women clients often tell us that their partners aren't consistent with stimulation. Find a consistent pattern and keep it up for several minutes at a time without change, except the changes we mention below.

Watch your partner's reaction. If a stroke is working, it arouses her. You see the arousal. Her genital area swells, adding fullness to the major and minor labia. Her clitoris enlarges and moves downward and inward. The clitoral glans engorges much as the glans of your penis does with erection. The vaginal area and the clitoris darken from the added flow of blood.

Your partner can guide you by making sounds. If what you're doing feels right, she can moan, hum, sigh with pleasure. Vocalizing during lovemaking is arousing in itself. It also lets you know that arousal is happening. Talking at this point is distracting; that's why nonverbal vocalizing is a valuable skill to learn.

Your partner will also guide you by moving her pelvis toward your hand or away. If your stroking is arousing her, if she is climbing toward orgasm, she will press her genitals into your hand because she is reaching for more stimulation. If the stimulation is ineffective or uncomfortable, or if she is resisting, she'll move her genitals away. These movements are subtle. They may amount to shifts of only a quarter of an inch or so, against your hand or away.

Look as well for larger signs of arousal, especially muscle tension. Pelvic muscle tension and general body muscle tension are signs of sexual arousal. So are sighs,

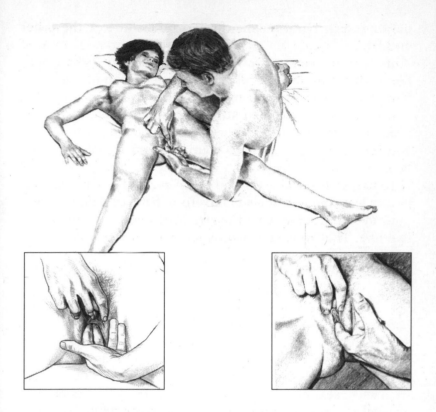

6 MALE STIMULATING FEMALE: LYING ON ELBOW

Comfortable. Easy access to clitoris and vagina with hands and mouth. Right hand demonstrates basic clitoral stimulation stroke with thumb and forefinger grasping clitoris. Thumb anchors clitoral base; forefinger strokes glans.

Left inset shows three-fingered variation of clitoral stroke. Thumb anchors base; forefinger and middle finger cradle clitoris and stroke sides.

Right inset shows another variation: heel of right hand on pubis, third finger pad on clitoris. Fingers of left hand stimulate G-spot area.

panting, jerky movements, sweating, curling of the toes and feet.

If your partner moves away even slightly from your hand, you need to back off. That doesn't mean lifting your hand completely away. It means letting up a little on pressure, slightly slowing your stroke or moving your fingers to a slightly different area of her clitoris. The clitoris is small. Your changes in response to your partner's signals need to be small too.

It helps to be able to see your partner's genitals. As you're learning ESO it also helps from time to time to close your eyes and sense what the structures you're stimulating feel like. That way, your hands learn as well as your eyes.

BUILDING AROUSAL

A teasing cycle builds arousal. When you've found a basic stroke that your partner likes, use it for about ten strokes and then relax to a resting stroke—lighter or slower or not so directly applied to the clitoris—for a stroke or two. That increases sexual tension. Your partner will signal her arousal by moving her genitals toward your hand, asking for the stimulating stroke again. Ten stimulating (climbing) strokes to one or two resting strokes is a good pattern to follow. It's not the only pattern. Six to one may be better for your partner, or three to one, or fifteen to one. Experiment and see.

You can build to extremely high levels of arousal with only your thumb and forefinger. For a variation, add the middle finger, so you have three fingers cradling the clitoris. (See illustration number 6 on page 117.) The thumb continues to anchor the clitoris from above; the forefinger and the middle finger then stroke the sides of the clitoris and its base. This is an excellent clitoral control stroke. The point is to find the best way to build arousal to higher and higher levels, always backing off when the climbing stops.

At any time during this initial stimulation you can insert one or two fingers of your other hand into your partner's vagina. That hand won't be especially active yet, although you may add to your partner's arousal by sweeping a finger around her vagina while you stroke her clitoris. Your forefinger or middle finger at least needs to be comfortably inserted into your partner's vagina by the time she begins orgasm.

Resistances

While you're stroking her clitoris, what's your partner doing? (Men: this discussion will apply equally to you when you're being stimulated. Read it carefully.)

She's actively aware. She's totally focused on her own experience. That experience is a combination of feeling and thinking. The more she can pay attention to feeling, the more she will feel. But part of the time your partner will be thinking, because thinking is a habit. Some of her thinking—especially her doubts, questions, and worries—will get in the way of arousal. That's resistance, and it blocks feelings. Your partner needs to learn to identify that kind of thinking quickly. When it's your turn, so will you.

A list of the things people tell themselves to deny themselves pleasure would be longer than this book. Ironically, everyone resists pleasure. Your partner struggles with resistances while you pleasure her. You will struggle with them when your partner pleasures you. Even men and women thoroughly experienced in ESO encounter resistances. Experience teaches them how to let go of resistances more quickly whenever they come up during sexual stimulation.

Your partner is resisting when she

1. subtly pulls away from you;
2. shows less engorgement or lubrication;
3. opens her eyes and looks bored.

Many resistances come in the form of intrusive thoughts. Sometimes such thoughts are continuous. At other times they occur intermittently—for a few seconds, perhaps, several times a minute. Here are a few common intrusive thoughts:

He's getting tired.
That's enough.
I don't deserve any more.
I'm afraid.
I feel like I'm going to burst.
I wonder what that sound was?
I wonder if the kids/parents/neighbors can hear?
This is wrong.
I want a cigarette/a cup of coffee.
I want to go to the bathroom.
I wonder if I smell?
I'm not attractive enough.
My stomach is too big.
My thighs are too fat.
I wish my breasts were bigger.
I wish my penis was larger.
Tomorrow I've got to . . .
Yesterday I should have . . .
I don't think I can do this.
I don't have time for this.
I should be:
    checking the kids
    cleaning the house
    getting ready for work tomorrow.
He has time for me only when he wants sex.

He's just using me.
He/she doesn't care how I feel.
This is boring.

Resistances are ways we limit ourselves. But resistances are normal. They're the necessary friction of love. In the context of sexual pleasure they're not wrong or bad and they're no one's fault. They're simply barriers that have to be worked through, every single time they arise.

Don't blame each other for resistances. If you do, you won't trust each other. If you don't trust each other, you can't fully let go to pleasure. Avoid criticizing and finding fault with your partner. You'll get much further by being understanding, supportive, and patient, and by providing gentle encouragement.

For a thorough discussion of resistances, see chapter 8, "Overcoming Resistances," page 195.

CONTROLLING THOUGHT I

There are two basic ways to control the thoughts that make up resistances. Your partner needs to apply both of them while you're stimulating her.

One way is to change the thought. The technical term for deliberately changing thoughts is "cognitive restructuring." When a distracting thought pops into your partner's head, she needs to replace it with a positive thought: "This feels good. I'm safe. I'll let that thought go." Cognitive restructuring isn't mumbo jumbo. It's a commonplace of psychology, and it works.

A variation of cognitive restructuring is replacing a distracting thought with a neutral thought. That's the basic technique of meditation systems that teach the use of mantras—of neutral, sometimes nonsense words. The neutral thought can be a relaxation phrase—"I'm calm"—

or a repeated number, or a sound like the classic mantra "Om." The neutral thought isn't sexually arousing, but it displaces the distracting thought and allows your partner to pay attention again to sensation.

That's the other basic way to control thoughts: by redirecting attention *inward* to sensation and allowing the physical experience to take over again. Your job is to make sure the sensation is steadily available when your partner needs it.

Many men, when they sense their partners leveling off or coming down from arousal, try to crash through the resistance by speeding up their stroke or by pressing harder. It's usually much better to let your partner work through her resistance herself. If you supply steady, rhythmic, reliable, pleasurable stimulation, she'll have the sensation she needs to find her way.

When you feel your partner resisting, back off slightly. The slight change should help her refocus her attention on the sensation you're providing.

See page 202 for additional instructions on controlling negative thoughts.

WHEN YOU'RE STUCK

After a while, if your partner is still coming down, try backing off a little more. If the blockage continues—if your partner continues to lose arousal—you may then want to try the opposite approach, increasing stimulation to help her push through. Do it subtly. You certainly don't want to create pain. You don't want your partner to feel that you're demanding she go on. Pay attention to the effect you're causing. If increasing stimulation makes your partner even more resistant, then back off once more.

Many couples get stuck at this point. It's a tricky, difficult moment, loaded with frustration. Couples get stuck and eventually give up. The man's tired, the woman's tired, they're angry with each other. He silently accuses her of resisting him. She silently accuses him of trying to force her to respond. Both people forget the point, which is pleasure. No one benefits.

If your partner is obviously coming down from arousal in a major way—if the resistance has completely taken over and she can't find her way through—you both should stop what you're doing and talk about what's happening.

Be affectionate with each other—be loving. Don't make accusations. You've hit a snag. Everybody does. Discuss it. Resistance is normal. It's part of the process. If it weren't, we'd all have sex all the time and forget to eat. You can even have fun with resistance by making overcoming it a game.

See what you can find out about what you were doing and what your partner was feeling. Then begin again if your partner feels more comfortable. Or switch roles and move on. Since you're working on ESO at least three times a week, neither of you ever needs to feel left out for long. You can always complete lovemaking in your usual way. ESO isn't exclusive. It adds range and depth to what you already have.

USING KEGEL EXERCISES

Another way your partner can overcome resistance is to contract her PC muscles deliberately by doing Kegel exercises while you are stimulating her. Resistance often shows up as muscle tension—tightening muscles, deliberately or unconsciously—which, when prolonged, works against arousal. But then relaxing those same muscles after tension usually leads to an increase in arousal. Many people, to build arousal, find themselves alternately tensing and relaxing their muscles—the PC muscles at least, and often their entire bodies.

Kegel exercises add an important third step to this process because they're a three-part exercise. The first step is tension, the second is release, and the third is pushing out—bearing down. Your partner can work through resistance by doing all three steps while you're stroking her. Not only does this help to increase arousal directly, it also focuses your partner's attention on muscular sensations rather than negative thoughts.

Do what it takes to overcome resistance, remembering the cautions we've mentioned. Even a light slap on the clitoris or the opening of the vagina can sometimes help startle resistance away. It shouldn't be hard enough to cause resentment or pain. It's another variation to experiment with.

Breakthrough Breathing

People frequently block orgasm by holding their breath. Breath holding usually follows from muscle tensing. A woman pushes out with her PC muscles to build arousal. When she pushes out and bears down, she holds her breath. Up to a point, holding her breath increases arousal, but some women hold their breath for half a minute or more.

If your partner has the habit of holding her breath when she's tensing her body or clamping her PC muscles to reach for arousal (you can tell if she does by noticing her breathing while you're stroking her), she should practice breathing more deliberately. We normally breathe about twelve times a minute. Climbing in sexual arousal, your partner should still breathe at least six times a minute. The best way to pay attention to breathing is to experience it. Your partner should *feel* taking in a breath—air moving into her nose and mouth and filling her lungs and abdomen—and then exhaling it down toward her genitals. You can help by reminding her to breathe when you notice she's holding her breath.

Learning how to breathe more with your abdomen than with your chest muscles is the most effective type of breathing. Imagine your belly is a bellows. As you inhale, expand your abdomen (open the bellows), then expand your chest. When you exhale, reverse the process. Contract your abdomen (close the bellows) and then contract your chest. Athletes, singers, and many meditative disciplines practice deliberate abdominal breathing. However, even normal chest breathing, when done with your conscious attention to it, will help increase and diffuse sexual energy throughout the body.

Breathing to a counting rhythm is another very useful technique your partner can use for breakthrough breathing. She counts silently to six (or four, or ten—whatever is comfortable), about one count per second, as she breathes in and again as she breathes out: IN two, three, four, five, six, OUT two, three, four, five, six, IN . . .

Paralleling her change in breathing, your partner should practice keeping the rest of her body relaxed when she tenses her pelvic muscles. That puts the muscle tension in her genitals, where it's useful, and makes breathing easier. Doing Kegel exercises while counting breaths teaches this technique. We can't stress too much the importance of Kegel exercises. The more of these exercises you and your partner do and the more regularly you do them, the better for sex. The bigger and stronger the PC muscle gets, the more feeling you'll have. Combining the two powerful techniques of breakthrough breathing and Kegel exercises will add a turbocharge to your sexual experience.

Switching to the Vagina

Eventually—building arousal, working through resistances, climbing and leveling and climbing—your partner will begin the regular one-second contractions of brief, Stage I orgasm. At that point *switch your attention to her vagina.* She may want you to continue clitoral stroking during these first contractions. If so, do, but you'll probably need to lighten up. Any but the lightest stimulation will probably be uncomfortable. You may need now to lift your hand entirely away from the clitoris.

Continue vaginal stimulation through these first orgasmic contractions and after they taper off. You can move your fingers in and out of your partner's vagina in a motion imitating the thrusting of your penis, or sweep them around the vaginal barrel. But the most effective stimulation is rhythmic stroking with one or two fingers of the area called the G spot. (See illustration 1, "Female Anatomy," page 38.)

An anatomy refresher: the G spot is the area about one and a half inches inside the vagina just behind the pubic bone in the center and front of the vagina. It's one to two fingers wide, rubber- or sponge-like, firmer than the rest of the vaginal wall. It gets firmer still when it's stimulated, which makes it easier to find. Remember, some women identify a general area rather than a particular spot. That's the area to stimulate.

By stimulating your partner's vagina when her orgasm begins, you'll cause a sharp increase even then in her arousal. If you directly stimulate the G spot much before orgasm, your partner may find it uncomfortable. But once orgasm begins, G-spot stimulation is arousing rather than uncomfortable. The G spot can then take hard pressure, while the clitoris, which was stimulated before by regular stroking, now responds to more than the very lightest touch with something like pain. You've probably noticed a similar sensation. Most men find touching the glans penis painful immediately after ejaculation. So pay attention to your partner's vagina rather than to her clitoris at this volatile time.

Female Extended Orgasm

When you switch attention to your partner's vagina while she's having orgasmic contractions, you continue to supply her with a high level of stimulation. Whether you're moving your fingers in and out of her vagina or stroking her G spot with your fore- or middle finger, you should continue the regular, once-per-second rhythm you established when you stroked her clitoris earlier. Continue building on that ten-to-one—or six-to-one, whatever worked best—cycle, increasing and decreasing pressure.

This internal stimulation creates a deeper kind of contraction than the superficial (outer one-third) vaginal muscle contractions of brief, Stage I, or multiple orgasm. The deeper contractions involve the deep pelvic musculature, including the big muscles of the uterus. These deeper contractions are a pushing out, bearing down. They last longer and are more pleasurable. They represent the physical basis for female extended sexual orgasm: ESO. The push-outs in this first phase of ESO are variable in length, lasting from one to ten seconds each.

The vagina responds to single orgasm by tenting—by enlarging at the back and lifting up into the body. To a finger inserted into the vagina, that response feels like a loosening and a pulling away. (See illustration 1, "Female Anatomy," on page 38.)

With the beginning of ESO your partner's vagina will respond to your stimulating finger by *pushing out*, as if the uterus were pushing toward the opening of the vagina and closing the vaginal space. (See illustration 8, "Push-out Response," on page 133.)

When you feel that pushing, your partner is beginning to have the deep pelvic orgasmic push-outs that may herald the beginning of ESO.

When you feel your partner's vagina drawing back—pulling away—then she's leveling, and you should lighten the pressure you're applying inside the vagina and slow your stroke. Soon your partner will begin to want more stimulation again. You add pressure and speed up your stroke, and she begins to push out against your fingers again. That means you're supplying the right amount of stimulation. You can continue at that level. Or you can increase the pressure and rate to bring on more climbing. Higher arousal may eventually lead to resistance, and you will feel your partner's vagina again withdrawing, signaling you to lighten and slow your stroke.

When she starts to level—when there's a pause in her climbing—switch your attention away from the vagina and return your attention to stimulating the clitoris.

Stimulating the clitoris at this point usually results in one or more squeeze contractions. Those contractions signal that you should once again switch your attention to the inner trigger area of the vagina. Look for a push-out response then—that will mean your partner is experiencing her most rapid form of climbing. You should continue the kind of stimulation that best works to produce continuous waves of push-outs.

Two factors determine the intensity and frequency of your partner's push-outs: the speed, pressure, and location of your stimulating inner finger or fingers; and your partner's skill at letting go of her resistances to climbing continuously toward more pleasure.

When your partner's climbing stops—when her push-outs cease—once again immediately shift your attention from the G spot and focus more on the clitoris. Within a few seconds you should notice contractions, either squeeze or push-out. That's your signal to redirect your stimulation to the vaginal trigger area again. If your pattern of rhythmic stimulation is correct, the periods of time between contractions, squeeze or push-out, will be very brief—approximately one to five seconds. Your partner's experience of continuous contractions of either kind will be longer—in the range of ten to thirty seconds.

As you continue this pattern for fifteen minutes or more you will find that the brief resting—leveling—periods occur less and less frequently and your partner has contractions more and more of the time. When the leveling or resting periods disappear and her contractions are all deep push-outs, she has entered the expanded orgasmic phase, Phase II ESO.

During ESO practice *you* will be more in control of the stimulation than your partner. She will have some control of voluntarily pushing out and withdrawing her pelvis, just as she had some control of moving toward your hand or away when you were stroking her clitoris earlier. She can also be conscious of her breathing.

But much more than before, she will be lost in feeling and will be doing very little thinking. She'll be reacting rather than controlling. You'll be in charge of supplying the right stimulation. You need to feel in command. As you learn what you're doing, you will. As long as you don't do anything to cause pain, your partner will let you—and should let you—control. When the stimulation is right, she won't move toward you or away. She'll stay where she is, on the "orgasmic track," and enjoy what she's feeling.

One of our clients, a young woman named Roberta, beautifully articulated the experience of breaking over into ESO. She commented pointedly at the same time on the subtleties of resistance.

"I was amazed at what happened," she told us about her

first ESO experience with her boyfriend, Albert. "Instead of *trying* to make myself have orgasm, or being annoyed with Albert for not stimulating me right, I just kind of blanked out for a moment—and I started to have orgasm instantly. Then, instead of tightening up after a few seconds, as I used to do just by habit, I remembered to *breathe* and let my mind blank out again. And I kept on having orgasm! I kept breathing and letting my body do what it wanted to.

"It felt so good," Roberta finished with a grin, "I thought to myself that I never wanted it to stop. Then I got scared. Then, instantly, it *did* stop!" We're glad to say it started again for Roberta as she gained more experience at letting go.

Communication can continue during ESO just as it did before—with body movements, with your careful reading of your partner's responses, with vocalizing. Your partner's body movements and vocalizing are likely to be much more obvious now, because she's experiencing much higher levels of arousal. Moaning, jerky motions of her arms and legs, tossing her head, curling her toes and feet, panting, all are signs you should expect to see in the climbing stages as ESO continues. *The main sign that should guide your stimulation is the vagina pushing outward against your fingers.*

During *leveling* periods of ESO, your partner will usually be more quiet, her body stiller, and her pelvic contractions of the squeeze type.

The graph on page 131, "Female Orgasmic Response Stages," shows the differences in arousal and response through time of brief orgasm, multiple orgasm, and extended orgasm (Stage I, Stage II, Stage III).

In single, brief orgasm (Stage I), arousal increases with stimulation through an excitement phase to an orgasm of one-second contractions lasting from about three to twelve seconds. Contractions are the vaginal-squeeze, clenching type in the outer one-third of the vagina and reflex contractions of the anal sphincter. Blood, which has been pooling in the pelvic area (vasocongestion), is pumped out and experienced as powerful, throbbing pulsations. Then arousal declines steadily down to baseline, within a few minutes. This is orgasm as Masters and Johnson describe it in *Human Sexual Response.* Sexual researchers William Hartman and Marilyn Fithian have called it discrete orgasm.

7 FEMALE ORGASMIC RESPONSE STAGES

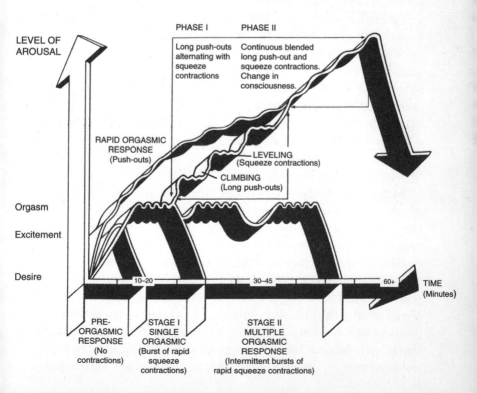

STAGE III
EXTENDED ORGASMIC RESPONSE

PHASE I   PHASE II

LEVEL OF AROUSAL

PHASE I
Long push-outs alternating with squeeze contractions

PHASE II
Continuous blended long push-out and squeeze contractions. Change in consciousness.

RAPID ORGASMIC RESPONSE
(Push-outs)

LEVELING
(Squeeze contractions)

CLIMBING
(Long push-outs)

Orgasm

Excitement

Desire

10–20   30–45   60+   TIME
(Minutes)

PRE-ORGASMIC RESPONSE
(No contractions)

STAGE I
SINGLE ORGASMIC RESPONSE
(Burst of rapid squeeze contractions)

STAGE II
MULTIPLE ORGASMIC RESPONSE
(Intermittent bursts of rapid squeeze contractions)

In multiple orgasm (Stage II), arousal doesn't decline rapidly to baseline after brief orgasm. Instead, the woman's response drops to the high-excitement level for half a minute to two minutes or more. Then, with continuing or renewed stimulation, her arousal level climbs back to orgasm and she experiences another three- to twelve-second burst of vaginal squeeze contractions and anal contractions. Heart rate, blood pressure, and muscle tension throughout the body remain at moderately elevated levels. This process may repeat several times for several minutes—in some women, for thirty minutes or more. After a series of two or more bursts of squeeze contractions, each lasting about three to twelve seconds, arousal returns to baseline. Hartman and Fithian have termed this response discrete multiple orgasm.

Extended orgasm (Stage III) follows a different development. The early phase of this orgasm has been called continuous multiple orgasm by Hartman and Fithian and blended orgasm by other researchers (i.e., Ladas, Perry, and Whipple). A woman experiences a Stage I orgasm first: desire, excitement, and a burst of rapid squeeze contractions; then she moves to Stage III. Or she may experience a Stage II multiple orgasmic response with several bursts of squeeze contractions over several minutes before moving to Stage III orgasm.

Extended, Stage III orgasm has two phases. The first phase is characterized by the occurrence of push-outs of the deep pelvic muscles of the uterus and back of the vagina (see illustration 8 on page 133). These alternate periodically with squeeze contractions of the outer vaginal muscles. The term "blended" refers to the blending of the squeeze and the push-out sex muscle responses. Compared with the briefer bursts of squeeze contractions, push-outs have longer cycles, varying from two seconds to thirty seconds or longer. As push-outs continue, they become stronger, are sustained longer, and feel increasingly

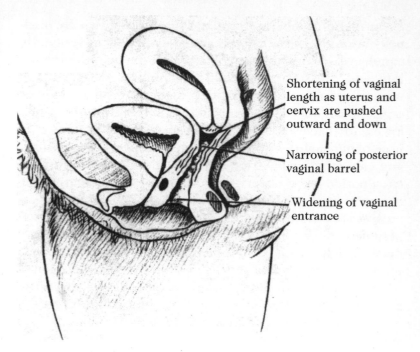

Shortening of vaginal
length as uterus and
cervix are pushed
outward and down

Narrowing of posterior
vaginal barrel

Widening of vaginal
entrance

8 PUSH-OUT RESPONSE OF DEEPER
PELVIC MUSCLES

*(A characteristic of Stage III—Extended Orgasmic
Response)*

more powerful. Their intensity and strength vary, depending upon the level of stimulation provided and the woman's ability deliberately to let go of mental resistances. Sex muscle push-outs during extended orgasm are slower and longer-lasting cycles than the bursts of squeeze contractions of Stage I and Stage II orgasm.

The duration and intensity of the deep pelvic contractions depend on the effectiveness of stimulation and on the woman's skill at focusing her attention on genital sensations and avoiding thoughts. The man influences the duration of a contraction when he stimulates his partner, usually manually or orally, in the climbing process we will describe. He can decrease the intensity of contractions by reducing the rate and pressure of vaginal and clitoral stroking. The woman climbs to increasingly higher levels of orgasm during push-outs. At times she may mentally resist by allowing intrusive thoughts to distract her and level off, the back of her vagina withdrawing subtly from the man's finger and clenching—squeezing—around it instead. During leveling periods, she experiences bursts of squeeze orgasmic contractions for a number of seconds. When the man increases stimulation, she refocuses and climbs again and experiences push-outs. If she stops climbing, the man may need to lighten his stimulation for a number of seconds until she subtly signals she is ready for more stimulation.

Generally, stimulating the clitoris encourages the squeeze contractions of the outer vagina; stimulating the inner-trigger areas encourages the deeper push-out response. A combination of alternating and simultaneous stimulation of the clitoris and the inner trigger areas is the basic method of stimulation in the first phase of extended orgasm. We also call this phase the "staircase phase" because of the way it looks on a graph—climbing, leveling, climbing, leveling.

The first phase of extended orgasm may last fifteen minutes or more. When a woman finally lets go of enough mental resistances for a sufficient time, she enters the second phase of extended orgasmic response, the continuous-climbing phase. This second phase is characterized by smooth, long waves of deep push-outs. The anal sphincter muscles are relaxed and open rather than closed or reflexively contracting as in Stages I and II. Her partner influences the intensity and duration of these push-outs by the way he stimulates the vaginal trigger areas. Pressure that is too hard, too soft, or off target will result in diminishing or cessation of orgasmic response. Furthermore, what stimulation is effective is not a fixed formula and frequently changes from minute to minute. The dedicated partner must give his full attention to his partner, adjusting his actions to her reactions.

Phase II, extended orgasmic response, is sometimes referred to subjectively by women who experience it as being on an "orgasmic track" or being "immobilized by pleasure."

To the woman this phase feels timeless. She feels as if she is on a track of continuous and smoothly rising pleasure. Like a meditative state, the feeling is of an altered state of consciousness—floating without effort. In the first phase of extended orgasmic response, the "staircase phase," the woman consciously and actively reaches for more pleasure. In the second phase, continuously climbing, she has no sensation of effort. This experience can last from several minutes to half an hour or more.

A small percentage of women are able to experience both Phase I and Phase II extended orgasm with clitoral stimulation alone. They can sustain the push-out response with very light clitoral stimulation. However, vaginal stimulation still usually adds to the intensity of their experience.

Electrical brain recordings show characteristic changes in brain waves that occur during extended sexual response. There appears to be a possible shift in relative activity between the left and right hemispheres of the brain, which become more synchronized with each other. The right side of the brain, which is more involved with intuition and feelings, becomes more active. These changes are similar to those seen in states of deep meditation. All who experience ESO agree it's a sustained state of changed consciousness.

One of our clients, Natali, calls the experience of second-phase ESO "being nailed." "At a certain point," she told us, "I finally gave up and let go completely. It's as if André had me nailed to the spot and I couldn't move a

single muscle. I didn't want to. I wanted to stay there forever." Another client compared the sensation to "floating
in space." A third found "no questions, only answers. Problems that had been bothering me for a long time suddenly
seemed clear."

After your partner has enjoyed a few minutes of second-
phase ESO, she may need less stimulation to maintain the
continuous climb. The orgasmic process becomes more
self-sustaining. Light stimulation of the vagina and clitoris
or of either area alone is usually sufficient then. Push-outs
may even continue for thirty seconds or more with no
stimulation at all.

Women who have experienced ESO report a level of
arousal with extended orgasm stronger than that of brief or
multiple orgasm. Each orgasm in a series of multiple orgasms, they say, feels much the same as the last one. But
ESO feels more and more intense as the stimulation continues. The vagina feels as if it is taking over. But remember, heart rate and blood pressure actually go down.
You won't explode.

We've left both time and level of arousal open-ended on
the graph on page 131 because we haven't yet seen any
limit to the level or duration of the female orgasmic experience.

How long you continue in the ESO state will depend on
your time and energy. Sooner or later one or both of you
will get tired or decide you've had enough for now. You'll
choose then to come down.

Before you do, however, finish your partner by taking
her up to an extra-high peak of orgasmic arousal, a final
climax.

Women experienced with ESO tell us that they continue
to feel occasional pelvic contractions for up to twenty-four
hours after extended orgasmic experience. Which is to say,
they continue to be aroused above the baseline state and
even feel occasional subtle orgasmic contractions as they

go about their day-to-day lives. That's why they may begin orgasm almost immediately upon penetration during intercourse. This is called the Rapid Orgasmic Response. It catapults a woman right back into ESO again. (See graph on page 131.)

Some women or their partners who read this may wonder about how they might act in this post-ESO period, when they are aware of increased sexual energy. Women are *not* more likely to seek other partners. Women who regularly experience ESO function better than ever, whatever their work. And they're healthier, less irritable, more relaxed, and much happier.

Another note about resistances: It's possible that toilet training early in life encourages the habit of keeping pelvic sphincter muscles tight. Tight pelvic muscles may be the equivalent of squeeze contractions in the orgasmic response.

A child's earliest muscular training is learning to respond to any feeling of pressure in the pelvic area by automatically tightening pelvic sphincter muscles. A child is strongly rewarded for learning to control his/her sphincter muscles. This control is reinforced throughout life. Inadvertent loss of sphincter control, resulting in accidental urination or defecation, is among the most socially embarrassing events anyone ever experiences. The only acceptable times for relaxing pelvic sphincter muscles are alone in the privacy of a bathroom.

Given this conditioning, if one assumes that the natural orgasmic response is in fact a push-out, the onset of a push-out would immediately be followed by a counter reflex—a squeeze reaction, trying to hold in. For this reason, a woman may resist or even fear the natural push-out response characteristic of the extended orgasmic response. This learned reflex resistance could equally explain as well males' resistance to experiencing spontaneous extended orgasmic responses.

6

Male ESO:
How to Stimulate
a Man

This chapter will tell you, the woman, how to stimulate your male partner to ESO.* "You" here will mean the active, stimulating partner. As before, both partners should read this chapter carefully.

You've enjoyed a time of ESO. Now it's the man's turn. You may want to proceed immediately to changing places and switching roles. Or you may want to take a break—for refreshments, to use the toilet, or simply to rest.

There's no law that says both partners have to experience ESO every time either one of them does. It's usually advisable. In the long run the books of sexual attention need to be balanced. Otherwise one or the other partner will feel cheated. Certainly, in practicing for ESO, you and your partner should pleasure each other for more or less equivalent periods of time.

---

*These directions apply equally to same-sex couples where male stimulates male.

Accepting Pleasure

Many men resist being pleasured. They're used to *taking* pleasure. If they're loving men, they're used to giving pleasure. They need to learn to accept lying back and relaxing and letting someone pleasure them. A man's goal at this point is to be totally passive and receptive, like a sponge, to see how much pleasure he can absorb. Men need to learn that sex doesn't always have to be a performance (so do you, if you're used to thinking of your partner as a performer).

Rodney was a client of ours who had difficulty accepting pleasure. He was forty-seven when we first saw him. His wife, June, was thirty. The age difference sometimes bothered Rodney, but he was more subtly troubled by the difference in his and June's body sizes. June was slightly larger than he, taller and heavier. The size difference intimidated him.

The problem didn't show up at first as Rodney progressed from early ejaculation to sustaining twenty- and thirty-minute erections and June progressed to beginning ESO. Then the time came for Rodney to allow June to stimulate him manually and orally. He balked. He felt dominated. He was happy to stimulate June. He was happy with intercourse. But he could only accept manual and oral stimulation from June for two or three minutes at a time before he became too uncomfortable, too anxious, to continue.

It wasn't an enormous problem to solve. Rodney concentrated on relaxing through his resistance. We suggested that June use one of the lower-profile positions we'll be telling you about, so that she didn't seem to tower over her husband as he lay on his back. She reassured him verbally that she found his body attractive. Rodney eventually learned to accept pleasure from June. They're doing very well.

Men who feel uncomfortable lying back and taking should remember that they've just given their partners an intense time of pleasure. They've done their duty. It's fair and right that they should have pleasure in return.

Men: your partner deserves the same experience of giving you intense pleasure as you had giving pleasure to her. If you don't allow her this privilege, you are denying her unfairly as well as denying yourself.

The highest levels of pleasure possible with ESO can be achieved only with a partner's stimulation. They can't be achieved if the man is actively taking or controlling, only by giving up control. Difficulty with giving up control is a resistance, to be dealt with like any other resistance. (For further discussion see chapter 8, "Overcoming Resistances," page 195.)

ROMANCING THE MALE

Music, flowers, scents, can help build your partner's anticipation of pleasures to come. Avoid interruptions. No serious subjects! Kiss, pet, caress. Bathe together or lovingly wash your partner's genitals. Remove any unnecessary jewelry either of you may be wearing. Be sure your fingernails are trimmed—at least both index fingers and thumbs. If appropriate, do a body massage.

Differences—Controlling the Two-Stage Reflex

Male ESO is different from female ESO. In female ESO you moved up to and through brief orgasm to a higher level of orgasm. In male ESO a male moves up to and into first-stage orgasm: the emission stage, where he remains for a period of time. There is hard erection, obvious arousal, and an intermittent secretion of clear fluid from the penis, which signals the presence of highly pleasurable internal contractions.

These contractions are from the prostate and Cowper's gland that contribute to semen production. You will help your partner reach this stage and extend it to even higher levels of arousal *without cresting over into ejaculation.*

The Prostate—A Man's Hidden Trigger

The role of the prostate gland in male sexual response has largely been ignored. Most men and their partners don't realize that stimulating this organ can add significantly to sexual arousal. We will discuss prostate stimulation in some detail in this chapter. Here we'd just like to explain why that stimulation is important.

Stimulating the male prostate is similar in some ways to stimulating the female G-spot area. Both areas have a similar nerve supply. Both areas may derive anatomically from the same fetal tissue. The G spot is still a subject of study. Of the existence and function of the prostate gland there is no doubt whatsoever.

Stimulating the prostate along with stimulating the penis produces a deeper, more powerful, longer orgasm in most men. Prolonged stimulation results in greater semen volume, and semen volume is one important factor in a man's sense of the intensity of his orgasm. Alternately or simultaneously stroking the penis and the prostate also produces high levels of continuous arousal. That's very much like the pattern of stimulation we described for women that involved alternately or simultaneously stimulating the clitoris and the vagina. Although the first or middle finger may be used, the thumb works best because considerable pressure is required to stimulate the external prostate spot (EPS). When one thumb gets tired, you can change positions and use the other thumb. For EPS stimulation, start with a dry hand for three to five minutes, then add lubrication for additional sensations.

Some couples may want to experiment with direct prostate stimulation. A woman can stimulate her partner's prostate directly by inserting a lubricated finger into the rectum and pressing upward toward the scrotum. (See illustration 2, "Male Anatomy," on page 44 for guidance.)

A specially shaped plastic device is available that simultaneously stimulates the internal and external prostate areas. Called the Aneros, it is inserted before solo or partner sex and can help a man more easily learn to have deep prostate-focused extended orgasms (see "Products and Where to Find Them" on page 269).

Positions

As you did before when it was your turn to be pleasured, your male partner now finds a comfortable position lying on his back. He props his head on a pillow if he likes. He separates his legs. You then have several options.

You can sit facing him between his legs with his legs flexed, knees up, and his thighs resting over yours. You may sit on your haunches, or cross your legs, or extend your legs. That allows both your hands access to his genitals. (See illustration 12 on page 151.)

Or, with your partner on his back, you can stretch out on your stomach or side, perpendicular to him—so that the two of you make a T—with your head and hands at the level of his genitals. You may also sit between his legs, resting your left elbow over his right thigh. His left leg can be between your legs or resting on top of your right thigh. In this position you have both hands free; you can also

9 FEMALE STIMULATING MALE: BETWEEN LEGS, HEAD ON THIGH

Right hand stimulates the upper penis; left hand stimulates base and root of penis/external prostate. Good for adding oral stimulation.

easily add oral stimulation. (See illustration 17 on page 175.)

Or you can start from a position sitting sideways between your partner's flexed legs. His legs are between or on top of your thighs. This position also makes it possible to add oral as well as manual stimulation. (See illustration 10 on page 145.)

Finally, and especially later in your ESO training, you can use a modified sixty-nine position, both of you resting on your sides turned toward each other with your heads at the level of each other's genitals. If your upper legs are flexed, each of you can then alternate manual as well as oral stimulation. You can take turns being active and being a receiver or you can stimulate each other simultaneously. (See illustration 4 on page 108.)

It's important to be comfortable; otherwise you won't give your partner your full attention. Feel free to shift position when you begin to feel uncomfortable—to bend your legs more or less, to prop your elbow, to add or subtract a pillow. Shifting positions also changes the stimulation and helps your partner maintain ejaculatory control. Moving around is part of your sexual dance together. Try to continue genital stimulation even while you are moving to another position to reduce the distraction.

These are good, basic starting positions. From them you can both move easily into variations.

Achieving Erection

Your partner won't necessarily have an erection after pleasuring you. The reason he won't is that he's been paying attention to you, not to himself. He'll be aroused, but it's a myth, and a destructive one, that men automatically become erect in sexual situations. They don't. Most need their penises directly stimulated to achieve erection, especially men beyond their twenties who have been with a familiar partner for a few years. That's not a sign of inadequacy. It's normal. Men who are immediately erect without penile stimulation in every sexual encounter make up only a small minority of the general population.

Once you and your partner are comfortably positioned, you should proceed to do whatever you usually do to stimulate him to erection. One obvious thing you can do is to apply lubrication.

If, in the course of stimulating your partner, you plan to

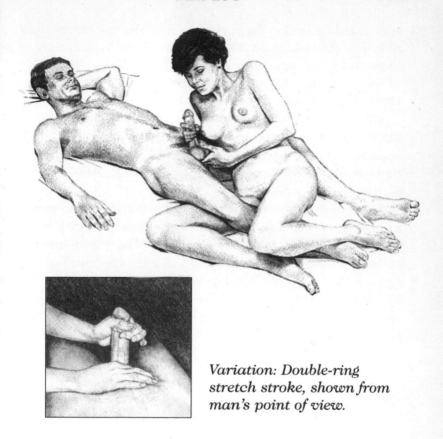

*Variation: Double-ring
stretch stroke, shown from
man's point of view.*

10 FEMALE STIMULATING MALE:
BETWEEN LEGS, ELBOW OUTSIDE

*Good access to genitals with hands and mouth. Right
hand stimulates penis, left hand stimulates external
prostate spot, testicles, and scrotum. Allows intimate eye
contact. In easy variation, woman shifts body downward, still resting on elbow. If woman's neck tires, she
can lower head to rest on man's thigh while stimulation
continues. If one hand tires, woman can easily shift to opposite elbow. Allows easy shift to oral stimulation.*

stimulate him orally, we suggest you do not use petrolatum now. Petrolatum tastes like . . . petrolatum. It lasts a long time, but it has neither a gourmet flavor nor texture. Use Albolene or our homemade lubricant recipe and add flavoring if you prefer. See "Lubrication," page 257.

Lubricate the penis thoroughly, as well as the scrotum, the perineum, and the external anal area. Lubricate both your hands. Use plenty of lubricant. Too much is better than too little. The pre-ejaculatory fluid that men produce is insufficient for lubrication.

Begin now to stroke your partner's penis, remembering what you learned from him during Sexual Exploration exercises about the strokes he prefers. The basic manual stroke finds your dominant hand circling the glans of the penis with the thumb emphasizing the lip. Strong pressure and a heavy stroke are often best at the beginning. Most of the nerve endings in the penis are concentrated in the glans. Remember, the glans is like your clitoris. It's a small area but very sensitive to stroking and pressure.

THE DOUBLE-RING STRETCH STROKE

This is an excellent stroke to use to coax a reluctant penis into full erection, as well as to harden an already full one. (See illustration 10 on page 145.) Make a ring with the thumb and index finger of each hand, one above the other, around the shaft of the penis at its base. Use enough pressure to constrict some of the outflow of blood from the penis. If your left hand is ringed around the penis base, move your right-hand ring upward toward the head of the penis. Then remove your right hand and again place two fingers in a ring just above your left hand near the base and again pull upward. Be sure to use enough pressure to trap some blood above your fingers and to stretch the penis as you stroke it. Develop a rhythm. You may find it useful to add a twisting motion to the stroke as your fingers move up the shaft. Another variant is repeatedly starting both hands in a ring around the middle of the shaft of the penis (rather than near the base) and moving them in opposite directions, one toward the base and the other toward the penis head. As the penis gets fuller, more than two fingers may be used to form the rings. To avoid fatigue, you may switch hands. The important thing is to move the rings up and down the shaft away from each other.

You should also experiment. Let your partner's penis be your guide. If his penis is hardening and stiffening, you're doing fine. But don't stop until you have given him a few minutes to respond. He may be working through resistance and need more time.

Adding Stimulation

When he's arrived at full, hard erection and stayed that way for at least fifteen minutes, you can begin to stimulate your partner's scrotum and the area closer to the anus, behind the base of the scrotum—the perineum—where it's possible to push in without pressing against bone. The prostate gland is located inside your partner's body directly behind that area. For convenience we'll refer to that external area as the "external prostate spot" or "EPS" from now on. (See illustration 2, "Male Anatomy," on page 44.)

Pressure on the external prostate spot usually isn't comfortable until a man is fully aroused and his scrotum is elevated and hard. Then stimulation there can cause additional arousal.

So you can add to your partner's pleasure by caressing his scrotal and external prostate areas in several ways.

One involves pulling the scrotum (not jerking; pulling). Women usually avoid handling their partner's testicles.

They've been taught that the testicles are extremely sensitive and can be easily hurt. Under other circumstances that's true, but during sexual arousal they enlarge and engorge and sensitivity to pain becomes, within limits, sensitivity to pleasure.

The testicles still shouldn't be squeezed, but they can be pulled, along with the entire scrotum. Don't hold on to the testicles themselves when you pull them. Make a loose clamp of your thumb and first fingers above the testicles on the scrotum, closer to the body, and apply traction that way. Or take firm hold of the scrotum with thumb and forefinger deeply *between* the testicles and pull. This method also works. You can pull lightly in rhythm either way as you stroke your partner's penis. (See illustration 11 on page 149.)

Scrotal pulling has another value. It's an excellent way to help your partner avoid ejaculating. Males usually don't ejaculate until their testicles are fully drawn up against their bodies.

While you're applying scrotal traction you can lightly tease the penis by tickling the glans with a circle of fingers. You're pulling on your partner's scrotum to stop him from ejaculating, so you need to lighten stroking his penis. Teasing the glans can add to arousal even while you're holding your partner back from going over the top.

Another way to caress your partner is by applying pressure with your thumb to his external prostate spot. Steady pressure feels good. So does stroking pressure in rhythm with stroking his penis. How hard you should press depends on how aroused he is. The more aroused, the more pressure is comfortable. Watch your partner's response. If you're applying too much pressure, he'll pull away. If he wants more, he'll move toward you. Many men complain that their partners are *too* gentle when handling their genitals. Don't be afraid to experiment.

A third caress we call the "prostate pincher." You can do

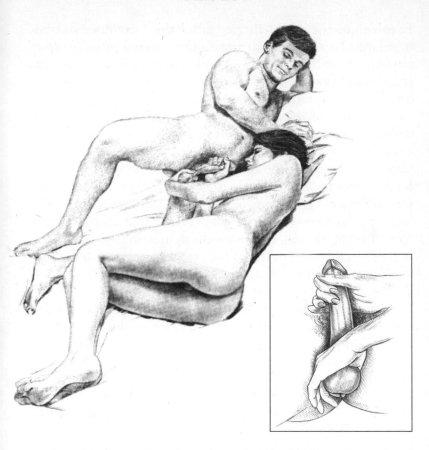

11 FEMALE STIMULATING MALE: SIDE BY SIDE

*Pillow supports woman's head, allowing relaxation, free
from exertion. Excellent position for long-term stimulation. Easily adaptable for oral stimulation. Woman can
lock elbows at waist and stimulate shaft and base of
penis with hands while applying oral stimulation to
penis head. Gently rocking back and forth provides almost effortless stimulation for extended period.*

*Inset shows detail of scrotal pull for stimulation and
for ejaculation control.*

it two different ways. Either press the forefinger of your dominant hand into your partner's external prostate spot, with the thumb of the same hand anchored hooked around the base of his penis; or reverse the position of the digits, anchor your forefinger around the base of the penis, and push in on the external prostate spot with your thumb. (See illustration 12 and inset on page 151.) One method works better for some people, the other for others. If your prostate-pushing forefinger needs more support, you can back it up with your middle finger. Either way, stroke your partner's penis with your other hand at the same time. The more pressure on the external prostate spot and the faster the stroking, the faster the climb to arousal.

Change stroke rhythm every ten to thirty seconds. If your partner's level of arousal is steady or climbing, your stimulation at that point is perfect.

While stimulating the EPS, divert your thumb or fingers forward occasionally to the penile bulb at the back of the buried penis base using lighter pressure. Your other hand can milk the penis. One of the most effective manual strokes is the whole-penis milking stroke: your lower hand pumps fluid from the EPS forward along the underside of the buried penis; then your upper hand picks up the motion and carries it, stroking upward. When your upper hand strokes back down, your lower hand relaxes pressure. Alternate hard and firm with soft and slow every three to twelve strokes.

With continued, climbing stimulation, your partner will approach ejaculation. You don't want him to ejaculate, or his orgasm will end until he can return through the refractory period to arousal. At this point do *not* stimulate the glans of the penis. Concentrate instead on other genital areas.

You have several means of control. One is the scrotal pull. A second is pressure on the external prostate spot, which distracts him. A third is squeezing firmly at the base

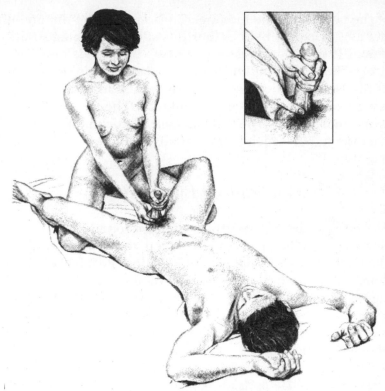

12 FEMALE STIMULATING MALE: KNEELING BETWEEN LEGS

Illustration and inset show left hand stimulating penis, right hand applying prostate pincher with thumb anchored at upper base of penis and index finger pressing on external prostate spot below.

Suggested for beginning or early stage of stimulation. Good for woman's alertness and focus of attention to create and maintain erection. Easy access to male genital area with both hands. Oral stimulation may be added by bending over. Intimate eye contact possible. Disadvantage: requires relatively more physical energy for woman to support body in upright position. Man may equally well utilize position when stimulating partner.

of the penis with the forefinger in front and the thumb on the EPS or penile bulb. A fourth is simply stopping stimulation. It may be necessary to take your hands away entirely. Stop stroking and simply pause, hands on or off, until his arousal decreases slightly, which may take only a few seconds or as much as a minute. Then begin stimulating him again. Try all these control techniques. Alternate them. See which combinations work best.

Controlling Ejaculation

At first you and your partner will have to pay close attention to controlling ejaculation. When you bring him up to the high level of arousal near ejaculation, he'll feel close to going over. You have to be very careful then, watching his signs of arousal and stopping or lightening and changing stimulation when he gets too close. Watch for his hands moving toward his genitals to push you away. Listen for changes in his sounds.

The man, for his part, is also attentive to how near he is to ejaculation. He pulls away from your stroking. He shifts mental attention away from his sensation. Or he uses Kegel exercises to help with control.

There'll be slips along the way. It's like learning how to ski or roller-skate—you fall a lot at first. The man should enjoy his orgasm when it happens by relaxing and letting go. Then you both should discuss the experience to find out why it happened and to plan for more effective control. The primary responsibility for control at this point is yours.

Just as women do, men contract their pelvic muscles to build arousal. When your partner feels ejaculation approaching, one way he can regain control is to hold his breath momentarily and push his pelvic muscles out—bearing down. This process is like straining for a moment to move his bowels. Breath holding and bearing down (pushing out) can momentarily stop the climb to ejaculation. Combining contracting the pelvic muscles with slow, deep breathing may also be effective. Then it's up to you to reduce the stimulation momentarily until your partner regains ejaculatory control.

Some men find deliberate, slow, deep breathing or, contrarily, faster panting helps control ejaculation. They may combine deliberate, slow breathing with bearing down, or deliberate, slow breathing with clenching. Making pleasure groans can help diffuse genital arousal, and also informs his partner about his arousal level. Each man must determine for himself the most effective combination of breath holding, deliberate breathing, and tightening or relaxing of the pelvic muscles.

It's important to remember that the man's ejaculation *isn't* your goal. In ESO, when your partner approaches ejaculation, you should *reduce* stimulation, not increase it.

Having regained control by bearing down while you reduced stimulation, your partner can now maintain control as you begin stroking again by again contracting his pelvic muscles. It's a question of shifting attention. Anything that shifts your partner's attention will momentarily level him off.

Control becomes a matter of teamwork: you sense his level of arousal and change rhythm and stroke to help him with control; at the same time, he responds with muscular contractions and relaxations and by bearing down. In the first stage of ESO, men can never quite lose consciousness to the extent women can. This first ESO stage is still extremely pleasurable, and it's more pleasurable the more *you,* his partner, learn to take control of preventing ejaculation. In the second stage of ESO, control of ejaculation becomes more automatic. It proceeds without effort or anxiety, and a man feels as if he has entered an altered state of consciousness that can last as long as he and you wish.

If he is becoming more and more aroused—climbing— his legs will usually flex more as his body reaches for stim- ulation. When he wants to level or come down to avoid ejaculating, he will usually extend his legs and pull away. You must learn to read these motions accurately.

The goal for the man is to relax his PC muscles totally while experiencing deep, continuous, prostate-focused pleasure. The feeling state of orgasm continues. Every con- traction urge is converted into an active push-out, lifting him into a higher level of orgasmic pleasure that can last five, ten, fifteen, twenty minutes to an hour or more. So after pushing out for five minutes or more whenever he feels the urge to contract, his goal should be to *relax into* the urges to contract, falling backward (so to speak) into emission-stage orgasm rather than falling forward into ejaculation. Your goal and his should be to keep him as close as possible to the point of ejaculatory inevitability, thoroughly enjoying the emission-phase orgasm without cresting over into ejaculation, feeling the pleasure and re- lease of prostate contractions, PC contractions, and anal- sphincter contractions. His mind and body will become amazingly relaxed, and he will have to make little effort to avoid ejaculation. This process is analogous to the mental discipline of meditation, where you redirect your attention away from passing distractions.

If you have agreed in advance on how much time you will spend stimulating your partner, don't change that agreement now. He may indicate by his arousal that he wants to ejaculate quickly. Don't encourage him or give in to his sense of urgency or pressure. If a man doesn't know about the much greater amount of pleasure possible in ESO, he pushes for ejaculation. You must be strong and help him resist this urge. If you give in too soon and stim- ulate him to ejaculation, you will be robbing him of greater pleasure, and he may feel responsible for failing to control himself.

Resistances

While you're building arousal, your partner will be working through resistances. They're the same resistances we listed before: worries about work, time, propriety, and distraction. Males also often have to deal with their chauvinisms:

Am I letting her run me?
Can she handle me?
Can I trust her to do it right?

Or they may be dealing with their doubts:

Is she really enjoying this?
She must be getting tired.
Am I reacting properly?

Men learning ESO have an additional and opposite problem from women learning ESO. Women mainly have to learn to let go. Men first must be able to let go, to allow arousal and erection, but then men have to learn *not* to let go, to prevent early ejaculation. For each sex the learning leads to greater pleasure. There's a promise of much more on the other side. Men who are hesitant to give up control should remember the reason for doing so: it feels good, and better and better.

So your male partner must deal with resistances somewhat differently from you. When he finds himself losing arousal because of resistances or any other distractions, he needs to turn his attention deliberately inward again to sensation. *He needs to concentrate and reconcentrate on*

sensation, adding the control mechanisms of Kegel exer-
cises and slow, deep breathing. Cognitive restructuring
doesn't work as well for the man because he needs to monitor his state of arousal continually at first to avoid ejaculating. If he switches to a positive thought or repeats a
neutral phrase, the sensation can catch him by surprise.

Men need to pay attention to breathing. They also sometimes hold their breath while they're concentrating their
muscles to build arousal. If they hold their breath too long,
they lose control. Remind your partner to breathe if you notice him holding his breath for longer than about ten seconds.

SNEAKING UP

If you've tried everything else and your partner still resists,
try making him *laugh*. At the same time keep stimulating
his penis very rapidly and with hard strokes. Sneak up on
him. Say something funny or kid him. Act silly. Make a
face. Do something unexpected. He can't resist as much
when he's laughing.

Achieving Male ESO

The graph titled "Male Orgasmic Response Stages" shows
the differences in arousal and response through time of
male single orgasm, multiple orgasm, and male ESO (Stage
I, Stage II, Stage III).

In single orgasm (Stage I), arousal increases with stimulation through an excitement phase to a three- to five-
second burst of pleasurable internal contractions
(emission-phase orgasm), which is experienced as a sense
of ejaculatory inevitability—the point of no return. Your
partner knows he's going to ejaculate and can't stop. Several seconds later ejaculation begins, with six to ten

13 MALE ORGASMIC RESPONSE STAGES

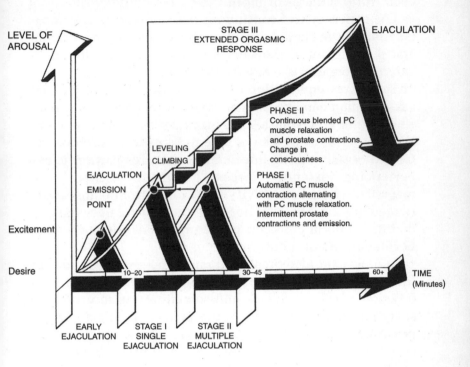

strong, propulsive orgasmic contractions and the expulsion of semen, lasting about ten seconds.

After a refractory period of several minutes or longer, when stimulation isn't effective, a man may have a second, similar orgasm. This is multiple orgasm in the male (Stage II).

For a man to reach extended orgasmic response (Stage III orgasm) he needs to learn to control the rate of his climbing arousal as he nears the emission phase of his orgasm. Repeated multiple peaking, involving "stop and start" or "fast and slow" stimulation, can lead into extended emission phase. The usual three- to five-second emission phase is prolonged in time. At first this extension is merely a second or two. With continued practice, it can be extended to many seconds, a minute, many minutes, even thirty minutes or more.

The experience of continuous male orgasm is one of relaxation of the genital muscles with a sense of opening up and pushing out at the same time. The anal sphincter in extended orgasm is relaxed and open, rather than closed or reflexively contracting as it is in brief and multiple orgasm. A man can experience extended orgasm most easily when he is receiving his partner's active oral or manual stimulation. He may also be able to learn to experience extended orgasm during intercourse when his partner is experiencing extended orgasm herself. Without the magnified vaginal sensitivity that comes from being in extended orgasm, she may not have the control necessary to maintain him in emission-phase orgasm as she does using her hands and/or mouth.

In male extended orgasm the man moves up to and into first-phase orgasm: the emission phase, where there is hard erection, obvious arousal, and sometimes an intermittent secretion of clear fluid from the penis, which signals the presence of highly pleasurable internal contractions. These contractions are from the prostate and other glands that contribute to semen production. The woman can help her partner reach this phase and extend it to even higher levels of arousal *without cresting over into ejaculation.*

The key to male extended orgasm involves having the man stay as close as possible to the point of ejaculatory inevitability—keeping him in emission-phase orgasm—without allowing him to crest and ejaculate. This is accomplished by creating multiple nonejaculatory peaks. When a man experiences fifteen or more of these peaks in close succession, they may become blended into a continuous emission-phase orgasm. Self-stimulation is effective to this purpose to a limited degree, but partner stimulation is more effective. The timing and pressure of external prostate spot stimulation is important in extending emission-phase orgasm. Firm pressure applied with a thumb or finger joint just prior to a peak will help block the ejaculation reflex. External prostate stimulation is equivalent to G-spot inner trigger sensation in a woman. Many men discover it to be remarkably pleasure-enhancing. The man uses various ejaculatory-control techniques to assist his entry into emission-phase orgasm. With experience and practice, this first-phase orgasmic response opens out from a narrow, unstable stage to a wide, stable platform of intense pleasure—which can last from a minute or two to thirty minutes or more.

In Stage III the reflex of ejaculatory inevitability is brought under control by deliberate training and practice. The emission phase of pleasurable internal contractions increases from a few seconds to a minute and then longer.

By learning to control the approach of ejaculatory inevitability, the man will be able to accept increasing amounts of stimulation during emission-phase orgasm. His level of arousal will continuously increase. He'll experience the stimulation as increasingly pleasurable, and he'll be able to accept more of it longer without ejaculating. He'll still be using some ejaculatory-control techniques himself—breathing, sex muscle exercises, switching attention, for example. During this time he may secrete larger-than-usual amounts of a clear fluid that is more watery than semen. He experiences a state of being pleasurably immobilized. When he ejaculates, his ejaculatory experience will probably be more intense and will also last longer. Instead of six to ten contractions, there may be fifteen to twenty or more. Continuous firm pressure on the external prostate spot during ejaculation can increase the number and intensity of expulsion contractions, which may go on for several minutes of climactic ecstasy.

Eventually, with ejaculation, the man trained in ESO also experiences a refractory period. But with mutual interest and continued, correct stimulation, he can reenter extended orgasm within several minutes. His penis may remain partly or fully erect.

His general level of arousal (and probably his levels of sexual hormones) will remain higher from day to day if both partners keep up their extended orgasmic skills. Then both partners will find even brief sessions of lovemaking more pleasurable.

Why is it that men don't spontaneously discover the ability to extend their orgasmic response more often? Lack of knowledge is one reason. In the discussion of ESO in the woman, we suggested another reason—early bowel training habits reinforced throughout life. For men, a third reason is that extended response requires unlearning still another reflex—the ejaculatory reflex. However, we know from discoveries in the medical field of biofeedback that many reflexes that had been believed to be automatic, beyond voluntary control, can in fact be brought under voluntary control through information, training, and practice. This reconditioning includes the orgasmic response.

Practice Schedule

During practice make it your goal to take your partner to a peak of arousal close to ejaculation at least fifteen times, on the average, during a thirty-minute session. You'll find as you and he learn control that he'll stay at higher and higher levels between peaks. Eventually there won't be much decline between peaks and you'll be supplying only very light, subtle changes in pressure and rhythm.

Male Extended Orgasm

After a while, as your partner works through his resistances and as you both learn the teamwork of ejaculatory control, you'll find it easier and easier to stimulate him to very high levels of arousal. He'll find it easier and easier to stay there.

The intensely pleasurable state close to ejaculation becomes more stable with experience and extends in time, as we saw in the graph of male response. You may begin to notice an intermittent secretion of fluid from your partner's penis. His penis is hard and engorged, and it doesn't soften unless you completely stop stimulating. He's not thrusting or straining. You're the driver, controlling his level of arousal and maintaining him just this side of ejaculation. He's the passenger, along for the ride—he's giving up control to you. In the early stages of ESO he may show the same signs of extreme arousal that you showed—moaning, panting, sweating, jerking his arms and legs. He's testing your sensitivity to his level of arousal and his feelings. He's learning that your goal is not to push him over that point of no return, but instead to extend his pleasure.

In Phase II ESO he will become more stabilized. The jerking and panting tend to diminish as he experiences quieter ecstasy. His blood pressure and heart rate drop moderately from their high levels in earlier stages of orgasm. His pelvic muscles relax. His anal sphincter relaxes and opens.

Eventually his penis may become so sensitized that a light touch, a teasing tickle, even simply blowing warm air on it or applying cool lubricant to it and letting the lubricant melt, give intense pleasure.

Your partner is experiencing Phase II ESO. You can keep him there for as long as you both like.

Changing Stroking

When we discussed giving the woman pleasure, we said it was important for the man not to vary his stroking too much—some teasing, but not a lot of variation. Nearly two-thirds of the women in a large survey by Carol Ellison reported needing steady, reliable stimulation before and through orgasm. The opposite is true for men. Steady, unvarying stroking will either reduce arousal or carry your partner straight to ejaculation. Because his ESO requires control, he needs lots of variety. Changing strokes prevents ejaculation. You may want to supply a steady, stimulating stroke when he's climbing to greater arousal. But change the stroking when he's close.

You'll find you need to change positions and switch hands for your own comfort. That has the added value of automatically changing the stroke.

Finishing

When you decide to end a session of ESO, take your partner on to ejaculation—if you both haven't decided to finish with intercourse—by giving him extra stimulation. Keep stimulating him lightly through ejaculation and afterward, paying more attention to his scrotum, his prostate, and the shaft of his penis when his glans becomes hypersensitive to touch.

If you keep stimulating after ejaculation appears to be over, you can extend ejaculatory orgasm by half a dozen contractions or more. You'll be *lightly* caressing the penis and pushing and milking the external prostate spot and Cowper's gland area. Part of your partner's pleasure during ejaculation comes from the sensation of fluid pushing up from the base of the penis. By pushing on the external prostate spot, you can mimic that good feeling. Then the pulsing of the deeper pelvic muscles can continue for several pleasurable minutes.

7

ESO:

More Ways to Give

Intercourse

The techniques you've just learned for male and female ESO are basic and central. They're ways to deeper levels of pleasure that should become a permanent part of your sexual repertoire. They're not a temporary substitute for intercourse or a supplement. They're not "variations." Extended sexual orgasm can best be learned when both partners pay attention to one sexual arousal at a time. In terms of levels of arousal, ESO by manual—and oral, which we'll talk about in this chapter—stimulation is more intense than intercourse that has not been preceded by manual stimulation. The blind, blunt penis, the mitten of the vagina, honorable apparatus that they are, can't initially match two skilled hands and a mouth.

That certainly doesn't mean you should abandon intercourse. Quite the contrary. Intercourse is an important part of ESO. These techniques, practiced at least once a week, are a desirable prerequisite to intercourse. If ESO by manual means is more intense than intercourse, it's also, necessarily, less intimate. Making love locked together in each other's arms is deeply satisfying emotionally and spiritually. The best possible lovemaking combines the intensity of manual/oral ESO with the intimacy of intercourse following. ESO continues into intercourse with even more intense contractions, making intercourse more pleasurable, less strenuous, more deeply satisfying, than ever before.

After each of you has pleasured the other to ESO, using manual or oral stimulation or both, you may want to move into intercourse. Even after a long period of ESO, partners often want to finish with intercourse—the grand finale.

If you've followed the pattern we've suggested—the man pleasuring the woman first, then the woman pleasuring the man—the woman will find it easy to return to a state of orgasmic arousal. The man's state will depend on whether or not his partner stimulated him to ejaculation. Even if he did ejaculate, he may find it easy to achieve another erection quickly and ejaculate again with intercourse, especially if he has been practicing Kegel exercises and semen-withholding exercises. Most men, up to at least their late forties, shouldn't have any difficulties. Older men may. That's a natural effect of aging. So, depending on a man's capacity, he may or may not elect to be stimulated to ejaculation at the end of a period of ESO. He may choose to save ejaculation for intercourse. Discuss arrangements beforehand, but don't worry if it doesn't go according to plan.

We've found that men who have learned ESO are more capable of recovery after ejaculation, in less time, than they were before ESO training. Men who have regularly practiced semen withholding also have an advantage. Sometimes they have to push deliberately through the resistance of *thinking* they can't have a second—or third, or fourth—ejaculation. But there's nothing wrong with saving ejaculation for intercourse either. It feels wonderful then, and it assures the woman a hard erection to enjoy.

After ejaculation, the man should continue his thrusting movements, even if his penis becomes less hard. Remember, engorgement of the female genitals magnifies the male's perception of size. Even a partially erect penis will feel extremely pleasurable and much larger than its actual dimensions. Keep the softened penis inside the vagina during these thrusting motions.

Control Positions

Imaginative men and women in every country and of every age have invented hundreds of different positions for lovemaking. We won't even attempt to list them all. We do want to mention a few, to point out their advantages for control. Then you can have the pleasure together of assessing the others on your own.

Some positions allow the man to control movement and therefore to control the amount of stimulation he's receiving. Others allow the woman to control her movement and her stimulation. And others make it possible for a couple to pass control back and forth, or to control movement mutually.

The "missionary" position—the woman on her back, the man on top between her legs—is a male-control position. The man thrusts, and the woman's movement is restricted, yet it's a good position, which is why so many people use it. A small percentage of men find it a position useful to help delay ejaculation, especially men intimidated by a more aggressive position of female control. It allows couples to look at each other and hold each other intimately.

A corresponding position where the woman is most in control finds the man on his back and the woman kneeling astride him. Here she moves, and his movement is restricted. In this position the woman can easily direct her partner's penis to stimulate her G spot. She can also rotate her pelvis to rub her clitoris directly against the base of her partner's penis. Many men resist this position. They falsely equate female control with emotional domination. But this is a good position for learning ejaculatory control. (See illustration 14 on page 167.)

Both partners kneeling with the man behind the woman (or the woman kneeling on a bed and the man standing on the floor) allows mutual control. (See illustration 15 on page 168.) The man may thrust; the woman may sway forward and back on her hands and knees or her forearms and knees; they both may move together. The man's penis can easily be angled to press against and stimulate the woman's inner trigger area.

A modification of the missionary position is also good for stimulating the G spot: the woman, on her back, positions a small, thick pillow beneath her buttocks to tilt the front of her pelvis up, increasing the angle of contact between her vagina and her partner's penis. The man mounts on top between her legs.

For prolonged intercourse, a side-scissors position can reduce fatigue. (See illustration 16 on page 169.) This position also makes it easier for the woman to stimulate her partner manually during intercourse. It allows the man to stimulate his partner's clitoris and vagina manually. Or he can hold his penis (erect or not) and use it for stimulation. The woman lies on her back, turned halfway on her left side (if she's right-handed); the man inserts his penis while he's between his partner's legs in the missionary position, then moves his left leg over her right leg so that his legs scissor her right leg and his perineal area is exposed. Her right hand is then free to stimulate his external prostate spot, the buried root of his penis, and behind his testicles, and to control his urge to ejaculate with a scrotal pull.

14 POSITION FOR INTERCOURSE: FEMALE ABOVE

Woman can control thrusting and penetration depth by moving torso from leaning forward (as illustrated) to sitting upright or leaning back, resting on outstretched arms. At least four distinct types of motion possible. Woman can use legs for heavy thrusting up and down. For less exertion, woman can slide or tilt pelvis forward and back. Can also rotate pelvis left and right. Range of movement allows for optimal internal stimulation of woman's inner trigger area (G spot) and can produce unique sensations for man.

Further advantages: intimacy of face-to-face contact and ability to kiss. If woman sits upright, man can caress clitoris.

Disadvantages: heavy thrusting may tire woman's thighs. Man is pinned down and has less freedom of movement. Slowing or stopping woman's thrusting to control ejaculation is more difficult.

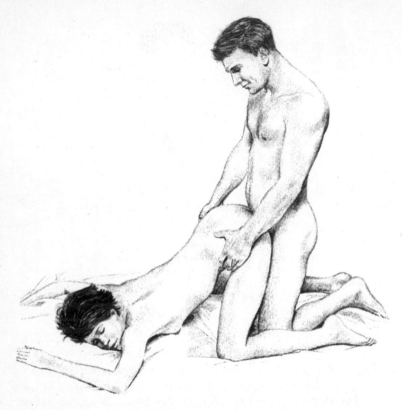

15 POSITION FOR INTERCOURSE: REAR ENTRY

Relatively mutual control. Woman can tilt or rotate pelvis for maximum stimulation of internal trigger area (G spot). Clitoris accessible to either partner for additional stimulation. Deep penetration possible. With hands on partner's hips, man can control woman's thrusting movements to delay ejaculation. Additional control of angle of entry possible when woman raises torso by resting on elbows or hands. Best position for "cervical tapping," repeated up-and-down movement while maintaining maximum penetration.

Disadvantages: penetration may be uncomfortably deep. Lack of face-to-face intimacy and caressing.

16 POSITION FOR INTERCOURSE: SCISSORS

Excellent longer-term position. Enter from man-above (missionary) position, with man rolling onto right side, woman rolling slightly onto left shoulder and side with right leg between man's legs. Both partners position hips for relatively equal freedom of movement. Woman can gain additional thrusting force by pushing right foot against bed for leverage. Woman's right hand is free to hold man's buttocks for guidance and leverage, or pull scrotum, or stimulate base of penis and external prostate area. Intimacy of face-to-face and extensive body contact possible.

Disadvantage: relatively less hip thrusting distance and force possible.

Several rear-entry positions allow the "cervical tapping" by the penis that has been demonstrated to be an orgasmic trigger for some women (Cutler et al.). The woman starts either lying facedown on a pillow or kneeling. These positions allow her partner to enter her vagina from behind. When he has penetrated deeply, she angles her buttocks as high as she comfortably can. Then, instead of thrusting with his hips—instead of pumping his penis in and out of her vagina—he keeps his body straight and pushes up toward her head for the forward stroke and then lowers down for the back stroke. This sliding motion with the penis buried causes the penis to lever up and down, bumping across the cervix. The object is to keep the penis pressed against the cervix while moving it in a levering, up-down motion rather than in and out.

Men who have good ejaculatory control report that when they have intercourse they make frequent *subtle* adjustments in their movements. These adjustments may include slightly speeding up or slowing down their thrusting, changing their angle of penetration, or syncopating their rhythm. Doing Kegel exercises also helps increase control—tightening, relaxing, and pushing out.

After enjoying intercourse for ten minutes to half an hour or more, depending on your desire and your energy levels, you may wish to conclude by taking each other to a peak of pleasure. Do this by increasing the depth and speeding up the rate of your thrusting. At this point the man may choose to ejaculate. During the man's maximal thrusting, the woman pushes out her sex muscles, angles her pelvis for the maximum amount of feeling, and breathes slowly and deeply to allow herself the most pleasure possible. Both of you please remember to vocalize your pleasure during your finale as loud as your environment allows. An "aaaaaHHHaaaa" typed of sound from deep in your abdomen can give you an extra boost.

Intercourse with a soft penis can be useful and pleasurable when a couple bypasses oral or manual ESO and the man is not erect but wishes to proceed directly to intercourse. See "Soft-Penis Intercourse," page 227, for a description of this technique. Illustration 19 on page 228 demonstrates it.

Women who regularly practice ESO often experience rapid orgasmic response with intercourse. When ESO is a regular part of a couple's practice—at least once or twice a week—natural lubrication and rapid orgasmic response may occur within a minute of penetration and thrusting. Women who don't always naturally lubricate quickly should use a lubricant to facilitate rapid orgasm. The rear-entry position, illustration 15 on page 168, works well. The woman should *push out*, opening the vagina to the penis and allowing her to accept penetration and find it immediately arousing. Rapid orgasmic response turns the "quickie" from an appetizer into a pleasure. The memory of recent ESO allows a woman to reproduce that ESO experience with minimal foreplay.

Couples often find themselves routinely making love in the same position week after week. That's fine as long as it's a deliberate choice among other positions, communicated and agreed upon. But choosing other positions for lovemaking can be useful, and arousing, from time to time, to see what new pleasures you can find in them. You don't necessarily need a book. You can make up your own. Fantasize about what you might like, then discuss your ideas with your partner and experiment.

Further considerations for improving intercourse:

When a woman who is not usually orgasmic during intercourse experiences intercourse, she will probably find it pleasurable, but she may also not find it interesting enough to continue for longer than about ten minutes. Without having orgasm during intercourse, she has little incentive to continue if she feels she's running out of energy or time. That's when she's likely to speed up her thrusting to stimulate her partner to ejaculate.

She can assist her approach to orgasm during intercourse by practicing internal squeeze contractions, particularly the slow-clench type (not push-outs, which are more useful for helping to intensify and extend orgasm). Her partner can stimulate her clitoris manually while they're having intercourse in the rear-entry position. She can stimulate herself manually or with a vibrator. Or man and woman together can organize some combination of these additional sources of stimulation.

The woman's deliberate internal squeeze contractions can help the man as well. He's stimulated by her internal movements, but not as intensely as he is from pelvic thrusting. This continuing but low-level stimulation may allow him to approach the emission phase more closely while remaining in control of ejaculation. This slower climb toward his ejaculation makes him more sensitive to pleasure because he has more time to study and experience the subtleties of his own arousal. The goal is for him to climb slowly to ejaculation using minimum physical movement. His attention is focused entirely on the intensely pleasurable sensation he is experiencing from her internal movements. As the man gets closer to ejaculation, he feels a greater level and intensity of arousal. The longer he experiences that feeling, the more he is able to control the speed of his arousal. More subtle and slow movements may be sufficient to take him steadily to higher levels of arousal without ejaculation. His partner will be considerably more sensitive to his level of arousal if she is experiencing orgasm or has had an orgasm in the previous several minutes.

When a woman has had an orgasm prior to or during intercourse, her vagina becomes more engorged and sensitive. This change helps her to pace her partner's sexual climbing and produces a more pleasurable environment for the penis. The most desirable situation is when the woman is able to have extended orgasm during intercourse.

The woman in orgasm, because of her greater sensitivity to the man's communications through his penis, is able to assume some resposibility for initiating or stopping pelvic movements, based on his level of arousal. If the woman experiences orgasm during intercourse for more than a minute or so, the man may need little or no pelvic thrusting. Her automatic contractions, combining both push-out and squeeze type, may provide all the stimulation he needs along the entire length of his penis. He can experience relatively slow, steady climbing toward emission-phase orgasm by enjoying the exquisite, relatively predictable rhythms and pressure of her spontaneous, continuous internal contractions, occurring without conscious effort. Without pelvic movements, he may occasionally brake his arousal simply by relaxing or pushing out his genital muscles.

Oral Lovemaking

You can increase pleasure two ways: by feeling more intensely through the channels of pleasure you already know and by opening up new channels. The entire surface of your body is a sensing organ. It feels. It can learn to feel more. That's not oversubtlety or mysticism. That's simple fact.

Oral lovemaking—genital "kissing"—can be a source of great pleasure. It isn't necessary to ESO, as we've mentioned. It adds to the pleasure. Combined with manual stimulation, it adds intensity and improves control. It's an additional channel and a delightful one.

Some men and women strongly resist oral lovemaking, or haven't yet included it in their sexual repertoire. For a

discussion of oral techniques, see "Learning Oral Lovemaking," page 262.

For men and women who already enjoy oral sex, we
offer the following suggestions.

STIMULATING A MAN

Orally stimulating your partner's penis during ESO can lift
him to higher levels of arousal. Kneeling between his legs
is one comfortable position for oral sex. (See illustration
12 on page 151.) While continuing manual stimulation,
you may want to shift his body and yours so that you are
both lying on your sides, facing each other, with your head
at the level of his penis. Rest your head on a pillow. You'll
be able to continue stimulating your partner manually, including his penis, his scrotum, and his prostate, while
adding oral stimulation to his penis. (See illustration 11 on
page 149.)

Another position you can shift to is lying on your side
with your head between his legs, resting on his thigh, with
his body partly turned toward you and his free leg flexed
over your body. (See illustration 9 on page 143.)

Or try lying on your side with your elbow outside his
thigh. (See illustration 17 on page 175.) This position gives
access to his entire genital area. The illustration shows one
hand pulling on the scrotum, which for many men increases arousal and helps to control ejaculation.

Either way, you can use whatever oral techniques your
partner finds arousing—licking the shaft of his penis,
mouthing the glans while you continue stroking the shaft
with your hands, moving your head up and down on the
glans and as much of the shaft as you can comfortably take
into your mouth. With your mouth stimulating the head of
the penis and one hand stimulating the shaft, use the other
hand to stimulate the scrotum and the bulb at the base of

17 FEMALE STIMULATING MALE: LYING ON SIDE, ELBOW OUTSIDE THIGH

Left hand stimulates penis; right hand uses scrotal pull for stimulation and for ejaculation control. Easy stimulation of external prostate spot is possible. Comfortable oral access.

the penis. Massaging stimulation of the Cowper's gland often results in your partner producing pre-ejaculatory fluid. You can massage the external prostate spot as well. This combination of mouth and hands is the ultimate male control stroke.

Keep your partner reaching for more. Your aim is to take him to erection Stage III, full erection, and keep him there, not advancing to erection Stage IV, rigid, swollen, in which ejaculatory control is more unstable. Try ringing the scrotum with your index finger and thumb and gently pulling down and teasing it while orally stimulating the glans. Be sure you're in a comfortable position.

If your partner is resisting and not responding, apply more oral and manual stimulation. Take as much of the penis in your mouth as you can. Try ringing the penis at the base, partially trapping blood in the shaft, which makes it more rigid and increases the sensation. Change frequency or pressure on the area being stimulated, depending on the fullness of the erection: go faster if you were going slower, go slower if you were going faster. Remember that the average attention span is seven seconds. Another variation involves positioning your hands under your partner's buttocks with your index fingers pressing against the spine at the level of the coccyx (tailbone). This pressure pleasurably stimulates the sacral nerve that runs just below the surface of the back.

Stay connected physically, hand or mouth, if you need to change positions. Otherwise your partner could lose his erection.

Experiment. If you stimulate your partner to a high level of arousal by hand before you begin oral lovemaking, he won't be thrusting now. If he is, he's asking for more stimulation, which you can best increase manually. At peak levels of sensation you'll need only the lightest touch with mouth and tongue. That's when oral stimulation works best with ESO.

Men usually prefer heavier stimulation than women, both manually and orally. Women tend to stimulate a male too gently and then hold him responsible for not achieving erection. If your partner has trouble achieving erection with oral stimulation, it may be because you aren't stimulating him vigorously enough for long enough periods of time to help him through his resistances. Once he knows that you are able to stimulate him through his resistances to full erection and that you intend to do just that no matter how much he resists, he will let go of resistance more quickly and allow himself to become erect.

To stimulate erection, experiment with stronger pressure and more rapid oral and manual strokes. Add pressure with your hands on the shaft of your partner's penis and with your mouth on the glans. Surround the entire glans with your mouth. Protect the penis from your teeth by covering them with your lips. Move your head rapidly up and down and simultaneously stroke the penile shaft with your lubricated hand. The motion of your hand on the shaft should follow the motion of your mouth, as if your hand were a continuation of your mouth. This technique feels like deep-throating: as if you were encompassing the entire penis in your mouth.

Your other hand can simultaneously stimulate the external prostate area. That stimulation—pressing inward and upward toward the penis, stroking as if squeezing fluid from the prostate gland inside—need not necessarily be coordinated with the rhythm of oral stimulation.

Your partner may not become aroused and erect the moment you begin stimulating him. He may need ten minutes or thirty minutes to let go of resistances and to clear away intrusive thoughts. This time corresponds to the time of continuous, reliable stimulation that many women need to reach Stage I orgasm. So you should prepare yourself in terms both of physical comfort and of personal determination to provide strong, effective oral stimulation for up to half an hour, even if your partner's penis doesn't become erect during most of that time. You'll need to change hands and vary strokes to avoid getting tired. If your jaw becomes tired, take your mouth off the glans. Substitute a well-lubricated hand on the glans alone. Use a squeezing, pulling, and milking stroke to create a mild suctionlike sensation. Your other hand should continue to stroke the shaft rhythmically. Along the way you might remind yourself of how long you take to let go of resistance when it's your turn to be stimulated.

Once your partner is fully erect and nearing ejaculation, you'll want to lighten stimulation. That sustains arousal without encouraging ejaculation. You'll need to stimulate only very lightly with your mouth and your tongue during ESO. When you notice arousal dropping even slightly— penis softening, testicles lowering, pre-ejaculatory fluid stopping—immediately increase oral and manual stimulation by adding pressure and speeding up the stroke.

Your partner's testicles as well as his penis are sensitive to oral stimulation. You can lightly stimulate his testicles, one at a time, by taking one into your mouth and gently moving your tongue around it. Stimulate the scrotum as well: use your lips to pull on the scrotum while your lubricated hands stimulate the penile shaft and glans.

Deep-throating, the technique Linda Lovelace made famous in the notorious film, isn't difficult to learn and can be an exciting variation in oral technique.

Most women find that taking more than an inch or two of penis into their mouth triggers the gag reflex in a plexus of nerves at the upper back of their throat. To control your gag reflex, simply *swallow* when you feel the urge to gag. Don't be afraid. You won't swallow your partner's penis. Instead, swallowing constricts your throat and stimulates the penile glans.

Deep-throating your partner's penis blocks your breathing, so take a good breath first. When you need to exhale, move the penis out of your throat back into your mouth. Breathe, then take the penis in deeply again. By alternating these two motions you set up a stroke. You hold your breath for five or ten seconds with your partner's penis deep in your throat, blocking breathing. Then you slide the penis out of your throat, still keeping the glans fully in your mouth, and exhale, breathe, slide the penis as deep into your throat as you can take it (keeping your neck extended and straight helps), and slide the penis out again. You can continue for as long as your partner finds the process pleasurable and you find it comfortable.

STIMULATING A WOMAN

Especially at higher levels of arousal, women usually prefer lighter rather than harder stimulation. *Most men use too much pressure.* Heavy suction, pressure, or motion may quickly become uncomfortable. Men probably overstimulate because they like strong stimulation themselves and assume their partners feel the same way. They're wrong. In our experience most complaints from women about manual and oral technique concern roughness. Even if a woman has told her partner to lighten up, she shouldn't be afraid to remind him each time he stimulates her uncomfortably and incorrectly. She should be tactful, but you should be receptive. When your partner's clitoris is erect and hard, it requires only very light stimulation.

Regular, predictable, rhythmic stimulation is good basic technique. Explore with your tongue to find the most sensitive areas on and around your partner's clitoris, then alternate tongue stimulation with suction, pushing with your tongue and then lightly sucking the clitoris into your mouth. Experiment with rapidly flicking your tongue. The most effective pressure is sometimes so light that you'll make hardly any contact between your mouth and your partner's vulva. Your mouth's warmth and the motion of the air from your breathing may be enough to stimulate her arousal for seconds at a time.

Your mouth and tongue effectively replace one hand when you switch to oral lovemaking during ESO. Your other hand can continue to stimulate the vagina, especially the G spot. You can alternate primary stimulation

18 MALE STIMULATING FEMALE: KNEELING OVER

Oral access to genitals. Free hand may stimulate breasts and other body areas. In minor variation, man extends legs and lies on stomach.

between the clitoris and the G spot just as you did with your hands before.

As always, let your partner's responses guide you. If she is climbing to arousal, continue whatever you have found that is stimulating her. If she is leveling off or coming down from arousal, change what you are doing. Try stimulating the clitoris less. Or try stimulating the clitoris more. Or add more or less G-spot stimulation.

The important rule to remember is to change stimulation when you sense that your partner is coming down from arousal. Sometimes what you have to change is your attention. If you're thinking of something else while you're stimulating your partner, she may unconsciously sense your distraction and respond by becoming less aroused. Pay attention to your partner at all times.

RESISTANCES

Men and women: Be alert for resistances to oral sex (see chapter 8, "Overcoming Resistances," page 195). Talk about them before you begin. If you encounter them during lovemaking, talk them out afterward. A good rule to follow is that either partner should feel free to signal a return to regular lovemaking or to manual ESO whenever he or she becomes uncomfortable, physically or emotionally, with oral sex.

Focus on Arousal

Both partners should focus intently on their own or their partner's arousal to prevent diversions of attention. Make sure your answering machine is on, your children are self-sufficient, no appliances need attention, and your doors are locked. If interruptions do occur, see how smoothly you can redirect your attention to what you were doing and experiencing before you were interrupted.

When a woman is pleasuring her partner, she takes control of his attention through genital stimulation. Her goal is to keep his thoughts focused on the sexual stimulation she's supplying, to cause him to prefer her not to be doing something else, whether that something else is a harder, softer, faster, or slower stroke or something altogether different. She judges the effect she's having on him by his response. Paying attention includes looking at his genitals, feeling their rigidity, sensing their warmth, and noticing their throbbing. Her silent self-talk reports her findings, the pleasure she's feeling giving her partner pleasure, and where she wants to take him. By this interior monologue she creates a two-way, nonverbal communication process. She doesn't have to explain what she's doing, but she does need to stay focused. When her thoughts are diverted, she'll miss feedback cues. Her partner's arousal level may drop, and he may lose his erection. Or she may miss the cues to ejaculatory urgency and unintentionally stimulate him prematurely to ejaculate. When all is said and done, it is *her* intention and attention, from one second to the next, which control his level of arousal. Many women are unaware of the necessity of keeping their attention focused on their partner's response. You can't do ESO mechanically while planning dinner or a shopping trip. If your partner's level of arousal is dropping, that's usually because your attention has wandered. You need to redirect it to what you're experiencing through your senses, your hands, and your mouth.

Men similarly need to stay focused while being stimulated. You begin by focusing on your genitals. Each and every time your mind wanders, you need to let go of that distracting thought and redirect your attention back to the physical sensations you're feeling. You need to monitor your arousal level closely, so that when physical arousal is too intense, when your erection becomes a rigid Stage IV and you're close to ejaculation, you can communicate that fact to your partner verbally or nonverbally. Relax your PC muscles and breathe deeply while your partner slows or stops stimulation and presses on your external prostate spot.

Safer Sex

Couples who wish to begin a sexual relationship today confront worries that simply did not exist twenty-five years ago. Sex continues alive and well, however.

New would-be partners who are unsure of their AIDS status may choose to be tested for HIV infection. In the meantime, they may want to take precautions to protect themselves. These precautions collectively are popularly labeled "safe sex." Since risk is relative, we'd prefer to call them "safer sex." Most of the exercises described in this book are uniquely adaptable to safer sex, because the ESO program involves techniques for sexual pleasuring that do not depend on intercourse or spontaneity. The full pleasures of extended orgasm can be experienced even when using latex gloves, condoms, and other barriers to viral transmission.

Safer sex practices are recommended for those couples who have some reason to suspect that at least one partner has been or could have been exposed to HIV infection. Six months without sexual contact outside the relationship— some public health officials suggest a year—and with negative HIV tests at the beginning and end are considered moderately reliable measures of freedom from HIV infection. While couples wait to determine their AIDS status, they may choose to enjoy and practice the ESO program using a condom for intercourse and oral sex. Pleasuring and sexual knowledge and control are characteristics of both the ESO program and safer sex.

Two people considering beginning a sexual relationship today should understand that the best guarantee of their safety from HIV infection is mutual AIDS testing at the outset, before any sexual interaction has occurred, followed by six months of using only safer sex practices, followed by a confirming HIV test. If both tests are still HIV-

negative for both partners, then the probability is high that
both people are not AIDS-infected. The six-month wait is
recommended because six months may have to pass after
infection before a test shows positive.

If the initial HIV test is negative for both partners, and
neither has apparently been engaging in high-risk behavior
in the past six months, they may feel relatively confident
in engaging in "probably safe" practices. Negative tests
again for both, six months later, would allow a couple options of fewer sexual practice restrictions. Alternatively, a
couple starting a relationship may decide to have only a
single HIV test after six months, while they engage in only
"safest sex" practices for six months. These recommenda-
tions are only suggested guidelines. There is some indication that a small percentage of HIV-infected carriers do not
develop positive tests for up to three years.

We see couples who come for AIDS testing together,
without guilt. They do so as a sensible precaution, not
from suspicion that either one is infected. Couples who
care about each other and who wish to begin an intimate
sexual relationship want to protect their partners as well
as themselves. If it should happen that one partner turns
up HIV-positive, the couple has a serious problem. The
couple may choose then to continue to practice safer sex.
But even condoms cannot be considered absolutely safe,
and each encounter increases the odds of eventual
condom breakage or slippage. Certain facts must be
faced. In the end, HIV-positive people are probably going
to have to confine their sexual relationships to each other
or practice celibacy and self-stimulation. These limitations are hardly solutions. They're probably necessary ac-
commodations until science finds means of prevention or
cure.

EXTENDED ORGASMIC RESPONSE
AND SAFER SEX

Many of the exercises in the ESO program emphasize manual stimulation. Manual stimulation alone by a knowledgeable partner can carry both men and women to extended orgasm. That distinction makes following a modified ESO program a highly desirable safer sex practice. Oral stimulation and intercourse can be omitted entirely from ESO program exercises if you choose. Thus the ESO program can provide wonderfully pleasurable techniques for couples who wish to practice safer sex but still want to experience higher levels of sexual response than they've ever experienced before. If they want to, they can work through the ESO program, without oral sex or intercourse, during the three- to six-month period when they're waiting out their voluntary quarantine before their first or second HIV test. If they test negative, they can then go back and incorporate the oral stimulation and intercourse exercises.

SAFER SEX CATEGORIES

The Institute for the Advanced Study of Sexuality promulgates three categories of sexual practices in the context of AIDS risk: safe, probably safe, and unsafe. Medical practitioners generally accept these categories as valid based on current information.

Sexual practices considered safe, or *very* low risk, are: social or dry kissing (kissing without the exchange of salivary fluids); hugging; body massage; nongenital petting; mutual manual stimulation of the genitals without anal contact; exhibitionism and voyeurism by consent; and the use of mechanical sex aids (such as vibrators and dildos), also by consent.

Considered probably safe are: vaginal and anal intercourse with the use of a condom and the spermicide nonoxynol-9; fellatio with a condom; oral-vaginal or oral-anal stimulation using a latex barrier such as a dental dam (so long as the skin is unbroken); and French kissing (tongue inserted) with the use of nonoxynol-9. Nonoxynol-9 is effective in destroying the viral agent HIV when used in intercourse with a condom. To make it effective in French kissing, it would have to be spread on the tongues and lips of both parties involved. That may be aesthetically unpleasant given the substance's medicinal taste. The HIV virus rarely appears in saliva. Nevertheless, French kissing can't be considered entirely safe.

Considered unsafe are: anal or vaginal intercourse without a condom; swallowing semen or accepting semen vaginally, orally, or anally. Manual anal contact without latex gloves is also considered unsafe because there's evidence that anal stimulation causes bleeding. If the manipulator has a break in his or her skin, blood could then be passed either way. A hangnail could be deadly.

CONDOMS

Lovers interested in practicing safer sex beyond manual stimulation should probably acquire a stock of two different kinds of condoms—dry for oral sex and lubricated with nonoxynol-9 for more assured protection during intercourse. Nonoxynol-9 has proven effective in destroying a wide spectrum of sexually transmitted disease agents. A great many condoms available on the market today contain nonoxynol-9 as an ingredient of their lubricant. In the past this information has not always been clearly indicated on the label. With greater public concern about safer sexual practices, manufacturers have begun identifying nonoxynol-9 as an ingredient. Condoms with nonoxynol-9 may not contain a sufficient amount. As added protection we recommend that you purchase a spermicidal jelly or cream containing at least a five percent concentration of nonoxynol-9 and spread it generously on the outer surface of the condom-clad penis.

Some people are sensitive to nonoxynol-9, unfortunately, and develop a bright red inflammation of the penis or vulva after repeated use. If you experience such a reaction, you will need to use untreated condoms and exercise greater care during vaginal or anal penetration.

Condoms sometimes fail. They slip off or tear. A condom slips off because it hasn't been put on correctly, because sex has been particularly strenuous, or simply because of careless withdrawal. Withdrawal after intercourse with a condom should take place while the penis is still erect. The man reaches down and holds the condom in place while he's withdrawing.

Condoms don't commonly break because of manufacturing defects or even incorrect application. The most common cause of breakage is corrosion from petrolatum, the ingredient in Vaseline. Petrolatum products should be avoided when using latex condoms, surgical gloves, dams, or diaphragms. The sexual lubricant we recommend, Albolene, also contains a small amount of petrolatum. It's safe for short periods of time, less than ten minutes of intercourse with any of the thicker latex condoms. In doing your own personal evaluations of different types of condoms, consider packaging accessibility, thickness, size, lubrication, design, color, cost, and any special features.

OTHER BARRIER MATERIALS

Wearing a latex glove on any hand that touches your partner's genitals can substantially reduce risk. Most dentists and ophthalmologists now wear gloves as a precaution against the transmission of disease. It's encouraging to note that none on record has contracted AIDS through patient contact. Latex gloves come in three sizes (small, medium, and large) and are available at many pharmacies. Using latex gloves may seem strange at first, but you'll probably find that you lose only a little sensitivity. Your partner may find additional pleasure in the subtly different sensations. Worrying about disease transmission can be a powerful inhibitor of sexual pleasure; using safer sex techniques can increase your feeling of security. Vinyl, "one size fits all" gloves may also be used, although they are made of heavier material and blunt sensitivity.

Anyone who has experienced dental surgery or root-canal work is probably familiar with the latex dam. It's a square of surgical latex stretched over the teeth in such a way that only the tooth being operated on is exposed. As an aid to safer sex, the thin latex square can be stretched over the opening to the anus or the vagina to serve as a barrier to viral transmission during oral stimulation much as a condom serves during fellatio. As with a condom, the latex dam to some degree reduces sensation. Many people find that latex dams are less acceptable for routine use than condoms or latex gloves. ESO can help overcome this obstacle to sexual pleasure by teaching you ways to work through your resistance and by improving your ability to concentrate on the stimulation you do receive. For men who wish to stimulate a partner orally who isn't documented to be AIDS-safe, a latex dam can offer a safer compromise. Alternatively, clear plastic food wraps can be used for cunnilingus.

You can add playing with latex as a component of foreplay during the initial encounter between you and your partner. Use your imagination to turn a necessity into an opportunity for pleasure. Blow up a dry condom and tie it off like a balloon, as most of us did on the sly when we were children. Rub the inflated condom over your partner's body. Use it to stimulate his/her nipples and genitals (use a separate condom for each person). It's an interesting sensation.

Play with a latex dam as you played with the condom before. Surgical gloves are hardly any hindrance to stimulation, and if you ever wanted to play doctor, now's your chance.

A significant sexual minority has always used latex materials and other rubber goods as adjuncts to stimulation. Such use may be fetishistic for some people, but it depends at least in part on sensual qualities inherent in the material—its similarity to skin.

LEARNING TO LOVE CONDOMS

To bring condom use into happy sexuality and intimacy, it's important to become comfortable with this sometimes intimidating stranger. Once you've accepted its importance as protection, you need to embrace it as an accessory to sexual enhancement. You need to decide to have fun with condoms. Remember, sex is fun no matter what you do.

Start by purchasing or collecting a variety of condoms. Discovering their qualities can be fun. Even going into a drugstore and buying them can be a new and interesting experience for the uninitiated. They're much easier to buy now than they used to be. In most pharmacies they're not hidden behind the counter anymore; they're out on display in a variety of colors, textures, and shapes. Some have ribs and little bumps molded in to add to sensation. Some are lubricated, some are dry, some are treated with the spermicide nonoxynol-9. Be willing to spend five to fifteen dollars on a collection. Spread out a variety of condoms in their original packages within easy reach, then close your eyes, reach into the pile, and pick one. With your eyes still closed, practice quickly and gracefully opening the package. If you're single, you may want to try this exercise alone first. Among its other qualities, the type of condom you ultimately select for regular use should be one you can open easily with your hands or teeth. If you need any kind of sharp instrument to open the package, select another brand.

Before you roll a condom onto the penis, notice how it smells and tastes. Different condoms smell, taste, and feel differently. Be sure you handle, smell, and even lick the condom while it's still rolled. Evaluate it for bouquet the way you would a glass of wine.

Appearance. Condoms are produced in various colors. Most are transparent; others are milky white or yellow. Decide what color or appearance you like. Partners should make this decision together.

Lubrication. Lubricants are important to how a condom feels. Albolene and Crème de Femme are oil-based lubricants that appear to be relatively safe for use with thicker-style latex condoms for brief periods—less than ten minutes. Lotions and creams are generally acceptable but some may also be oil-based; check ingredients. More specialized and longer-lasting products that can be used with condoms are listed in "Products and Where to Find Them" on page 269.

For improved disease protection and for contraception, you may want to use a lubricant that contains nonoxynol-9. This spermicide is not an attractive taste to most people and isn't likely to be acceptable for oral sex. The man should try applying it to his condom-covered erection so that doing so becomes a familiar experience and feeling. Enjoy the fun of applying it with stimulation supplied by the man himself or by his partner.

Nonoxynol-9 has been found to kill herpes simplex virus, genital herpes, and perhaps HIV, cytomegalovirus, hepatitis B virus, chlamydia, gonorrhea, and syphilis as well as sperm. Condoms alone are very good protection, since they help prevent viruses from entering the partner's body. Nonoxynol-9 is additional protection in case of condom breakage.

Texture. Some condoms are made up with textures: ribs, fine bumps, coarser bumps. Manufacturers claim in advertising that textures add to female pleasure. Most women don't notice any significant difference between condoms with or without these embellishments, but they may be fun for a change.

Tearing. Some people are inhibited from using a condom because of concerns about tearing. Condoms are surprisingly sturdy, particularly the thicker American brands. (Japanese brands are sometimes thinner and a little less sturdy.) We suggest you sacrifice several condoms to learn their tear strength. Go ahead and try to tear one. In fact, tear several. See what it takes to do so. Stretch one until it covers not only all four fingers, but your entire fist. Try putting one over your head. Clamp one around a faucet and fill it with water until it bursts. Fill one with a small amount of water, tie off the end, put the condom in your mouth, and chew on it. (It produces the same satisfying crackle and snap as chewing gum.) Some men brag about being "just too much man" for any condom to contain. Once they've seen a tiny latex tube stretched over a person's head, they may want to reconsider this boast. If you think that the intensity of your sexual activity is too great for condoms, you may need to reexamine your opinion after you've stretched, popped, and chewed a few.

Applying condoms. Many men learned how to put on condoms when they were adolescents, as part of their self-stimulation ritual. They used condoms as a way of disposing discreetly of their ejaculate. If you didn't discover condom use in this way, it's not too late to learn now.

With fantasy or friction, get yourself erect. Open the package. If the condom is dry, you may apply a small amount of lubricant to the end of your penis. Using a small amount of lubricant on the head of the penis adds to the male's sensitivity but may somewhat increase the possibility of the condom's unintentionally slipping off during intercourse. You may find your erection subsiding while you're distracted with putting on a condom, but don't be concerned. Get yourself erect again.

Slowly roll the condom onto your penis shaft all the way to the base, leaving a small reservoir end at the tip if there isn't one in the condom. Enjoy the sensation of the condom sliding over your penis. Notice the pleasurable feelings and concentrate your attention on the arousal sensations that the condom provides.

For men without a foreskin, using a condom helps to duplicate to a degree the experience of having one. Try moving the condom at the penis head up and down. Rotate it back and forth from side to side between your thumb and forefinger at the glans. This stimulation can be highly arousing.

Use your condoms during self-stimulation. Wear one for the full time you're self-stimulating.

For women with or without partners, incorporate opening condoms and exploring and playing with them into your self-stimulation activity. Put one on your fingers and use it to touch yourself on your outer and inner lips, on your clitoris, and inside your vagina. It may be interesting to roll a condom over the head of your vibrator or dildo. Apply a condom over your fingers and suck on them. Try blowing one up, tying a knot at the end, and creating your own phallic toy. You may also enjoy learning to put a condom on your partner with your mouth, turning a responsibility into a game. Practice on your fingers first.

Couples can have fun exploring and playing with condoms together, laughing together. Remember, lovemaking is communication. One kind of communication is playing. Playing with condoms together can be a part of lovemaking.

Condom Use: A Checklist

Some people find condoms easy to use. Others find them frustrating. Careful attention to handling them can maximize protection and increase your self-confidence. When condoms fail, they generally do so because of incorrect use. Proper usage will substantially increase effectiveness. The basics of safer sex with condoms:

1. Always use condoms for vaginal or anal sex.
2. Always put on the condom *before* penetration.
3. Use only water-based lubricants.
4. Avoid use of oil-based lubricants such as mineral oil, cold cream, skin lotion, or petrolatum jelly (including Albolene).

Steps in using a condom:

1. Select a brand that you have pretested for relative convenience of packaging and opening, for taste, texture, presence or absence of lubrication and nonoxynol-9 spermicide.
2. Add a small amount of lubrication to the head of the penis before putting on a condom to increase sensation without causing significant slippage.
3. Leave a little room at the head of the penis as you unroll the condom. Don't leave too much—air bubbles can cause breakage. Plain-end condoms should have half an inch of free space. Reservoir-end condoms have this space designed in.
4. Unroll the condom so that it covers the entire erect penis. If uncircumcised, pull back the foreskin before rolling on the condom. Smooth the condom to eliminate any air bubbles. Add extra water-based lubricant on the outside of the condom before beginning intercourse. Insufficient lubrication can cause condoms to tear or pull off. If the condom begins to slip off, you

can clamp it with your fingers at the base to hold it in place.

5. After intercourse, hold the base of the condom to avoid spillage, withdraw gently, discard the condom, and wash.

6. Communicate. Discussing using condoms with your partner can make it easier for both of you. Be honest about your feelings and needs.

When condoms break:

1. Stop what you're doing, withdraw, and examine the condom closely. If the man has not ejaculated or if the tear is near the base of the condom, there's little to worry about. Simply remove the torn remains, replace the condom with a new one, and continue. (Breakage during intercourse is why we recommend that the man try to break a condom deliberately during self-stimulation. He needs to learn to feel the difference between intercourse with and without.)

2. If the breakage occurs during or after intercourse with released semen, insert a generous amount of spermicidal foam or spermicidal jelly into the vagina (or anus, if intercourse was anal) to help destroy sperm or germs. Don't remove this spermicide for at least an hour.

With care and deliberate attention to detail, sex can be safer. The experience of practicing ESO program stimulation techniques adds to the intense physical pleasure and intimacy possible even through the protection of mechanical barriers.

8

Overcoming
Resistances

We began talking about resistances in chapters 5 and 6. In this chapter we'll discuss them in more detail.

Resistances are the mental conditions, conscious and unconscious, that determine what experiences we allow ourselves to have. They include the attitudes, the rigidities, the rules, the fears, and the misinformation that limit our ability to experience more pleasure. Everyone has sexual resistances, or all of us would automatically experience extended orgasm the first time we were aroused. You're aware of some of your resistances. Others—probably the majority—you're unaware of. Some resistance is normal and essential to survival.

The first step toward overcoming specific resistances is identifying them. The simplest way to do that is to make a written list. The resistances you're aware of you can identify easily. The ones you're unaware of you'll have to discover as you go along.

Religious Prohibitions

Many people encounter resistances connected to past or present religious prohibitions. You must finally decide if any form of sexual pleasuring violates your faith, and, if so, whether or not you want to accept that prohibition and the limitation on pleasure it enforces.

You should be aware that all religions and all societies have arranged to control sexuality, usually by limiting it to specified acts and partners. The key word is *control*. The basic purpose of that control is to remind you of the religion or society and to demonstrate your voluntary respect for its power. In an intimate, strongly emotional context like sexuality, a rule restricting you from making love in a certain position, for example, forcefully recalls you to your faith and emphasizes the reach of that faith into the most private center of your life.

Unfortunately, some men and women who learned religious prohibitions as children find themselves inhibited as adults. They find they've emotionally generalized specific rules until all of sexuality is permeated with a sense of sin, even sexuality permitted within the context of their faith and even, in some cases, after they've given up that faith.

If that's a serious problem for you, you may need to consider consulting a counselor. It is often possible with short-term therapy to understand and work through beliefs acquired earlier in life that cause unnecessary guilt, shame, and fear in the present. If you discover more specific and limited relationship-based resistances, the techniques for overcoming resistances we'll discuss here should work for you.

Resistance to self-stimulation in particular can be a religion-based anxiety. Besides the relaxation techniques we'll discuss here, the best way we know to work through that resistance is to realize that you aren't learning self-stimulation only for yourself. You're learning it to improve your relationship with your partner, to improve your ability to give and receive pleasure, to add to intimacy and commitment. In any religion, intention is crucial in judging behavior. The intention of the self-stimulation exercises here, which serve as a kind of extended foreplay, is to strengthen your bond of love with your partner.

Dealing with Children

Another resistance that plagues many men and women is concern for what their children know and hear of their lovemaking. Children of every age can severely inhibit couples trying to arrange time and privacy for lovemaking. Fear that children can hear them can paralyze parents. Anxiety that time set aside for pleasure is time stolen from children can make sex furtive and all too brief.

The children problem breaks down into several separate problems with different solutions.

You can usually arrange time for sex while very young children and infants are sleeping, since they sleep so many hours. Infants up to the age of perhaps eight months can even sleep in the same room if neither of you finds that inhibiting, thus eliminating the worry that they've waked and you've failed to hear them.

Older children need first to be provided for. You need to do whatever must be done—dinner served, assistance supplied with homework, transportation arranged—to convince yourselves that your children are fine and you're not shirking parenting by pleasuring each other. If providing for your children consistently gets in the way of private time together, then you need to discuss rearranging and simplifying your schedules. No matter how demanding your responsibilities as parents appear to be, *all* parents need, and must take, some private time to devote exclusively to each other. Your children will benefit in the long run.

Tell children why you're leaving them alone: "Mommy and Daddy need time by themselves to enjoy and love each other." The important word is *love*. Children feel safer when they know their parents love each other.

If your child's response is, "Why do you and Daddy need private time? Why can't I be there? I love you too," then one answer is, "When we can give each other love privately, we feel closer and that helps us love *you* more too." Another answer is, "Everyone gets a turn. Sometimes I'm just with you. Sometimes Daddy's just with you. Sometimes I'm just with Daddy."

Another question children ask that the word *love* helps answer: "Why were you crying when you and Daddy were alone? Was Daddy hurting you?" You answer: "Those were love sounds. Daddy and I make them when we're loving each other a whole lot." The child understands that you weren't in pain and learns that vocalizing during lovemaking is good. If the thought of being overheard is personally inhibiting, you can always mask your vocalizing with music.

Sooner or later children test their parents' resolve to be alone. All those little knocks on the door. You can help forestall them, and allay the guilt you may feel about them, by giving the child loving attention before the door is closed. But when you hear the knock and the call, be definite. Tell the child you meant it when you said you were having private time. You don't want to be disturbed. The child can do whatever you arranged beforehand for him to do—watch TV, nap, go out and play. You'll be with him again in half an hour, an hour. Not "in a minute," unless that's literally true. Then follow through. Afterward give the child extra attention to show him that he's loved.

Once you've dealt with the little knocks, you may have to deal with the resistance of your overconcern: "I really should stop now." Use the techniques developed in this chapter. Remind yourself that you can give your children far more love when you have a strong, fulfilling relationship with your partner and feel good about yourself than when you don't. After ESO time especially, you're likely to return happy and relaxed to caring for your children.

Common Resistances

All resistances are partly thought and partly feeling. They won't instantly disappear if you change the thought. They also have to be worked through emotionally, and that takes time. But to the extent that they're based on misinformation and bad communication, you can start working through them by rethinking them. In chapter 5 we listed a few common resistances. Here's that list again, with additions and with some discussion:

1. *My partner's getting tired.* If you've agreed ahead of time that each of you will stop when you feel tired, trust your partner to keep the agreement. In the meantime enjoy yourself. There's nothing wrong with going ahead even when you're tired, by the way. Sometimes that pushes through resistances and generates a welcome sense of achievement.
2. *I don't have time.* Arrange time in advance. Remember, if you want to learn ESO you must give sex higher priority than you probably have in the past.
3. *I feel silly.* That's because you're doing something new. Do it anyway. When it's familiar to you, you won't feel silly anymore. Silliness can be fun if you let it be. Watch how children play.
4. *I look unattractive.* Women have this worry more than men, but it's not uncommon among men. You like your partner's sounds and movements and expressions in

lovemaking. You like your partner's body. Why assume that your partner doesn't like yours? If you need reassurance, ask for it. If you think your partner wants reassurance, offer it: "You're beautiful." "You're sexy." "You're wonderful." For people who love each other, one or more of those statements is bound to be true.

5. *I'm afraid.* Feeling afraid usually means fearing letting go of old habits and rules that put limits on what you're willing to do and to feel during sex. The program of ESO practice we've outlined in this book is designed to give you a sense of safety as you explore. It's an opportunity to check out whether those prohibitions you've always had still apply today. Once you have experienced the rewards of pushing through a personal barrier, you may find it gets easier to do.

6. *I have my period.* You can practice ESO during menstruation if both of you find that practice comfortable. Discuss it and agree in advance, then trust your partner to have been honest in his agreement.

   ESO during menstruation may decrease the number of days and the volume of flow. The intense and prolonged uterine contractions of extended orgasm help move the menstrual material more efficiently from the uterus. A towel will protect the sheets.

7. *I'm angry.* Why? If it's old anger, leave it outside the bedroom door and discuss it in communication exercises at neutral times. If it's anger that came up during lovemaking, deal with it like any other resistance, using the techniques we consider in this chapter and in chapters 5 and 6.

Other thoughts you can similarly reason out with yourself include: *I feel like I'm going to burst./ This is wrong./ Tomorrow I've got to . . . / Yesterday I should have . . . / I don't think I can do this.*

Changing Behavior

Behavior arises in thought and feeling. Resistance is one kind of behavior. Given time and attention, any behavior can be changed. At our clinic in California we help people with smoking, weight control, blood-pressure control, headaches, asthma, chronic pain, alcohol and drug dependency, sleep disturbances, bed-wetting, muscle tics and spasms, depression, anxiety, anger, phobias, dieting, sexual problems, and more. What can't be changed can at least be modified.

Many of the same methods of change work for all these problems. Anxiety is part of all unwanted behavior, so we help people free themselves from anxiety. Misinformation or lack of information usually complicates unwanted behavior, so we help people reeducate themselves. Behavior can usually best be changed in small, incremental steps rather than all at once, so we devise and supervise programs of gradual readjustment. And what applies to the relief of pain and unhappiness applies equally well to the relief of unhappy and sometimes painful resistances to increasing sexual pleasure.

Desi is a former client we remember with great fondness. He was a successful thirty-four-year-old businessman from India who had lived in the United States for five years when we first saw him. He was charming and humble; he was also a virgin. He had self-stimulated three or four times when he was fourteen; that was the extent of his sexual experience. He was extremely anxious because his parents had arranged a marriage for him, and he was sure he'd be a failure on his wedding night. He wasn't aware of having erections and he had very little interest in sex, but he wanted to learn.

We began at the beginning with education. Desi was raised in a religious culture that taught that sex is evil. His parents had punished him severely when he was a child for playing doctor with his friends. We reminded him that he was conceived through sexual intercourse and entered the world through a sexual orifice. Could sex be so evil, we asked him, if nearly all of us depend on it for our very lives?

We showed Desi training films, instructed him in self-stimulation techniques, reduced his anxiety with hypnosis and biofeedback, taught him to fantasize. In time he was able to produce strong, sustained erections and had mastered full information about how to stimulate his bride-to-be. He needed then to practice what he knew, but he lacked a partner. Since his marriage was arranged, and his future bride was therefore a stranger, far away in another country, we encouraged Desi to work with a surrogate—a woman trained in sex therapy who was willing to help him learn. He agreed. He and the surrogate progressed through five meetings from simply talking and touching to full, satisfying intercourse. In their last meetings Desi was able to stimulate the surrogate to extended orgasm for as much as ten minutes at a time.

Desi went home to his arranged marriage. We heard from him once more. He wrote us that he and his wife were both very happy with his sexual skills.

Controlling Thought II

We talked earlier about controlling your thoughts—"cognitive restructuring"—when you encounter a resistance (see page 121 for review). It takes about three seconds, after a thought arises in the brain, to identify the thought content, to decide to change it, and to make the change. We've watched the process in our office in clients attached to biofeedback equipment. Their galvanic skin response, which is a sensitive measure of emotional arousal, suddenly changes. The equipment registers the change with an audible tone, and the meters jump. The client hears the tone and says, "Yes, I did just have a thought. I was wondering if I can handle this training."

At that point the client can change his response most simply by reversing the thought: instead of thinking, "I'm really scared," he can deliberately think, "I'm really comfortable. I can handle it." Instead of "This is terrible," he can think, "This is exciting." *Even if he doesn't believe it.* People finally believe what they choose to believe, what they tell themselves to believe. That's why coaches give pep talks and politicians make appearances to the crescendo of a band playing "Happy Days Are Here Again." In the context of our work a client's deliberate reversal of a thought is founded on a provisional truth: "I'm really comfortable" is what he *hopes* to be and what he *will* be after successful training.

Reversing negative thoughts works well in sexual situations. You should tell yourself, "I like being pleasured," "I feel good." Your partner can encourage you too. Make a habit of using such phrases as a bridge to feeling good.

A second way to move past a point of resistance, mentioned earlier, is to replace a distracting thought with a neutral thought. The neutral thought can be a nonsense sound: "Ahhh." "Ommm." It can be a phrase: "I'm calm." "My mind is quiet." Repeated over and over, mantras such as these push distracting thoughts aside. Like solid objects, two thoughts can't occupy the same space in consciousness at the same time. A neutral mantra allows your body's natural responses to reassert themselves. When you're being sexually stimulated, that means a greater sensation of pleasure.

A third way to restructure thoughts, we said earlier, is to switch your attention inward to *feelings* and allow the physical experience of being stimulated to take over your awareness.

Paying attention to feeling means just that: paying attention to your body and the sensation that your partner is creating for you. Some people resist pleasure by telling themselves that their partners aren't stimulating them correctly. Assuming that their partners aren't causing them pain, and assuming they've taught their partners what feels good, that expectation is probably misguided. One kind of stimulation may feel better than another, but *you can take any amount of stimulation and use it to build arousal by paying attention to it.* Every time you find yourself thinking—especially negative thoughts—switch your attention back to sensation.

We've treated preorgasmic women—women who haven't yet learned to have orgasm—who have driven their partners to distraction looking for the perfect touch and the perfect stroke. We've treated men with erection problems who have similarly burdened their partners with blame. They don't recognize that if they're getting *any* physical stimulation at all, they're getting as much as they need. After all, men have erections and ejaculations, and women experience lubrication and arousal, during sleep, with no physical stimulation whatsoever.

If you doubt this point, try an exercise. Ask your partner to stimulate you lightly and steadily and see what you can experience. You may be surprised how aroused you can let yourself become. Use the sensation that's there. It's more than enough to climb if you decide to let it be.

Similarly, when you find yourself face-to-face with a resistance, *concentrate on feeling.* If you're completely feeling, you won't be thinking about anything else. Your whole experience will be feeling. In a way your *thought* at that time is to *feel.* That's a strong, positive suggestion in itself, and by consistently willing it, you push resistance aside.

Your last experience with severe pain is a grim but vivid example of what we mean by "completely feeling." Maybe you smashed your thumb with a hammer. Maybe you stubbed your toe or cracked your shin. When the pain arrived, it overwhelmed thinking. Afterward you probably had a thought or two about it. But before those thoughts came, you were completely aware of pain and only of pain.

With ESO, you're working toward a state of complete, conscious awareness of pleasure—toward letting pleasure overwhelm you. The object of ESO practice is to learn to achieve that state and then to stretch it out through time: to reach a place where you're not thinking *about* anything but simply, consciously, *experiencing*. Experiencing pleasure, where your entire experience is permeated with feeling and sensation.

Which isn't to advocate mindlessness. We don't. We think everyone needs a clear head to live decently and well. Your mind will be all the sharper later for having had the experience of an interlude of intense pleasure. You'll feel centered, relaxed, fulfilled, at peace. You'll probably also feel loved and loving.

Breathing

As we have emphasized earlier (page 124), breathing is a good way to work through resistance. Paying attention to breathing, especially deep, regular belly breathing from the diaphragm—with the stomach rising and falling rather than only the chest—helps, because it brings you back from thought to sensation, to your body. It helps because many people hold their breath when they're reaching for sexual arousal, tightening their muscles and reducing the oxygen supply to the brain.

Breathing also helps because the breathing reflex is complex, and many bodily systems involved in sexual arousal are hooked into it. Breathing produces relaxation by changing the state of the body's autonomic nervous system. Relaxation reduces anxiety. And remember: there's anxiety behind each and every one of your resistances.

Visualization/Fantasy

Visualization can be a way of relaxing. Close your eyes while you're being pleasured and imagine you're somewhere else—on a Tahiti beach listening to the regular, smooth breaking of the waves, warming in the South Pacific sun. In a suite in a Swiss ski lodge on a fur rug before a crackling fire. In Paris between satin sheets in an elegant hotel. Choose someplace that makes you feel good and makes you feel peaceful and go there.

Sexual fantasy involves a variety of visualization techniques. Fantasy can chase resistances away. You imagine a desirable sexual experience with your partner or with someone else, or you recall a pleasurable sexual experience you've had in the past. Some people fantasize more easily than others. Everyone can learn.

If you think you have difficulty fantasizing, try this exercise: start by closing your eyes and seeing yourself as you are right now, at this very moment, with your eyes closed, doing just what you are doing. Then experience your breathing. Notice your lungs filling and emptying and the sensation of your breath passing in and out of your nose. Now, eyes closed, picture the objects in the room around you. Can you see them almost as if you had your eyes open? Picture yourself in the room among these objects. What are you wearing? Visualize your clothes.

Now change the scene. Visualize yourself on a soft, sandy beach, lying on powder-white sand in warm sun. Then picture someone with you on the beach.

Now switch to a sexual fantasy. Recall in detail a desirable sexual experience with your partner or with someone else. Or imagine a sexual experience that you would like to have at some future time. These memories and experiences may appear to you as snapshots, as movies, as fragmented and impressionistic images. They may involve feelings or words more than visual images.

Keep the fantasy in mind and build on it by adding new details. You can change the setting or add new experiences to real experiences you remember.

Knowing what other people fantasize about can help you learn to fantasize. Everyone has sexual fantasies some of the time. Here are common fantasies, listed in the order of their popularity:

1. *Sex with your regular partner.* Pleasures you've enjoyed together in the past. Pleasures you'd like to enjoy but can't because you or your partner finds them unacceptable. Real experiences with imaginary embellishments. Feel free to invent any activities you think you would enjoy with your partner, however unlikely. They're your private fantasies and yours alone.

2. *Sex with other opposite-sex partners.* Someone you have met or known. Screen stars, sports heroes and heroines, your high school prom king or queen. Since this is fantasy, not reality, it's safe to pick anyone you want. Imagine where you are, what you're doing, what you say to each other. Visualize how your imagined partner looks and how touching and caressing feels. Decide what you would like to do. Mentally write an entire shared scene. You may be more comfortable with this fantasy if you also fantasize that your regular partner is having sex with someone else.

3. *Sex with more than one partner.* A friend as well as your regular partner. A movie star, a famous man or woman. A man may fantasize a woman with full, sensuous lips stimulating him orally while his regular

partner watches or joins in. A woman may imagine two men loving her physically at the same time, or a man and a woman. One may be a stranger and the other her regular partner.

4. *Rape.* Fantasies of being taken sexually against your will. Women particularly enjoy this fantasy. It's perfectly acceptable. It has nothing to do with real rape, which is an ugly, violent act of criminal assault. Imagine being kidnapped, or someone breaking into your house. A stranger or someone you know takes you forcefully. Perhaps your regular partner is made to watch. You resist at first, then give in. You may be tied up and totally helpless but become sexually aroused along the way.

5. *Sex with same-sex partners.* Most people fantasize occasionally about having sex with people of their own gender, although many strongly resist acknowledging these thoughts. If you aren't too threatened to explore this fantasy, picture in detail whom you would enjoy having sex with, what you would do, and where you would do it. Same-sex fantasies aren't an indication of homosexuality, conscious or unconscious. They're simply exercises in human imagination, a normal part of life.

6. *Fantasies left over from childhood.* Vivid memories of fantasies and experiences may return to you from childhood if you let them. Our first sexual experiences and feelings are often overwhelmingly powerful; you can tap some of that residual emotion by recalling them. They may be only fragmentary: a girl's hair brushing a boy's face; a glimpse of someone naked. You may have thought of playing doctor with another child, or of having sex with an adult. Recall those fantasies now.

Fantasies have great value in sex. They're private, so they affect no one else and depend on no one else, and they actually change body chemistry. They stimulate arousal;

they can give you a head start on pleasure with your partner. The image comes before the reality and begins preparing the body for that reality.

If you find a fantasy arousing, continue that fantasy. If you find a fantasy neutral or negative, switch to another fantasy until you discover one that gives you pleasure.

Start with a fantasy that feels safe. Mentally write the scene. What time is it? Where are you? What does your partner (or partners) look like? What do both of you (or all of you) do? Begin dressed and enjoy undressing—even fantasies deserve time for foreplay! Don't rush your fantasy. Extending it will add pleasure and benefit arousal. If you are fantasizing about sex with someone other than your regular partner, choose someone with whom you feel comfortable. If the fantasy works, keep it going. If it doesn't work, change it.

Use fantasy in sexual situations. First fantasize alone while you self-stimulate. Then add fantasy while you're with your partner making love.

Some people fear they will act out their fantasies. Fantasies are almost always safe. Very few people ever act out fantasies they believe to be taboo.

Some people fear that fantasizing is dishonest. They believe they owe their partners one hundred percent of their physical and mental attention. They believe fantasizing is disloyal. They think that their partners would feel rejected and excluded if they knew. In fact, sharing fantasies often increases a partner's excitement. Partners should trust each other enough to share some fantasies. One way to test the water is to share a relatively safe fantasy and see what happens—a fantasy, for example, that involves only your partner and yourself, doing something together that you don't usually do. The sharing can develop from there.

Sharing fantasies can help enliven long-standing relationships when partners feel stuck sexually and bored.

Fantasies add excitement and may also improve communication. Your partner may find renewed interest.

It's likely, in any case, that you and your partner both use sexual fantasies from time to time. Sometimes your partner's fantasies include you, sometimes not. Feel good about your fantasies—they'll enhance your shared pleasure.

Most of our clients find that regular fantasy helps them break through resistance. Replace resistance with fantasy to stimulate yourself to higher levels of arousal. That gives you more pleasure; it also gives your partner more pleasure.

Remember: fantasies are normal and healthy. You don't necessarily have to tell your partner about them. You're responsible for what you do in this world, not for what you think. By fantasizing during lovemaking, you're helping yourself and your partner do what you both want to do, which is increase your mutual pleasure.

Suggestion

Suggestion is yet another way of relaxing, a way through resistance. If you see that your partner is struggling with resistance, you can offer positive suggestions. "You're getting more and more aroused." "You're really wonderful." "I love you." "Let yourself go." "That's nice." "Breathe—in and out." "Every time you breathe, you'll get higher." "Relax." "Trust me." "Yes, yes." "That's it." The right words, suggested quietly and with confidence, can help your partner through.

Telling your partner what you're going to do and then doing it can help build anticipation and arousal. "I'm going to tease you with timing—stroke the head of your penis for a while, stop, and then start again until you beg me for more." "Now I'm going to stroke your clitoris with the lightest possible touch and drive you crazy."

Monitoring Tension

We've said a lot already about Kegel exercises. We haven't talked about the more general question of pelvic muscle tension. Tension in the genital area strongly influences your level of sexual arousal. There's always pelvic muscle activity during sex, with tension either increasing or decreasing, so staying aware of that level of tension is always useful. Doing so won't be distracting. To the contrary, it focuses your attention on the area where you're receiving stimulation.

Then, when you encounter a resistance, you can add tension by contracting your PC muscle, holding it for six to eight seconds, relaxing it, and then pushing out. That shifts your attention from the resistance to a physical activity. It returns your attention to your genital area. It boosts arousal directly by stimulating the sexual tissues themselves.

Working your pelvic muscles to push through resistances and to build arousal has an important advantage over cognitive restructuring: it doesn't require thinking. You don't have to identify a resistance first and then decide how to deal with it. You only have to move from a resistance to a habitual muscular process. That automatically distracts you from resistance. Each and every time a resistance appears, you can start doing Kegel exercises or increase their intensity. You can always squeeze a little harder or a little longer.

Remember to breathe.

Changing Position

Finally, you can work through resistances by shifting your position and by subtle changes in movement. You can rotate your pelvis, arch your back, shift your legs, move to an entirely different position. That redirects your attention. Add a pillow. Remove a pillow. Turn to one side. Turn to the other side. Your partner can move along smoothly with you and can usually continue stimulating as you go.

The more time you spend at a point of resistance, carefully working through, the more progress you'll make. But stop before the experience becomes physically or psychologically painful. Otherwise you won't want to try it again.

Sensitive Encouragement

A majority of men report deriving their greatest sexual satisfaction from "making my partner come." Men need to remember that they are not "giving" their partners an orgasm. Just as men do, a woman experiences orgasm in her own mind and body. What a man *can* do is encourage and motivate his partner to pursue ever more intense and lengthy experiences of physical pleasure. If he wants that to happen, though, he needs to be exquisitely sensitive to her feelings and needs. The way to do that is to work for good communication during sex and afterward, to help keep him tuned to his partner's experience. If he "encourages" her too forcefully to go beyond her comfort level, he will find her even more resistant in the future to what she experiences as excessive pressure from him. Such resistance will slow the couple's rate of progress. A man must practice patience, use gentle, consistent encouragement, learn to read and adjust to his partner's physical and nonverbal signs of arousal and periodically check his estimates by requesting brief verbal communication. Men don't *give* women sexual pleasure; they help them find it.

At different periods in their lives people move through their resistances in small steps and at different speeds.

Couples in a committed relationship have an advantage over casual couples because they have more time and experience together. Couples in a casual relationship, on the other hand, have the advantage of less emotional baggage—fewer past resentments—to deal with. Emotional baggage can be managed with regular practice of the Appreciations and Resentments communication exercise (page 88).

9

ESO: The Future

ESO and Health

Since the dim beginnings of human history, men have looked for miracle cures for the diseases and conditions that beset them. They've sought from one continent to the next, from one discipline to the next, from one fad to the next, for fountains of youth and magic diets and miracle cures, despite their general failure.

It's just possible that regularly experienced ESO could supply some of the missing magic. We've seen improvement, often dramatic improvement, in an astounding variety of symptoms in people who have regularly practiced ESO. These are some of the symptoms and problems that ESO seems to have improved and in some cases eliminated:

Physical symptoms:
    headaches (migraine, tension, allergic)
    chronic pain (back, neck, pelvis)
    menstrual pain syndrome
    arthritic pain

stomach and gastrointestinal complaints
prostatitis
high blood pressure
asthma and bronchitis
skin eruptions (dermatitis and psoriasis)

Emotional problems:
depression, "low energy," constant fatigue
anxiety
alcoholism and some drug dependencies
insomnia
marital conflict
explosive anger

This list is incomplete and expands as we gain experience in the effects on men and women of ESO practiced over longer periods of time.

Why these broad and profound effects? It's really not that surprising. The sexual response system is linked to many different bodily systems: the nervous system, both central—brain—and autonomic—self-regulating; the circulatory system and the heart; the musculature; the system of hormone production; the gastrointestinal system. Sex also involves all the body's organs. Sexual responsiveness is every human being's birthright, an intrinsically natural, healthy function. ESO gives the body a vigorous workout, restoring natural balance. It's at least as effective as regular exercise—jogging, for example. Jogging feels like too much work at first. But after you practice, after it becomes a habit, it's easy, fun, and automatic. Regular joggers find that when they stop jogging, even for only a few days, they feel the loss mentally and physically. This acclimation is also true of ESO.

The beneficial health effects of regular exercise are well documented. Exercise operates to restore the balanced functioning of a variety of bodily systems. Regularly practiced ESO reaches into the depths of emotional life as mere physical exercise can never do; it's far more influential on health and happiness. Frequent practice of ESO is the strongest as well as the safest, and certainly the most pleasurable, medicine we know. Unlike other treatments or medications available, ESO is *totally safe*. There are *no* reported bad side effects.

Discovering, by experience, that vastly more pleasure is possible than you imagined, even in fantasy, always has a powerful impact. When the intensity of your sexual responses and the practiced excellence of your sexual skills exceed anything you have heard or read or seen, your personality and your values change. You gain self-confidence. You discover optimism. You're happy.

Sex and Aging

Age is no barrier to sex. It's also no barrier to ESO. None of us uses more than a small fraction of his sexual potential. By learning to use more, men and women of any age can increase their response, often beyond the levels they achieved when they were younger.

One of our favorite clients is a seventy-year-old former professional actor. Mike came to see us one day because, as he said, "It just hangs limp." He had erection problems.

Mike had all but given up sex. We assigned him daily self-stimulation exercises. We coached him that better functioning was possible. He began to trust us. He began dating. He's discovered now that he can have three or four separate ejaculations a day, which is more than he'd enjoyed for thirty years.

Mike didn't stop there. He learned ESO. He taught it to a variety of partners. He became one of the most popular widowers in town. He was a very happy man.

We've seen many couples and individuals who have increased their sexual abilities to high levels, more than compensating for their natural decline with aging. Regular self-stimulation for fifteen minutes or more at a time is crucial to that increase. So are Kegel exercises. The first and most important requirement is giving sex time and priority in your life.

Studies show that people who have frequent sexual activity in their younger years have sex much more frequently in their older years than do people whose sexual activities have been limited all along. The best guarantee of a good sex life in your later years is making sure you have a good sex life in your earlier years. But even if your sexual activities have been limited, you can usually improve significantly by following the guidelines in this book. Every activity and experience we've discussed here should be available to you, regardless of your age. It's good for your health. It's good for life.

A Final Word

As with all challenging journeys, not everyone who starts out to learn ESO will arrive there. Some of you will decide you don't want to begin the trip. That's fine. No one should travel who isn't intrigued by newness, adventure, and the excitement of uncertainty. Even if you decide not to attempt any of the training programs described in this book, simply having read it may begin to improve your sexual experience in subtle ways.

Others may give up and turn back before reaching ESO. We encourage you to talk over your fears and resistances with your partner. Every journey faces the traveler with periods of discouragement and disillusionment. *Keep going!* If you share your doubts with your partner, he or she may help you find the incentive you need to continue. Even the process of sharing is likely itself to improve your relationship. When your partner is the one discouraged, your encouragement may be the critical factor that supplies a reason to go on. Remember as well that getting there is half the fun, and even when you arrive, you won't have come to an end. There's always more pleasure to discover in lovemaking, we're delighted to say.

If you have just read through this book for the first time, congratulations on your willingness to come this far in developing your sexual potential. We encourage you now to begin to practice what you've learned.

Sexual energy may be like nuclear energy, a vastly powerful force hidden in history until it was accidentally discovered and tapped. If it is, it is energy entirely on the side of life. Your natural resistances will assure that you will unfold your sexual potential only gradually and safely. What we are learning, studying, and teaching is a new *human* technology for increasing *human* pleasure. The important human experience of sexual intimacy no longer has to be left to accidents of self-discovery and the vagaries of ancient prescription. The blind no longer have to lead the blind. The new sexual technology seeks to understand sexual responses and find ways to make them better under a variety of conditions from handicapped to optimum. Some will not be surprised, and others will be relieved, to hear that the highest forms of sexual response seem to occur between two people who love and trust each other.

In all that we've said here and in all that you do, remember to enjoy yourself. Don't be too programmatic. Don't turn pleasure into work. Goals help, in sex as elsewhere, but choose pleasure first when you're making love. That's what this book is: a program for pleasure—fluid, fluent, and deeply human.

Enjoy your journey. We certainly are!

ACHIEVING ESO:
A CHECKLIST

1. Assume that ESO is possible.
2. Acknowledge that you want and deserve more sexual pleasure.
3. Decide to learn for ESO.
4. Have a partner who shares equally in wanting to experience ESO.
5. Learn the procedures and techniques of ESO.
6. Practice ESO training for two to four hours a week.
7. Talk frequently with your partner about your positive and negative sexual feelings.
8. Find courage to continue training despite possible setbacks along the way.

10
Solving Problems

We've included this section in our book because some aspects of sexual functioning need to be changed before ESO becomes possible. We won't go into as much detail here as we did in previous chapters. Many men and women will be able to work through their problems with the information we supply here. Some won't. For them we advise counseling with competent sex therapists.

Many people with sexual problems will find it helpful to practice the exercises and procedures described in chapters 3 and 4. Some people with problems will find that following the ESO training program can be useful to improve their functioning, without making extending orgasm a goal. But there's much to learn as well in this appendix. We strongly recommend that everyone read it through at least once, regardless of your level of sexual functioning and your degree of sexual sophistication.

Sexual Problems

DEFINING SEXUAL PROBLEMS

You have a sexual problem if there's a significant gap between what you expect your experience should be and what it actually is.

That's a much more accurate description than the ugly labels that self-appointed authorities sometimes still use, labels like *frigid, impotent, incompetent.* Sexual functioning isn't fitted to some universal standard. The range is enormous. So is the potential, as we've seen. No one—not even men and women trained in ESO—achieves full sexual potential. In that sense we all have sexual problems.

The only person who can validly identify a problem area in your sexual functioning is you. A man might define himself as an early ejaculator if he ejaculates sooner than he and his partner wish and doesn't know how to delay orgasm. A woman might define herself as situationally nonorgasmic if she can stimulate herself to orgasm but doesn't know how to have orgasm with her partner during intercourse and wants to.

MEDICAL PROBLEMS

Not all sexual problems are psychological. Some are medical and physical. Diabetes can cause sexual problems. So can prostate surgery, chronic infections, torn ligaments, excessive alcohol, chronic illness, chronic pain, and many physical difficulties. A variety of medications can interfere, particularly tranquilizers and drugs for high blood pressure. If you suspect your problem is medical, visit a physician for a thorough examination.

Even if you have a physical condition that can affect you sexually, deliberate effort to improve your sexual functioning—such as by following the exercises and programs described in this book—can improve your sexual experience. There are very few people, even with severe medical disabilities such as diabetes or paraplegia, who cannot learn to have better-quality sex than they now think possible. Unfortunately, their doubts are often reinforced by their doctors, families, and friends. Our advice: don't believe prophets of sexual doom. Give pleasure a try.

ANXIETY

Most sexual problems arise from lack of knowledge, emotional concerns, or lack of experience. Most can be corrected, then, with information and practice.

Anxiety is the root cause of sexual difficulties. It shows up as fear, tension, stress, and resistance. That's why we've emphasized relaxation techniques throughout this book. We'll refer to those techniques again here as we discuss what to do about problems.

Most problems can be solved—most gaps can be closed—using basically the same skills as those you develop for ESO. So what you learn here can be carried forward directly into that training. You'll even have an advantage over many people, because you'll already have learned how to work through tough problems of resistance.

TRAUMATIC EARLY EXPERIENCE

Some sexual problems can be worked through best with an experienced licensed psychotherapist. These are usually problems that go back to childhood: a background of severe punishment for sexual behavior; severe conflict about sexual behavior; traumatic incest; other traumatic early sexual experiences. These experiences can produce anxiety that's too deep-seated to give way to the self-training methods we discuss here. If you find yourself unable to make progress by these methods, you may want to work with a knowledgeable counselor. But most people can greatly improve their sexual skills without psychotherapy.

MALE PROBLEMS

Since women go first in ESO training, we'll talk about gentlemen first here: erection problems, then problems with timing ejaculation.

Erection problems come in two degrees of severity: the primary problem of the man who has *never* been able to maintain an erection in intercourse and, less severe, the secondary problem of the man who *sometimes* can't maintain an erection in intercourse.

Primary Erection Problems

A man with primary erection problems has *never* been able to sustain an erection for intercourse with any partner. Erections are usually possible with masturbation and sometimes with manual or oral stimulation by a partner. Often primary erection problems originate in deep-seated emotional conflicts about sex or about women. Although the methods for improving secondary erection problems described below are frequently helpful, men who experience primary erection problems may benefit from longer-term psychotherapy.

Secondary Erection Problems

More commonly, men who complain of erection difficulties have functioned relatively well at some time in the past. About fifteen percent of the men in this category are likely to have a problem with their health.

At least once a week, do you find yourself moderately to fully erect when you awaken from sleep at night or in the morning? Can you get an erection when you self-stimulate? If the answer to both these questions is no, then you should certainly consult a medical doctor. If the answer to both these questions is yes, then the chances are good that the problem is psychological.

No male, throughout his entire life, maintains an erection during intercourse one hundred percent of the time. The erection mechanism isn't that reliable. Sex therapists usually call it a problem if a patient has difficulty maintaining an erection during intercourse more than twenty-five percent of the time. That's one out of four. If your difficulty is less frequent than that, you're probably normal. The majority of men function more or less the same. Your problem can be dealt with by learning to overcome resistance and to take in more pleasure. ESO training is a good way to do both.

But twenty-five percent is only a general rule of thumb. One patient of ours is, quite literally, a rock star, who showed us how subjective these rules can be. He came to us complaining of erection problems. When we sat down and charted the difficulty, it averaged out at about twenty percent. We didn't consider twenty percent a problem, but in his world that percentage was catastrophic. His professional image is highly sexual. His female partners expected him to show them the best night of their lives. They expected one-hundred-and-twenty-percent function. When he couldn't produce and maintain an erection, he felt humiliated.

We asked him to list the times he could and the times he couldn't. A pattern emerged that he hadn't noticed: he had trouble with erection when he'd been using drugs and alcohol. He agreed then not to put himself into sexual situations when he had recently used alcohol or drugs. That helped. With relaxation training he was soon back to his high-average normal.

Our first point, then, is simply reassurance: no one maintains erection successfully all the time. Fatigue, tension, stress, anxiety, distraction, and chemicals all can intervene.

Your partner needs to recognize that her pleasure is not totally dependent on your erection. You can stimulate her by other means. One of the advantages of ESO training is that it relieves you of performance pressure. If you feel you have secondary erection problems, go ahead and get started with ESO training.

A ban on intercourse can be extremely helpful. Ideally you'll want your partner's cooperation. Otherwise she may begin to wonder why you've lost interest.

We'd suggest you agree with your partner not to have intercourse for at least six sexual encounters. You can find pleasure, and give your partner pleasure, any other way you care to, but during that time you won't have intercourse. This simple agreement is the single most useful method we know of for dealing with erection problems.

If you don't have a regular sexual partner, or if your sexual partner can't be included in your decision, you can decide unilaterally to ban intercourse. If you do, you should give your partner more attention in other ways sexually so that she won't miss intercourse as much and won't put so much pressure on you to have intercourse. This unilateral ban isn't as desirable as a ban with your partner's agreement, but it's better than none at all.

With a ban on intercourse you'll probably notice that your erections return. You shouldn't expect them to return all at once. But eventually, with other sexual stimulation, they will. It's important then that you don't try immediately to use your erection for intercourse.

Along with an intercourse ban you should follow the self-stimulation program in chapter 3, "Developing Skills." Don't try to achieve advanced levels of extended arousal yet. Concentrate on achieving and sustaining an erection by self-stimulation for fifteen minutes and then go on to ejaculation.

The Sensory Focus exercise on page 253 is very useful to help reduce performance anxiety in men who have trouble achieving and sustaining erection. Go through all four steps at least four different times. Then you may concentrate on steps 3 and 4, with ejaculation allowed as a conclusion.

When you are able to achieve reliable erection during Sensory Focus, step 3, you and your partner have a choice. You may proceed to intercourse at the end of this period of manual stimulation by your partner, or you may go on with ESO training. Refer to the discussion on page 110, "Are You Ready for ESO?" to guide you in determining your readiness to go on with ESO training. You may then want to resume intercourse when you are able to experience extended orgasms lasting twice as long as those you experienced before training. Men who learn to experience Phase I ESO for several minutes, several times a week, are likely to have fewer problems with erections during intercourse.

Erection problems often occur because a man believes he should automatically experience an erection whenever he's in a sexual situation. Women often believe that too.

It's a myth. Most men need their penises directly stimulated for erection. The need increases with age. A partner is the best source of that stimulation, so you should continue self-stimulation training through the stages when your partner watches you to learn how and then takes over the process.

You are responsible for arranging enough stimulation. You have to make sure you give yourself enough or your partner gives you enough. Then, even if you don't begin a sexual encounter with an erection, you can produce an erection with self-stimulation. If you've done that in front of your partner in training, then you won't be embarrassed to do it again when it's needed. And yes, it's okay, many men stimulate themselves in order to achieve a working level of arousal. It's more fun if your partner does it for you, but not all women are willing to agree. It's your penis, your pleasure, and ultimately your responsibility.

Soft-Penis Intercourse

This can be a useful exercise for erection problems. Both partners experience pleasure from penile stimulation that isn't dependent on erection. It's also a pleasurable variation for any couple to use near the beginning of a sexual encounter, because it establishes sexual intimacy without rushing sexual performance.

The woman lies on her back with her right leg tented over the man's hips. The man lies at a forty-five-degree angle to her body on his left side, facing her. He holds his penis in his right hand and rubs the glans up, down, and around the woman's clitoris. Both areas, penis and vulva, should be well lubricated. (See illustration 19 on page 228.)

The man should concentrate on stimulating his glans, focusing his attention on the pleasurable sensations he receives from rubbing it against his partner's genitals. The woman should allow herself to enjoy the clitoral stimulation she's receiving without thinking ahead to what she hopes or anticipates should happen—to her arousal or to his.

If you, the man, happen to develop an erection during this exercise, don't be concerned. Continue the stimulation. If you sustain an erection for five minutes or more, you may partly insert yourself—no more than one inch—into your partner's vagina. If you do partly insert yourself, continue to use your right hand to move your penis from inside the vagina to outside, up, and around the clitoris—in, out, around and around.

19 POSITION FOR INTERCOURSE:
SOFT-PENIS INTERCOURSE

Training and foreplay exercise. Man rhythmically rubs soft penis against woman's vaginal opening and clitoris. If penis lengthens, man rhythmically inserts up to one inch and withdraws.

After five minutes or more of partial insertion and clitoral teasing, if you are still sustaining an erection, you may gradually increase penetration while decreasing clitoral stimulation.

Do this exercise at least three times a week for at least fifteen minutes each session, even if you or your partner resists doing it, even if it bores you. Don't expect an erection. Soft-penis intercourse is a training exercise. Boxers jump rope for training to develop their reflexes and stamina, not because they expect to jump rope in the ring.

Men with erection problems should make a list of the times when their penises rise to the occasion and the times when they don't. You may identify a pattern. The pattern our rock star found involved drugs and alcohol. He hadn't noticed that pattern before. Alcohol is a very common cause of erection problems. The classic alcohol-related disability is failing to achieve erection because you're anesthetized with alcohol and then panicking and assuming your penis is permanently disabled. Performance anxiety after that sustains a self-fulfilling prophecy. Up to two drinks in any three-hour period can help rather than hinder sexual experience, but more than that may interfere.

There are other difficulties you might discover by listing occasions. Some men find they have no difficulty with a familiar partner but difficulty with a new partner. For other men it's the other way around.

Especially with a familiar partner, you can solve your problem by finding ways to make sex feel new, different, and more exciting. Change the time, change the setting, change the position. One certain new adventure that you and your partner might arrange for yourselves is agreement to train for ESO.

You need to learn how to reduce anxiety. We've discussed methods in chapter 8, "Overcoming Resistances." Learn to relax. Work on cognitive restructuring. Practice breathing exercises. Work on visualization. Have your partner use positive suggestion. All those techniques will help.

Just as you're responsible for arranging enough stimulation, you're also responsible for deciding when you feel up to lovemaking. Don't have sex just because you think you ought to. If you're feeling pressed, if you have a deadline the next morning, you should recognize that you're in conflict and aren't likely to give pleasure your full attention. It's great to agree never to say no to sex, but if you have an erection problem, you're not ready yet for that agreement.

Men have more trouble saying no than women do. It's important to say no in a way that won't hurt your partner's feelings. Be honest. Don't tell her you have a headache. Admit you have a deadline to meet the following day and you're preoccupied. Offer an alternative: "Can we agree to make love tomorrow night instead? Because then I'll be more attentive."

This approach applies as well to situations that provoke anxiety. You're not required to make love where you're uncomfortable. Some years ago we worked with an adventurous woman married to a conservative man. Melanie would propose making love in the woods in broad daylight or in a car parked on a city street, and Arthur would be appalled. We suggested compromise. They both moved a little toward the middle. Now they make love in the woods at night or parked on a back-country road. Arthur's working toward becoming more adventurous because Melanie likes it, and he's finding he likes a touch of it too.

Drugs other than alcohol can also cause problems. We don't mean only illegal drugs. We're often surprised to find clients taking several prescribed medications without realizing that they may affect sexual functioning. Tranquilizers and sleeping pills are serious offenders. So are drugs for high blood pressure. If you're taking medication and have erection problems, you should discuss that medication with your doctor. Doctors are often reluctant to tell you in advance about possible sexual side effects of the medications they prescribe, because the information itself can trigger problems in anxious patients.

If you use marijuana, don't use too much too frequently. Used recreationally, no more than once a week, it can be helpful, creating some slowing of the time sense, loosening inhibitions, and allowing you to focus more on feelings than on thoughts. On the other hand, some people have bad reactions—more anxiety and sometimes paranoia. And reliable research has shown that chronic—daily—marijuana use decreases testosterone levels and thus decreases libido.

In general we favor natural pleasures over chemical pleasures. Your body produces hormones and other substances when it's sexually stimulated that enhance pleasure and increase libido—endorphins, androgens. The best way to maintain healthy hormone levels is to enjoy frequent sex.

If, however, you have erection problems and haven't had your testosterone level checked, you might discuss that measurement with your doctor (both "total" and "free" testosterone should be measured). If he finds low levels of testosterone for your age, discuss hormone replacement therapy with him. Methods include biweekly injections or daily applications of testosterone gel or five percent cream, the latter available by prescription from a compounding pharmacy. Testosterone precursors such as DHEA and androstenediol are available as dietary supplements. However, before using them, and several months after regular use, it is wise to get a blood test, or the new salivary test, for testosterone and DHEA levels.

Viagra

Viagra can help you to achieve an erection with direct stimulation of the penis and to maintain an erection so long as stimulation continues. It works by increasing levels of nitric oxide in the penis, a neurotransmitter essential for stimulating erection. Viagra is effective for about seventy-five percent of the men for whom it's prescribed. It does not increase desire or libido, nor does it directly affect orgasm. It should be taken on an empty stomach about an hour before you anticipate having sex, and you shouldn't eat for at least an hour after you take it. You'll probably only notice its effect with direct sexual stimulation. Some men experience mild head pressure or flushing, without significant discomfort. The effects of Viagra persist for several hours—sometimes as long as six to twelve hours. Men with any form of heart disease should be especially cautious about using Viagra. There have been several hundred deaths worldwide attributed to Viagra, mostly but not exclusively in men with some form of heart disease. While this number represents only a small fraction of one percent of users, it does emphasize that this prescription medication should be used prudently and with medical supervision.

Another prescription product that can aid erection is Yohimbine, an herb available under the trade name Yocon, which is taken three times per day, every day. About a third of men who use it report useful results. Side effects, while not common, include an increase in pulse and increased blood pressure.

Herbal sexual enhancers that some men find useful include Tribulus Terrestris, Maura Pauma, and Vigorex Forte. Three grams of the amino acid L-arginine taken one hour before sex has been shown, like Viagra, to increase penile nitric oxide, but by a different mechanism.

Other Products

Erection strength and longevity can frequently be helped with properly sized silicone erection enhancement rings.

The ones designed for the medical market are more effective than those advertised and available in the consumer market.

Some men with persistent erection problems benefit from using a medical-grade vacuum pump and erection ring. See "Products and Where to Find Them" on page 269.

Early Ejaculation

Early ejaculation is a timing problem. You ejaculate before you want to or before your partner wants you to. In sports we admire quick reflexes. In bed they can cause difficulties. But it's not far-fetched, in the context of ESO, to say that all men are early ejaculators. Very few of us can make love for three hours at a stretch.

It's possible to learn. You only have to want to. You'll be able to give your partner more pleasure in lovemaking if you can last longer. That's the traditional rationale. It's true and valid. But less often emphasized is another reason for learning to delay ejaculation, equally valid and perhaps even more in your interest: you'll give yourself more pleasure too. Go back to page 157 and look at the graph of male orgasmic responses. It demonstrates that the longer your erection can last, the higher your arousal and the more total pleasure you'll have.

In chapter 4, "Getting Together," we discuss foreplay. A formal exercise in foreplay is Sensory Focus, page 253, which is a good way to begin dealing with early ejaculation problems. Many men ejaculate sooner than they and their partners would like because they focus all their attention on their genitals. They fail to realize that their entire bodies are available for sexual stimulation. To the degree that you can allow your whole body to participate in lovemaking, you'll be able to take in more pleasure longer without tripping the ejaculation reflex.

Sensory Focus involves your partner. She needs actively

to caress you. Some women don't think that's their job. They see themselves as simply a receptacle, or they look out for their own orgasm and expect a man to do the same. Don't accept those terms. If your partner wants you to last longer, she should be willing to help you learn how.

After Sensory Focus, you and your partner can go on to ejaculation-control training. You lie on your back, knees bent or extended, and your partner sits or kneels between your legs. She lubricates your penis and scrotum and begins stimulating your penis—stroking it—until you approach orgasm. She concentrates on learning the signs of approaching orgasm: thrusting hips, jerky body movements, lifting of the testicles upward against the body, pulsing of the penis itself. You can help her by quickly withdrawing your pelvis as a signal or by telling her where you are: "I'm getting close." "Stop." But eventually she needs to learn to know without being told.

When you're close to orgasm, your partner simply stops stimulating you—stops stroking, or even takes her hands away for a few seconds, up to a full minute. Your level of arousal will decline. When it has declined to where you feel in control, she starts stimulating again. She might stop and start at least six times in fifteen minutes.

If you go over to orgasm and ejaculation, open your mind and body. Relax, flowing into the ejaculation experience. Afterward discuss with your partner what happened and how both of you can achieve better control next time. The exercise in semen withholding on page 74 can help you achieve better control of ejaculation. It's the opposite of letting go and relaxing.

Another control technique your partner can learn is the scrotal pull, which is discussed on page 147 in chapter 6, "Male ESO: How to Stimulate a Man." As you may have noticed by now, early ejaculation-control training is similar to ESO training. The one leads directly to the other.

Practice ejaculatory control by the Sensory Focus steps

3 and 4 and stop-start methods at least twice a week until you achieve control. When you can last thirty minutes with your partner stimulating you, you may be ready to go on to ESO training.

Manual stimulation is different from vaginal. A man might have no problem with early ejaculation during manual stimulation but will ejaculate as soon as he enters his partner's vagina. To desensitize yourself to intercourse, here's a ten-step training program you can follow. It incorporates as steps 3 and 4 the stop-start method we just discussed. Stop whenever you feel ejaculation is near and then start again.

Ten-Step Training Program for Early Ejaculators

1. Stimulate yourself with a dry hand until you can last for thirty minutes.
2. Stimulate yourself with a lubricated hand until you can last for thirty minutes.
3. Have your partner stimulate you with dry hands until you can last for thirty minutes.
4. Have your partner stimulate you with lubricated hands until you can last for thirty minutes.
5. Lie on your back. Have your partner kneel facing you, astride. Keep your penis in her vagina, moving only enough to maintain erection, until you can last for thirty minutes.
6. Lie on your back. Have your partner kneel facing you, astride. With your penis inside her, she thrusts gently, stopping when necessary for control, until you can last for thirty minutes.
7. Lie on your back. Have your partner kneel facing you, astride. With your penis inside her, you thrust gently, stopping when necessary for control, until you can last for thirty minutes.
8. Lie on your back. Have your partner kneel facing you,

astride. With your penis inside her, both of you thrust, stopping when necessary for control, until you can last for thirty minutes.

9. Make love lying on your sides until you can last for thirty minutes.

10. Make love in the missionary position for thirty minutes.

Use this program at least twice a week for six months. Complete ejaculatory control may require two to six months of practice. You'll regress sometimes. That's normal and nothing to worry about. Just go back to Sensory Focus and stop-start. You may also find yourself experiencing occasional problems maintaining your erection. That's normal too. Look over the section entitled "Secondary Erection Problems," page 223, for guidance then.

You'll also want to learn to relax. Reread chapter 8, "Overcoming Resistances," for instruction.

Do Kegel exercises faithfully. They're an excellent way to control ejaculation.

If you're clenching your pelvic muscles when climbing to arousal, then quickly push out and stop breathing for a moment to control the urge to ejaculate. If you're pushing out to climb to arousal, then momentarily clench your pelvic muscles as tightly as you can and hold your breath to control the urge to ejaculate. These controls are much easier if you've regularly practiced Kegel exercises.

Delayed Ejaculation

Delayed ejaculation is a relatively less common problem. If you often have vaginal intercourse with an erection for thirty minutes or more but then are unable to ejaculate vaginally even if you want to, you may have a problem with delayed ejaculation. Delayed ejaculators can usually ejaculate in other situations—when self-stimulating, for example.

The problem is almost always caused by a severe resistance to allowing semen to enter the vagina, and it's often best dealt with in psychotherapy. Relaxation techniques can help. So can self-stimulation exercises fitted to intercourse.

Those work this way: you stimulate yourself almost to the point of ejaculation and then insert your penis into your partner's vagina at the final moment to finish. When you can ejaculate inside the vagina that way, then at later sessions of lovemaking, insert yourself at earlier and earlier stages before ejaculation. After a month or more, you may find you won't need to stimulate yourself at all prior to intercourse, except possibly to achieve an erection.

Another approach to delayed ejaculation is by way of Sensory Focus (page 253) and partner stimulation. Your partner should do Sensory Focus with you. Follow the self-stimulation and partner-stimulation training program we describe in chapter 3, "Developing Skills." When your partner has learned how you like to be pleasured, she should practice stimulating you by hand to orgasm. Then, at a later session, she should take you up to the point where you're ready to ejaculate and then insert your penis into her vagina with you on your back and her kneeling facing you, astride. At successive sessions she should insert you progressively earlier. She can also help by doing rhythmic push-outs to increase penile stimulation.

FEMALE PROBLEMS

Women experience two basic kinds of sexual difficulties: problems with orgasm and painful intercourse. Problems with orgasm divide between those women who have never had orgasm and those who have it only in some situations but not in others.

Preorgasmia

If you have never learned to have orgasm, either with a partner or alone, by any means, you're preorgasmic. Preorgasmia is the easiest of all female sexual problems to correct. More than ninety percent of preorgasmic women can learn to have orgasm through a directed program.

The key is self-stimulation. To learn to have orgasm you need to be willing to practice regular self-stimulation. All the advantages of sexual pleasure, for yourself and for your partner, follow from that decision.

You should practice relaxation techniques and anxiety reduction. See chapter 8, "Overcoming Resistances," for guidance.

You need to learn Kegel exercises and to do them faithfully, as discussed on page 57.

You can learn to have orgasm, and then to have orgasm during intercourse, by following a ten-step program. Practice each step until you complete it successfully before going on to the next step.

Do these exercises every day.

Ten-Step Training Program for Preorgasmic Women

1. Stand nude in front of a full-length mirror. Look at your body as if you were another person. Be neutral, not critical. Assess yourself. Find your good points. Very few women ever take time to look at their bodies. See if you can agree to appreciate your body as it is, as worthy of pleasure.

Look over your genitals. Examine them. Learn where things are.

2. In a comfortable, private place, such as lying alone in bed, touch yourself for pleasure, not sexual arousal. Include your genitals in your touching, but with no expectation of arousal. Enjoy touching and being touched. Notice what feels good.

3. In a comfortable, private place, touch yourself for arousal. With your eyes and your hands, explore your body and your genitals to discover the areas that are most sexually sensitive. Touch your scalp, your neck, your shoulders. Touch your nipples to see what feels good. Does firmness feel best? Does rolling your nipples between thumb and forefinger feel best? Touch your belly. Touch the insides of your thighs, your labia, your clitoris. Learn what feels good so that later you can teach your partner. He won't know what you like unless you teach him. You can't teach him if you don't know yourself.

4. In a comfortable, private place, stimulate yourself for arousal (without seeking orgasm) in the areas you identified in step 3 as sexually sensitive. Use a lubricant when you stimulate your genitals (see "Lubrication," page 257).

5. Stimulate yourself more intensely over a longer period of time, at least thirty minutes or more every day. Allow orgasm to happen naturally. If, after two weeks of daily stimulation, you haven't had orgasm, go on to step 6.

6. Using a vibrator, stimulate yourself in turn on each of the sensitive areas you've identified, working your way to your genitals. (See "Vibrators," page 266.) Include clitoral stimulation and bring yourself to orgasm. If one type of vibrator doesn't seem to work for you, try another kind. If the vibrator feels too intense, put a towel between it and your genitals. Or use water from a tub faucet or flexible shower hose. A flexible shower hose with the head removed is a superb tool for sensual pleasure. Relax in the bathtub and adjust a warm soft flow from the hose. Direct the flow all over your genitals, then focus the flow on your clitoris for exquisite sensations. Start with a gentle flow and later experiment with greater pressure.

If, after two or three weeks of daily exercises, you are

unable to have orgasm using a vibrator, consult a sex therapist or a training group. Many women's organizations offer group counseling for preorgasmia. That's the least expensive form of treatment, and it gets results. Call around.

When you achieve orgasm with a vibrator (congratulations!), see if you can then learn to have orgasm without a vibrator. Use the vibrator to get close to the point of orgasm. Then switch to your hand. When you can take over orgasm with your hand, stop using the vibrator a little earlier each week. Eventually you should be able to give yourself orgasm using your hands alone.

7. Stimulate yourself to orgasm with your partner observing.

8. Allow your partner to stimulate you to orgasm as you demonstrated in step 7.

9. During intercourse allow your partner to stimulate you to orgasm as he learned in step 8. The best position for this exercise is the rear-entry position with both of you kneeling (see illustration 15 on page 168) or with the man standing beside the bed. He can reach around in this position to stimulate your clitoris with his hands.

10. Stimulate yourself to orgasm during intercourse.

Orgasm Sometimes, but Not with Intercourse

Women who have orgasm with self-stimulation or partner stimulation but not with intercourse need first to consider how assertive they are. They are often women who have been taught to believe that the man's pleasure always comes first. One practical problem with that conviction is that when a woman encourages a man to ejaculate before she's had orgasm, she no longer has an erect penis available to work with.

First of all, then, be sure you're taking what you need. You may want to extend the time you spend in foreplay and intercourse. You may want to make sure the conditions of lovemaking suit you. (See chapter 2, "Creating the Conditions for Pleasure," page 11.) You may want to choose a more arousing position for lovemaking. Subservience doesn't work in bed. Your needs are just as important as your partner's.

Another approach is to assign yourself the pleasure of having orgasm in ways different from what is usual for you. Find a different position or make subtle changes in the angles and movements within positions you are already using. If you haven't been using a vibrator with intercourse, try it. If you've been making love only in bed, make love somewhere else. Deliberately alter some habitual patterns. Focus on the pleasurable sensations you *do* feel during intercourse rather than on the ones you *think* you should be feeling. This will encourage sensations to grow.

ESO training is an excellent way to deal with this problem. Your ability to experience orgasm with manual vaginal stimulation is enhanced. If you are able to experience an orgasm of several minutes or more by manual stimulation, your vagina will become heavily engorged with blood and pleasurably sensitive. It's much easier then to continue the orgasmic experience with a thrusting penis.

Situational Nonorgasmia

If you've had orgasm in the past, but are presently unable to have orgasm by any means at all, this is your category. Situational nonorgasmia usually signals a change in your health, your relationship, or your attitude. It is not a result of simply "getting older."

Has your physical condition changed? Do you have an infection? Are you taking a prescription medication for high blood pressure, depression, or other problems? Have you started to have a problem with drugs or alcohol? Some diseases can develop silently that affect your sexual functioning. Diabetes is the most common. You may want to arrange a complete examination to rule out physical causes.

If health isn't a problem, then you and your partner need to talk about what's changed in your lives. You may not be getting what you want from your relationship. Maybe you've moved. Maybe you've added children to your life. You may be feeling isolated and angry. Use the communication exercises we discuss in "More Communication," page 247, to help work through your problem. Work on relaxation and anxiety reduction as well.

Pain with Intercourse

An early step to take when intercourse is painful is examination by a gynecologist or other physician. If your pelvic area is normal, then you need to take control of your lovemaking.

Painful intercourse very often occurs because your partner is controlling the timing, position, and depth of thrusting in intercourse. The vagina lengthens and enlarges with sexual arousal to accommodate almost any size penis, but it doesn't respond instantly. You need to be properly stimulated first.

1. You should be thoroughly lubricated. (See "Lubrication," page 257.)
2. Have your partner insert a lubricated finger into your vagina. You should *push out* against his finger. Pushing out opens up your vagina for easier penetration. Your partner can start with a smaller finger and work up to a larger finger. At first he should insert a finger without moving it. Then he should begin moving it, imitating the thrusting of a penis, slowly increasing depth of penetration and speed.

3. Allow yourself to be the receiver, totally. Have your partner stimulate you manually/orally to the best and longest orgasm possible. He should stimulate you vaginally as well as orally. If possible, locate and have your partner stimulate your internal trigger area or G spot. Don't allow this important step to be rushed. See chapter 5, "Female ESO: How to Stimulate a Woman," for more instructions.

4. Now take charge. If your partner is not erect at this point, stimulate him manually/orally until he is. See chapter 6, "Male ESO: How to Stimulate a Man," for appropriate techniques.

5. Choose a position for intercourse where you have a greater degree of control. Rear-entry, female-on-top, and side-to-side positions are usually best. *You* control the speed and extent of penetration. *You* determine the amount and type of thrusting, ranging from none at all to vigorous. Feel perfectly free to stimulate your clitoris at the same time. Remember to keep pushing out against your partner's penis.

6. Practice this exercise until you have an orgasm with your partner's penis inserted. You need your partner's cooperation. He should realize that this problem can be solved more easily if he's helpful and nonjudgmental. The process can be as enjoyable for him as it is for you.

PROBLEMS COMMON TO BOTH SEXES

Discrepancy of Desire between Partners

The most frequent common problem is a discrepancy of desire between partners. One partner wants to make love more often than the other.

Not long ago we worked with a stockbroker and his wife, Scott and Rebecca. Scott's interest in sex had declined with a drop in the stock market, and he experienced occasional loss of erection. The couple's lovemaking decreased to once a month, and Rebecca missed it. We encouraged Scott to allow himself to have sexual fantasies—specifically, to recall past pleasurable sexual experiences. Fantasizing awakened his interest to the extent that he agreed to practice ESO training assignments with his wife. We assigned a schedule of days as well as of exercises and asked Scott to follow the schedule regardless of fluctuations in the Dow Jones average or in his mood. He resisted at first, but as Rebecca got more sexual attention from him and began having several orgasms a week, he began enjoying her reaction to his attention. She, in turn, was so pleased with the improvement in their sex life that she started complimenting and encouraging him again. Scott's confidence returned. He returned to his previous level of sexual interest and to reliable, longer-lasting erections. The stock market's caprices bothered him much less than before.

Communication is crucial when there's a difference of desire between partners. Often the problem isn't sexual at all. It's a problem in some other area of the couple's lives. One partner may be angry with the other. Both people need to talk. Use the communication structures discussed in "More Communication," page 247, to help you get started.

You may need to arrange to focus more attention on sex. You can do that by deliberately creating sexual times together, as we discussed in chapter 2, "Creating the Conditions for Pleasure."

It can help a partner with lower sexual interest if partners share erotic media—X-rated magazines, books, videotapes, video discs, Web sites, or even phone sex. The materials may not be intensely arousing in themselves—that's a matter of personal preference—but they serve to focus both partners' attention on sex. Any number of people go through their lives struggling simply to handle

every day's complex details. They find it difficult suddenly
to switch to a mood of sexual arousal. Erotic material can
help them make the transition, because it calls attention
to sex without concentrating that attention on the immediate relationship—it's shared rather than confrontational.

Ideally both partners should share erotic media. It's a
myth that women aren't interested. Studies show that
women respond to erotic media with increased lubrication
even when they report no interest. Couples who see X-
rated films together are more likely to make love in the
next twenty-four hours than couples who see non-X-rated
films.

ESO training is an excellent way to equalize differences
in desire. All it requires of you is the willingness to follow
the ESO exercises that you both agree to do. After you
have both thoroughly understood the content of this book
by reading it through twice and discussing it, agree on
which exercises you will do on which particular days. You
should do the agreed-upon exercises at least three times
every week, though more often is better. However, if three
times per week seems too frequent, doing an exercise even
once per week will be of value. Your goal is not specifically
orgasm. Your goal is more general: pleasurable feelings and
pleasurable thoughts. Tell yourself, "This feels good; I'm
enjoying myself." *It's okay if one of you enjoys the experience more than the other.*

No Partner

Men and women without a partner can improve their
sexual skills and the quality of their sexual experiences.
These improvements will help them move to higher levels
of pleasure when they select a partner who shares a desire
to extend orgasmic experience. It's possible to experience
Phase I ESO without a partner. But Phase II ESO requires
a partner of like mind. That's because two partners fully at-

tending to one of them creates a synergistic effect that multiplies each partner's sexual power.

Even without a partner you can extend your range of arousal and increase your pleasure significantly beyond your present level. You can do this by refining your self-stimulation skills. The basic information you need to do so is contained in chapter 3, "Developing Skills"; chapter 5, "Female ESO: How to Stimulate a Woman"; and chapter 6, "Male ESO: How to Stimulate a Man."

A man, for example, can practice lasting longer, setting five minutes as a goal, then ten, then fifteen, until he can maintain himself at a high level of arousal, near the point of ejaculatory inevitability, for thirty minutes. He should practice "peaking" himself—stopping just short of ejaculation—many, many times. Most men give up after about six peaks. A man should be able to peak himself at least fifteen to thirty times at a single session. He can experiment with different positions, different strokes, different locations, different lubricants, different kinds of erotic media. He can learn to increase the number of contractions with each ejaculation and the number of ejaculations during each session of pleasuring. All these activities train him for sex with a partner and, equally important, keep him sexually active. Both body and mind require sexual stimulation for optimal health and well-being. Older men especially should keep up sexual stimulation, because it's harder to recover with age when it's neglected. The saying "use it or lose it" has some validity.

Men and women both tend to use self-stimulation quickly for tension relief. A woman without a partner should also push beyond her present sexual limitations. If she's preorgasmic, she can become orgasmic. If she hasn't tried a vibrator, she may buy one and use it. If she's orgasmic but not multiorgasmic, she can learn to have several orgasms when she stimulates herself. She can usually also increase the number and strength of contractions she experiences with each orgasm. This in turn will prepare her for ESO with a partner.

An orgasm a day is a healthy, pleasurable goal for men and women of every age, with a partner or alone.

More Communication

Good communication is vital to good sex. Without open, honest discussion between you and your partner, the information in this book will be less useful to you. Changing your sexual relationship will bring up fears, hopes, anger, anxiety, resistances. It will lead to changes that extend beyond the sexual into the personal and even the social areas of your lives. You must not only practice to learn ESO: you must also talk. You must *listen* to your partner. Talk and listen objectively, without anger, fear, or condemnation.

Besides the very useful Appreciations and Resentments exercise we discussed on page 86, we've included some communication exercises here. We've met people who consider such exercises silly. We've discussed that sense of self-consciousness before. You can find your way through silliness by accepting it and even enjoying its temporary relief from dignity. These exercises are games with big rewards. They're also a way of formalizing good communication. Do at least one of them every day. If you do them regularly, you'll find eventually that you've incorporated them into your routine communication. Then they won't be exercises anymore. They'll be skills you've mastered.

AGREEMENT

The first step to take with any communication exercise is agreeing to do the exercise. That means asking your partner, "John, I'd like to do an Appreciations and Resentments exercise with you. Okay?" And John then has the option of saying, "Okay, I'm listening," or "No, this isn't really a good time. How about an hour from now, after I've finished this work?"

If a partner doesn't want to do an exercise immediately, he should propose an alternative time. A flat *no* cuts off communication.

THE VOLCANO

The Volcano is a general blowing off of steam. You're mad as hell, and you aren't going to take it anymore. You aren't mad at your partner. Your partner's role is to listen sympathetically. You propose a time limit—one minute, two minutes, three minutes. Your partner agrees to listen for that long. Then you blow: your job, the traffic ticket you got, the tax returns due next week, the unfairness of it all. In this exercise you can give your emotions free rein. When you're finished unloading, your partner says only, "Thank you," using a neutral tone of voice and without further discussion. And because your partner listened, you feel better and you both feel closer.

THE TRIM

It's particularly important to deal promptly and openly with anger, which is always a component of sexual change. The Trim can serve that purpose. It's a Volcano exercise directed at your partner. You spend a minute or two or three letting your partner know how you feel about something that concerns his or her behavior.

"I'm really angry about what you've been getting away with lately. You're not paying attention to me and you never care about me and you're always critical and you're not giving the kids any time and you're not taking care of your responsibilities around the house and I hate it. What the hell is wrong with you?" Your partner then says, neutrally, "Thank you."

You agree not to hit below the belt: not to bring up subjects that you know are particularly painful, unfair, off-limits, such as a previous spouse or an old relationship, a lost job, a weight problem.

Your partner agrees to listen and not to comment beyond saying "Thank you." Your partner also agrees not to discuss your criticism unless you agree to allow that discussion, and in any case not for at least thirty minutes after you've finished.

After those thirty minutes, your partner may ask you if you're willing to discuss one or more of your criticisms. You may then say yes, you're willing, or no, you're not. If you're not willing to discuss your criticism yet, you can indicate when you will be. One response, of course, is "Never." Your partner then has the option of discussing your "Never" when *your* turn comes around to be Trimmed.

The Trim isn't meant to cause gratuitous pain. You'll be cheating if you use it purely to wound. It serves two purposes: it allows you to express anger you might otherwise keep to yourself for fear of starting a major argument, and it allows your partner to think about your criticism before responding, which reduces defensiveness and increases understanding.

APPRECIATIONS AND RESENTMENTS

We discuss this exercise in detail in chapter 4, "Getting Together." Turn back there to learn it or for review. You might notice again that it's important to do sexual Appreciations and Resentments regularly when you're learning

ESO. You can use Appreciations and Resentments to deal with feelings of anger. Most people can accept anger more comfortably if it's preceded by appreciation. Note that unlike the Volcano and the Trim, Appreciations and Resentments are delivered by both partners, giver and receiver, in a *neutral* tone of voice.

MIND READING

We're all constantly reading each other's minds. Why not formalize the process? You ask your partner, "Jane, I'd like to read your mind. Is that okay?" Jane says, "Yes." You say, "I feel as if you're angry with me. I think you don't think I've been paying enough attention to you lately." Jane says, "Thank you." Then she categorizes your Mind Reading with a percentage: "You're one hundred percent right. I have been feeling that." Or "No, that's one hundred percent wrong. I don't know where in the world you got that." Or "That's about twenty percent right, but it's not a big issue. I'm not mad about it. I know you have lot on your mind."

Mind Reading is a way of checking how your partner is feeling. It's also a way of reminding yourself how impossible it is to read someone else's mind and how impossible it is for someone else to read your mind. Reminding yourself, in other words, how important communication is.

YES/NO

This exercise is individual rather than mutual. It helps people who defer to their partners so often that they privately feel walked on.

Very simply, you make an agreement with yourself to say no to three things each day that you would ordinarily agree to with unspoken reluctance. You can say no to someone else's request; you can say no to yourself about something you "should" do.

Similarly, you make an agreement with yourself to ask for three things each day that you would like but usually wouldn't seek or accept or feel you deserve.

Some people find it hard to say no. They're afraid they'll be disliked or rejected if they do. They learn by practicing, beginning with small refusals and building as their fear of rejection fades. Some people find it hard to ask, to say yes. That limits risk, too, because if you don't ask for something, you can't be rejected. In fact, the more you ask for, the more you're likely to receive. As with saying no, start with small requests and increase their scope as your fear of rejection fades.

Learning to ask is especially useful sexually. Each time you have sex, ask your partner to do something that your partner might not otherwise do and that you might not otherwise ask for. "I'd love you to massage my feet first," for example. Or "We haven't used the vibrator in a while— would you be willing to include it now?"

GETTING TO KNOW YOU

Communication isn't only verbal. It's also, or it should also be, physical. So we've included here several exercises that combine verbal and physical activities. You'll enjoy them. They're fun.

Sexual Exploration

This exercise allows you to familiarize yourself with your partner's genitals and the feelings they sense when you touch them in specific ways and with specific strokes. It's described in detail on page 102.

Pleasure Turns

This exercise formalizes learning to give each other pleasure. You alternate manual stimulation with discussion. It's a logical follow-up to the previous exercise, and puts what you learned there to use.

Find a comfortable position. Decide who's first. Agree how much time to allow, at least twenty minutes each. Apply a lubricant. Begin stimulating your partner for arousal. Your partner then directs you as you go: "A little higher. A little faster. Maybe slightly more pressure. There. That's good. That's wonderful."

Explore. Enjoy. Orgasm is optional.

Afterward, talk it over. Both of you will have feelings and discoveries to discuss.

This exercise is a genitally focused variant of the Sensory Focus step 4 exercise described on page 257.

An Hour of Pleasure

Very simple: intercourse is banned; every other kind of sexual pleasuring is encouraged, including oral, manual, fantasy, and role playing. The idea is to learn to express your body's full potential for pleasure and to help your partner to that pleasure as well. The hour may include resting and talking about feelings. Orgasm shouldn't be a specific goal. If it happens, enjoy it.

Requests

Also very simple: during a period you've set aside with your partner for pleasuring, ask for one new sexual pleasure. Take turns.

Taking Charge

Each partner spends half an hour doing whatever he or she wants with the other. Decide who's in charge. If it's the man, he can stimulate the woman in any way he desires. Or direct her to stimulate him in any way he desires. When it's the woman's turn, she can stimulate the man in any way that occurs to her or direct him to stimulate her exactly as she likes.

Please note that nothing specific is expected to happen during this exercise. It allows freedom to express assertive sexual feelings and to receive sexual stimulation passively. If you find yourself resisting, say to yourself, "I'm enjoying this. It's fun." Repeat the phrase each time your thoughts distract you from pleasure.

Taking Charge is a deceptively simple exercise. Used frequently, it will open up many possibilities that might otherwise be missed. It can lift couples out of sexual ruts, and it allows partners to express safely some of their fantasies.

Sensory Focus

Sensory Focus is light massage with ground rules. It's an excellent exercise in learning to feel pleasure over larger areas of your body. It's a simple way to relax, to move from distraction to intimacy with your partner, to pay attention to pleasure. It's always a good way to begin lovemaking.

We include here a graduated series of Sensory Focus exercises. We often direct our clients to spend a week or more on each step before going on to the next. When you begin practicing Sensory Focus you might follow the same procedure. Once you have moved through step 4 and are comfortable with all four steps, you can choose from week to week and from pleasure session to pleasure session which step you prefer at that time. Or you may want to combine one or more steps into one. Feel free to experiment. As always, the point of exercise is discovering more pleasure.

Step 1: Silent Touching (twenty minutes minimum each partner)

1. Woman lies nude on bed or floor on her stomach. She focuses on her sensations or listens to music with her eyes closed.
2. Man, nude, begins by touching and massaging woman's extremities—head, hands, and feet—working his way slowly toward the center of the woman's body.
3. Working from her shoulders down her back, man starts stroking woman's body lightly, increasing pressure as he progresses.
4. Man then gently turns woman over and repeats the process of touching and stroking on the front of her body. He does *not* focus on breasts and genitals. He may lightly touch the breasts but totally avoids the genitals.
5. Woman takes as much pleasure from the man's stimulation as she can. She shouldn't be doing anything but feeling as good as she can allow herself to feel.
6. Man should be experiencing the pleasure of caressing his partner and giving her pleasure.
7. When man is finished, he gently drapes a towel over his partner's body and allows her to lie quietly for about three minutes. Then he gives her a gentle, loving kiss and helps her up.
8. Now reverse the procedure, the woman giving the massage and the man relaxing and receiving.

Step 2: Touching with Feedback (twenty minutes minimum each partner)

Repeat the same procedure as step 1, but with the partner who is being massaged giving both verbal and non-verbal direction. Each partner in turn should say what he/she is experiencing and what he/she likes and dislikes.

Many men and women hesitate to experiment sensually because they're afraid they'll do something wrong. This exercise helps break through that resistance. Do touch the genitals, but not so rhythmically or at such length that you produce high sexual arousal. See if you can discover something that you weren't aware of before about your partner's preferences. The partner being touched may physically guide the hand of the massaging partner to show how best to stroke or touch a particular area: to the thigh, for example, saying, "Please massage me here, like this . . . that tickles a little . . . more with your palm . . . that's perfect." Or "That feels nice, but a little more [or less] pressure would feel better." Allow yourself to moan or sigh with pleasure when the stroking feels good.

Afterward, spend several minutes discussing the experience, talking about what you learned and what you felt.

Step 3: Genital Arousal without Feedback (thirty minutes minimum each partner)

Lovingly stroke and touch your partner's body from head to toe; then concentrate on stimulating the genitals for arousal. Be sure to use lubricant. Enjoy the experience *without talking.* Devote equal time to each step. No orgasms or ejaculation permitted. The positions demonstrated in illustrations 5, 6, and 18 are convenient for a man stimulating a woman. The positions in illustrations 9, 11, 12, and 17 are convenient for a woman stimulating a man.

Woman stimulating a man:

1. Concentrate on stimulating the penis. Enjoy stroking the shaft first with one hand, then with two.
2. Direct your attention to the testicles. Stroke and fondle first one, then both. Explore the effect of gently tugging and stretching the scrotum.
3. Explore the area behind the testicles, in front of the anus—the perineum. Stimulate and rhythmically pump the buried penile base.

4. Locate and stimulate the external prostate spot.
5. Experiment with the sensation of stimulating the anus. In response to loving, gentle stimulation it engorges and relaxes, opening up, just like your labia and vaginal opening. If it clenches tight, it is resisting and wants less stimulation.
6. Stop stimulation well short of orgasm.

Man stimulating a woman:

1. Stroke, tease, and massage the breasts and nipples. Does your partner appear to enjoy this stimulation? Do the nipples engorge and erect? Try to identify the most arousing ways to stimulate them.
2. Use one or two hands to touch, stimulate, stroke, and tease the pubic hair and inner thighs; the major labia; the minor labia.
3. Circle around the clitoral shaft without touching it.
4. Gently grasp the clitoral shaft between thumb and forefinger and roll it between your fingers at a rate of about once per second.
5. Stroke the glans clitoris with two fingers.
6. Insert your forefinger into the vagina and slowly sweep your finger clockwise and counterclockwise, noticing areas of sensitivity and response.
7. Stroke the anus. Notice if it becomes engorged. When the anus relaxes it is aroused and wants more stimulation. If it clenches tight it is resisting and wants less stimulation.
8. Simultaneously stimulate two of the areas you've explored, one area with each hand: the anus and the vagina, for example, or the clitoris and the anus.

Remember, *no orgasm* is permitted during this exercise. Talk about it only after you both have completed it.

Step 4: Genital Arousal with Verbal Feedback (thirty minutes minimum each partner)

This exercise proceeds from step 3, but each partner makes at least one comment to the other while each genital area is stimulated. "I like watching your labia swell." "That feels good but I can't tell exactly what you're doing." "I'm getting bored, but keep on going—I'll get back to feeling good soon." (This step is similar in some ways to the Sexual Exploration exercise, except that it doesn't necessarily involve identifying your partner's anatomy or using a rating scale.)

After you've both finished doing any one of the above Sensory Focus exercises and talking over your experiences, you may decide to have intercourse or any other sexual sharing. Make sure before you go on that you get explicit verbal agreement from your partner.

Lubrication

Lubrication is absolutely essential for ESO. Delicate tissues can't be stroked for thirty minutes or an hour without the protection and reduced friction of a good lubricant. Natural body lubrication isn't enough. Neither are lightweight water-based lubricants such as lotions, creams, and jellies. Neither are oils alone. That's why we recommend heavy-duty lubrication, either a commercial lubricant such as petrolatum or Albolene, or the inexpensive mixture of mineral oil, paraffin, and petrolatum for which we gave the recipe on page 33. Silicone-based lubricants, relatively new on the market, are condom-safe and a very good compromise between oil- and water-based in utility. They are mainly available through mail-order or online sources.

For a pleasant variation you can add a few drops of scented oil to your lubricant. Scented oils are sold in

health-food stores. Coconut, jasmine, lemon, and rose are
nice. You may also want to buy a decorative plastic, wood,
or ceramic container, with a lid, for the lubricant. Pour the
lubricant into the container while it's still liquid. It will
cool to its normal semisolid consistency in half an hour.
Store the container near your bed.

Some people dislike using lubricants. That's a problem.
Sex is basically slippery and wet—the body deals naturally
in the short term with the problems artificial lubricants
solve in the longer term—and it's not ever going to be dry.
If you dislike lubricants but want to extend sexual
pleasure, you need to work your way through your aversion. It's actually a phobia, and it can be treated by pro-
gressing through small, step-by-step changes.

Start with a lightweight lubricant such as baby oil. Rub
it only on your hands. Or ask your partner to rub it only
on your hands or on some neutral part of your body—your
arm, your knee. When you're comfortable with that application, which may take several sessions, gradually over a
period of weeks apply the lubricant closer to your genitals,
until you're comfortable having it applied to your genitals
themselves.

Then gradually increase the viscosity and amount of the
lubricant—from baby oil to a cream, from a cream to ESO
lubricant—until you're adjusted to using lubricant.

If at any time along the way you feel too uncomfortable,
go back one step until a sense of comfort returns. This
process of desensitization may take several weeks or more.
Along the way talk to your partner about how you feel, and
practice relaxation.

You can help yourself work through an aversion to lubricants by deliberately experiencing them in nonsexual
settings. Apply lotion to your body after bathing, for example, and pay attention to the pleasure sensations. Give
your partner back rubs with lubrication and let your
partner do the same for you. You might even consider

taking up finger painting for a time. It's fun and good therapy.

You may choose to let your partner take responsibility for the lubricant. If your partner applies it to your genitals for you, and you don't have to touch it, you may feel more comfortable using it in lovemaking.

Lubrication serves another useful purpose: it clearly communicates that you want to make love, that sex is going to happen and there's pleasure in store. Many men and women are deliberately tentative about approaching each other sexually. They brush shoulders or touch an arm to test the waters. If their partners don't respond, they can then pretend they weren't asking (and go away with their feelings secretly hurt). But when you take out the lubricant, you're stating very clearly what you have in mind. You can't be ignored. If no sex follows, at least you'll both have to face the question of why. Applying lubricant at the beginning of a sexual encounter is often enough to melt any resistance your partner may feel to having sex.

Adding Light

If you're uncomfortable making love with the lights on, you can work your way through the problem in a series of small steps.

First decide that you want to learn to enjoy higher levels of lighting. Then you won't be limited to making love only at night. Light will help you and your partner see what you're doing when you're giving each other ESO. And it's erotically stimulating, or can be, to see your partner's body naked in arousal. These are all good reasons for learning to accept more light.

Once you've decided, you can proceed step by step, allowing at least one week to each small change. Begin with the most light you can tolerate in the room without feeling anxious. That may be a tiny night-light. It may even be a tiny night-light covered with some translucent material, like a napkin or a towel. Begin where you can, and use the beginning light level during lovemaking until you're comfortable with it. If you feel some discomfort, practice the relaxation methods discussed in chapter 8, "Overcoming Resistances."

When you're comfortable with the first level of lighting you've arranged, increase it. If you started with a night-light, add another night-light. If you started with a covered night-light, uncover it. Practice lovemaking with this increased light level until you're comfortable with it.

Then increase it again, perhaps changing to a small lamp with a fifteen- or twenty-five-watt bulb, or a red bulb, or, more romantically, candles. Continue this stepwise increase in lighting until you reach a level that you and your partner both find acceptable. Dim lighting is desirable for a romantic effect, provided you can see your partner's body. Bright lights tend to be distracting.

If at any time your anxiety returns, go back to the previous light level until you're comfortable again.

Don't feel hurried. Take time to get used to each light level before going on to the next, and change levels only gradually.

It helps to discuss your feelings with your partner, especially if you've kept the lights low because you're concerned about your body. Use the communications exercises we describe in this section to guide your discussions.

Learning to Vocalize

It's useful and freeing in lovemaking to vocalize, to let out the sounds that come to your throat when you're feeling pleasure. We'd all do that naturally if we didn't grow up having to take our pleasures in secret. Silence is a learned inhibition. It keeps you from letting go, and it interferes with breathing. It's easily unlearned.

Making natural, unforced groaning, moaning, or sighing sounds during sex serves at least three functions. Sounds force you to remember to exhale deeply. Producing sounds can help you diffuse sexual arousal into your whole body. Vocalizations give your partner feedback about how you're feeling, without requiring of you the distraction of forming and speaking words—useful information that can also increase your partner's level of arousal. Try making different sounds as you exhale.

Practice vocalizing together in a nonsexual setting. That might be sitting in your living room. It might be lying together in bed after watching the evening news. You may want to screen your vocalizing with sound—a stereo, a radio, the TV turned up. You can practice, alone or together, in the shower, where the acoustics are flattering and the warm water helps you relax. Decide you're going to make sounds and then make them. Take turns.

Try making the sounds you think you'd make if you were feeling the most pleasure you could possibly feel, the ultimate ecstasy. Moan, cry, laugh, scream—whatever feels freeing. Breathe in and out, and as you breathe out, make a sound like an animal. Rattle the back of your throat. Laugh. Sob. Swear if swearing feels good. If you think you're making too much noise, hold a pillow over your face. Try vocalizing "aaaaHHHaaaa" after every three or four quiet deep breaths.

You'll feel silly, stupid, embarrassed. That's normal. Enjoy the experience. Talk about it.

Keep practicing in a nonsexual context until you're both comfortable with vocalizing. Then, when you're making love, don't fake it or force it, but let it come.

Learning Oral Lovemaking

Many men and women resist oral lovemaking. They've been taught that it's dirty or wrong. Or they're afraid they'll be rejected. They're concerned about the taste of their partner's secretions. Women may be afraid they'll gag.

Oral lovemaking is another way to pleasure. It can add to arousal and to intimacy. It's sad but true that prostitutes find eager and nearly universal interest in oral sex among their clients. That's because it's intensely pleasurable and, too often, because the men's sexual partners reject oral lovemaking at home. If you don't know how to do it, you can learn. If you're anxious about doing it, you can gradually free yourself from anxiety.

Begin by *imagining* oral lovemaking while you're making love or during self-stimulation. Imagine you are kissing and licking your partner's genitals. Imagine your partner is kissing and licking yours.

Agree with your partner that you both want to learn oral lovemaking. Agree further that while you're learning, if either of you becomes too uncomfortable, you'll return to familiar lovemaking for the rest of that period of time. *Agree to shower or bathe, separately or together. At minimum, agree to wash your genital area thoroughly before beginning oral lovemaking.* Hygiene comfort is crucial to this intimacy. Agree to take turns and to proceed in small, incremental steps.

CUNNILINGUS

Cunnilingus (kun-ih-*ling*-us), the man orally pleasuring the woman, can begin with both partners smelling and tasting the woman's natural lubrication when she's clean and fresh. Many women (and men) are concerned about genital odor. The best way to resolve that concern is to bathe or shower together or separately before making love, paying special attention to washing the genitals. If odor continues to be a concern, the man can apply scented oils or scented lubricants to his partner's genitals. He can adjust to the oil by applying it first to a nongenital area of his partner's body and licking it off.

We suggest you do a Sensory Focus step 3 exercise (page 255), followed by the man briefly brushing his lips over his partner's genitals. From session to session he then slowly increases the time and the intensity of his stimulating.

He should experiment with different kinds of oral stimulation: brushing with his lips, licking, light suction. Regularly alternating tongue pressure on and around the clitoris and clitoral hood with sucking the clitoris into the mouth can be highly arousing. Men usually err in the direction of excessive force. Women generally like lighter, more regular, predictable, rhythmic stimulation. Let your partner's responses guide you.

At first, orgasm shouldn't be the goal. Later, when both partners are comfortable with oral lovemaking, it can be.

Some women find their partner's physical position during cunnilingus unmanly. They can help themselves through that resistance by deciding it's mistaken and by applying the techniques discussed in chapter 8, "Overcoming Resistances." The kneeling-over position (illustration 18 on page 180) or the position for mutual stimulation (illustration 4 on page 108) can help alleviate this concern.

FELLATIO

Women often resist fellatio (fuh-*lay*-she-oh) because they don't like the idea of their partner ejaculating in their mouth. They may dislike the taste of semen. They may feel the penis is dirty because it's also used for urination. They may be afraid of gagging, possibly from previous experience.

Bathe or shower together to assure each other of cleanliness. Uncircumcised men should draw back their foreskins and carefully wash the area. Begin with Sensory Focus step 3 (page 255). The woman then kisses the penis without taking it into her mouth. When she's comfortable doing that, at the same or a later session, she can begin taking the erect penis into her mouth. She should position herself above the penis, her partner on his back, so she can control any thrusting. She can also place her hand around the shaft of the penis to limit its movement into her mouth. These controls help her avoid gagging.

Suction isn't necessary. Simply moving the glans penis in and out of the mouth, making sure her lips cover her teeth, is highly arousing. So is licking the glans and the shaft.

Women who fear accepting their partner's semen into their mouth and who don't trust their partner's ejaculatory control can practice fellatio with a condom over the penis. Later, when they gain confidence in themselves and their partner and learn to recognize the signs of approaching ejaculation, they can pleasure their partner without using a condom.

Some women may choose never to receive their partner's semen orally. They can still give him the pleasure of fellatio, returning to manual lovemaking or intercourse for ejaculation. An excellent alternative is for the woman to take her mouth off her partner's penis just before he begins to ejaculate but keep her warm, lubricated hand moving on the glans. Under those circumstances the man may not even know the difference. She may catch the semen in a towel or tissue, wipe it up later from the man's body, or simply not worry about it.

A woman who wants to learn to enjoy fellatio to ejaculation has to accept the taste and texture of semen in her mouth and throat without gagging. The mere thought of swallowing semen can trigger the gag reflex in some women. Others find that the taste and texture of semen has the same uncomfortable effect. A woman who wants to avoid swallowing semen can practice pressing her tongue against the back of the roof of her mouth. This arrangement closes and blocks her throat. She may then spit the semen onto a tissue or a towel.

Our experience, however, indicates that most men would prefer their partners not to spit out their semen. A woman can learn to hold both semen and penis in her mouth. Saliva begins to collect after a few seconds. It dilutes the semen, changing the taste and texture to make it more acceptable and pleasurable.

Some women who accept the taste of semen still have trouble swallowing it. Another way to get used to semen—taste, texture, and swallowing—is for the man to ejaculate into the woman's hand. She can then place a small amount of ejaculate in her mouth. She should savor its texture and flavor and gradually increase the amount she tastes and swallows until she can enjoy all of it.

A woman who finds it impossible to like the taste of her partner's semen can at least disguise it with flavored oil or by preparing her mouth with a flavor she prefers—a sip of wine, a piece of chocolate, a swallow of fruit juice. Semen may taste slightly sweet or slightly bitter. It may have hardly any taste at all. Alcohol, even drunk in moderation, most frequently causes bitter semen. If bitterness is a problem, a man can experiment with changes in diet.

A woman should recognize that swallowing her partner's semen can be an intensely intimate act for both partners. It can be a significant symbolic gesture of love, and many women find it a meaningful and even a spiritual experience. It can strengthen your relationship. If this possibility appeals to you, you can both train yourselves toward it.

For more on these techniques, see "Oral Lovemaking," page 173.

Vibrators

We tend to think of the Victorian era as prudish, and in many ways it was, but nineteenth-century physicians treated some female patients with "nervous" conditions by stimulating them to orgasm. Vibrators were originally developed to make that treatment less strenuous and intimate, much as stethoscopes gave the physician a less intimate alternative to pressing his ear directly to his female patients' chests.

Vibrators can be a godsend for women who want to have efficient, intense single or multiple orgasms. They can help women who have never had an orgasm learn to become orgasmic. And they can allow the orgasmic woman to have multiple orgasms more easily. But since most plug-in vibrators (as opposed to the battery-operated kind) available in retail stores are suitable for clitoral stimulation only, they are not significantly useful for learning and attaining ESO states.

The most versatile vibrators are those that have accessories specifically designed for sexual, and particularly G-spot area, stimulation. The Hitachi Magic Wand, a large dual-speed plug-in vibrator with a spherical head, and similar designs are the most powerful available. The Magic Wand has three useful attachments that slip firmly onto the head: a small knob, a straight shaft, and a well-designed curved shaft called the "G Spotter." Coil-operated plug-in vibrators such as the Sunbeam Coil are popular for their more compact, quieter operation. The Sunbeam offers attachments such as the Clitickler, the Twig, the G Spotter Plus, and the Come Cup. (The Come Cup is designed for male use.) G-spot-stimulating attachments are equally suited to stimulating the prostate gland, both externally and internally. The ultimate in automated self-stimulation is the Sybian, a comfortable, padded, saddle-like device with a built-in dildo on which the woman sits. The dildo, available in several interchangeable sizes, is adjustable for movement and vibration intensity.

Battery-operated vibrators, which go by such names as the Pocket Rocket and the Twig Vibe, offer portability and convenience. The smallest operate on one AA battery and are designed for clitoral stimulation. Penis-shaped vibrators use two C batteries, and may be used for vaginal insertion. (For ordering information, see "Products and Where to Find Them," page 269.) Vibrators of various types without special sexual attachments can be found in many department and drug stores. Those with sexual attachments are usually only available by mail or on the Web.

A man can also use a vibrator for pleasure, applying it or having his partner apply it to his penis, scrotum, external prostate spot, or anal area.

If a vibrator feels too intense, even on low speed, you can reduce the intensity by wrapping it in one or more thicknesses of towel.

Jacuzzi jets make good vibrators. So do handheld pulsating shower heads. Some women enjoy the dental appliance made by Water-Pik, normally used for oral hygiene. Its fine, precisely adjustable pulses of water can be directed pleasantly onto the clitoral area. An inexpensive rubber spray head and hose attached to the tub faucet can provide excellent stimulation. Try removing the spray head and directing the concentrated stream onto the clitoris. Adjust pressure and water temperature carefully. Start with gentle pressure and increase it as you gain experience.

Products and Where to Find Them

Lubricants

1. *Water-soluble, glycerin-based*. Latex compatible (can be used with a condom or diaphragm), all are similar and superior to plain KY Jelly; most are available in drugstores and pharmacies or online (www.safesense.com). AstroGlide is considered to be the best (and most expensive) in this category. Others are: Foreplay Sensual Lubricant, KY Liquid Personal Lubricant, Maximum Lube, PrePair Personal Lubricant, Probe, Slippery Stuff, Vagistim Intimate Moisturizer, Wet Light, Women's Personal Lubricant, Aqua Lube.

2. *Silicone-based*. Relatively new on the market, they do not become sticky or tacky, last longer than glycerin type, and are latex condom and diaphragm compatible. Usually available only from sexual specialty stores or online (www.safesense.com or www.goodvibrations.com): Eros Super Concentrated BodyGlide (www.erosusa.com), Liquid Silk, ID Millennium, Wet Platinum.

3. *Oil-based*. Longest-lasting and smoothest type (do not use with condoms, diaphragms, or latex sensual products): Albolene Cleanser (this inexpensive makeup re-

mover is similar to natural lubrication and longer-lasting than water- or silicone-based products; it's available in large drugstores in the cosmetics section), Crème de Femme, Men's Cream, Wet J/O (www.safesense.com).

Other Sensual Products

Sybian for women and Venus II for men (automated self-stimulation devices): Abco Research, Box 354, Monticello IL 61856-0354, (800) 253-6135, www.sybian.com.

Aneros male prostate stimulator (a well-designed plastic device for stimulating internal prostate and external prostate spot simultaneously): www.malegspot.com.

Vibrators, G-spot stimulators (including the Crystal Wand), and other products: Good Vibrations, www.goodvibrations.com.

Prescription hormone creams: Medical Center Pharmacy, (800) 723-7455.

Products and equipment: www.secretaffair.com.

Kegelmaster device for aiding PC muscle development: www.kegelmaster2000.com.

Erection enhancement rings (high-quality, silicone, various sizes, medical-grade): www.esoecstasy.org.

Vacuum erection devices, medical-grade: www.esoecstasy.org.

The Nine-Week
ESO Program Sequence

Some couples find they learn better with a structured sequence of exercises. For those couples, we offer the following nine-week program. Ambitious couples who are willing to devote at least two to three hours per week for sexual activities together can follow the program week by week. Couples with less available time should spread the weekly practice sessions over a longer period. Be honest with yourselves; don't go on to a subsequent week until you both agree you've done the current week's exercises satisfactorily.

Couples may take two, three, or even more weeks to do any individual weekly exercises, depending upon available time or life schedule.

We suggest that couples refrain from their usual sexual activities for the duration of the program, limiting themselves to the interactions described. This limitation may be difficult for couples used to having intercourse or other sexual interactions frequently. But even the most active sexual relationship benefits from occasional periods of abstinence from intercourse or habitual sex, just as fasting occasionally detoxifies and cleanses the body. If giving up your habitual sexual activities for a few weeks seems unimaginable to you, here's an alternative: after working through any exercise, declare and agree that you have completed it and then proceed to any other activity you choose.

WEEK 1

SOLO EXERCISES

20–0 Countdown (page 53), three minutes every day.

Sex Muscle (Kegel) exercises (page 57), two times per day, every day (may be combined with routine daily activities).

COUPLES EXERCISES

Appreciations and Resentments (page 86), with script, nonsexual subjects. Two rounds each, every day.

Kissing exercise (page 100), with script.

Sensory Focus step 1 (page 254), silent, nongenital. Twenty minutes per person, forty minutes total.

WEEK 2

SOLO EXERCISES

20–0 Countdown, three minutes every day.

Sex Muscle with Breathing exercises (page 60), two times per day, every day (may be combined with routine daily activities). Increase number of repetitions as you are able.

COUPLES EXERCISES

Appreciation and Resentments without script, nonsexual subjects. Two rounds each, every day.

Kissing exercise with script.

Sensory Focus step 2 (page 254), verbal, nongenital. Twenty minutes per person, forty minutes total.

WEEK 3

SOLO EXERCISES

20–0 Countdown, three minutes every day.

Sex Muscle with Breathing exercises, two times per day, every day (may be combined with routine daily activities). Increase number of repetitions as you are able.

Self-Stimulation I (Basic Techniques, page 67 for men, page 76 for women), thirty minutes, three times per week minimum.

COUPLES EXERCISES

Appreciations and Resentments without script, nonsexual subjects. Two rounds each, every day.

Kissing exercise without script, minimum three times per week.

Sensory Focus step 3 (page 255), genital, verbal. Twenty minutes per person, minimum three times per week.

WEEK 4

SOLO EXERCISES

20–0 Countdown, three minutes every day.

Self-Stimulation I combined with Sex Muscle with Breathing, minimum three times per week for thirty minutes.

COUPLES EXERCISES

Appreciations and Resentments without script, nonsexual subjects. Two rounds each, every day.

Kissing exercise without script.

Sensory Fous step 4 (page 257), genital, verbal. Twenty minutes per person.

WEEK 5

SOLO EXERCISES

20–0 Countdown, three minutes every day.

Self-Stimulation, Advanced (male, page 73; female, page 78).

COUPLES EXERCISES

Appreciations and Resentments without script, nonsexual subjects. Two rounds each, every day.

Sexual Exploration (page 102), thirty minutes per partner, three times per week.

WEEK 6

SOLO EXERCISES

20–0 Countdown, three minutes every day.
 Self-Stimulation, Advanced.

COUPLES EXERCISES

Appreciations and Resentments, sexual subjects only, every day.
 Mirroring Your Partner (page 81), thirty minutes per partner, one hour total, three times per week.

WEEK 7

SOLO EXERCISES

20–0 Countdown, three minutes every day.

COUPLES EXERCISES

Appreciations and Resentments, any subject.
 Mutual Stimulation (page 107), thirty minutes, three times per week.

WEEK 8

SOLO EXERCISES

20–0 Countdown, three minutes every day.

Couples Exercises

Appreciations and Resentments, any subject, every day.
   The Volcano (page 248).
   The Trim (page 248).
   Male Stimulates the Female (Female ESO, page 112), thirty minutes, three times per week.
   Female Stimulates the Male (Male ESO, page 138), thirty minutes, three times per week.

WEEK 9

Solo Exercises

20–0 Countdown, three minutes every day.

Couples Exercises

Appreciations and Resentments, any subject, every day.
   The Volcano, three times per week.
   The Trim, three times per week.
   Male Stimulates the Female (Female ESO), thirty minutes, three times per week.
   Female Stimulates the Male (Male ESO), thirty minutes, three times per week.
   Proceed to Intercourse (page 163).

Communicating with the Brauers

Y ou can stay current, learn about training programs for individuals and couples, order selected products, link to other sites, and communicate with Alan and Donna Brauer and other *ESO* readers by logging on to

www.esoecstasy.org.

Sources

General Guides

Adams, Carl. *Secrets of Marathon Masturbation.* New York: Helios Press, 1979.

Anand, Margo. *The Art of Sexual Ecstasy: The Path of Sacred Sexuality for Western Lovers.* Los Angeles: Jeremy P. Tarcher, 1989.

Brenton, Myron. *Sex Talk.* Briarcliff Manor, N.Y.: Stein & Day, 1977.

Brylin, Brian Richard. *Orgasm—The Ultimate Experience.* New York: Dell, 1973.

Campbell, H. J. *The Pleasure Areas.* New York: Delacorte Press, 1973.

Comfort, Alex. *The Joy of Sex.* New York: Simon & Schuster, 1974.

———. *More Joy of Sex.* New York: Simon & Schuster, 1975.

Kulliger, J. L. *Masturbation—The Art of Self Enjoyment.* Canoga Park, Calif.: Omega Press, 1975.

Reich, Wilhelm. *The Function of the Orgasm.* New York: Simon & Schuster, 1974.

Renshaw, Domeena. *Seven Weeks to Better Sex.* New York: Dell, 1996.

Rosenberg, Jack. *Total Orgasm.* New York: Random House, 1976.

SAR Guide for a Better Sex Life—A Self-Help Program for Personal Enrichment/Education. National Sex Forum, 1523 Franklin Street, San Francisco, CA 94109, 1975.

Schwartz, Robert, and Leah Schwartz. *The One Hour Orgasm.* Houston: Breakthru Publishing, 1999.

Tideman, Debbie. *The X Spot Orgasm: Extended Ecstasy.* Chicago: Jetex, 1995.

Male

Chia, Mantak, and Douglas Abrams Arava. *The Multi-Orgasmic Man: Sexual Secrets Every Man Should Know.* Harper San Francisco, 1996.

Cohen, Harvey, Raymond Rosen, and Leonide Goldstein. "Electroencephalographic Laterality Changes during Human Sexual Orgasm." *Archives of Sexual Behavior* 5, no. 3 (1976): 189–99.

Kinsey, Alfred C., et al. *Sexual Behavior in the Human Male.* Philadelphia: Saunders, 1948.

Kolodny, Robert C., et al. *Textbook of Sexual Medicine.* Boston: Little, Brown, 1979.

Nowinski, Joseph K. *Becoming Satisfied: A Man's Guide to Sexual Fulfillment.* Englewood Cliffs, N.J.: Prentice-Hall, 1982.

Penney, Alexandra. *How to Make Love to a Man.* New York: Dell, 1982.

Pietropinto, Anthony, and Jacqueline Simenauer. *Beyond the Male Myth.* New York: Signet, 1977.

Richards, Brian, M.D. *The Penis.* New York: Valentine Press, 1977.

Robbins, Mina, and Gordon Jensen. "Multiple Orgasm in Males." *Journal of Sex Research* 14, no. 1 (1978): 21–26.

Schulz, R. Louis. *Out in the Open: The Complete Male Pelvis.* Berkeley, Calif.: North Atlantic Books, 1999.

Zilbergeld, Bernie. *The New Sexuality.* New York: Bantam, 1999.

Female

Barbach, Lonnie G. *For Yourself: The Fulfillment of Female Sexuality.* Garden City, N.Y.: Doubleday, 1976.

————. *Women Discover Orgasm: A Therapist's Guide to a New Treatment Approach.* New York: Free Press, 1980.

Cutler, W. B., M. Zacker, N. McCoy, E. Genoveses-Stone, and E. Friedman. "Sexual Response in Women." *Obstetrics & Gynecology* 95 (April 1, 2000): S19.

Fisher, Seymour. *Female Orgasm.* New York: Basic Books, 1973.

Heiman, J., L. LoPiccolo, and J. LoPiccolo. *Becoming Orgasmic: A Sexual Growth Program for Women.* Englewood Cliffs, N.J.: Prentice-Hall, 1976.

Kassorla, Irene. *Nice Girls Do.* New York: Playboy Press, 1982.

Kegel, Arnold H., M.D. "Sexual Functions of the Pubococcygeus Muscle." *Western Journal of Surgery, Obstetrics & Gynecology* 60, no. 10 (1952): 521–24.

Kinsey, Alfred C. *Sexual Behavior in the Human Female.* Philadelphia: Saunders, 1953.

Kline-Graber, Georgia, and Benjamin Graber. *Woman's Orgasm.* New York: Popular Library, 1976.

Ladas, Alice Kahn, Beverly Whipple, and John D. Perry. *The G Spot and Other Recent Discoveries About Human Sexuality.* New York: Holt, Rinehart & Winston, 1982.

Schubach, Gary. *Urethral Expulsions during Sensual Arousal and Bladder Catheterization in Seven Human Females.* Doctoral Research Project, Institute for Advanced Study of Human Sexuality, San Francisco, 1996.

Relationships

Bach, G., and P. Wyden. *The Intimate Enemy.* New York: Avon Books, 1968.

Butler, Robert N., and Myrna Lewis. *Sex After Sixty: A*

Guide for Men and Women in Their Later Years. New York: Harper & Row, 1976.

Gottman, John M., and Nan Silver. *The Seven Principles for Making Marriage Work: A Practical Guide from the Country's Foremost Relationship Expert.* New York: Crown, 1999.

Love, Patricia, M.D., and Jo Robinson. *Hot Monogamy.* New York: Penguin Putnam, 1994.

Masters, William H., et al. *The Pleasure Bond: A New Look at Sexual Commitment.* Boston: Little, Brown, 1975.

Massage

Downing, George. *Massage Book.* New York: Random House, 1972.

Inkles, Gordon. *The New Massage.* New York: Putnam, 1980.

Inkles, Gordon, and M. Todris. *The Art of Sensual Massage.* San Francisco: Straight Arrow Books, 1972.

Montagu, Ashley. *Touching: The Human Significance of Skin.* 2d ed. New York: Harper & Row, 1978.

Whelan, Stanley. *Art of Erotic Massage.* New York: Signet, 1979.

Other Sources

Cutler, Winifred. *Love Cycles.* New York: Villard, 1991.

DeMartino, Manfred F. *Human Autoerotic Practices.* New York: Human Sciences Press, 1979.

Ellison, Carol Rinkleib. *Women's Sexualities*. Oakland: New Harbinger, 2000.

Hartman, William, and Marilyn A. Fithian. *Treatment of Sexual Dysfunction: A Bio-Psychosocial Approach.* Long Beach, Calif.: Center for Marital & Sexual Studies, 1972.

Hite, Shere. *The Hite Report.* New York: Macmillan, 1976.

Kaplan, Helen S. *The New Sex Therapy: Active Treatment of Sexual Dysfunctions.* New York: Brunner/Mazel, 1974.

————. *Disorders of Sexual Desire.* New York: Brunner/Mazel, 1979.

Katchadourian, Herant A. *Fundamentals of Human Sexuality.* 4th ed. New York: Holt, Rinehart & Winston, 1985.

Masters, William H., and Virginia E. Johnson. *Human Sexual Response.* Boston: Little, Brown, 1966.

————. *Human Sexual Inadequacy.* New York: Bantam, 1979.

Michael, Robert T., John H. Gagnon, Edward O. Lauman, and Gina Kolata. *Sex in America.* Boston: Little, Brown, 1994.

Thorne, Edward. *Your Erotic Fantasies.* New York: Ballantine Books, 1971.

Index

About the Authors

ALAN P. BRAUER, M.D., is a psychiatrist, a graduate of the University of Rochester and the University of Michigan School of Medicine. He interned at New York University's Bellevue Hospital in New York City and completed his psychiatric residency at Stanford University in California in 1976. He is board certified by the American Board of Psychiatry and Neurology in both adult and geriatric psychiatry. Additionally, he has board certifications in pain management, psychopharmacology, and antiaging medicine. He is the founder-director of TotalCare Medical Center in Palo Alto, California, a pioneering multidisciplinary center with more than two decades of experience in using integrative and alternative medical approaches to treat psychological and physical problems.

DONNA J. BRAUER, a trained psychotherapist, is his cotherapist and wife. Together, the Brauers have led numerous professional seminars and helped many individuals and couples reverse sexual dysfunctions or explore their sexual potential.

52 SATURDAY NIGHTS
Heat Up Your Sex Life Even More with
a Year of Creative Lovemaking
by JOAN ELIZABETH LLOYD

Let Joan Elizabeth Lloyd, whose fabulously popular books and delicious fantasies have helped countless couples put the blaze in their bedrooms, take you on a spice-filled, week-by-week course in pleasure that begins with sweet, romantic scenarios, gets progressively sexier with each Saturday night, and offers down-to-earth, how-to advice every sensual step of the way. Saturday night is for lovers . . . and it comes fifty-two times a year.

SATISFACTION GUARANTEED
What Women *Really* Want in Bed
by RACHEL SWIFT

Finally—here is a book that reveals what women truly want during sex. Based on confessions and stories from hundreds of women, it tells you everything: from how to become the perfect lover to what moves to avoid when wooing and seducing the woman of your dreams to what kinds of men women like most. Best-selling sex author Rachel Swift gives you reality-tested advice that's fun, candid, and crucial to satisfying the woman in your life.

WOMAN'S ORGASM
A Guide to Sexual Satisfaction
by GEORGIA KLINE-GRABER, R.N.,
and BENJAMIN GRABER, M.D.

Do you know what a woman's orgasm is—and can be? There is widespread misinformation among women about their own bodies and capacity for pleasure. This classic guide candidly explains female sexuality and anatomy and includes an amazingly easy and successful self-help program developed by a doctor-nurse sex therapist team . . . all to help every woman fully explore and enjoy one of life's peak experiences.

NOW AND FOREVER—LET'S MAKE LOVE
From First Kiss to Fiftieth Anniversary . . .
Making Sex Hot at Every Stage of Your Life
by JOAN ELIZABETH LLOYD

Making love with the one you adore should be hot, fun, and exciting—at every stage of your life, from twenty-one to seventy-one. Showing you the sensible and sensual way to always keep the sizzle in your sex life, this book is spiced with erotic stories that couples can enjoy and embellish. It is filled with intimate advice from a woman who's been there, done that, and made it work for her relationship—and can guide everyone, from newlyweds to grandparents, to the most passionate lovemaking of a lifetime.